THE ROYAL HAMPSHIRE

The *River Clyde*

REGIMENTAL HISTORY

THE ROYAL HAMPSHIRE REGIMENT

VOLUME TWO

1914–1918

BY

C. T. ATKINSON

1952

PRINTED FOR THE REGIMENT BY
ROBERT MACLEHOSE & COMPANY LIMITED
THE UNIVERSITY PRESS GLASGOW

TO THE MEMORY OF
ALL MEMBERS OF THE ROYAL HAMPSHIRE REGIMENT
WHO HAVE FALLEN IN ITS SERVICE

AND OF

GENERAL SIR RICHARD C. B. HAKING
G.B.E., K.C.B., K.C.M.G.

COLONEL OF THE REGIMENT FROM 1924–1945
ON WHOSE INITIATIVE THE HISTORY
WAS WRITTEN

PREFACE

To try, over thirty years after the last events to be recorded, to put together an account of the share of a regiment of the Line in the war of 1914–1918 is to meet certain difficulties which would have been less serious had the attempt been made even ten years earlier. Time has made many gaps in the ranks of the survivors of that war, and not only are many who might have done much to supplement the available information no longer with us, but of those who are left many find that memories are getting dim, especially when it is a question of fixing accurately some doubtful detail. With others touch seems to have been lost, and though the compiler of this account has reason to be grateful to those who have been able to correct and expand the story, what help has been received only emphasizes how much more might have been obtained had more survivors been here to give it. A further loss is that during the war of 1939–1945 the Part II Daily Orders were destroyed in a ' blitz ', so that the very useful information contained in them has gone beyond recall. For things like changes in the officers with a battalion, dates and numbers of casualties, the award of honours, the arrival of drafts, the disposal of the officers and men of disbanded battalions, the Part II Orders would have been invaluable. Working through them was rather laborious work but, in other cases, it amply repaid the time spent on it and without their information many gaps must remain unfilled.

It is some compensation that the completion of the Official History provides much useful information about the main story of the campaigns in which the different battalions of the regiment took part. It should now be easier, with its help, to give a more correct and balanced picture of the background, to assess what the different campaigns and battles contributed to the ultimate result and to see what the whole was of which the regiment's achievements formed part. To keep the balance between that whole and the regiment's share is far from easy, there is always a danger of giving too much of the background and going into things which may seem to be outside the province of a regimental history. Still the opposite danger also exists, some regimental histories fail to show why certain sacrifices were demanded of individual units or what the reasons were for certain things which need explaining. A writer of a regimental history can be quite sure that whichever line he takes he cannot hope to please more than some of his readers, and perhaps it is better to insert than to omit.

The main sources for this account are the war diaries kept by the different battalions, supplemented to some extent by those of the brigades and Divisions in which they served, with the information contained in the regimental Journal. This last was particularly useful for 1914 and 1915 ; after that the exigencies of the censorship prevented it from being as definite and precise as it had been. After 1915 it contains few of the extracts from letters from the front which were so helpful for the retreat from Mons and for events up to the middle of 1915. The

' citations ' for the award of decorations are not very helpful when the date of an incident is not given and when it cannot even be certain with which battalion the recipient of an award was serving when he won his M.C. or D.C.M. Here the battalion diaries sometimes provide the answer, but by no means always. Two of the awards of the V.C. are not mentioned in the battalion diaries in which it might be expected to find them recorded. It is feared, therefore, that many gallant actions have not been recorded because they could not be dated with any accuracy.

The battalion diaries naturally enough vary greatly in their usefulness. Keeping them was hardly a matter of extreme urgency and clearly there were times of stress when more important things took up the attention of those responsible, when the diary was written up later on by someone who had not been in the action in which crippling losses had been incurred. It may also be that while the diaries were supposed to be kept in duplicate, the copy which has got to 'Records' has not been furnished with maps, orders and reports and other things which were attached to the top copy. But instead of complaining if some diaries fail to give any account of quite important engagements or to mention the names of officers killed and wounded in a major action, it is more reasonable to be grateful to those diary keepers who did insert these things and have provided much useful and detailed information. The diaries of the 1st Battalion for much of 1917 and 1918 and of the 2nd Battalion for a good part of 1916 and for 1917 may perhaps be mentioned as deserving of gratitude as having been very helpful. If there is some lack of proportion between the accounts of different operations it is because for some little information is to be had, whereas for other episodes the diaries are fuller and provide more of what the compiler needs.

I have occasion also to be grateful to several officers who have answered queries, sent me information and in particular to Mrs May for letting me see some most interesting and helpful letters from Captain H. W. M. May, which were of great assistance. Of published works Captain Bacon's *Wanderings of a Temporary Warrior* has been of great help and the short account of the 10th and 12th Battalions published in 1930 makes me wish that Major Cowland would have followed Captain Bacon's good example and written of those battalions at greater length. Of other regimental histories, Major Stacke's very detailed history of the Worcestershire Regiment has been very helpful for the doings of the 2nd Battalion and Captain Berkeley's account of the Rifle Brigade for those of the 1st Battalion, while for Salonica Colonel Jourdain's story of the 5th Connaught Rangers has been useful. It is odd that only one of the Divisions in which Hampshire battalions served has had its history written. The story of the Fourth Division is one which it is strange to find has not been tackled and among " New Army " Divisions the Forty-first had a record well worth telling. That of the Twenty-Ninth Division, which has been written, would have been more helpful if it had been more liberally furnished with maps and had it gone into certain episodes in rather fuller detail.

The cost of maps is so great and the need for them to illustrate the story is so imperative that I have provided a large number of more or less skeleton maps, in preference to a few really elaborate maps. Some of these are composite productions based on two or three sketches in diaries, and they do not claim to be more than diagrams in which I have tried to show really relevant features. If there are some discrepancies in spelling between maps and text this is partly because my authorities have varied considerably in the spelling they adopt, especially in those for the Macedonian, Mesopotamian and Palestine campaigns.

I have deliberately omitted initials except where officers of the same name might be confused ; this has been done to avoid the really large amount of space which the printing of initials in other cases would have taken up. Space also implies cost, for which reason the names of those who lost their lives have been omitted and no attempt has been made to provide a Roll of Officers for those who only held ' temporary ' commissions or for the Territorial Battalions. To produce them would also have greatly delayed the production of a work which has already been over long in labour. I have to thank Mr Holland of the Royal United Service Institution for his help in producing the list of Regular and Special Reserve officers which carry on from the lists in Volume I.

The Colonel of the Regiment has been very patient over the long time this volume has been in production. I owe him many thanks, as also to Major Jeffery, who has been unfailingly helpful in every way.

C. T. A.

Band Pouch Badge, 1887

CONTENTS

CONTENTS

PLATES

MAPS AND DIAGRAMS

Drum Carrier Badge

BATTLE HONOURS

THE GREAT WAR

LE CATEAU

RETREAT FROM MONS

MARNE, 1914, 1918

AISNE, 1914

ARMENTIÈRES, 1914

YPRES, 1915, 1917, 1918

ST. JULIEN

FREZENBERG

BELLEWAARDE

SOMME, 1916, 1918

ALBERT, 1916

GUILLEMONT

GINCHY

FLERS-COURCELETTE

THIEPVAL

LE TRANSLOY

ANCRE HEIGHTS

ANCRE, 1916

ARRAS, 1917, 1918

VIMY, 1917

SCARPE, 1917, 1918

MESSINES, 1917

PILCKEM

LANGEMARCK, 1917

MENIN ROAD

POLYGON WOOD

BROODSEINDE

POELCAPPELLE

PASSCHENDAELE

CAMBRAI, 1917, 1918

ST. QUENTIN

BAPAUME, 1918

ROSIÈRES

LYS

ESTAIRES

HAZEBROUCK

BAILLEUL

KEMMEL

BÉTHUNE

TARDENOIS

DROCOURT-QUÉANT

HINDENBURG LINE

HAVRINCOURT

CANAL DU NORD

COURTRAI

SELLE

VALENCIENNES

SAMBRE

FRANCE & FLANDERS, 1914–18

ITALY, 1917–18

KOSTURINO

STRUMA

DOIRAN, 1917, 1918

MACEDONIA, ~~1914-18~~ 1915-18

HELLES

LANDING AT HELLES

KRITHIA

SUVLA

SARI BAIR	SHARON
LANDING AT SUVLA	PALESTINE, 1917–18
SCIMITAR HILL	ADEN
GALLIPOLI, 1915–16	SHAIBA
EGYPT, 1915–17	KUT AL AMARA, 1915–17
GAZA	TIGRIS, 1916
EL MUGHAR	BAGHDAD
NEBI SAMWIL	SHARQAT
JERUSALEM	MESOPOTAMIA, 1915–18
JAFFA	PERSIA, 1918–19
TELL 'ASUR	ARCHANGEL, 1919
MEGIDDO	SIBERIA, 1918–19

Old Hampshire Title

THE HAMPSHIRE REGIMENT 1914–1919

CHAPTER I

LE CATEAU AND THE RETREAT

WHEN, in August 1914, the German violation of the Belgian neutrality, which the German Empire was pledged to defend, forced Great Britain into war to fulfil her treaty obligations, both Regular battalions of the Hampshire Regiment had spent nearly a year at the new stations to which the previous ' trooping season ' had transferred them. By shifting it from the Second Division to the Fourth [1] the 1st Battalion's move from Aldershot to Colchester had influenced its fortunes in the war far more than the 2nd's move from Mauritius to Bengal affected that battalion's doings, as the 1st Essex, who replaced the 2nd Hampshire at Mauritius, were actually in the same brigade of the Twenty-Ninth Division. The 1st Battalion's move meant that it missed Mons and the first great struggle in the Ypres Salient but fought at Le Cateau and helped in the stubborn defence of the British line in the Lys valley, that if not at Neuve Chapelle or Loos it was to be sorely tried in ' Second Ypres ', and that throughout the war its experiences were very different from those it would have met if still in the Second Division.

The gravity of the approaching crisis had hardly been generally appreciated in England before the Austrian ultimatum to Servia, news of which, appearing in the Sunday papers on July 26th, suddenly competed for seriousness with the grave developments in Ireland, on which most people's attention had till then been focused. The issue of orders on July 29th to adopt the ' precautionary period ' measures made it clear that the authorities were taking the gravest view of the situation, and therewith at all military stations preliminary preparations for mobilisation began to be put in hand.

The ' precautionary period ' measures included the recall of all those on leave and the manning of coast defences, the 1st Hampshire sending parties to Felixstowe and Purfleet. For political reasons actual orders for mobilisation were delayed as long as any faint chance of averting war remained, but meanwhile those actually with the Colours could be given medical examinations, equipment could be checked and other work got through before the great influx of Reservists [2] which followed quickly on the actual declaration of war on the evening of August 4th. Even before that Reservists had begun to report at the Depot, and on the Wednesday afternoon (August 8th) a large party left for Colchester under Captain Unwin, followed next day by another batch under Captain R.W. Harland ; amounting in all to 500 men. That left nearly as many to join the 3rd Battalion, whose mobilisation was completed by the evening of August 7th, so that it could leave for its war station at the Isle of Wight next

---

[1] The Fourth Division was commanded by Major General Snow and the 11th Brigade by Brigadier General Hunter-Weston. The 5th Brigade of the Second Division was under Brigadier General Haking.

[2] The Brigade and battalion War Diaries do not cover the period between mobilisation and the move overseas, and the unfortunate destruction by German air action of all the Part II Orders makes it impossible to supplement these gaps from this invaluable source.

3

day.   Another 50 men from the Regular establishment of the Depot under Lt. Kent were also transferred to the 1st Battalion, which in turn sent back to the 3rd the few unfits and all those too young for service overseas.

The 11th Brigade's mobilisation was not impeded as was that of the 10th and 12th, which were sent off to York and Cromer as a precaution against a German raid.   At Colchester the 11th was in position to meet a descent on Essex and did not therefore have to move, so all proceeded 'according to plan'. As the 1st Battalion had been at home nearly nine years most of the Reservists had done the bulk of their Colour service with the 2nd, so that many officers and N.C.O.s of the 1st, unless recently transferred from the 2nd, had seen little of them, but they fitted quickly into their places, while the fortnight that elapsed before the Fourth Division went overseas gave plenty of time for any unfamiliarity to pass off.

By August 17th the Special Reserve had taken over its coast defence duties, the Territorials had also been mobilised and their Divisions were at or on the way to their war-stations.   The Fourth Division could therefore be relieved from its temporary role as the spear-head of the Home Defence Force and concentrated in readiness to follow the rest of the British Expeditionary Force overseas.   August 18th found it assembling round Harrow, where its entrainment began on August 21st-22nd, the 1st Hampshire leaving soon after midnight and embarking at Southampton, headquarters and the right wing in the *Braemar Castle*, the left wing along with the Rifle Brigade in the *Cestrian*. Sailing before midday they were at Havre before midnight and before dawn had disembarked and moved out to a rest camp outside the town.

Before leaving Colchester orders had been received to find a Captain, a subaltern and 15 selected N.C.O.s to form a nucleus for the new 'Service Battalion' which every regiment was to raise as part of the 'New Army' of six Divisions, whose formation Lord Kitchener, now Secretary of State for War, had ordered.   Captain Morley and Lt. K. A. Johnston were the officers detailed, along with 2nd Lts. Hudson and Waddington, recently appointed and due to take the next draft out to India, and to complete the war-establishment Captain Richards and Lt. Halls, home on leave from the 2nd Battalion, accompanied the 1st overseas, along with two Special Reservists, Lts. Rose and Griffiths.

The officers who went out to France were Colonel Jackson, Majors Hicks (2nd in command) and Barlow (O.C. C Company), Captains Palk (D), Baxter (B), Moore (A), Richards (A), Connellan (C), Perkins (Adjutant) [1] and Harland (B), Lts. Dolphin (B), im Thurn (D), Le Hunte (machine guns), Kent (A), Knocker (C), Halls (D), Edsell (transport), Cecil (A), Trimmer (C), Rose (C), and Griffiths (D), 2-Lts. Cowan (B), Sweet (C), Westmorland (D) and Nicholson (A) and Lt. and Qr. Mr. Hackett.   Captain Williams (R.A.M.C.) accompanied the battalion as M.O., Captain R. D. Johnston being in charge of the first reinforcements.[2]

[1] He had just succeeded Captain Baxter, whose three years were up on August 6th.

[2] Besides the six Regular officers on the establishment of the 3rd Battalion, two Majors (Williams and Mackay) and three Captains were in Staff posts or at the Staff College, seven Captains were doing duty as Special Reserve or Territorial Adjutants, three Captains and seven subalterns were employed with the Egyptian Army or Colonial forces.

✱ L⍓ E.M.S KENⰽ(ᴀ) K.I.A 26.8.14

The Fourth Division was not long at Havre. The B.E.F. was already in touch with the Germans at Mons, and before the whole Division had arrived in France entrainment had begun. Divisional Headquarters and the artillery were to detrain at Busigny, the 10th and 11th Brigades at Le Cateau and the 12th at Bertry. The 1st Hampshire entrained in the small hours of August 24th and after spending over 24 hours in the train, reached Le Cateau about 4 a.m. next day.[1] The men travelled uncomfortably, crowded in vehicles 'rather after the style of our guards' vans' one officer wrote, but their discomfort did not prevent their being in high spirits. Detraining promptly the battalion had just time for a hurried breakfast before marching off N.W. to Solesmes, where the Division, or such of it as had arrived, was taking position to cover the B.E.F.'s retirement from Mons. It was very hot and the men, tired by the long journey, found a six miles march very trying.

Regimental officers and men naturally knew little even of the local situation, except that the 'B.E.F.' had been in action at Mons and was retiring Southward, while Sir John French's headquarters had left Le Cateau for a position further South. Of the miscarriage of the French counter stroke in Lorraine they knew nothing or of the unexpected strength of the German advance through Belgium, before which General Lanrezac's French Fifth Army was retiring, its retreat having been successfully covered by the British success in holding up von Kluck's First Army at Mons (August 23rd), after which the B.E.F. had itself to retire to avoid the envelopment which its stand had enabled Lanrezac to evade.

The Fourth Division's arrival at Le Cateau was the more timely because on that day Smith Dorrien's Second Corps and Haig's First had diverged, having to pass on either side of the great Forest of Mormal, while with von Kluck's Army bearing more SW. than South, the Second Corps was being followed by overwhelming forces ; indeed its situation would have been highly perilous had not the Fourth Division been there to cover its retirement and then prolong its line to the Westward.

Actually on August 25th the Fourth Division was not seriously engaged. The 11th Brigade's leading battalions, the 1st Somerset L.I. and 1st East Lancashire, were in position SE. of Solesmes quite early on, and the Hampshire's first orders were to support the E. Lancashire. Accordingly they dug in South of Solesmes about Bellevue Farm with the E. Lancashire on their right and the Somerset on the left, and awaited developments. C. Company was in advance of the rest just outside Solesmes. Heavy firing could be heard away to the Northward, and from parties of British troops who, mixed up with a flood of civilian refugees, were passing through the Fourth Division's line, a little news and rather more in the way of rumours could be picked up, but of the pursuing Germans next to nothing was to be seen. Captain Connellan took two platoons of C Company forward North of Solesmes to reconnoitre but merely met British cavalry, who reported that the Germans were keeping their distance.

[1] The battalion's first casualty occurred on the journey : the Adjutant's groom, trying to control his frightened charger in passing through a tunnel, was kicked out of the train and killed.

But until the rear-guards were through its line the Fourth Division had to retain its positions, the 10th Brigade S.W. of Solesmes, the 11th on its right and the 12th in reserve at Viesly. Early in the afternoon the Hampshire were moved Westward to Briastre where they remained till after dark, No. 15 Platoon from D Company under Lt. Halls being sent forward to a cross-roads North of Briastre on outpost.[1] Details of the Third Division were passing through and the enemy were shelling Solesmes, where towards dusk the Third Division's rear-guard became somewhat sharply engaged, the only time during the day when the Germans really came to grips with the British infantry. By 9 p.m. this rear-guard had been successfully withdrawn and the Fourth Division was free to fall back also. When the 11th Brigade's retirement started, A and D Companies under Major Hicks were left as rear-guard, two platoons of D Company under Lt. Halls being detailed as rear party in Briastre, while the brigade moved off SW. to the new position assigned to it. This was on the left of the Second Corps, whose line ran from Le Cateau Westward to Caudry and was to be continued by the Fourth Division from Fontaine au Pire to Wambaix on the rising ground North of the valley of the Warnelle brook. In this position the 11th Brigade was to be on the right, with the 12th on its left and the 10th in reserve across the Warnelle.

Moving off about 10.30 p.m. the Hampshire's rear-guard had to halt for a time, as the 10th Brigade was delayed ; it then had to toil along over a pavé road full of holes and ruts which a terrific thunderstorm late in the afternoon had left muddy. After their tiring journey and the intense heat and being drenched by the thunderstorm, while no supplies had been issued, all ranks were nearly exhausted, and on reaching the straggling village of Beauvois—Fontaine au Pire, in whose winding streets it was easy to go wrong in the dark, about 2 a.m., the men lay down in the streets to get what poor rest they could and eat a mouthful of biscuit. Here the rear party arrived about 3.30 a.m.; they had been attacked several times by cavalry patrols whom they had driven off each time. The battalion's rest was short enough, before dawn it was moving out NW. towards the position assigned to it further to the left. Parties of German cavalry were hovering about, so B Company with one of the Rifle Brigade were detailed to cover this move, and directly they got into line upon a ridge they came under artillery fire, B having several casualties.

Sir John French, in ordering the retirement from Mons, had originally intended to attempt a stand on the Le Cateau position. The rapid development of the German advance, its unexpected strength and the retreat of Lanrezac's Fifth Army on our right had made this impossible, and overnight G.H.Q. had ordered General Smith-Dorrien to continue the retreat as early as possible on August 26th. During the night information had come in, both about the Germans and about the British troops,[2] which convinced General Smith-Dorrien that to attempt to retreat as ordered would invite disaster and that he must stand and fight, in the hopes of inflicting such a check on the enemy that he would eventu-

---

[1] No. 15 made a road-block here ; perhaps the first made by the B.E.F.
[2] Some of the Third Division's rear-guard only reached the Le Cateau position about 4 a.m.

ally be able to disengage and withdraw in his own time. He had accordingly asked General Snow to place the Fourth Division under his orders and co-operate with the Second Corps in ' giving the enemy a wipe ', as Sir John Moore called it. General Snow had promptly agreed, but the news of his decision had barely reached his brigades before his infantry was already hard at it, keeping off the enemy's attacks.

The 11th Brigade's transport [1] was just starting off for the village of Ligny across the Warnelle ravine, when the German attack developed, and it had some difficulty in getting clear of Fontaine au Pire and suffered some loss, while about

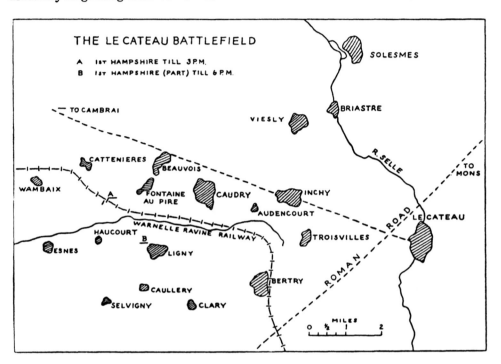

this time the machine gun section got detached from the battalion but eventually took up position along with that of the Rifle Brigade on the South of the Warnelle ravine somewhere between Ligny and Haucourt. Here it was to remain in action till evening, getting several opportunities of opening fire with good effect at rather long range. Meanwhile the battalion was taking up its position roughly facing NW. towards Cattenières and astride a light railway running NW. Major Hicks had been able to carry out a hurried reconnaissance, and A and D were soon in position and were working hard with their ' grubbers ' [2] to throw up a little cover when the battalion came under machine gun and artillery fire.

---

[1] It could not accompany the battalion across country but some of the S.A.A. carts did reach the battalion's position and issued their ammunition, one being destroyed by a shell in getting away.

[2] The small entrenching tool then carried by the infantry.

The Fourth Division, or such portions of it as were coming into action, was engaging in battle at great disadvantage. The nicely adjusted organization of a British Division of all arms provided cavalry and cyclists for protective work, R.E. to direct working parties and supply skilled labour, R.A.M.C. to attend to the wounded, a Signal Company to provide its commander and his brigadiers with the means of controlling their commands. At Le Cateau the Fourth Division was unfortunately short of these vital elements and had not even the heavy battery of 60 pounders to supplement the fire of its 18 pounders and 4.5 inch howitzers. If the 12th Brigade, on the 11th's left, had most reason to regret the absence of the Divisional squadron and cyclists, who might have saved the heavy losses it suffered from having one battalion surprised in mass by machine guns, the Signal Company's absence [1] was probably on the whole the biggest handicap from which the Division suffered and was responsible for losses which with proper means of communication might have been averted.

The 11th Brigade, covered by its rear parties of the Hampshire and Rifle Brigade, took up its position without much delay or loss, the Hampshire on its left being separated from the 12th Brigade further West by a wide gap, but not too wide as to allow the enemy to advance into it, while again and again the battalion lent the 12th Brigade effective assistance by fire. Its line ran roughly along the crest of the ridge North of the Warnelle ravine, from which ridge the ground sloped slightly down to the Northward towards the high-road to Cambrai. The country, though under cultivation, largely with beet and clover, not yet harvested as other crops had been, was open, with few trees and hedges, and gave a fair field of fire, particularly to D Company, North of the railway, as the Germans[2] found when they tried to advance, British rifle-fire soon discouraging them and checking efforts to work round towards our left. Accordingly against the 11th Brigade they relied mainly on shell fire and machine guns and only very occasionally was the Fourth Division given targets like those by which the Second Corps had profited so much at Mons. Even so by the next morning many of the men proved to have had occasion to use up most of their ammunition.

After the brigade had taken up its position the covering parties were able to fall back. B Company had been quite sharply engaged and had several casualties. As they fell back one detachment had the satisfaction of wiping out a platoon of Jäger [3] who had incautiously emerged from Fontaine au Pire in pursuit. Half the company under Captain Baxter became separated from the rest and joined the Somerset, alongside whom they fought till that battalion had to retire on Ligny, Captain Baxter, whose party was about the last to retire,

---

[1] Being without the Brigade Signal Section, the Brigadier kept in touch with his forward troops by riding freely about : his charger having been shot under him he borrowed B. Company's charger which also was hit and with it were lost the company's Field Conduct Sheets in a wallet on the saddle.

[2] Dismounted cavalry in the early stages of the fight, infantry of the IVth Reserve Corps coming into action later.

[3] Jäger battalions were attached to the German Cavalry Divisions, whose fire-power they substantially augmented.

being badly wounded.[1] The rest of B under Captain Harland were now placed in reserve behind D, who had to endure the main ordeal of the German shell fire. The line here, on top of the ridge, was very much exposed, though a sunken lane leading down to the railway cutting gave the supports some shelter. However, Captain Connellan brought two platoons of C up to reinforce, and he and Captain Palk set a splendid example of leadership and coolness,[2] encouraging the men to

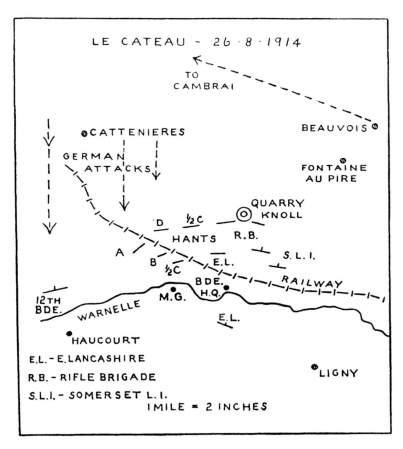

LE CATEAU - 26·8·1914

TO CAMBRAI

○CATTENIERES

GERMAN ATTACKS

BEAUVOIS ⊘

FONTAINE AU PIRE

QUARRY KNOLL

D   ½C

HANTS   R.B.

A   B   ½C   E.L.   S.L.I.

BDE.   RAILWAY

12TH BDE.   WARNELLE   M.G.   H.Q.   E.L.

●HAUCOURT

E.L. - E. LANCASHIRE

R.B. - RIFLE BRIGADE

●LIGNY

S.L.I. - SOMERSET L.I.

I MILE = 2 INCHES

endure the ordeal and keeping them ready to take advantage of any targets which presented themselves. About 9 a.m. D had the satisfaction of seeing Germans coming forward in large masses. Reserving the fire of his left half-company till the enemy were quite close, Lt. Halls then opened rapid fire with great effect, the surviving Germans falling back to a ridge nearly 300 yards away, but after that few such targets were given again, and the Germans, apparently dismounted cavalry, merely maintained a desultory fire at a very respectful

[1] He got back to the dressing station at Ligny but was one of those who in the absence of the Division's ambulances were so unlucky as to fall into German hands.

[2] Captain Palk is said to have read Scott's *Marmion* aloud to his men.

range. South of the railway the left company (A) had rather better cover, thanks to sunken lanes, and its men dealt very effectively with efforts to creep forward along the line. Some Germans creeping up under cover got near enough to call out ' Retire ', which for the moment deceived a few men, but they gained little from their ruse.

On the Hampshire's left the 12th Brigade had recovered from the unfortunate opening of the battle, even the battalion which had been caught in quarter-column had managed to extend along the shelter of a lane and had replied effectively to the machine-guns which had smitten it, and though about 9 a.m. the brigade had to retire across the Warnelle valley this movement was successfully carried out. In this two platoons of the Hampshire gave useful help ; pushing forward a little they got a good target in a battery which had unlimbered in the open near Cattenieres, shooting so effectively at a range of over 1200 yards that it was forced to limber up and get away. With the Germans chary of pressing home their attacks, the Hampshire, though prompt to take advantage of any targets, got but limited chances. The best marksmen of D Company were able to pick off some of the machine-gun crews and occasional officers who marked themselves out by carrying drawn swords, and the men were very steady and fired with good effect. One German machine gun was put out of action and the efforts of their infantry to cross the railway line or advance along it were effectively checked, while heavy as the shell fire was, much went high and our casualties were less than might have been expected from such a volume of fire. At one moment a battery got the range of the hedge along the railway cutting with disastrous results, Lt. Kent and 2/Lt. Cowan and several men being killed and many wounded, but this was luckily exceptional. Later on, however, when infantry were pressing forward against the 12th Brigade, now back between Ligny and Haucourt, parts of A and B Companies tried a counter-attack to take this advance in flank, but their move drew down on them so fierce a storm of shrapnel that the Brigadier had to stop the advance and bring the men back to their line, several casualties having been suffered.

All through the morning the Fourth Division maintained its ground though more German batteries [1] had reinforced those of the Cavalry Divisions already in action in this quarter. With the 12th Brigade back across the Warnelle ravine and with the Third Division hard pressed to maintain its hold on Caudry, fully a mile to its right, the 11th Brigade's position was none too satisfactory, but any attempts of the German infantry to close with it were promptly checked, and if sometimes parties of our men were shelled out of their positions, these were soon re-occupied, the supports in the Warnelle ravine providing reinforcements.

Elsewhere the Fifth Division on the right was having an even harder time, being in a nasty salient under heavy enfilade artillery fire, and before 2 p.m. it had become clear that it could not hold on much longer. Its retirement necessarily involved that of the Third and Fourth Divisions, who could otherwise

---

[1] Those of the IVth Reserve Corps who had pushed on ahead of their infantry. These came into action later, early in the afternoon.

have held on,[1] as they were keeping their own opponents at bay, a counter-attack having recovered a large part of Caudry after that village had been evacuated by order. Somewhere about 3 p.m. General Hunter-Weston, seeing that his right flank was much exposed by the German lodgement in Caudry, while more German infantry were now moving up in his front,[2] ordered the 11th Brigade to retire across the ravine and re-form in front of Ligny. The Hampshire and East Lancashire were to go first, covered by the Rifle Brigade and such of the Somerset L. I. as were not already in the back position. As the Hampshire started to retire it seemed, as one officer wrote,[3] ' as if every gun and rifle in the German Army had opened fire ', but the movement was steadily carried out, the German infantry had been kept at too respectful a distance to press the retiring troops, who were soon in dead ground, though in mounting the slope towards Ligny they again came into view, whereupon the German gunners redoubled their efforts, inflicting more casualties, though with the men well extended the loss was not really heavy. When the rear-guard in turn fell back German infantry pushed forward, to be promptly checked by our guns. Renewing their effort a little later, they were met not only by our guns but by the rifles of such of the 11th Brigade as had reached Ligny and faced about there. Trying another advance they again failed in the face of our rapid fire and after that the 11th Brigade was left unmolested. It was, however, by this time rather split up ; companies and even platoons had got detached, and without the Signal Company the Divisional and Brigade commanders had found the controlling of the troops almost impossible. Consequently when, about 5 p.m., the 11th Brigade started to retire from the Ligny position, the orders failed to reach several parties and all its units were broken up into disconnected detachments, and though the Brigadier was able before long to collect a substantial body at Selvigny, many parties continued detached for some days.

About 300 Hampshire under Major Hicks, with whom were Captains Connellan, Moore and Richards and Lt. Dolphin, were still holding on at Ligny about 6 p.m., without any orders or any knowledge of the situation, when the Adjutant made his way back to order them to retire, the rest of the brigade having already moved off. As they left the village [4] it was very heavily shelled but otherwise the party was unmolested. Before long, touch was regained near Caullery with another party under Colonel Jackson, which had hung on even longer near Ligny, not retiring till 7 p.m.[5] From Caullery the battalion made its way across country, the road being blocked at Clery by troops of the Second Corps, and till nearly midnight the men tramped on, worn, weary and hungry. A halt was then called near Serain, where the main body of the brigade was near

---

[1] Captain Palk and his company were reported as being most reluctant to retire—they had not let any Germans get near them.

[2] Of the IVth Reserve Corps.

[3] Lt. E.J.W. Dolphin, for whose valuable letters I have to thank his brother, Colonel H. C. Dolphin.

[4] Most of the wounded of the brigade had been collected in the school at Ligny where the majority had to be left behind in the absence of the Division's ambulances.

[5] The Germans were not pressing them even then.

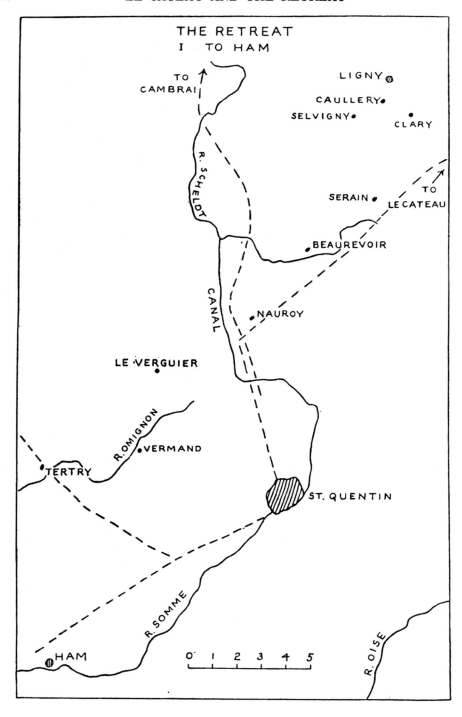

THE RETREAT
I TO HAM

at hand, and the weary men got a brief but welcome rest, before resuming the march about 2 a.m. The people of the place did what they could for them in providing bread and hot water for tea or soup. The retreat had so far been quite unmolested, the Germans, after the reception they had met, were in no mood to press forward in pursuit.[1]

Over 100 years had passed since the Thirty-Seventh had last been in action against a European enemy, and never since the Flanders campaign of 1794 had they been as severely tried or suffered so heavily. Their losses, when finally established, came to nearly 200. Lt. Kent and 2/Lt. Cowan had been killed, Captain Baxter, Lts. Rose, Halls, Griffith [2] and Le Hunte [3] were missing, with the M.O., Captain Williams, who had stayed behind with the badly wounded. Major Hicks, though continuing at duty, had been wounded, as had Lt. Cecil in leading a small counter-attack. Of other ranks 46 were killed and missing and 126 wounded, D Company having suffered the most severely.

However, the battalion with the rest of the brigade could congratulate itself in having maintained itself in one unfavourable position after another for ten hours and more, on having held its immediate opponents and punished them heavily and on having helped to foil their effort to envelope and corner the left wing of the B.E.F. Heavy as the British losses at Le Cateau were, the Fifth Division's losses in guns being specially serious, it may be claimed that at Le Cateau General Smith-Dorrien had achieved his main purpose ; his men had checked von Kluck's greatly superior force and hit it so hard that it made no serious attempt at pursuit and in consequence lost touch with the B.E.F. Moreover, as the German commander was confirmed in the erroneous conclusions he had formed about our movements, intentions and line of retreat, the stand at Le Cateau contributed appreciably to the foiling of the German effort to secure a ' knock-out ' victory. If for the moment the B.E.F. had to make a hurried and exhausting retreat, Le Cateau helped to secure it from molestation and was to yield no small harvest before many days were out.

Before dawn on August 27th such of the 11th Brigade as were together, including most of the Hampshire, were stumbling along Southward again, weary and hungry, moving across country by Beaurevoir to Nauroy, where they halted rather after 7 a.m. for such breakfast as was possible. About 9.30 the North Irish Horse, who were covering the position, reported that German

---

[1] They did not actually occupy Ligny till that morning, and a few Hampshire remained on outpost there all night without being molested ; but were mostly captured next morning.

[2] Originally reported killed.

[3] The machine-gun section, after remaining in position until dark, had then started to retire as all other troops near were doing. It had some difficulty in getting the limbers along a bad track but after a time met a Frenchman, who offered to guide it to Clery, where he said the English were concentrating. He may have been a German agent, for when the party, increased by stragglers to a dozen, reached Clery it was to run into the Germans in force and be taken. The two machine-guns, left for the time lying in a courtyard, were discovered there by a civilian, M. Fernaud Lerouf who concealed them so successfully that the Germans never found them. Eventually in 1921 the then Maire of Clery informed the local military authorities of the existence of these guns and Captain Le Hunte had the satisfaction of going to Clery to recover them for the regiment and express its thanks to M. Lerouf for their preservation : he had risked his life for it, as he would have been shot had they been discovered.

cavalry were approaching. The Brigadier not being on the spot at the moment, Colonel Jackson as senior officer present promptly sent the East Lancashire to take post East of the village and was preparing to post the Hampshire North of it when the Brigadier arrived and gave orders for the immediate resumption of the retreat. The troops were moving off when German guns opened fire at about 1000 yards range. The Brigadier thereupon directed Colonel Jackson to engage these guns and cover the retirement, to which end A Company of the Hampshire took post North and East of Nauroy and opened fire on the guns but was almost immediately fairly sharply engaged with cyclists and dismounted cavalry. This company, with about 50 details of all units whom the Brigadier had placed under Colonel Jackson, held on for some time, giving effective cover to the retirement of the main body. This, in moving across country to avoid the shell-fire, inevitably became split up again ; one large party, including most of the Hampshire under Major Barlow and guided by the Brigade Major, Captain Boyd, made its way by Le Verguier to Tertry. Major Hicks, still carrying on despite his wound, now took charge of about another 120 Hampshires with some details, having with him Lts. Knocker and Nicholson, and this party, having got away without much loss, eventually joined on to the tail of the Third Division, in whose company it reached Vermand that evening, having covered 25 miles in the day. Another 100 of the battalion under Captains Moore and Richards, most of whom had been part of the rear-guard and had been East of Nauroy, made their way back separately, getting across the St. Quentin Canal and joining some of the Rifle Brigade and East Lancashire under the Brigadier. Of the rest of the rear-guard the majority had become casualties and among them Colonel Jackson himself, who had the bad luck to be hit in the leg and disabled and had to be carried into the house of a curé, where he was found and taken by the enemy. It was hard on the battalion to lose so competent and trusted a C.O. and hard on an officer of his record and attainments to lose all chance of earning distinction in the war. Had he escaped he would in all probability have before long been removed from command of the battalion by promotion ; his good services in controlling his battalion at Le Cateau had been brought to notice by General Hunter-Weston, to be disabled and captured was a cruel misfortune.

Apart from this clash at Nauroy little was seen of the enemy all day and the different detachments plodded along unmolested. Supplies had been dumped at the road-side to be picked up as the troops passed by, while some lucky individuals were given eggs, coffee and apples by kindly farm-house people. All were terribly weary : one Hampshire subaltern, who was given a ride, found himself falling asleep in the saddle, though he managed not to fall off, and those men who were picked up in carts or lorries were likewise promptly asleep. Some got rides on gun-limbers and had to keep awake. The brigade's scattered detachments had remained separated all day, but at Ham, which they reached early on August 28th after starting from Vermand in the dark and covering ten miles, mostly in heavy rain, Major Hicks and his party found the Brigadier with Captains Moore and Richards and their men, and when, about 8 a.m., the march was again resumed most of the 11th Brigade was together again. Another long and trying march followed to Freniches, six miles short of Noyon, where after covering 15 miles on indifferent roads in great heat the brigade eventually halted, dead beat and very grateful to some R.A.M.C. who, having arrived there earlier, had prepared a hot meal for the later arrivals. Here also the Hampshire had the satisfaction of rejoining their transport which had got safely away.

It was a great relief next morning, after the first night's rest the Hampshire had known since leaving England, not to start off again at once. Apart from other reasons, it indicated that the B.E.F. had some freedom of choice in its actions and was not merely conforming to the enemy's moves. Regimental officers and men might be quite in the dark as to the general situation, this at least was some small encouragement. The Second Corps and the Fourth Division had by their exertions got clear away from the enemy, whose pursuit was being mistakenly directed Westward and SW. rather than following the Southward line of the British retreat, and so General Smith-Dorrien's men could get some of the rest they needed so badly. Their rest was broken into that afternoon by a sudden order to resume the march, but the roads were blocked with transport and little progress was made, the brigade eventually halting at Les Cloyes, where it spent the night in bivouac and where the Brigade Major's party, including Major Barlow and nearly 500 of the Hampshire, rejoined during the night, having made their way by Voyennes and Esmery-Hallon [1] to Sermaize, which they had reached on August 29th. Many individuals were still detached, some having attached themselves to other regiments, others having been given lifts in empty lorries and taken on well ahead, [2] but the Division was now largely re-assembled, having been rejoined by most of the units whose absence had cost it so much at Le Cateau.

The retreat was resumed about 6 a.m. next day (August 30th) with officers and men still in doubt about the situation, very weary and short of sleep but plodding doggedly on, getting occasional chances of supplementing their rations with fruit and eggs. Crossing the Aisne the Fourth Division reached Pierrefonds that evening, moved on Westward (next day) through the Forest of Compiegne, welcoming the shade on the hottest day yet, and halted at its SW. corner, covering St. Sauveur and Verberie. Here the battalion, posted East of St. Sauveur, had to picquet and obstruct roads leading NW. in which direction German cavalry were in evidence again, the picquets having a few brushes with their patrols. Major Hicks' wound had now forced him to retire to hospital, Major Barlow taking command.

While these days had seen the gap between the First and Second Corps virtually closed and the danger of their separation averted, since Le Cateau contact with the enemy had been almost lost, von Kluck's First Army having pushed on South Westward, and if our First Corps had had some clashes with Bülow's Second Army, these had not really impeded its Southward move. On August 29th Lanrezac's Army had attempted to check the German pursuit by standing at Guise, but this had not sufficed to do more than delay Bülow, and

---

[1] I.e. well West of the line taken by the rest of the brigade.

[2] These accounted for most of the stragglers who subsequently rejoined.

next day Lanrezac had to resume his retreat. His halt at Guise had, however, exposed him to envelopment should von Kluck's Army now wheel round to its left and, moving SE., fall on him before he could cross the Marne. This von Kluck was attempting and it was his cavalry advanced-guards that the Fourth Division's outposts had encountered on August 31st.

Sir John French's orders for September 1st prescribed for the Fourth Division and the 19th Brigade, now forming the Third Corps under Lt. General Pulteney, an early start for the area round Baron, ten miles South of Verberie. Many units of his Corps having reached their billets late on August 31st, General Pulteney had now to postpone his start, and the Hampshire outposts had not yet moved when about 6 a.m. cavalry [1] began pressing in on them. These they effectively kept at bay until, about 8 a.m. orders were received for the battalion and the East Lancashire on its left to fall back through the Rifle Brigade and Somerset, who were in a covering position on high ground in rear. As the Hampshire fell back, A Company furnishing a rear-guard, a company of the Somerset on their right rear gave the battalion useful help, being quite sharply engaged, while when the covering battalions retired in their turn C Company under Captain Connellan on a ridge at Vaucelle assisted the Somerset effectively, checking the Germans and then taking over the rear-guard. On getting away through a wood, the Hampshire's rear-guard rounded a corner to find dismounted cavalry in force only 200 yards away. These blazed away without much effect, the Hampshire replying with one ' area shoot ' at a well-concealed enemy, while at another point some men under Lt. Dolphin lined a bank and had ' some very satisfactory shooting ', with some hand to hand fighting in a turnip field. Orders reaching the detachment to retire, it did so, breaking off the engagement quite successfully. One party, with which were Captains Richards and Harland, Lt. Knocker and 2/Lt. Nicholson, now crossed an unfordable stream by means of a life-line formed by linking rifle-straps together for the non-swimmers. Increased by details from other units to nearly 150, this detachment made its way to Nery, passing close to the site of the morning's action there, and rejoined the battalion that evening at Rosieres.[2] Lt. Dolphin's party had also got away, crossing the same stream by using a fallen tree as their bridge.

' The Germans seemed to have suffered severely and did not press the pursuit ' is the Somerset's account, and once the rearward movement had started it was not molested. Elsewhere all along the B.E.F.'s line, at Nery, Crepy en Valois and Villers Cotterets, our rear-guards had been more or less sharply engaged but had punished the Germans appreciably. One effect of these engagements was that von Kluck, having to his surprise encountered stiff resistance from the British, whom he had reckoned to be a negligible factor incapable of offering serious opposition, was distracted from his original plan. Instead of pressing on Eastward to fall on Lanrezac before he could cross the Marne, he swung his men round South to pursue the retiring B.E.F. but failed to

[1] The German 2nd Cavalry Division and the advanced troops of their IInd Corps.
[2] N.E. of Baron.

bring it to action, and when he resumed his Eastward move it was too late to intercept the French Fifth Army.[1]

That evening the Hampshire bivouacked at Rosieres [2] and got a really good meal, the more appreciated because it had been in preparation for some German cavalry, who had retired discreetly on their approach. They were glad also to rejoin their transport ; it had come under shell-fire, but Captain Hackett struck off across country and brought it through safely. Major Barlow had had the misfortune to be taken prisoner : going back through the forest to look for a missing company, he had run into German cavalry. Captain Palk therefore took command.[2]

Mere marching without any more fighting now followed ; the first day's march, still Southward and in stifling heat, brought the B.E.F. to the line Dammartin[3] (Third Corps)—Meaux, on the next it crossed the Marne, the Hampshire at Ligny, to get a welcome rest on September 4th, with a chance to wash and shave. That afternoon, however, the Hampshire were ordered to take up an outpost position near Couperey to cover the crossings of the Marne. An alarm that the enemy were bridging the river proved to be unfounded, but the battalion remained in readiness to dispute the passage till about 3.30 a.m. (September 5th) when it started off again. This early move was ordered partly to avoid hostile observation, partly to benefit by marching in the cool of the night and early morning.

As things turned out this had far-reaching consequences, as this move carried the B.E.F. to points SSE. of Paris, from Brie Comte Robert on the left (Third Corps) to Rozoy, well SW. of the line facing East which should have been taken up had General Joffre's orders for September 5th reached G.H.Q. in time for our march to be stopped and its direction altered. Could Joffre's orders have been carried out, the B.E.F. could have hardly avoided serious contact with the Germans directly it started forward on September 6th. What had happened was that von Kluck's effort to intercept Lanrezac and roll the French line up from its left had carried his Army SE., leaving on its flank the garrison of Paris with Maunoury's newly formed French Sixth Army and the B.E.F., the last not as incapable of an offensive as von Kluck seems still to have imagined. The would-be enveloper was thus lending himself to envelopment, and General Joffre, having substantially reinforced his left by reverting to the defensive in Lorraine and thus freeing many units for use elsewhere, was now in position to pass over to the offensive and fall on the weak flank-guard von Kluck had left facing Paris. Joffre's attack had actually started on September 5th, Maunoury's men advancing North of the Marne to engage Kluck's IVth Reserve Corps on the Ourcq, separated as it was by a substantial gap from the rest of his First Army. Realising its peril von Kluck had on September 6th to halt his advance and order his right and right centre, the IInd and IVth Corps,

---

[1] As the *Official History* (1914. I. p. 266) says, Kluck's Army had advanced ' under 10 miles and had not struck to any purpose either the French Fifth Army or the British '.

[2] This day's casualties only came to half-a-dozen.

[3] The Hampshire halted at this place.

to retrace their steps and recross the Marne, thereby opening a gap between them and his two remaining Corps, who were engaged South of Montmirail with the French Fifth Army, now under General Franchet d'Esperey. Had the B.E.F. been where General Joffre wished it to be, the IInd and IVth Corps could hardly have carried out their move unimpeded but must have become engaged with the B.E.F. somewhere SW. of Coulomniers.

As it was, the early start had carried the B.E.F. well to the South and out of immediate contact with the enemy. Its units had mostly reached their halting places [1] early in the day and were taking the opportunity to get a real rest and even a wash. During the day most battalions and artillery brigades picked up their ' first reinforcements ', the Hampshire being joined by 52 men under Captain R. D. Johnston,[2] a much smaller reinforcement than most battalions received. Their arrival was welcome, while the news that the retreat was over and that the B.E.F. was taking the offensive next day was even more cheering. If this meant fresh efforts and fresh exertions, at least the men would be going in the right direction. The battalion had been marching almost continuously for nearly a fortnight, in which it had covered nearly 200 miles, often short of food, always short of rest and sleep, and the small number of sick and stragglers were a great testimony to the fitness, discipline and splendid spirit of the men. It had been hard for regimental officers and men to understand why they were retiring before an enemy on whom they had inflicted substantial losses and whom they were ready to meet again. A ' strategical retirement into the interior of the country ' may have been the only solution for the serious situation which had confronted the Allies after the unexpected strength developed by the German thrust through neutral Belgium and the failure of the French counter-stroke in the Ardennes and Lorraine : it was not easily appreciated by those who had to carry it out and to endure the toils and hardships of the ' Retreat from Mons '. That retreat with all its exertions and difficulties had tested the the training, discipline and soldierly qualities of the British troops even more severely than their actual encounters with the enemy. Those who emerged from it unshaken and undismayed, fully ready to turn and hit back effectively, had deserved well of their country and had more than sustained the regimental traditions and spirit which had helped appreciably in what they had accomplished.

[1] The Hampshire at Chevry, but with two companies on outpost to the NE. at Gretz, on the road to Tournan.

[2] Lt. J. F. Gwynn, R.A.M.C. had joined on the previous day to replace Captain Williams.

CHAPTER II

THE MARNE—THE AISNE—THE MOVE TO FLANDERS.

THE position in which the B.E.F. found itself on September 6th put its right ten miles too far West, while the Third Corps on its left was double that distance from its intended place, so that the first move had to be a wheel to the right, pivoting on the First Corps, which could not venture to push forward far until the Second and Third had come up into line on its left and were ready to support it. The advanced guards did indeed get into touch with German troops, those covering the move of von Kluck's IInd and IVth Corps back across the Marne, but they had to confine themselves to pushing these flank-guards back and were unable to press against their supports, still less to interfere with the main bodies beyond them. Rather after midday the Second and Third Corps came up into line with the First, the Third getting to Villeneuve le Comte, whence in the afternoon it advanced to Villiers sur Morin. The Hampshire had the satisfaction of seeing many signs of the hasty movement of the Germans, dead men, more dead horses and much evidence of damage, if they did not encounter the enemy. The B.E.F. was now in a position to advance NE. across the Grand Morin and Petit Morin into the gap now opening in the German line. This gap was widened during September 7th and 8th, when Maunoury's menace to von Kluck's right flank and rear brought the latter's two remaining Corps back Northwards across the Marne to join in the battle now developing on the Ourcq. This move uncovered the right flank of Bülow's Second Army, but, undervaluing once again the B.E.F.'s fighting capacities, von Kluck expected to check our advance with a screen of cavalry, reinforced by Jäger and cyclists with many machine-guns but quite inadequate, as it proved, for its task. The B.E.F., which had reached the Grand Morin on September 7th without meeting serious opposition, though the cavalry had several successful encounters, had quite stiff fighting next day, when its passage of the Petit Morin was stubbornly disputed, and some sharp actions resulted in our breaking through the enemy's lines at several points and inflicting quite substantial casualties.

The Third Corps on our left had met less opposition than the other two. On September 7th, the 11th Brigade had reached Montdenis beyond the Grand Morin after an exhausting march in great heat and very short of rations, and the next day's advance took it to Les Corbières. It was behind the leading brigades of its Division, which found the enemy in some strength at La Ferté sous Jouarre, where the Petit Morin joins the Marne. These brigades eventually crossed the Petit Morin and got into La Ferté, after some fighting, but the 11th did not come into action, and the Hampshire, who bivouacked at Les Corbières about 7 p.m. on high ground overlooking La Ferté, had a tiring day without firing a shot. Captains Palk and Moore having had to go sick, Captain Connellan took command, with temporary rank as Major.

The success of the First and Second Corps in forcing the passage of the Petit Morin and thrusting aside the opposing cavalry and Jäger was exploited next day (September 9th), when both Corps crossed the Marne unopposed at several several places above La Ferté sous Jouarre and established themselves on von Kluck's left rear, his whole Army being now across the Marne and closely engaged against Maunoury.   Unluckily an inaccurate air-report of large columns moving NW. from Chateau Thierry caused the First Corps to halt just when another short advance promised to catch von Kluck's left at a great disadvantage.   This unfortunate halt allowed von Kluck, now fully aware of his precarious situation, to break off his battle against Maunoury and thereby to extricate his army from its dangerous position, so that it got back across the Aisne, somewhat shaken and disorganized but with all its fighting formations intact ; it could therefore profit by the advantageous tactical position presented by the high ground on the right bank of the Aisne immediately East and West of Soissons, familiar as the Chemin des Dames ridge.

It may be idle to speculate on what might have happened had the B.E.F. closed with von Kluck on September 9th or if the night march of September 4th/5th had not prevented our engaging his main body in the act of retracing its steps Northwards across our front : still on the Aisne we fought at tactical disadvantages we should have escaped in either of the other situations, and even if we had had as heavy fighting and even more serious losses than we incurred in establishing ourselves across the Aisne, much more might well have been achieved.

September 9th did not bring the Third Corps, least of all the 1st Hampshire, much fighting, though the Germans were still hanging on to La Ferté sous Jouarre and were strongly posted North of the river.   The Rifle Brigade were sent forward to clear up La Ferté, the Hampshire covering their advance from high ground to the SW., where they came under some fire from across the river, mainly snipers, and got occasional chances of replying.   However the clearing of La Ferté took some time and not till late afternoon could the Hampshire move down into the town.   Before this the 12th Brigade had got across at a lock some way upstream, whereupon the defenders of La Ferté, fearing to have their retreat cut off, had withdrawn.   While they had destroyed the stone bridge, they had been in too great a hurry to put out of action the many rowing boats available, and in these the Hampshire and the East Lancashire began about 9 p.m. an unopposed passage.

B Company, now under Captain Harland, were the first Hampshire across, to find many wounded Germans but none to fight, and, covered by the screen B threw out, the rest were all across by 11 p.m., two men getting drowned in the process.   There was no wasting time, by 2 a.m. (September 10th) the battalion was advancing again and before daylight had secured a line on high ground two miles to the Northward.   But for one Uhlan patrol the only Germans encountered were dead or badly wounded and again the road-side was littered with the debris of their hasty retirement.   The enemy was not standing on the order of his going, and the Third Corps, having been delayed at La Ferté, was slightly behind the Second and First, whose advanced-guards had sharp fighting with rear-guards, whom they handled quite severely besides capturing many

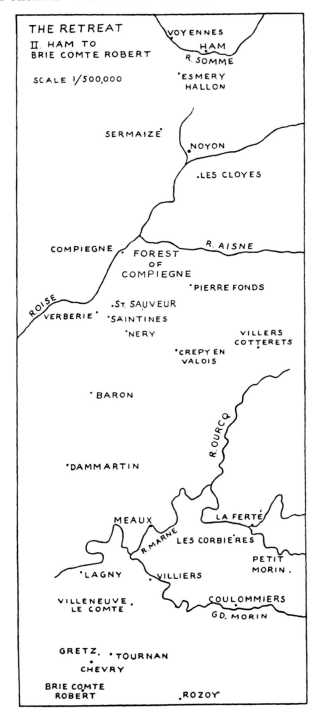

THE RETREAT
II. HAM TO
BRIE COMTE ROBERT

SCALE 1/500,000

VOYENNES
HAM
R. SOMME

'ESMERY
HALLON

SERMAIZE'

.NOYON

.LES CLOYES

COMPIEGNE . FOREST
OF
COMPIEGNE

R. AISNE

'PIERRE FONDS

.St. SAUVEUR
VERBERIE' 'SAINTINES
'NERY

ROISE

VILLERS
COTTERETS

'CREPY EN
VALOIS

' BARON

'DAMMARTIN

R. OURCQ

MEAUX
R. MARNE

LA FERTÉ

LES CORBIE'RES

PETIT
MORIN .

'LAGNY   .VILLIERS

VILLENEUVE .
LE COMTE

COULOMMIERS
GD. MORIN

GRETZ. 'TOURNAN
.
CHEVRY

BRIE COMTE
ROBERT
.ROZOY

stragglers, but neither on September 10th or 11th did the Hampshire come into conflict with the enemy. They toiled on, often through pelting rain and short of rations, cheered to be advancing and strengthened by a ' second reinforcement ' of 137 men under Captain Sandeman (3rd Battalion) who joined on September 9th.

September 12th brought the B.E.F. into contact with the enemy again, the First and Second Corps meeting opposition along the Vesle, a tributary which joins the Aisne near the bridge at Condé, where a spur of the high ground North of the river juts out almost to the bank. The Third Corps, whose line of advance was bringing it to the Aisne below Condé, did not meet this opposition, and by 3 p.m. its leading brigade, the 12th, had reached Septmonts, only three miles from the Aisne, and the Divisional cavalry, scouting ahead, were reconnoitring the bridges on its front, that at Venizel being found damaged but not destroyed. Brigadier-General Wilson, now commanding the Fourth Division as General Snow had been disabled by an accident, determined to see if this bridge could be used and detailed the 11th Brigade to attempt a crossing. Accordingly, about 10 p.m. the Hampshire, after three hours in billets at Septmonts, had to turn out and lead the way down to the river. As a preliminary Lts. im Thurn and Knocker were sent to reconnoitre the bridge, to find that though the main girders had been cut through, the reinforced concrete of the road-way offered a passage to men in single file. Lt. im Thurn thereupon cut the fuses of a charge of explosive which had apparently failed to work, an Uhlan patrol, which appeared while he was in the act of cutting the fuse, fortunately retiring without trying to interfere.

About midnight, therefore, the Hampshire started to lead the brigade across. It was a tedious business and tricky ; as one officer wrote, ' to cough on the bridge was to set the whole structure shaking ', while the ammunition carts had to be unloaded and taken across empty, their contents being carried over separately. The first men across formed a covering screen, but no German patrols troubled them, and by 3 a.m. (September 13th) General Hunter-Weston could order an advance towards the higher ground [1] beyond the two miles of water-meadows and flat ground immediately North of the river, the Hampshire in the centre making for Bucy le Long.

It was a daring move in the dark, over unreconnoitred ground, with no idea of what Germans were ahead or where they were, but its daring was fully justified. No opposition was encountered and after D Company (Captain Johnston) had found Bucy le Long unoccupied, the Hampshire reached the foot of the heights just as day was breaking : sweeping up them, the battalion established itself on the crest, German outposts, completely surprised, retiring in haste. A position was promptly taken up and entrenching begun, the Hampshire being around La Montagne Farm, with the Rifle Brigade and the Somerset on right and left respectively. The men were nearly dead beat, having marched over 30 miles since starting off on the 12th, but theirs was the only brigade of the B.E.F. across the Aisne.

---

[1] The ridge was about 300 feet up from the river.

Unluckily the position the Fourth Division had so enterprisingly secured had serious tactical defects, above all the difficulty of finding good artillery positions North of the river,[1] while the heights South of it were so far back that guns posted on them could not reach the German gun positions. Accordingly when, early on September 13th, the Germans started a heavy bombardment of the 11th Brigade's line, little reply could be made and the men could only hang on despite the shell-fire and do their best with their ' grubbers ' to im-

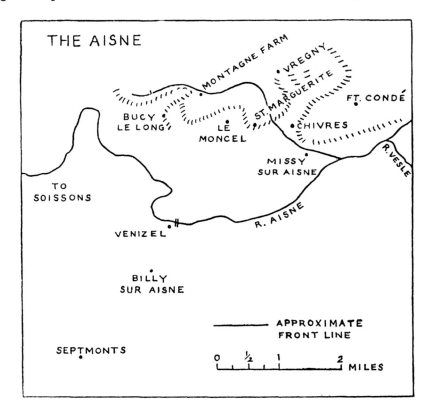

THE AISNE

MONTAGNE FARM
VREGNY
ST. MARGUERITE
FT. CONDÉ
BUCY LE LONG
LE MONCEL
CHIVRES
R. VESLE
TO SOISSONS
MISSY SUR AISNE
R. AISNE
VENIZEL
BILLY SUR AISNE

——— APPROXIMATE FRONT LINE

SEPTMONTS

0   ½   1   2   MILES

prove their position. This lack of artillery support effectively forbade any advance by the Fourth Division or by the Fifth on its right, between it and the Condé spur, and though the Fifth Division with some help from the right brigade of the Fourth made several efforts the little ground gained was not worth the casualties, and during the three weeks the Hampshire spent on the Aisne no major advance was attempted, though a forward line was entrenched by night. Some wooded ground on their left front was a weak spot and at first a gap separated them from the Somerset L.I. This was filled on September 14th by two companies of the Dublins who assisted to drive off some enemy who were

[1] Some guns were eventually brought across and even found positions almost in the firing line, but the advantage in artillery positions was all with the Germans.

pushing forward, but after that the line remained virtually unchanged apart from readjustments between battalions, the Hampshire after spending four days at La Montagne side-stepping about a mile to the left.

The Hampshire's ' opposite numbers ', part of the IInd Corps, showed little inclination to give them a chance to show their shooting powers by attacking. With all their advantages in numbers, in position and in artillery, the Germans here were singularly unenterprising.   One officer wrote that ' but for sniping and occasional scrapping by outposts at night we have not had much infantry fighting.   The Germans have made one or two disjointed attempts at attacking but have been beaten back each time.'   On September 19th, for example, a wiring party was heavily fired on and this was followed by an attack, which was repulsed with only two casualties, including one man who ran his bayonet into his own nose.   It was upstream of the Fourth Division's position that the critical fighting took place and that the timely arrival of German reinforcements only just forestalled the B.E.F.'s advance into the still open gap between the Ist and IInd German Armies and so prevented it making the Aisne what the Marne had just missed being, a decisive victory over the German right wing.   The counter-attacks which endeavoured to throw back into, and across, the Aisne the British troops established on the slopes of the Chemin des Dames did not extend below Condé, so the Fourth Division was denied the chance of hitting back effectively by which the First Corps and the Third Division profited.

To the 1st Hampshire the Aisne was therefore mainly notable as their intro-duction to that ' trench warfare ' of which they were to have so much stern experience.   For ' trench warfare ' the British Army was but ill-equipped, all the apparatus it required, from periscopes onward, had to be improvised some-how and the technique and routine of this type of fighting painfully acquired. The Germans may not have expected the war to develop like this nor had they trained their troops for it, any more than we had, but being far better equipped for sieges they could utilise siege-warfare equipment for the new purpose.   The 1st Hampshire in common with the whole B.E.F. had to learn the trade by experience.   They busied themselves in consolidating systematically their position North of Bucy le Long, improving their trenches, connecting them, digging communication trenches leading back from the front line, putting up pointed stakes to serve as an obstacle, while they had to strip the neigh-bouring fields for wire.   No Man's Land was open ground, under cultivation, but behind the front line there were woods and the steep slopes of the ridge contained caves, one ' weird and huge cave and quite romantic ', it was said, gave quite good cover for battalion headquarters, another sheltering the reserve company.   By night patrols pushed out towards the German trenches, here over 1000 yards away, and obtained much useful information, if encounters with hostile patrols were infrequent.   Very occasionally a German patrol approached our trenches and gave our men something to shoot at; thus, early on October 1st, 'the first day of pheasant shooting ', a patrol reported having ' bagged seven and half brace ' of ' Pomeranian Grenadiers ' at the cost of only one wounded, and on another occasion our machine guns got a chance when a haystack was set on fire and several Germans bolted from it. Our snipers also were busy. As one officer wrote ' we know when a German relief arrives, as they walk about on the sky-line but they don't do it a second time.' ' Things are pretty quiet here ' another wrote : ' we sometimes bag a German or two.' At first, before entrenching tools could be brought across so that the battalion was really well dug in, the shelling, which was often heavy, caused nearly all the casualties,[1] as our guns could not silence the German batteries which were mainly beyond their range. After that, with our position much improved, casualties decreased, while despite wet weather and the discomforts and bad conditions in the trenches fewer men went sick than might have been expected. Sleeping in the open, often on wet ground, with no chances of a change of clothing and the scantiest opportunities of washing, did not seem to disagree over much with the men's health, and once the retreat was over rations were plentiful and good. With the troops stationary in trenches, mails and parcels containing many ' comforts ' could be delivered regularly, while large supplies of clothing and equipment arrived, including two machine guns, and the battalion was soon pretty well refitted, though boots were slow to appear. Every new arrival commented on the extraordinary cheerfulness of the men and their endurance of the conditions. After a bit every-one got quite used to the shelling, which was largely ineffective, and life was developing into a regular routine. Two large drafts, amounting to 266 other ranks, many of them ' Section D ' Reservists, under Lts. Wade and Twining (3rd. Bn.) and 2/Lt. Gill [2] arrived before the end of September [3] and with them Major Parker, who had been commanding the new 10th (Service) Battalion, to take command, taking over from Major [4] Connellan who had been commanding for several days and doing admirably. Several vacancies among the subalterns were filled up by the promotion of N.C.O.s who had done good service in the field, including R.S.M. Fidler and C.S.M.s Coulter and Sprake.

Within a few days of the British reaching the Aisne it became evident that a deadlock was being established on that front. We had just failed to exploit our opportunity on the Marne but we had definitely foiled and thwarted the German effort at a ' knock-out ' blow on the Western front. A new phase in the operations was now developing : both the French and Germans trying to turn their opponents' uncovered Western flank. Each in turn prolonged the outer flank, the French extending their line Northward beyond the Oise to get round behind von Kluck's right. The Germans parried this threat by bringing troops across from their left and left centre, threatening in their turn to outflank the outflankers. They were still not without hopes of sweeping round the French left and with this were combining projects for seizing the almost uncovered ' Channel ports.' The ' Race to the Sea ', into which this developed, was going

---

[1] Up to September 18th 11 men were killed and Captain Richards, Lt. Westmorland and 54 men wounded. September 13th was the worst day.

[2] Newly commissioned from the R.M.C.

[3] The arrival of 20 ' stragglers ' is recorded on September 23rd, mainly foot-sore men who had fallen out during the retreat and had been given lifts in lorries. The battalion had fewer than any other in the brigade.

[4] Temporary rank.

on in the last fortnight of September and creating a new front line Northward from the Oise over the Somme into Flanders, so that it seemed possible that our line might gain touch with the Belgians, still in the occupation of Antwerp and of the Belgian coast line. British reinforcements, a Seventh Division, mainly composed of troops withdrawn from South Africa and our Mediterranean garrisons, and the two Divisions which India was sending to Europe would soon be available, and it was desirable that all our troops should be together under our Commander-in-Chief. Other considerations, mainly administrative, partly political, made it expedient to get the British forces on to the left flank again, instead of having them in the middle of the French line, and before the end of September it had been decided to relieve the B.E.F. by French troops and to transfer it to Flanders.

This move was begun by the Second Corps on October 1st, the Fourth Division extending to the right to take over the Fifth's trenches ; five nights later the Third Corps followed the Second, having been relieved by the French, the Hampshire, who had left their position North of Bucy le Long after dark on October 4th and crossed the Aisne at Venizel, bivouacked South of Ville Montoire ; starting off again at 1 a.m. they had reached Billy sur Ourcq before dawn. Five marches, mostly by night or in the late afternoon, in hopes of evading German air observation, then carried them Westward to the railway at Estreé St. Denis, where they entrained early on October 11th. Journeying by Montdidier and Amiens they reached Wizernes about 10 p.m., detrained there and marched to billets at Oiselle two miles away. Three weeks in the trenches had not been good preparation for marching, as it had been difficult to keep men properly exercised and many men's feet and boots had suffered from the mud and wet which so much rain had caused, some men indeed had to march in gym shoes and with bandaged feet, but the battalion was not much below establishment [1] and was very ready to give a good account of itself.

[1] Captains Beckett and Unwin and Lt. Prendergast (3rd Battalion) had joined just before the battalion left the Aisne, and Captain Cope and Lts. Standen, Morgan and Harrington (all 3rd Battalion) joined on October 11th, against which Captain Moore and 2/Lts. Sweet and Nicholson had been invalided home. Lt. Aitchison also joined in October.

THE FIGHT FOR THE CHANNEL PORTS
—WINTER IN THE TRENCHES.

THE B.E.F.'s move to Flanders had placed it on the left of General Maudhuy's Tenth Army, whose line extended Northward East of Arras and West of Lens almost to Bethune and the La Bassée canal. When the B.E.F. reached Flanders the German right extended no further Northward, except that large bodies of cavalry, stiffened by Jäger and cyclists, were advancing Westward from Lille and SW. up the Lys valley, threatening to sweep away the thin screen of French cavalry and Territorials facing them on the line Bethune—Aire—St. Omer. It was this cavalry that the Second and Third Corps were now to encounter, the Second astride the La Bassée canal but not reaching quite to the Lys, on whose left bank the Third, after detraining about St. Omer, would advance. Ahead of them and between them and the great industrial area of Lille lay the Aubers Ridge, only a slight rise but sufficiently above the level of the low and rather water-logged Flanders plain to possess tactical and even strategical importance.

The Third Corps completed its concentration in time to advance on October 13th, the Second, which had started two days earlier, being already in conflict with the enemy. The 11th Brigade had been taken in motor buses to Hondeghem on October 12th, a very bumpy journey being punctuated by many stops and some loss of direction and taking nearly five hours, time enough to have marched the 14 miles and been little more fatigued. Next day, when the enemy were encountered at Meteren and driven back, the brigade was in reserve, and though about 9.30 p.m. the Hampshire were ordered forward to reinforce the 12th Brigade, they were not engaged. Later on C Company came up between the 12th Brigade and the Sixth Division on its right, with whom a patrol under Captain Twining gained touch during the night, while the company covered a night advance by the Lancashire Fusiliers, who cleared Meteren, taking some prisoners,[1] thereby completing the previous day's work. The next day (Oct. 14th) took the Hampshire forward to Bailleul ; they were advanced-guard to the Division but the only opposition came from cavalry patrols and cyclists, who were soon pushed back, a few prisoners being taken : the enemy apparently had been sharply punished at Meteren and had gone back behind the Lys. The inhabitants' joy at being delivered from German brutalities found expression in their readiness to provide the troops with fruit and eggs and hot coffee at any moment. The battalion spent most of October 15th on outpost, to the South of Bailleul, and it was dark before it received orders to push on to the Lys and occupy Nieppe. It started forward therefore about 6 p.m. C Company leading and securing a covering position South of Nieppe, after which B Company (Captain Unwin) advanced direct upon the village to be received by machine-gun

[1] One was captured by C.

fire. They quickly established themselves in the village, however, having only a dozen casualties. Pressing on towards the bridge, Lt. Knocker's platoon found it strongly barricaded and came under machine-gun fire but escaped casualties, though Lt. Knocker was so unfortunate as to fall into a cesspit in avoiding the bullets. It was difficult to understand why the Division was not being directed to press forward more vigorously : the Germans did not seem to be in great strength and were retiring. Next day, (Oct. 16th) however, the Division secured the passages over the Lys at Pont de Nieppe and at Erquinghem, a little way upstream. At Pont de Nieppe C Company worked forward into a flanking position to cover the main advance by A and D ; this was also covered by the machine-guns, now under Lt. Wade, and after a 18 pr. had been brought forward and had demolished the barricade across the bridge with its first shot, the

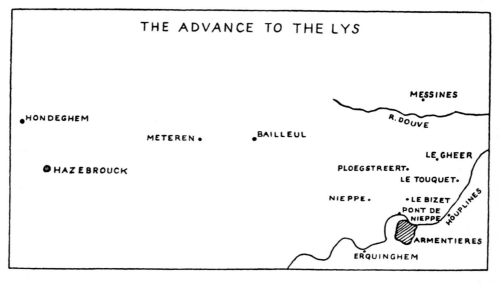

THE ADVANCE TO THE LYS

Germans retired hastily, assisted by 'five rounds rapid' from C. The Sixth Division on the right was also across, and during the day the cavalry gained touch with the Seventh Division, which, after a fruitless effort to help Antwerp, was now in front of Ypres and ready to co-operate in the main operations.

That evening found two companies of the Hampshire holding a forward line from Erquinghem along the railway to the Nieppe—Armentieres road, the other two being on the main road behind the left.

The next three days (October 17th—19th) the 11th Brigade spent in reserve, the 10th advancing through Armentieres to Houplines, while on its left the 12th reached a line East of Ploegsteert Wood ; the Hampshire, in Divisional reserve, came up to Armentieres on the 18th, waiting there next day. Some 'spy hunting' went on, parties searching the town for Germans in and out of uniform left behind to signal and get information, several being captured. The First Corps was now arriving from the Aisne and getting ready to advance beyond Ypres, to make what Sir John French optimistically hoped would be the successful out-flanking movement against the German right, but though to the Southward the Second Corps was established on the Aubers Ridge at Herlies, its right was meeting stiff opposition opposite La Bassée and it was only prudence to keep something in reserve. Already the B.E.F. was covering a front out of all pro-portion to its strength and its attacks had nothing behind them. That this imposed on the Germans and caused them to credit the B.E.F. with reserves it did not possess may be admitted, but when our offensive encountered opposition it could not overcome and we were thrown back upon an unprepared defensive, our long and thinly held line presented many weak spots and gaps.

This was evident when on October 20th the Germans, having been substanti-ally reinforced, passed to the offensive and thrust hard at both Second and Third Corps. Both had to give ground ; even if the Fourth Division slightly improved its position across the Lys, on its right the Sixth was thrust back and the Fourth had to prepare to see the counter-attack extended to its front. The 11th Brigade was held in reserve ' as long as possible ',[1] though a battalion had to be sent to help the hard-pressed Sixth Division. Of the Hampshire three companies were sent forward to entrench positions in support East of Armen-tieres ; in doing this they were heavily shelled and the casualties unfortunately included one of the battalion's mainstays, Major Connellan, now commanding C Company. He had given proof of his capacity when in temporary command on the Aisne and was much regretted.

October 21st brought no real relaxation of German pressure, though the heavy price their gains had cost them had taken some of the sting out of their attacks. Overnight General Hunter-Weston had been ordered to take all the available troops of his brigade to Le Gheer and Ploegsteert to support the hard-pressed left of the Division, but the Hampshire remained in Divisional reserve, having been detailed to be ready to help the Sixth Division, and they thus missed a share in the highly successful counter-attack by which their Brigadier restored the critical situation at Le Gheer where the Germans had broken through the 12th Brigade's front. About 10 a.m., however, A and C Companies under Captain Unwin were ordered up to Ploegsteert, to support the left of the Division's line against which the enemy were pressing. The rest of the battalion followed them in the evening, to be put into billets in Ploegsteert village and then turned out in the small hours (October 22nd) to relieve the King's Own, who had had a very hard, if successful, day at the Le Touquet cross-roads. This relief was not made easier by difficulties in finding the way and was not quite finished by daylight, when the Germans opened a heavy fire and started to advance against a trench which B Company was taking over from some of the 11th Hussars. Lt. Dolphin, however, rushed the leading men of his platoon up into the trenches in time to bring the German advance to a standstill by some accurate shooting and the German rifle-fire, though heavy, proved harmless and inflicted no casualties.

The Hampshire now started to improve their trenches and take any chances

[1] H.Q. Diary, Fourth Division.

offered by the Germans, whose line was about 700 yards away, too far for their snipers to do much damage. It was some satisfaction to see how heavily previous German attacks had been punished, the ground being covered with their dead. A and C Companies meanwhile were away to the left beyond Ploeg-steert Wood, between St. Yves and the Douve. Neither detachment was seriously troubled during the day and after dark both were relieved and drawn back into reserve at a chateau near Ploegsteert, where the battalion remained for

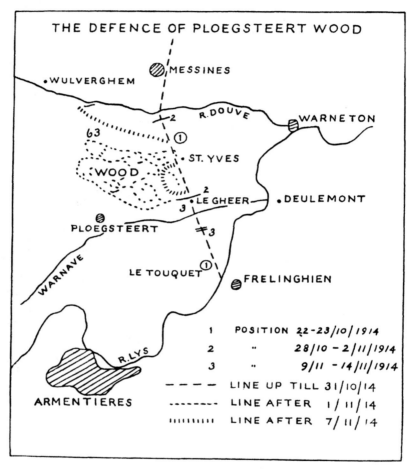

THE DEFENCE OF PLOEGSTEERT WOOD

	POSITION 22-23/10/1914
1	POSITION 22-23/10/1914
2	" 28/10 – 2/11/1914
3	" 9/11 – 14/11/1914
– – –	LINE UP TILL 31/10/14
- - - - - -	LINE AFTER 1/11/14
ııııııııı	LINE AFTER 7/11/14

four days, digging a reserve line. The Division had meanwhile taken over more line on the right of the Lys and was thus extended over an eight miles frontage, thinly held and almost without reserves. Fortunately in its musketry the B.E.F. had still a substantial asset; if the last Regular Reservists had before this time come out, the trained Special Reservists, now providing most of the drafts, had also learnt to shoot. Shortage of artillery ammunition, however, was forcing our guns to restrict their firing to the absolutely essential, making our chances more dependent than ever on our infantry's staunchness and good shooting, but in this we had something the enemy could not overcome.

But for persistent shell-fire the Fourth Division was not much troubled during the four days the 1st Hampshire spent in reserve at Ploegsteert. Something could therefore be done to improve the line, dig communication trenches and generally prepare to meet another thrust. Very heavy fighting had now developed East of Ypres, where the First Corps and the Seventh Division were deeply involved in their great defence of the Channel ports, while further South the Second Corps and the Lahore Division, just arrived from India, were almost as hard pressed, and though the Fourth Division only had to beat off several small attacks, especially against its right and centre, it could not expect much more of the comparative quiet it was experiencing.

On the evening of October 28th the Hampshire relieved the Somerset L.I. East of Ploegsteert Wood past St. Yves, their left (B Company) resting on the Douve and their right (A) reaching to Le Gheer. But for one platoon of A Company the whole battalion was in the firing line, over 2000 yards in length, which consisted mainly of separate trenches, not a continuous line, and was almost without communication trenches. The enemy's line was about 1100 yards away. The first day here passed quietly enough, but about 6 p.m. an attack developed on Le Gheer, in repulsing which the battalion was effectively assisted by the 68th and 88th Batteries, R.F.A. This was only the prelude to a tremendous bombardment, which started about 6.30 a.m. (Oct. 30th) and was maintained with varying intensity throughout the day. It was the heaviest the battalion had yet endured and the trenches and their garrisons suffered heavily, but the men held on unflinchingly and whenever German infantry attempted to advance our rifles were ready for them. About 7.30 a.m. the 11th Brigade reported one such unsuccessful attack and at 10.30 another had been repulsed. The most dangerous attack came about 4.30 p.m. when the Germans swarmed forward in masses, trusting perhaps to the failing light to handicap our shooting. ' They came on so thick you couldn't miss them ' one man wrote ' It was just like shooting rabbits on Shillingston Hill.' They were checked nearly everywhere, the right centre in a good position soon stopped them getting near but in our left centre dead ground helped them and they rushed an isolated trench, in advance of our line, to which Lt. Trimmer and No. 10 Platoon had been clinging with magnificent tenacity, taking a heavy toll of the attackers before being killed or taken almost to a man. The Hampshire lost another fine officer when Captain Harland was killed here, exposing himself gallantly to direct the defence, and the Germans, having overwhelmed the last survivors of No. 10,[1] threatened to break right through. They were prevented from exploiting their success, largely by 2/Lt. Fidler's platoon who, though attacked in flank and rear, disposed of the Germans who were breaking through and by the machine guns under Lt. Wade, while Captain [2] Aitchison, now commanding C, threw up a barricade across the end of the next trench and planted a machine gun to enfilade the

---

[1] A few wounded men were taken, the majority, including Lt. Trimmer, had been killed.
[2] Promoted October 21st.

captured trench. This foiled the effort to roll up our line from the left, and any Germans who ventured to advance across the open were promptly sent back to cover by our unfailing shooting,[1] while eventually Lt. Trimmer's trench was won back by the brigade reserve, two companies of the Somerset, who drove the Germans out, inflicting heavy casualties, to find practically all the original defenders dead at their posts. The battalion's tenacious gallantry was most warmly acknowledged by the Brigadier, who was loud in his praise of its stubborn defence. Several prisoners were taken, whose capture revealed the presence on the Third Corps' front of a fresh German Corps.

That night much of the line was re-dug, from which the battalion benefited next day, when the trenches were subjected to another tremendous bombardment, followed once again by an infantry attack. This time the enemy again reached the wire in front of our trenches but they were driven back without the brigade reserve being called upon ; they had suffered heavily, 75 of their dead being counted in front of one short trench only. A company of the Somersets had occupied the left centre trenches which C had been holding and assisted in the repulse, while the battalion's left was now covered by bringing the Inniskillings up from reserve. That evening a small patrol under Lt. im Thurn went forward some 200 yards and brought back trophies from an evacuated trench.

If the Fourth Division had managed to maintain its line intact, beyond its left across the Douve the Germans, attacking in greatly superior force, had driven our cavalry and some attached infantry units off the Messines ridge, the loss of which (November 1st) necessitated the flinging back of the Fourth Division's line along the Northern edge of Ploegsteert Wood, so that it presented a distinct salient at St. Yves, while the Hampshire's left could be enfiladed from the ridge. Could the Germans have exploited their capture of Messines by advancing Westward up the Douve, the Fourth Division's line would have become untenable, but this they failed to do, and the line which the Hampshire had managed to maintain on October 30th and 31st was to remain, save for one small loss of ground, virtually unchanged until the German offensive of April 1918 drove us back almost to the outskirts of Hazebrouck. It was only maintained after further stubborn resistance to renewed attacks. On November 1st and again next day the line was again heavily bombarded and infantry attacks again followed. Though suffering severely from the bombardment, the Hampshire were quite ready for the infantry and punished them heavily whenever they tried to take advantage of the shell-fire and advance. With infantry attacks our rifles could deal, even one particularly violent effort early on November 1st was repulsed without having to call on the brigade reserves. Next day (November 2nd) the Germans actually broke in, driving back a platoon of D, but they were soon expelled by about 40 men under Captains Unwin and Beckett, Lt. Prendergast and 2/Lt. Standen, who promptly counter-attacked and cleared them out, Captain Unwin being wounded but remaining at duty.[2]

[1] One man claimed to have fired 150 rounds, despite being wounded in the left hand.
[2] Lt. Standen also was wounded, more seriously.

Two platoons of B had reinforced D, whose right platoon, No. 14, had held stoutly on, while the left half company had supported the charge with most effective covering fire, catching the enemy as they rose to meet it.

The shell-fire was a more formidable ordeal, but the G.O.C. Fourth Division reported that the battalion's conduct under very heavy shelling had been excellent. The trial was indeed severe, the trenches had not yet been linked up into a continuous line and isolated detachments often found themselves under very heavy fire without any chance of help. Sergant Williamson, for example, held on most tenaciously with a few men in one isolated trench and maintained his position intact. But the Hampshire were weary and worn after enduring all this bombarding, and it was well that on the evening of November 2nd General Hunter-Weston could give them a well-earned and urgently needed relief. The Indian Corps had now taken over the front held by the Second, whose battered units after the briefest of rests were now thrown into the fight again at critical points, two being placed at the 11th Brigade's disposal. November 3rd therefore found the Hampshire resting in bivouac at Ploegsteert. Since going into the line on October 28th they had lost, besides Captain Harland and Lt. Trimmer, 46 men killed, 51 missing[1] and 121 wounded. Captains Unwin (at duty) and Johnston, Lts. Wade and Harrington [2] and 2/Lt. Standen had been wounded and during October the Quartermaster, Captain Hackett, and 40 men had gone to hospital.

In November 1914 to be ' relieved ' usually merely meant to be shifted to another point in the line, and on the evening of November 4th the battalion took over the trenches held by the East Lancashire on the Ploegsteert road at Le Gheer, B Company being in reserve and the rest in the firing line. This time the battalion had about half a mile to hold with well under a man a yard for the purpose. Two ' quiet ' days followed, with an attempt by Germans dressed in kilts to pass themselves off as Scottish Rifles, not very successfully, and then on November 7th came a fresh attack in force, advantage being taken of a mist to launch no less than eight battalions against the 11th Brigade. Against the Hampshire they made no impression ; ' we poured volleys into them ' writes one account ' and a long line of dead marked the position they had reached '. On the left in the Southern part of Ploegsteert Wood they broke through a weak and weary battalion of the Second Corps, fitter for a long spell in reserve than for the line, and a large party began advancing round the Hampshire's flank. However, this did not shake the battalion's hold on its line. Once again Sergeant Williamson and a small party held on firmly in an isolated trench, and A Company, recently relieved from the firing line, promptly counter-attacked. Headed by Captains Unwin and Dolphin,[3] they quickly cleared the intruders out, capturing an officer, though Captain Dolphin was killed, being shot as he went forward to receive the surrender of men who were calling out ' Don't shoot ' and pretending to be ready to give in. This reception effectively discouraged further German efforts at this point, and eventually the brigade reserves

---

[1] Many probably buried under demolished trenches.
[2] Died of wounds.
[3] He had just been promoted.

recovered most of the lost ground except for some houses North of Le Gheer, the blunt salient thus left in our line, soon christened the ' Birdcage ', proving very troublesome thereafter.

The Hampshire's success had not beeen cheaply obtained, the casualties including Captain Dolphin and 34 men killed and missing and Captains Unwin (second time), and Aitchison and 2/Lt. Weston wounded with 20 men. Of the officers who had come out with the battalion only Captains Perkins and im Thurn [1] and Lt. Edsell now remained, though the campaign was well under three months old.

The attack of November 7th was the enemy's last serious venture against the Fourth Division. If the Germans, despite several efforts, maintained their hold on the ' Birdcage ', where the houses were sheltered by the wood from our artillery fire, even if ammunition had been available for demolishing them, they had had enough of attacking and did not repeat the experiment. Trench warfare conditions thus began some ten days sooner on the Fourth Division's front than in the Ypres Salient, where the German Guard had yet to make the supreme effort of November 11th which the remnant of the First Corps was to repulse so dramatically.

The Fourth Division's share in foiling the great German autumn offensive is apt to be overlooked, but attention should not be exclusively concentrated on the great struggle in the Ypres Salient to the extent of disregarding the achievement of the Second and Third Corps. They too had to struggle in most adverse conditions against very heavy odds, being at a great disadvantage as regards the volume of artillery support available, though so far as their limited means allowed our over-matched artillery shot extraordinarily effectively, earning the gratitude of our hard-pressed infantry : perhaps the attacks to be faced in this quarter, vigorous as they were, may have lacked just a little of the weight of numbers and thrust of those delivered against Ypres, but those two Corps and particularly the Fourth Division, had a much greater length of line to hold and this greatly enhanced the strain on them.

Those in the trenches in November 1914 may have hardly appreciated that the ' battle ' was over and that a stalemate was setting in. The 1st Hampshire continued in line at Le Gheer for a week after repulsing the attack of November 7th. The Germans, having evidently abandoned any idea of renewing their attacks, were busily improving their line, their working parties occasionally providing our rifles with good targets ; if shelling slackened, snipers were troublesome and caused most of our 30 casualties, which included four killed and two missing. We did some retaliatory sniping but were mainly occupied in working at the line, now becoming fairly strong, though bad weather severely impeded our efforts, trenches in that low-lying area rapidly becoming water-logged. Rain and mud greatly increased the strain of trench-warfare but despite all hardships and discomforts the men were extraordinarily cheerful, their patient endurance being really remarkable. ' The men are wonderful ' one

---

[1] Promoted Nov. 1st. besides him and Captain Aitchison, Lts. Venour and Wade had been promoted while most ' pre-war ' 2/Lts. had before this received a step.

company commander wrote, ' how they stick the wet and the cold with no sleep for days on end beats me.'

After three days out of the line, the battalion [1] then spent the last fortnight of November directly in front of Le Gheer and just North of its last trenches. Heavy rain had reduced the line to a dreadful state and hard as all worked it was difficult to produce much impression. Two companies were usually in front line, being relieved from support at regular intervals, the relief often taking several hours owing to communication trenches being so narrow and muddy and men going in ' loaded up like Tweedledum '. With the enemy so near nearly half the trench garrisons had to ' stand to ' all night, in hourly reliefs so that few got any real rest. Here also snipers were the chief trouble, causing another 20 casualties, nine fatal, while the Adjutant was wounded on November 18th when battalion headquarters was severely shelled, Captain im Thurn taking over his duties. The sick-rate was naturally high, Captain Cope (3rd Battalion), Lt. Edsell and 2/Lts. Coulter and Gill being sent to hospital with 92 men, while only 20 recovered sick returned to duty.

December brought little change. Our patrols were active, Lance Corporal Irish and Private Glasspool both distinguishing themselves by obtaining useful information about the enemy's defences, Glasspool locating a machine-gun.[2] Bad weather was more troublesome than the enemy, even constant pumping could not prevent the trenches from being flooded. They were continually caving in and needing revetting and even when temporarily free from water were knee-deep in slush. Some had to be abandoned and sandbag breastworks built up instead, while many experiments were made with bricks and wooden floors to keep men above the water level when in trenches. However, arrangements had now been made to give the men baths and clean clothes when they came out of trenches absolutely plastered with mud. Brewers' vats made excellent baths and ample supplies of clothing and ' comforts ' arrived regularly, supplementing the ample but rather monotonous rations. The clothing included ' some extraordinary fur garments with the fur outside ', ' one has only got to go on one's knees and growl to be like the bear in the pantomime ' one officer wrote. It was hard to be smart in such conditions. Considering the wetness of the trenches the sick-rate, 180 admissions to hospital in December, was hardly excessive, and the arrival of 260 men from the 3rd Battalion at the end of November went far to replenish the ranks. Major Hicks came back on December 12th and resumed command [3] and Captains Palk and Unwin also rejoined, while Captain Garsia, hitherto on duty as R.T.O., had joined on November 26th and taken over C Company. Several new subalterns appeared, of whom Lt. Smythe came from Sandhurst,[4] the others being from the 3rd Battalion, mostly Gazetted since August 4th but qualified to take their places in the field by a good deal of previous O.T.C. training.

[1] The Divisional Diary gives its strength on November 15th as eleven officers, no other battalion having as few, and 800 other ranks, two other battalions only being weaker.
[2] Both received the D.C.M.   [3] Promoted to temporary Lt. Colonel Nov. 29th.
[4] 2/Lts. Wyld (who was out with another regiment), Smythe and Gill, all commissioned from the R.M.C. in August, were promoted temporary Lts. in November.

The Birdcage was still a sore thorn in our flesh, its occupants could enfilade the left of the Hampshire line, which here formed a T, from 150 yards away, while it was too near our lines for our guns to range on it with any accuracy When therefore, in the middle of December, minor offensives were ordered at different points in our line to assist a French attack at Arras, the Fourth Division attempted to get rid of this constant cause of trouble, the Somerset

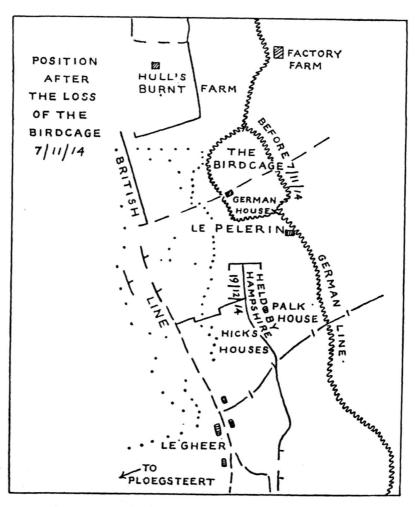

L. I. and Rifle Brigade being detailed for the attack, the Hampshire co-operating with fire and having a platoon of D company (Captain Palk) ready to dig in on the Rifle Brigade's right and connect the position captured with our main trench, now held by C Company (Captain Beckett).

Only a miserable allowance of ammunition was available, a mere 100 rounds for the howitzers, nothing like enough to give the attack a fair chance. Nevertheless, attacking at 2.30 p.m. on December 18th, the Rifle Brigade took the two nearest houses but could get no further, partly because our own shells fell short and caused several casualties. One Hampshire platoon caught several shells, but Captain Beckett steadied the men, setting a splendid example of coolness, and Sergeant Haydon backed him up well, C Company doing some effective shooting at Germans retiring from the forward houses, while the digging platoon under 2/Lt. Reeves got quickly to work, though the ground they had to entrench proved such a swamp that they soon had to come back. Unluckily, while directing machine-gun fire from our front trench, Major Parker was killed, the regiment thus losing yet another valued officer of much experience, ' a born leader ' who had commanded the battalion most successfully and was much missed by all ranks. In all, the Hampshire had 40 casualties, including Lt. Prendergast wounded and 15 men killed, and as the Rifle Brigade had over 70 casualties and only retained a small portion of their objective, the operation could hardly be reckoned very successful, though it was something to have ousted the German snipers from one coign of vantage. Both sides had by now constructed defences which could hardly be taken without a much larger ammunition expenditure than either could afford for a minor enterprise, and troops in trenches were now enjoying some respite from bombardment. Snipers, however, were very active : the flooding of the trenches which drove both sides to construct breastworks above ground naturally increased their opportunities, which neither side neglected, and of the battalion's 50 casualties in December, in addition to those of the 19th, snipers caused the majority, while ours claimed a good many hits, though the Saxons of the XIXth Corps, now facing the 11th Brigade, were not aggressive enough to offer many targets.

Trench mortars and hand grenades were now being brought into use, and with both the Germans were better prepared and better provided, while the British had to improvise, the ' jam-tin ' and the ' hair-brush ' patterns being among the earlier experiments, while if the ' drain-pipe ' brand of trench-mortar was as damaging to the enemy as it was dangerous to its crews, its use would have been amply justified.

The end of 1914 found the 1st Hampshire with only six officers present who had come out with the battalion in August, Lt. Colonel Hicks and Major Palk,[1] both of whom had rejoined, and Captains im Thurn and Knocker,[2] who had served continuously, as had 2/Lts. Fidler and Sprake, commissioned in October. Of original other ranks 366 were still present, the largest number in the brigade : 265 N.C.O.s and men had been killed or were missing, 390 had been wounded. Altogether eight officers had been killed, six were missing [3] and fifteen had been wounded.

The New Year brought the Hampshire little change. The Fourth Division's main problem was water, which the occupants of trenches in Ploegsteert Wood

[1] Promoted November. 20th.
[2] Captain Knocker had been off duty sick for a short time. He had been promoted temporarily on Nov. 15th
[3] All six were known to be prisoners of war.

had always with them, bale or pump as they would. A wet January ended with frost and snow, which went on into February and at any rate dried up the mud and reduced casualties, because with the communication trenches allowing of progress the temptation to risk crossing the open was less.

Spending hours in wet and muddy trenches was a constant cause of sickness, though from January extra rations, pea soup and more tea and sugar, were issued to men actually in the trenches. Though rheumatism and bronchitis were prevalent with a lot of ' trench feet ' and frost bite, for which new remedies had to be devised, pneumonia cases were remarkably few, and the admissions to hospital, 150 in January, 120 in February and 100 in March, were not as high as might have been feared.

Casualties in action came to Captain Knocker, who was hit by a sniper, and 11 men killed, Lt. Cecil,[1] 2/Lt. Lambert and 34 men wounded. That these were no higher was largely due to the steady improvement of the line, now showing the effect of all the hard work devoted to it. The men were becoming very expert at their work on the trenches, ' as good as R.E.'s ' one officer wrote. The houses behind the front line had become quite formidable ' strong points ', and though, as time wore on, the German shelling increased in volume it inflicted few casualties and did little damage to the defences, which were gradually becoming less uncomfortable as well as stronger. Conditions behind the lines also were being much improved, notably the arrangements for bathing and for providing dry clothing, and in February the arrival of a travelling kitchen or ' cooker ' was much appreciated.

Drafts came out in a fairly steady stream, though while some recovered sick came back straight from hospital in France, the majority of the sick and wounded were sent home, joining the 3rd Battalion on recovery. The drafts contained some re-enlisted old soldiers but now consisted largely of men enlisted since August 4th, good material if their musketry hardly reached ' mad minute ' standards, the trained men of the Special, as well as the Regular, Reserve being by now pretty well exhausted. Ten officers arrived in January, among them Captain Perkins and Lts. Cecil, K. A. Johnston, Capel, who had been with the Dorsets, and Wyld, who had been with the Bedfordshire. The R.M.C. was now turning out large batches after a shortened but intensified course, and the Special Reserve was well off for officer material, if many had to go overseas rather short of training. At the end of March the battalion had nine ' pre-war ' Regulars with it, the C.O., Major Palk and Captains Perkins and im Thurn having come out with it, together with eleven Regulars commissioned since August 4th, of whom 2/Lt. Sprake was acting Quartermaster, and eight Special Reservists, two of them attached from other regiments.

Opportunities of harrassing the enemy, though few, were not neglected, occasionally the machine-guns got at working parties while our snipers were always on the alert, but the enemy was not disposed to risk much.

Between the end of November and the re-opening of active operations with the British attack at Neuve Chapelle (March 10th) the Fourth Division's line

[1] Second time : he had rejoined on January 1st.

changed less and saw less activity than the rest of the front. Elsewhere, February saw much ' liveliness ', especially at Ypres, where the Fifth Corps [1] had relieved the French. On our right also, at Givenchy and Cuinchy astride the La Bassée canal, fighting had reached quite serious dimensions, both in December and in January, but the Fourth Division's opponents were content not to provoke it into an activity, which it, for its part, was in no position to initiate. The water-logged ground largely accounted for this, but the Division [2] had so long a front that it could not have collected the force required for a minor enterprise without weakening its defensive strength unduly. This inactivity gave its units a good chance to assimilate their drafts, while as they had more old hands to be a leaven to the new-comers, it was easier for the Fourth Division to maintain the old standards than for a Division even more depleted by constant serious fighting. The Division was to reap the benefit of this in the severe ordeal now close ahead of it.

A welcome sign of better things to come was the arrival in February of parties of the 7th Sherwood Foresters (North Midland Territorials) and of Canadians to be attached for instruction,[3] two companies of each going into the trenches at a time to be initiated into trench warfare by experienced old hands. This showed that at least some help was to be given to the much-tried ' Old Army ' and Special Reserve who had so long sustained their heavy burden without rest or relief. Every winter of the war may have its own title to have been the worst, weather conditions and increased German shell-fire, bombing behind the lines, the menace of the impending mass-attack, that of 1914–15 can at least claim to have imposed the most continuous strain with the fewest facilities for meeting it.

A re-arrangement of the Division's line and of the method of holding it, so that each battalion did six days in trenches and then six either in reserve or support,[4] was introduced early in March but made little difference, except that any new trenches the Hampshire had to take over fell distinctly short of their own high standards of cleanliness, comfort and defensibility. The Hampshire's line had been a real model of what trenches could be, its condition had won them much praise from the authorities and they had rightly prided themselves on their work. The enemy's shell-fire and sniping had both slackened off and our patrols found little trace of him in No Man's Land. From April 5th to 11th the battalion was in rest billets at Nieppe and then had its last spell in the Ploegsteert trenches, coming out on April 15th on being relieved by South Midland Territorials, under Brigadier General Nicholson, lately C.O. of the 2nd Battalion, some of whom the 11th Brigade had introduced to trench warfare earlier in the month. They were loud in their praise of the Hampshire trenches, ' the best and cleanest we have seen ', one account says, while a senior officer wrote of the vast improvement made in the lines ; ' where one used to have to

[1] It was mainly composed of Regulars who had been relieved from India and other stations overseas by Territorials, including both the original Wessex Division and its ' Second Line '.
[2] The London Rifle Brigade had joined the 11th Brigade, a picked Territorial battalion being attached to each brigade.
[3] Colonel Bewsher of the 10th Battalion was another visitor ' for instruction '.
[4] This had the advantage of having a complete battalion in reserve, not four separate companies.

crawl on one's knees one can stand upright in broad daylight.' The battalion now went back to Noote Boom near Bailleul. Here it spent a week, comfortably billetted in farms and well out of the line, carrying on general training, getting a little leave and doing some route-marching, badly needed after so long a spell in trenches. Several officers joined, including Major Humphery (3rd Battalion) and Captain Twining and Lt. Prendergast from hospital, with about 50 men. The battalion had been promised a longer rest, but on April 22nd the brigade was suddenly warned to be ready to move at short notice. The Germans had just attacked at Ypres, using the gas they were pledged not to employ and the collapse of the surprised French holding the Northern flank of the Salient had created a most dangerous situation.

CHAPTER IV

THE 2ND AND 3RD BATTALIONS—THE TERRITORIALS— EXPANSION

AUGUST 1914 had found the British Regular Army better trained and organized than for any previous war and with the Special Reserve behind it to provide for draft-finding, while from the other branches of the old ' Auxiliary Forces ' a ' Home Defence ' force had been constructed which, whatever its deficiencies in numbers, equipment and training, was a great advance on any earlier ' second line of defence' . But these forces, even if India could to some extent supplement them and if the King's Dominions overseas contained considerable potential reserves of fine fighting material, were at best an inadequate contribution to the cause in which we and our allies had taken arms. The original B.E.F. had admittedly rendered invaluable services to that cause in the opening crisis of the war, but if we were to pull our weight and give our allies the support which, in our own interests no less than in fairness to them, was so urgently needed, the military forces of the Crown must be enormously expanded. It was a gigantic task, beset by every possible difficulty and obstacle, with little to forward it but the good-will and readiness to serve of the great majority of the King's subjects, and it is perhaps the greatest of Lord Kitchener's services that he determined that, despite almost overwhelming handicaps and hindrances, the tremendous expansion needed could be not only attempted but carried through. Vision and determination were both essential and fortunately he possessed both.

Of the measures he now set on foot two particularly affected the Hampshire Regiment, his decisions to raise the needed new forces on the basis of the old existing regiments, utilizing their great traditions and characters to help build up the new units and to set them standards to which to aspire, and to invite the Territorials, though specifically raised for Home Defence only, to undertake service overseas. By doing so they would relieve the Regular units in India and at Colonial stations who thus became available for the formation of new Regular Divisions, five of which eventually reinforced the original six, the 2nd Hampshire being allotted to the Twenty-Ninth Division, by no means the least in fame and achievement, if the last formed.

The 2nd Hampshire had had only eight months in India when war broke out. It was in the middle of the leave season, so several officers were at home, one, 2/Lt. Silk, was in Australia, and two, recently Gazetted, were due to join with the next draft, so the battalion was rather short of officers, though not much below establishment in other ranks. The Fifth (Mhow) Division, to which it belonged, not having been selected for employment either in France or in Mesopotamia, the battalion at first talked rather gloomily about ' being out of it ' and though on August 31st it was directed to leave Mhow at once for Bombay, this was merely to take over from the Sherwood Foresters, who were embarking for England. The battalion had received a very complimentary farewell from Major General Lloyd Payne, G.O.C. Mhow Division, praising its excellent conduct, smartness and manoeuvring and regretting its departure, but, though mobilised, the 2nd Hampshire remained at Colaba until the middle of November, when their own 7th Battalion relieved them and they also embarked. A variety of duties had kept them busy at Colaba, including the removal of ammunition from a ship on fire in the dockyard. Before leaving Bombay 20 N.C.O's and men had been detailed for service, some with ' Force D ' in Mesopotamia as signallers or with the Divisional Field Hospital, others for Base duty with the force proceeding to France, and ten picked N.C.O.s, among them Colour Sergeants Gawn and Wells, had been sent home for duty with ' New Army ' units. Another five, Sergeants Dalton and Moorse and Corporals Peckham, Ginn and Thorn, were commissioned into other regiments and five new 2nd Lieutenants, O'Brien, Parker, Lord, Howard and Hillis, were appointed to the regiment, three joining in time to embark in the *Gloucester Castle* on November 16th. In all 21 officers embarked, with 43 sergeants, 15 drummers and 816 rank and file, Lt. Smith and 24 other ranks being left to introduce the 7th Hampshire to the unfamiliar conditions of Indian service.

The voyage home, in company with many other transports, was uneventful, and on December 22nd the convoy reached Plymouth. A dozen N.C.O's and men, among them R.S.M. Holdway, had embarked with the battalion for Malta in September 1903 and had never been home on leave, while Major Leigh, Captains Addison, B. S. Parker and Reid and 22 men were still present but had not served with the battalion throughout the tour.

From Plymouth the battalion went to Romsey, where it was made very welcome, while the opportunity was taken to give most men short leave. Then on January 13th it moved to Stratford-on-Avon to join its Division, which was being collected in Warwickshire in preparation for active service. The 2nd Hampshire were allotted to the 88th Brigade, under Brigadier General Napier, and found themselves in company with the 4th Worcestershire, the 1st Essex, who had replaced them at Mauritius,[1] and the 5th Royal Scots, a fine Territorial battalion from Edinburgh. Several more officers joined, mostly from the 3rd Battalion, which supplied two drafts, one of them of 181 on January 31st, another of 50 on February 20th, to complete the battalion to establishment. Battalion and company training were carried on, as far as the difficulty of finding suitable manoeuvre ground allowed, and some musketry, while the Division's equipment was being completed. It was at first intended for France, but on the decision, eventually taken in March, to dispatch it to Gallipoli, several changes became necessary, mule transport having to be substituted for wheeled. However, this did not hold up mobilisation seriously and by March 20th the battalion left Warwick, whither it had moved a fortnight earlier, for Avonmouth, where it was to embark. Just previously, on March 12th, the

---

[1] Thus the Sixty-Seventh found themselves again serving alongside the 44th, who had stormed the Taku Forts along with them.

whole Division had passed in review of the King. It was a magnificent spectacle, a whole Division at war strength, the majority of its men seasoned soldiers of several years' service, the last formation provided by the Old Army, which had already suffered so severely and achieved so much.

In the various schemes for Army re-organisation brought forward in the ' Nineties ' and immediately after the South African war, the Militia had formed a substantial part of the field armies, leaving the work of draft-finding rather to the regimental depots, though during the South African war ' details ' of battalions on service were usually attached to the Militia battalions of their regiments when embodied.[1] In the scheme adopted in 1907 the Militia was converted into the Special Reserve, to be relegated to draft-finding and coast-defence duties and not to be invited to undertake the service overseas so many Militia battalions had seen between 1900 and 1902.

Accordingly upon the mobilisation order the 3rd Battalion, now under Lt. Colonel Powney, after assembling at Winchester upon August 7th, moved at once to the Isle of Wight to take up its war station at Parkhurst. It had only just been disembodied after its month's training at Christchurch, where it had encamped on the estate of Lord Malmesbury, a former officer of the battalion. Though much under establishment in men, many of the year's 200 recruits having already passed on to the Regular Army, it was well off for officers, both in numbers and experience, several of them having put in some years of training. On mobilisation it was joined by the surplus Reservists not required to complete the 1st Battalion to war establishment, nearly half the 950 who had reported being left to accompany the 3rd Battalion to ' the island ', while the ' details ' left behind by the 1st Battalion, ' young soldiers ', recruits in training and the very few found medically unfit, also joined it. On orders being issued to form a new ' Service ' battalion Major Parker and the other Regular officers with the 3rd Battalion, except the Adjutant, Captain Middleton, were posted to the new unit. But in their places came several ex-officers who had rejoined, with a flood of subalterns, nearly all with some training in the O.T.C., as well as several newly Gazetted Regular subalterns from Sandhurst.[2] Recruits rolled in as fast as the Depot could enrol them and do as much as was possible towards clothing and equipping them, though the influx was so large that any surplus supplies were soon exhausted and all sorts of makeshifts had to be adopted until the country's industries could get down to the prodigious task of fitting out a nation in arms.

The Depot had had nearly 1000 Reservists to deal with, some had even antici-pated the mobilisation order by reporting on the Tuesday, August 4th, before it was actually issued. On the 3rd Battalion leaving Winchester, Major Playfair (Reserve of Officers) assumed command at the Depot, with Major Bowker

---

[1] Cf. Vol. I, p. 393
[2] On September 10th thirty subalterns were with the battalion at Parkhurst, two-thirds of them Gazetted since August 4th.

(Reserve of Officers) as second in command, Captain Coddington becoming Adjutant, with Major Westmorland as District Recruiting Officer. Even with the demands of the ' New Armies ' for N.C.O.s of experience to help start the new units along the path they should take, a highly efficient staff could be maintained at the Depot, as any number of ex-N.C.O.s of the regiment hastened to re-enlist and do invaluable service. Not many of these veterans proved physically equal to the strain of active service overseas : trench warfare made demands on physical fitness which were beyond the older men, however willing and self-sacrificing, but these old soldiers did work of vital importance and the regiment and the country owed them a great debt. To many who took part in this attempt to expand the Regular Army into a force adequate to all that was at stake the task seemed almost insuperable, so great were the difficulties involved. That so large a measure of success was achieved was largely due to many who bore the heat and burden of the day at home, denied opportunities of active service but carrying on with the unending and arduous work of licking the new material into shape despite shortage of arms and equipment, even at times of absolute essentials, often in terribly overcrowded quarters with little room for training, and meanwhile having no small amount, especially in the early days, of defence work, patrolling the coast, digging trenches and keeping watch. Both the Depot and the 3rd Battalion did a good job of work and did it well.[1]

Draft finding began almost directly the 3rd Battalion settled down in ' the island '. The first drafts were composed of the surplus Reservists, with the ' details ' as they completed their training and qualified for the front ; but Special Reservists were soon finding their way overseas and long before the end of 1914 men enlisted since the outbreak of war were being included in the drafts. Lt. Sandeman [2] was the first Special Reserve Officer to go to the front, and by the time the 1st Battalion moved to Flanders Captains Cope and Twining and Lts. Lane, Harrington, Morgan and Prendergast and 2/Lts. Standen and Weston had all joined, while Captain Humphery had been attached to the Devons and Lt. Colebrook to the D.C.L.I. By October 440·men had already gone out in drafts, but their places were filled over and over again by the steady influx of recruits. On September 10th the battalion had 1600 men present, and soon afterwards its numbers passed the 2000 mark. It had taken over Albany Barracks at Parkhurst, which in peace-time held 700 officers and men, and to cope with the flood of new arrivals had to overflow into the criminal lunatics' ward at Parkhurst Prison, into which another 400 could be packed, the surplus being under canvas. The training was strenuous, though hampered by the shortage of weapons and equipment. Parades were a remarkable sight, every

---

[1] Besides those former officers who served either at the Depot or with a battalion of the regiment, many others were employed on various duties. Colonel Buckley was in charge of the Record Office at Hounslow, Colonel Munro on the Staff of the Eastern Command, Major A.C. Richards was a Railway Transport Officer, Major Tompson and Captain Kennedy Shaw were with the Remount Service, Captains Whitaker and Ennis were Recruiting Officers and Captain H.C. Dolphin served on the Lines of Communication in France.

[2] Promoted Captain in September, as was also Lt. Twining.

variety and combination of garments and head-gear, civilian and military. At the end of October 640 men could be turned over to a new ' Service ' battalion, the 13th, which for the time continued to share the 3rd's much over-crowded quarters. By this time convalescents from the 1st Battalion, officers and men, were joining the 3rd on discharge from hospital and were of great assistance in training the recruits. Despite the dispatch of 900 men to the 1st Battalion and the formation of the 13th, the 3rd ended the year with nearly 1400 men.[1]

The Territorial Force had been raised for home service only, though a few units had before August 1914 undertaken to serve overseas in case of war ; it was therefore asking a good deal of its members to present them within a few days of the outbreak of war with what was virtually a peremptory demand that that they should volunteer for the very service they had been repeatedly assured they would never be expected to undertake. The response of the Territorials to this none too tactfully presented request was a great tribute to their zeal and good sense. It was soon evident that an invasion of these islands was hardly to be apprehended : the German Navy was showing no disposition to try conclusions with our Grand Fleet, whom it was leaving in effective possession of that ' command of the sea ', which must be wrested from us before invasion could become a serious menace. It was clear therefore that Territorials were unlikely to find employment of the kind for which they had been raised. As was said on an earlier occasion[2] ' we are perfectly strong in point of home defence, our weakness lies in the want of Regular and offensive force'. To confine to home defence duties the large body of partially trained officers and men, many units of which had already reached a considerable proficiency, would have been a bad economy of force, and even if the Territorial Divisions were hardly ready yet, particularly as regards arms and equipment, as immediate reinforcements for the B.E.F., they were quite equal to relieving Regular units overseas to set them free to supplement the original B.E.F. In being asked to go out to India and undertake the duties of the Regulars normally stationed there, besides completing their war training, the Wessex Division was receiving a well-deserved tribute to its efficiency as well as undertaking work of the utmost value.

The four battalions in the Hampshire Territorial Brigade, of which Brigadier General G. H. Nicholson was in command, had duly assembled for their annual training at Bulford a week before the outbreak of war and were therefore already more than half mobilised. During the ' precautionary period ' detachments were found for guard duty at various key points, and on August 4th the brigade marched in to Salisbury and entrained for Portsmouth to take over the coast defences until they could be relieved by the Special Reserve units detailed for this task. Meanwhile at their respective battalion head-quarters every effort was being made to cope with the rush of recruits which was presenting itself and to complete mobilisation, no easy task, though willing helpers were plentiful.

[1] The highest figure it had reached was 2210 early in September.
[2] By David Dundas of the ' eighteen damned manoeuvres ' to Cornwallis in 1798.

Of the four battalions, the 4th and 7th were best off for officers, the 4th being three above establishment in subalterns, though one Captain short, and the 7th complete to establishment. The 5th lacked two Captains and four subalterns and the 6th five subalterns,[1] but all four had plenty of former officers with Volunteer and Territorial experience, many of whom now rejoined, though others went rather to the new Service battalions in hopes of getting sooner to the front. In other ranks again any shortage of establishment [2] was quickly made up by the re-enlistment of old members, including many who had just completed the four years for which they had engaged when the T.F. was formed.

By August 9th Special Reserve units had taken over the Portsmouth defences and the Hampshire Brigade could return to Bulford. It was here that the invitation to volunteer for foreign service was received and accepted by the great majority of officers and men. If a battalion could produce 600 volunteers it was to be accepted as a unit and brought up to an establishment of 1000 by recruiting,[3] those unable to undertake foreign service forming the nucleus of a ' Home Service ' battalion, on which the home defence duties should devolve and which should also provide drafts for the battalion abroad. All four soon produced the needed numbers. This meant some breaking up of companies and old associations, several officers and men being unable to pass the necessary medical tests for foreign service, while Colonel Naish of the 4th Battalion, being in Holy Orders, was at first refused ecclesiastical permission to go abroad. He was replaced in command of what now became the ' 1st Fourth ' by Lt. Colonel Bowker, who had retired as a Major in 1908, while Major Playfair took command of the 6th Battalion, Lt. Colonel Peters remaining with the 2nd/6th, as the Home Service units were soon re-named.[4]

The Wessex Division was so quick to form its ' Foreign Service ' units that on September 26th it was announced that it had been selected for service in India and that the Hampshire battalions would embark on October 9th. As they would replace Regular units in the Divisions already in existence in India, the Divisional and Brigade staffs did not accompany them but remained behind to take over the ' Second Line ' Division of Home Service units. These were to go into billets, the 2nd/4th (Lt. Colonel Naish) at Winchester, the 2nd/5th (Major Day) at Southampton, the 2nd/6th (Lt. Colonel Peters) at Petersfield and the 2nd/7th (Lt. Colonel Lord Montagu) at Bournemouth.[5] Before this the 2nd/5th had been sent at short notice to Lyndhurst to strike the camps of the Seventh Division, which had just gone overseas, and to guard the ordnance stores until they could be removed. This kept them in camp till nearly the end of October.

[1] The 8th (Isle of Wight Rifles) were three Captains and four subalterns short but had a supernumerary Major, the 9th (Cyclists) were one Captain and one subaltern short.

[2] The 4th was nearly 800 strong on mobilization, the 5th being down to 630, the 6th just under 700 and the 7th 760.

[3] They actually went out at an establishment of 800 other ranks.

[4] Lt. Colonel Burford-Hancock went out with the 5th and Lt. Colonel Parke with the 7th.

[5] The nucleus of the 2nd/7th consisted of about 400 of all ranks ; it was fortunate in that Captain Gribbon, the Adjutant, was left behind to train it. The Adjutants of the other battalions, Captain Barton (5th), Earle (5th), and Bowers (6th) accompanied their battalions to India.

The Territorials' voyage to India, though full of interest to all ranks, was not marked by any ' incident ', except for meeting large convoys of transports from India carrying some of the much needed reinforcements whom the Wessex Division was relieving. The *Emden* had not yet been ' liquidated ' but did not trouble the convoy which carried the Hampshires, though their closely packed ships gave [1] little chance of drill or exercise. A month after leaving England the convoy cast anchor at Bombay and the four battalions separated to their different destinations, Poona for the 4th, Allahabad for the 5th, Dinapore for the 6th and Colaba for the 7th. That battalion, as already stated, was actually relieving the 2nd Hampshire, whose band and drums played it into barracks, while the 2nd got a chance of seeing again many old friends, the senior N.C.O.s of the Territorials including many former Regulars.

Before the end of the year the ' Second Line ' Wessex formations were also invited to accept the overseas obligation and go out to India to relieve more Regulars. Though they were largely composed of recruits and as yet much handicapped in their training by lack of arms and equipment,[2] it showed that any amount of hard work had already been put in to make them fit to go overseas. The invitation was no small compliment.

The decision to send the Second Wessex Division to India was taken before the end of November, and on December 12th the 2/4th, 2/5th and 2/7th left. The 2/5th were made up to 740 all told by a draft of 150 from the 2/6th, but the 2/4th and 2/7th had managed to reach the Indian establishment of 800 other ranks without drawing on other units. They were rather less time on the way out than their predecessors, the 2/4th reaching Karachi on January 11th and going to Quetta, the 2/5th reaching Bombay on January 4th and going to Secunderabad, whither the 2/7th, who landed on January 7th, followed them.

The 2/6th, after completing the 2/5th, had been reduced considerably below the establishment for service in India and was therefore retained at home, partly to produce drafts for the Territorials overseas, though ' Third Line ' formations for this purpose were also organized before long. A Provisional Battalion, of which Colonel Peters took command, was formed early in 1915 of Home Service men left behind by the different battalions, and this after a brief training was sent to Scotland for duty on coast defences, moving in May to the N.E. coast and performing similar duty at Blyth and neighbouring places. Originally ' the Hampshire Brigade Battalion ', then the 84th Provisional Battalion, it was finally renamed the 17th Hampshire.

The two Hampshire T.F. battalions not in the Wessex Division had not as yet left England. Their ' Special Service ' sections had been called out as early as July 25th, the 8th for duty on the coast of the Isle of Wight and the 9th to provide patrols along the South Coast. On mobilisation, the 8th concentrated at Sandown and took over the forts in the East of the island from the 4th Royal

---

[1] The 4th and 6th shared the 10,000 ton Cunarder *Ultonia*.

[2] Thus the rifles the 2nd/5th took out were condemned as unfit for use, and not till it was re-armed with the ' long ' rifles then discarded by the 1st/5th could the battalion get any proper musketry instruction.

Fusiliers, whom they also relieved of coast duties. Consequently the battalion was much split up, nearly 200 [1] men being on detachment, and not till September 9th could it be brought together as a battalion at Nunwell Park. Recruits flocked in and the battalion was soon above establishment, so that early in December a ' Reserve ' or ' Second Line ' unit could be organised, of which Lt. Colonel Wallace, formerly a Major in the Militia, took command as from December 5th, with Captain Grigg, formerly of the D.C.L.I., as Adjutant. Before this the original Adjutant, Captain Stone, had rejoined his own regiment, the Norfolk, and Captain Veasey had replaced him as Adjutant of the ' First Line ' unit, which by this time had been reconstituted with foreign service men only. It adopted the four company organization as from January 10th, but remained in the Isle of Wight on coast defence duty well into the New Year.

The 9th (Cyclist) Battalion [2] was not left long on the South Coast, on August 8th it was ordered to Lincolnshire, establishing its head-quarters at Louth and patrolling the coast from Grimsby to Skegness. A raid was looked upon as far from unlikely, and every night patrols maintained a vigilant watch from dark to dawn, constant alarms and rumours keeping them much on the alert. Like other T.F. units the 9th was invited to undertake overseas obligations, which it did, whereupon, as in other cases, a ' Second Line ' unit was formed,[3] Major A. B. Perkins becoming C.O., with Lt. Talbot-Ponsonby as Adjutant. This moved back by road to Portsmouth, arriving on October 1st. Its head-quarters were then established at Chichester, but two companies were detached to join the Plymouth garrison and another to Corfe Castle, while a fourth crossed over to Ventnor, where it was soon expanded into two companies, two more being formed at head-quarters before the end of the year to complete the 2/9th to eight companies.

Meanwhile the 1/9th had moved back to Sussex in October, taking over patrol and coastal duties, its head-quarters also being at Chichester.

Except for Lancashire, London and Yorkshire, Hampshire had more Territorials than any other county, and with the Navy drawing so largely upon it for recruits its resources were severely tried to provide its quota to the ' New Armies '. The First and Second New Armies, ' K 1 ' and ' K 2 ' as they were generally known, were composed of six Divisions apiece, organized by localities, except for a Light Division of Rifles and Light Infantry, each Regular regiment contributing one battalion [4] to each New Army. Both New Armies had three purely English Divisions, with eight battalions over, mainly from the Southern counties, who became ' Army troops ' and were attached to different Divisions for training. The ' K1 ' and ' K2 ' battalions of the Hampshire were among the Army Troops and were both attached to the Irish Divisions,[5] the Tenth and the Sixteenth.

---

[1] On mobilisation it mustered 25 officers and 540 other ranks, under Lt. Colonel Rhodes.
[2] Lt. Colonel Johnson was in command.   [3] It originally had five companies.
[4] Some Irish and Scottish and four battalion regiments raised more.
[5] The 10th Battalion started life at Winchester but moved to Dublin on Sept. 8th.

When it came to forming a Third New Army, ' K 3 ', authorised in September, no Scottish, Irish or Light Divisions were formed, only one Division reproducing those of ' K 1 ' and ' K 2 ', and the Hampshire battalion, the 12th, found itself in a Twenty-Sixth Division, composed mainly of regiments from the South and West of England with a Scottish brigade. In the Fourth New Army, formed in October from the battalions thrown off by the Special Reserve, the allotment to Divisions was in the main not local, though the Thirty-Second Division, to which the 13th Hampshire were assigned, came mainly from Southern counties.

Raising these ' New Armies ' naturally became more difficult with each addition, as the demand for instructors, for weapons, for clothing and for equipment of every kind became harder and harder to meet. For ' K 1 ' a satisfactory nucleus of trained instructors was available from the Regular officers serving with the Special Reserve and the two officers and 15 N.C.O.s which each Regular battalion left behind on going overseas. Thus the Hampshire made a good start, being fortunate in having Major Parker, promoted temporary Lt. Colonel on August 9th, to command them, together with Captains Morley and Black-Hawkins, Lts. Berkeley, Capel and K. A. Johnston and 2/Lts. Waddington and Hudson, these last four belonging properly to the 2nd Battalion. To these were soon added Captains Faith, who became Adjutant, and Savage from the Reserve of Officers, and Erle, who had only recently retired from the 3rd Battalion, with Captain McCormick of the 72nd Punjabis, formerly in the regiment and home from India on leave, and Major Pilleau, recently retired from the 105th Mahrattas. In Sergeant Major Saunders, appointed to be its Quartermaster, the 10th had a tower of strength and in its senior N.C.O.s [1] it was also very fortunate.

The many old members of the regiment who had rejoined included several N.C.O.s of experience, and the fine body of recruits who had been collected were better off for instructors than for weapons or equipment. The subalterns were a fine lot, nearly all with some O.T.C. training, considerably augmented during a month of intensive training in camps of instruction organized by the Senior Division of the O.T.C., which enabled them to take charge of their platoons directly they joined. This they did early in October after the battalion had left Dublin, where it had completed its formation, for Mullingar, where it was to spend the winter. It had overflowed the accommodation at Beggar's Bush Barracks, Dublin, 300 of its 1070 other ranks having to be under canvas, but a shift to Royal Barracks improved matters. Before the 10th left Dublin Lt. Colonel Parker had gone out to the 1st Battalion. He had started the new unit admirably and his departure was no small blow, but in Lt. Colonel Bewsher, who joined on October 10th, he had an able successor, under whose direction the battalion's training made as rapid progress as the difficulties of arming and equipping it would allow. There was no want of willingness or hard work and the battalion was made quite welcome at Mullingar, whither it was

[1] R.S.M. J. Smith, R.Q.M.S. W Barnes, C.S.M.s Whitaker, Groves, King and Parkinson, C.Q.M.S.s Goodall, Mills, Lewis and Barton, and O.R.S. Barratt.

soon followed by the 11th Battalion. This had come into existence at Dublin on September 14th. Command went to Colonel Kemmis, formerly of the King's Own,[1] with Major Robertson (late Connaught Rangers) as second in command, and Lt. Berkeley, who transferred from the 10th Battalion, as Adjutant, while several Regular N.C.O.s and P.S.I's whom the Territorials had left behind were posted to the battalion and did invaluable service.[2] Some of the new officers had previous service with Special Reserve or Territorials and its subalterns, like those of the 10th had mostly had some O.T.C. training or had been through the camps of instruction and were of the type required.

The 12th Battalion's first commander, Colonel Walker, came from the Indian Army, having commanded the 20th (Brownlow's) Punjabis. Majors Wombwell and Bazalgette were old officers of the 3rd Battalion, Major Rake had been in the 6th Hampshire, Captain Buckley had formerly held a commission in the regiment, Captain Church had been Sergeant-Major of the 3rd Battalion and Captain Stevens had retired from the West India Regiment. Lt. Persse, who became Adjutant, had served in South Africa with Brabant's Horse and the Imperial Yeomanry, so that the battalion started with several officers of some experience, while its N.C.O.s included over 20 old Regulars of the regiment. It was not long at Winchester, a first detachment, 250 strong, under Major Wombwell, leaving on September 30th for Codford in Wiltshire, where a camp was being formed. It found tents and blankets but no floor-boards, and in general the 12th had to rough it and make the best of even graver deficiencies in equipment than the 10th and 11th had had to face. Substantial detachments soon followed the first and the battalion was soon up to establishment. It was posted to the 79th Brigade, along with the 10th Devons, 8th D.C.L.I. and 7th Wiltshire, and soon settled down to a strenuous programme of training, much impeded as the autumn advanced by heavy rain, which reduced the camp site to a quagmire and eventually, after an ineffectual shift to higher and, for a brief time, drier ground, drove the brigade into billets in the middle of November, the 12th Hampshire going to Basingstoke, where they were warmly welcomed and were most comfortable. On the 2nd Battalion's arrival in England half a dozen of its N.C.O.s were attached to the 12th to assist in the instruction of young officers and N.C.O.s. For subalterns ' K 3 ' got rather fewer with any substantial O.T.C. training : ' K 1 ' and ' K 2 ' had absorbed nearly all who had not gone to the Special Reserve or Territorials, but before long a large number of young men of the right type began to appear from overseas, having come back from the Colonies or the Argentine to serve, a class who were just what was needed, rather older than those of ' K 1 ' and ' K 2 ', men who had already knocked about the world enough to face difficulties.

[1] He had commanded one of its Militia battalions in S. Africa.
[2] The Warrant Officers and Senior N.C.O.s were R.S.M. Simmonds, R.Q.M.S. Rendell and C.S.M.s Hopkins, Murdoch, Glasspool and Lambert, C.Q.M.S.s Hafles, Purnell, Weale, Gawn and Simms (O.R.S.)

The 13th Battalion, formed on October 31st from surplus officers and men of the 3rd, had for its original commander Major Thornton, another ex-officer of the Indian Army. In November, however, Major Crofts, who had retired from the regiment in 1907, was appointed to the command as Lt. Colonel. Hardly any of its officers had any previous connection with the regiment but it was also fortunate in getting a good many ex-N.C.O.s to give it a start. The battalions of the Fourth New Army, though allotted to Divisions, were left in the coast defences in which most of them had been formed, the intention being to move them in the spring to hutted camps at training centres.

Meanwhile a 14th (Service) Battalion had come into existence, raised at Portsmouth by a strong local committee, which undertook all responsibilities for the battalion until such time as it could be presented complete for inspection and approval by the Army authorities, who would then take it over. This was being done all over the country, largely by local authorities and committees, sometimes by bodies like the Church Lads' Brigade, and in the end produced eleven Divisions. The 14th Hampshire, originally allotted to the 121st Brigade in the Fortieth Division, were transferred to a newly-organized Thirty-Ninth in April 1915, but this was not brought together for training round Winchester till August, long before which the 14th Hampshire had been accepted by the War Office, having reached its establishment. The 14th's first C.O., Lt. Colonel Ramsbottom-Isherwood, formerly of the 3rd York and Lancaster, had been Gazetted to command it as far back as September 1st, 1914, and by April 1915 it was nearly complete with officers, its original second in command being Major O'Farrell, formerly of the 6th D.G., with Captain Finlay its first Adjutant.

With the 2nd Battalion home and likely before long to be at the front and in need of drafts, the 3rd Battalion's task did not grow any easier, though as the 1st Battalion spent the first quarter of 1915 in relative quiet, its demands for drafts were less insistent. However, over 200 men had to be found in January to complete the 2nd Battalion to war establishment, besides three drafts amounting to 150 for the 1st. At the end of January the 3rd Battalion moved to Gosport, with head-quarters in Fort Gomer and detachments at Forts Gillicker and Monckton, Calshot Castle, Horsea Island and Southampton Docks, Calshot being a seaplane depot and Horsea a wireless station with a lake where torpedoes were tested. Recruits continued to come in steadily and the battalion seemed likely to top the 2000 mark again, but the 2nd Battalion's heavy losses at Cape Helles and the 1st's casualties in its determined defence of Ypres caused nearly 600 men to be sent off in May, six officers going to Flanders and five with six from the 13th Battalion to Gallipoli. Lt. Tarrant also left to join the 1st Battalion, Captain Hackett, now convalescent, succeeding him. The battalion was fortunate in having the services of several convalescent officers from the B.E.F. who joined it on becoming fit for duty, their experience being most helpful in training the recruits. Another 300 men left for the Dardanelles at the end of June, 350 were sent off in July, with nearly 800 in September, 600 going to the 10th Battalion which had lost so heavily at Sari Bair. Nevertheless on

September 30th the 3rd Battalion had still 1926 men actually on parade and had touched 2903 of all ranks on the 12th, while up to December 31st 5247 men had been sent out with 124 officers.

Before the end of 1914 it was decided to add Pioneer battalions to the New Army Divisions, the 5th Royal Irish becoming the Pioneers of the Tenth Division, whereupon the 10th Hampshire replaced them in the 29th Brigade under Brigadier General Cooper, its other units being the 6th Royal Irish Rifles, 5th Connaught Rangers and 6th Leinster. In the Sixteenth Division the 11th Hampshire were chosen as the Pioneers and had therefore to acquire a sound knowledge of military engineering, while not neglecting their training as infantrymen, Pioneers being fighting soldiers as well as craftsmen.

March brought the 10th a move to the Curragh; they left Mullingar with the good wishes of the townspeople, with whom their relations had been of the friendliest, the excellent behaviour and exemplary discipline of both 10th and 11th Battalions having made a profound impression. They remained at the Curragh until early in May, confortably housed in huts, training hard. With most of the Division in the neighbourhood much more elaborate and advanced exercises could be undertaken and orders to go overseas were expected daily. On leaving Ireland, however, the Tenth Division did not go straight to France but to England to undergo final preparations for 'the front' round Basingstoke, so that the 10th Hampshire found themselves back in familiar country, while some strenuous Divisional training considerably extended their acquaintance with Berkshire and Surrey. The Division was now in the Aldershot Training Centre and battalions went in turn to the Ash ranges for intensive musketry, besides being initiated into bombing. An inspection by the King on May 28th and another by Lord Kitchener a few days later gave the Division an opportunity of showing what remarkable progress it had made in well under a year's training and that it was ready to go overseas.

Meanwhile its destination had been under much consideration. The virtual failure of the Allied Spring offensive in France had been mainly due to the inadequacy of the ammunition supply, and until far more ample quantities were available the resumption of our attack could not be contemplated. This added force to the arguments of those who urged that far-reaching advantages might be gained by exploiting the opening secured at Gallipoli by the gallantry of the Twenty-Ninth Division and the rest of the Mediterranean Expeditionary Force and that therefore the New Armies should be sent to Gallipoli. However, three 'K I' Divisions had already crossed over to France before, on June 27th, the remaining three, the Tenth, Eleventh and Thirteenth, were warned to prepare for service in Gallipoli. The 10th Hampshire therefore found themselves preparing to assist the 2nd Battalion in its effort to reach Constantinople, instead of helping the 1st to expel the Germans from France and Belgium.

The change of destination meant much re-fitting and re-equipping, khaki drill clothing was issued and officers' chargers were withdrawn, helmets were fitted with Indian 'pagris', and the inferior American leather equipment, already virtually worn out by three months' home service, was replaced by good English accoutrements. Battalion staffs and more particularly the Quartermasters had a hectic time, but by July 5th the leading units of the Division had started for Devonport to embark there. Drafts from the Sixteenth Division had brought units up to establishment.

Two companies of the 11th Battalion, A and B, had already quitted Mullingar before the 10th left, moving to Birr in February, the rest of the battalion soon after shifting to Moore Park, Kilworth. In March, ill-health forced Colonel Kemmis [1] to relinquish command, his successor being Lt. Colonel Crockett, formerly of the Leicestershire, who was already known to the battalion, being on the Divisional staff. To the general regret Major Robertson, the second in command, died in March, and several changes occurred among the officers, while those Regular N.C.O.s who were not re-enlistments for ' duration ' were recalled to the 3rd Battalion. The first week in April saw the battalion re-united at Moore Park, with which it was to become only too well acquainted, remaining there until, early in September, the Division crossed to England to complete its training in the Aldershot area.

After spending most of the winter comfortably housed at Basingstoke, the 12th Battalion had in March moved to Bathwick near Bath. If still short of up-to-date weapons and equipment, it had at least got proper uniforms and was presenting a greatly improved appearance. It had been inspected by the G.O.C., Southern Command, General Pitcairn Campbell, who was very well satisfied with its progress, while it was kept up to establishment by an excellent draft from the 3rd Battalion. It remained at Bathwick until early in May, when it moved to Sutton Veney near Warminster, where it found quite good and comfortable huts and ample ground for training. Major Rake and Captain Stevens left on medical grounds, Captain Church transferred to the Royal Sussex and Captain Buckley was given command of the 7th Leinster in the Sixteenth Division, their departure causing a considerable flow of promotion, and several new faces had appeared in the Officers' Mess before, in September, the Twenty-Sixth Division started to cross to France.

The Divisions of the Fourth New Army were to have been concentrated for training in the spring of 1915, but by then it had become abundantly clear that the difficulty of maintaining the strength of the forces in the field in modern war had been underestimated, trench-warfare with its perpetual contact and conflict causing a heavy drain, sometimes quite heavy, against which more provision must be made. The Special Reserve was being fully taxed to provide the Regular battalions with drafts and could not possibly cope with the demands the New Armies were bound to make. Accordingly ' K 4 ' battalions were converted into draft-finding, or ' Second Reserve ', units and the Divisional organization was abandoned, the Divisions of the Fifth New Army, mainly

---

[1] He made the battalion a much appreciated gift of eight bugles.

composed of the specially formed ' local ' units, being re-numbered.[1] Thus the
13th Hampshire, who had remained in the Isle of Wight after the 3rd had left
in January but had crossed over in May to go into camp at Bovington near
Wool, had now to settle down to their new duties and were soon sending out
drafts almost as regularly as the 3rd Battalion. At Bovington the battalion had
better facilities for training than when it had also had garrison and coast defence
duties to discharge, good ranges were available and once effective rifles replaced
its ' D.P. ' weapons considerable progress was made in musketry. Many officers [2]
went off to the 2nd Battalion in the Dardanelles, to which theatre of war some
six drafts had been dispatched before October. It was the first two drafts from
the 13th Battalion that had the misfortune to be torpedoed on board the *Royal
Edward*, sunk between Alexandria and Gallipoli on August 13th, only 26 out of
the 250 [3] Hampshires on board being saved.

The 14th Battalion had meanwhile been taking shape steadily : during the
early months of 1915 its establishment of officers was completed, while recruiting
went well enough for the committee responsible for raising the battalion [4] to
embark on forming another ' Portsmouth ' battalion, a 15th Hampshire, to the
command of which Major O'Farrell was transferred as from April 20th 1915.
As already mentioned the 14th had been allotted in December 1914 to the 121st
Brigade of the original Fortieth Division,[5] but in April when the ' K 4 ' Divisions
were broken up and the ' K 5 ' re-numbered, the 121st Brigade, in which were
also three battalions of the Royal Sussex, the 11th, 12th and 13th (Southdown),
was transferred to a new Thirty-Ninth Division and re-numbered as the 116th
Brigade. The 15th was eventually allotted to the junior ' K ' Division, the
Forty-First, which was not really organized until September 1915, though its
formation had been authorised in April. Naturally these later formed ' New
Army ' units were handicapped as regards trained personnel to instruct them,
though before long wounded and invalided officers and men from overseas
became available, but as regards equipment they were perhaps at a less disadvantage, as the country's industries were adjusting themselves to the situation
and the necessary articles were being produced in some volume.

[1] Originally the Thirty-Seventh to Forty-Second they became the Thirtieth to Thirty-Fifth.
[2] The June Army List shows the 13th Battalion as having no less than 95 subalterns on its
strength, a total which makes the 56 of the 3rd Battalion seem quite modest.
[3] 50 came from the 3rd Battalion.
[4] Unfortunately the records of this committee do not appear to have survived the air-raids on
Portsmouth of 1940 and later.
[5] Re-numbered Thirty-Third in April 1915 and re-organised.

CHAPTER V

SECOND YPRES AND AFTER

THE winter of 1914–1915 had seen much greater activity in 'trench-warfare' than was to prevail in later winters, when there was less harassing of the enemy and more inclination to avoid provoking retaliation without some very definite purpose ; strategically, however, it had been mainly a time of waiting and preparing and, apart from some heavy fighting in Champagne, neither side had attempted anything of more than local importance. The Allies were confidently hoping that a large scale offensive in the spring might recover much of the French territory in German hands, even if it did not achieve decisive victory. The Germans' decision to make their main effort in 1915 against the Russians must be attributed to their distrust of the ability of their Austrian partners to withstand further attacks, if left to their own resources, but after 1914, and particularly after Ypres, they may have felt disinclined to incur the costs of renewing the 1914 offensive against the enemies who had thwarted it and whose powers of resistance they had good reason to respect. The wisdom of their decision may be questioned. France had paid heavily for what she had achieved in 1914 and had used up much of her man-power, while British unreadiness for war was to be more conspicuous in 1915 than in 1914. The Old Army had accomplished more at Mons and Ypres than our augmented but ill-equipped forces could achieve in 1915 : we had virtually exhausted our trained reserves and available supplies ; the Territorials and the improvised New Armies were deficient in equipment and training and had to acquire experience and practice in actual warfare before they could fairly be asked to undertake a major offensive ; above all, the terrible shortage of ammunition, which crippled every British operation as well as handicapping our men dangerously even when merely holding the line, might have produced disaster had the enemy attacked our line in force. Fortunately for us he postponed his next major effort on the Western Front until 1916, by which time the British Armies in France, if hardly really ready even then for a major offensive, could lend the French substantial help by taking over more line and so setting troops free to reinforce Verdun. This they could not have done in 1915, and the Allies were fortunate that that year's one German offensive on the Western Front, which began with the gas attack at Ypres on April 22nd, was apparently undertaken more or less as an experiment and that the German supreme command was not prepared to take full advantage of its success and exploit it really vigorously. In resisting it the 1st Hampshire were to endure even severer trials than they had yet faced ; the stubbornness of the fight which they and the whole Fourth Division put up, along with the equally tried Fifth and Twenty-Seventh and Twenty-Eighth, may well have contributed to discourage the Germans from trying to develop the opening their disregard for another 'scrap of paper' had secured them.

The gas attack (April 22nd) had completely surprised the French troops holding the Northern flank of the Ypres Salient, half Algerians, half Territorials.

55

Quite unprepared for this new form of attack, they gave way before it and their retreat uncovered the left flank of the Canadians, who had only just taken over from the French a very indifferent line roughly between the Gravenstafel–Passchendale and the St. Julien–Poelcappelle roads. The Canadian reserves hastily threw back a line to cover their exposed flank, those of the Twenty-Seventh and Twenty-Eighth Divisions were hurried to their help and something of a front was patched up across the wide gap left by the French collapse. Further reinforcements followed, and on April 23rd the Germans made little further

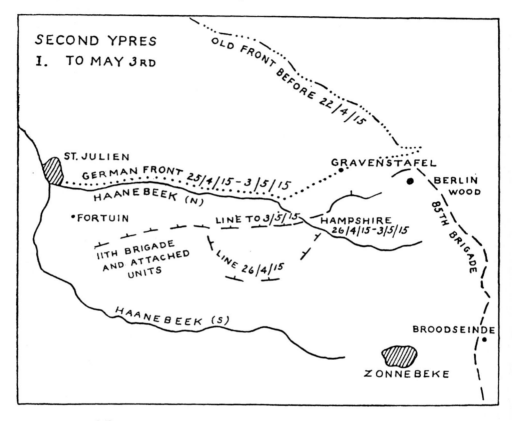

progress, while some ground was secured by gallant but terribly expensive counter-attacks. But the German attack was now (April 24th) extended to the Canadian front and, despite their stubborn resistance, it drove them back from all but their extreme right, next to the Twenty-Eighth Division's left at Berlin Wood. St. Julien was lost, and though a fresh line was somehow formed behind it, this was a mere improvisation and hardly continuous. Meanwhile the 11th Brigade had been ordered to Ypres [1] and about mid-day (April 24th) the Hamp-

---

[1] The battalion was warned to be in readiness to move on the afternoon of April 22nd and had spent the next 24 hours in listening to the sounds of distant gun-fire before getting definite orders late on April 23rd.

shire entrained at Bailleul. The 10th Brigade had preceded the 11th and were already across the canal. Detraining at Poperinghe the Hampshire found the rumours about the gas attack confirmed by the sight of French and Algerian stragglers, victims of the gas and suffering greatly, while the chlorine could be smelt only too distinctly. However the brigade was merely placed in billets South of Poperinghe, thereby escaping a wet night in the open.

April 25th saw the 10th Brigade's splendid if unsuccessful attempt to recover St. Julien. If plenty of infantry were available, the artillery support, especially from heavy artillery, was quite inadequate, while had more guns been ready ammunition was sadly short. But the whole situation in the Salient was precarious; if St. Julien could not be recovered and with it more ground Westward towards the canal the position would become untenable, and the French were insistent on a prompt counter-attack even if their own contributions to recovering the lost ground lacked weight and vigour. That the 10th Brigade's counter-attack, made over ground it had not properly reconnoitred, failed to recover St. Julien is merely to say that it did not accomplish the impossible, but the line it established was to hold up the German advance in this direction until the evacuation, by order, of the old front of the Fifth Corps. But in the two miles' gap between the 10th Brigade's right and Berlin Wood the position was particularly dangerous. With their left flank ' in the air ', the few Canadians still holding on NW. of Berlin Wood could not maintain their ground and were forced back, leaving the 85th Brigade's left exposed, only some details and mixed parties hanging on to the Gravenstafel ridge on its left rear with, beyond them but some distance away, two weak battalions of the Twenty-Eighth Division. Meanwhile, early in the day, the 11th Brigade had moved up to Vlamertinghe and had been placed under General Bulfin, commanding the Twenty-Eighth Division, who decided to use it to relieve the scattered detachments between Berlin Wood and St. Julien, and fill the dangerous gap in our line. Some delay occurred, largely owing to the scrappy and conflicting reports received at the Division's head-quarters, before definite orders could be issued. Eventually about dusk the 11th Brigade moved forward across the canal to St. Jean. The move took them North of the outskirts of Ypres, which was being shelled, while wounded and stragglers were coming back and congesting the road. After a brief halt at St. Jean the Hampshire, who were leading, went on to Wieltje where Canadian guides were expected to meet them and direct them to their new position. No guides turned up and an exhausted Canadian Brigadier who appeared could only give a confused picture of the situation. Something had to be done without delay, and after an hour's wait the Brigadier [1] ordered Colonel Hicks to take the battalion forward to get in touch with the 85th Brigade and extend to its left, the rest of the 11th Brigade moving up to Fortuin, SE. of St. Julien, and extending Eastward from there towards the Hampshire.

On reaching the 85th Brigade's head-quarters at Verlorenhoek, discovered

---

[1] Br.-General Hasler, who had in February replaced General Hunter-Weston, promoted to command the Twenty-Ninth Division, of which the 2nd Hampshire formed part.

with some difficulty through a glimmer of light at the road side, Colonel Hicks found that its left battalion, the 3rd Royal Fusiliers, was completely ' in the air ', the Canadians hitherto covering it having been withdrawn, and that the telephone wire to the Fusiliers had been cut, so that the exact situation in the front line was very uncertain. Two signallers who were going up to repair the wire were therefore ordered to act as guides, and the Hampshire pushed on across country with only the vaguest ideas about the situation while the guides proved quite uncertain where they were going, though Verey lights and bursts of rifle and machine-gun fire ahead showed that the battalion was nearing the front. It was 2 a.m. by now, and with daylight not far off it was essential not to be caught in the open, in column of route complete with first-line transport, a fine target for the converging fire German guns could concentrate on the salient in our line.

On reaching a slight rise and knowing that he must by now be somewhere on the Royal Fusiliers' left flank and rear, Colonel Hicks halted the battalion and went forward with the company commanders to reconnoitre the position as far as the darkness would allow. A more unpleasant situation could hardly be imagined but Colonel Hicks did not hesitate. As an officer has written ,' he rose to the occasion as few men would. The odds against him were overwhelming. We should have been justified in retiring to the Zonnebeke ridge where trenches existed '. But Colonel Hicks had been sent up to fill a gap and meant to do it. Having found a line which seemed to give a fair field of fire and placed markers to show the frontages of the companies, he moved the men up into position and set them to work to dig in. His imperturbable coolness made a grand impression on all ; grave as the situation was he tackled it with calm and resolution and the men responded splendidly. ' It was ', as he himself has written, ' a race with dawn ' : the men were naturally tired but they knew how much depended on their being in good cover before daylight and they dug splendidly while luckily the earth was fairly soft.[1] Some old trenches facing North were discovered which could be utilised, and by good fortune the morning proved misty and gave the battalion another two hours of concealment.

While the digging was going on a large party was detected approaching our right. Calling out that they were Royal Fusiliers, they deceived and knocked out a too credulous patrol, but Captain Beckett was not to be caught and C Company quickly and effectively disposed of the intruders. A Company on the left fared worse : it had occupied some houses on the flank, but Germans, approaching in the mist, rushed them, drove the survivors of their garrison in on top of the men digging away at the trench and tried to roll up our line from the flank. A confused struggle followed. Captain Sandeman, a Special Reserve officer of ten years' service, was killed in rallying the men and preparing for a counter-attack and with him fell Captain Chapman (attached from the E. Surrey), but Lt. Le Marchant headed a party of bombers, among them Lance Corporals Field and Hare and Pte. Winter, and checked the rush, holding on at a traverse, and Sergeant Ley led a counter-attack which drove the enemy

---

[1] As there were only 25 shovels per company most men had to use their' grubbers '.

back and restored the situation. A barricade was thrown up and the flank secured.

By 7 a.m. the mist was lifting and the battalion found itself with its right, C. Company, facing N.E. towards Berlin Wood, 400 yards away, where the Royal Fusiliers' thrown back left faced NW.[1] D in the centre faced nearly due North, A, whose left was now thrown back, facing almost West. B was in a second line just over the crest of the ridge, with its left also thrown back. On this flank a wide gap separated the battalion from the next troops, a mixed detachment of the Twenty-Eighth Division South of the Fortuin–Mosselmarkt road. In the short time available the battalion had really provided itself with reasonably good cover.

It was to reap the benefit of its labours. Directly the mist really lifted, a most tremendous bombardment started, salvo after salvo of heavy shell descending upon its line in rapid succession ; shells at times were coming down at the rate of 50 a minute and that anyone survived was a marvel. The German tactics were to drench the ground with shells and then push infantry forward, thinking to take easy possession of a destroyed line ; but heavily as they shelled the Hampshire they did not shift them and any effort to advance was promptly checked. In places the Germans could get up close by using old trenches and saps, but they could not oust the Hampshire. Casualties, however, were heavy, nearly all from shell-fire, though 2/Lt. Walford was shot by a sniper. One serious loss was that of Captain Fidler,[2] who had returned from taking a platoon of B out to clear up the situation on our left and was hit when standing on the parapet to see that his men got quickly down into the trench. Commissioned from R.S.M. in October, he had done admirable service. The battalion was also nearly losing its head-quarters staff, who were buried when a shell hit the parapet nearby. Fortunately the soil was sandy and light and the C.O., whose head was not covered, so that he could call for help, was dug out unharmed, along with the Adjutant and the orderlies.

There had naturally been no time to do more than provide the minimum of cover, with no conveniences, the trenches were too narrow to let people pass along them easily, indeed there was hardly room to move. Conditions, even apart from the shelling, could hardly have been more uncomfortable or difficult.

All day the rain of projectiles went on, beating down incessantly, along the whole front, but the Hampshire stuck to their line, effectively preventing repeated efforts to turn the flank of the Royal Fusiliers or to penetrate into the wide gap on the left where the mixed detachment was hanging on beyond the Haanebeek. Casualties, however, came to over 150 ; 59 men killed and missing (probably buried), Lt. Watts and Lt. Le Marchant being among the 100 wounded. Captain Beckett's [3] coolness and gallantry were conspicuous and greatly encouraged the men, Lt. Wyld, whose company, C, had about the worst part of the line, set a splendid example, and the machine-gun officer, 2/Lt.

---

[1] Touch was established with them by a patrol under 2/Lt. Stevens.
[2] Just promoted to a Captaincy in the R. Warwickshire.
[3] He was awarded the D.S.O.

Holroyd (3rd. Bn.) did useful work with his guns, one of which could enfilade the nearest enemy from a forward sap, part of an old communication trench. He had the last surviving periscope, which proved of great use, and for a time his trench was the only part of the line in telephone connection with headquarters and the brigade. Despite everything the coolness and steadiness of the men was quite remarkable. Whenever the shelling slackened they stood to arms, ready to deal with any attacks and effectively checking some efforts to advance, the right of D Company and the left of C both getting opportunities.

Night brought a welcome relief from the bombardment but no relief from labour. It was only at night that movement and work were possible. The wounded had to be got back to the clearing stations, three miles and more away,

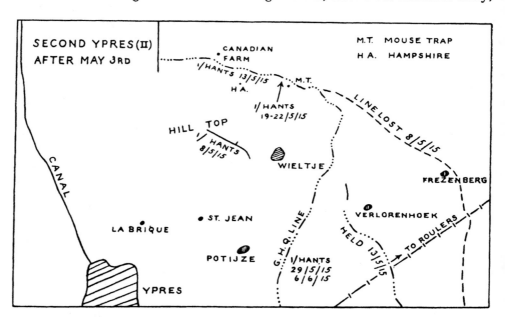

and that by stretcher bearers, no ambulances being able to get any nearer; rations, water and ammunition had to be fetched over the same distance, much of the route being swept by fire, unaimed but none the less dangerous, the trenches had to be repaired, and they needed it, while a vigilant watch was necessarily kept against a night attack. By daylight on April 26th the line had been substantially improved and, though the bombardment continued all that day and the next four, it never reached the same intensity and the total casualties, 27 men killed and missing and 59 wounded, were little over half those of April 26th; they included, however, another company commander, who could ill be spared, Captain Unwin, while Captain Beckett, who had again been conspicuous for good work, keeping his company steady under the heaviest fire, was wounded, as were Lt. Capel and 2/Lt. Weston. General Hasler having been killed early on April 28th, Colonel Hicks was away in charge of the brigade for three days, so Major Palk was commanding the battalion and setting a fine example of coolness and tenacity.

On the evening of April 27th two companies of the Durham L.I. (Territorials) were placed under Major Palk, who used them to extend his line to the left down to the Haanebeek, where good patrolling by Lt. Gill had helped to clear up the situation and gain touch with the troops who were now filling up the gap, and also to push out to the right. Two drafts, one of 25 and another of 143, who arrived on the 27th and 28th, were a welcome addition to the battalion's depleted ranks, while Lt. K. A Johnston rejoined from sick leave and took over A Company.

Meanwhile more counter-attacks had been made between St. Julien and the canal, in co-operation with the French and largely to comply with their wishes, but without appreciably improving the situation. Inadequate artillery support was again the main cause of our failures, while the Germans had had time to consolidate their positions and enjoyed great advantages in observation, besides having many more guns, and heavier guns at that, with ample ammunition. However, the position between Berlin Wood and St. Julien was much improved, the 11th Brigade relieving the details hitherto in the gap and establishing something like a continuous line, while the defence of the old Eastern face of the Salient remained unshaken, repulsing all attacks. The Germans were relying mainly on their artillery, and any efforts their infantry made to advance were promptly quashed, the Hampshire's machine-guns were well sited and quick to use any chance, Lance Corporal Collins doing some very effective shooting. Despite the shelling the trenches had been much improved and in consequence the casualties were much lower.

However, with the French unable to contribute effectively towards the recovery of the ground they had lost, the general situation remained very disadvantageous, and by April 29th it had been decided to evacuate the apex of the Salient and draw back to a more defensible line running Northward by Sanctuary Wood and East of Hooge to Frezenberg and thence N.W. by Mouse Trap Farm, NE. of Wieltje, to connect with the line now being consolidated on our left. Preparations for the withdrawal took some time and for another three days the 1st Hampshire had to hang on in their exposed position, maintaining it as best they could and keeping a sharp watch for any infantry advance. They owed much to the Transport Officer, 2/Lt. Hume, who never failed to keep them supplied with rations and ammunition despite many casualties among his men, horses and mules. The roads the transport had to follow were under constant fire and the men had great difficulty in controlling their frightened animals, but they stuck splendidly to their work with a determination which did them the greatest credit.

May 1st and 2nd saw the enemy's shell-fire increasing in intensity, adding another 50 to the battalion's casualty list, but though the enemy released gas against the 10th and 12th Brigades, the latter being now between the 10th's position and the canal, and followed this up with an infantry advance which was decisively repulsed, the gas was not extended to the 11th Brigade's frontage.

The 11th's trial was to come next day, when a bombardment of greater intensity than ever developed about day break and continued nearly all day. The Buffs, now holding the salient at Berlin Wood, got the worst of it, but the rain of shells on and behind the Hampshire's line was continuous enough, and it was a positive relief when, about 3 p.m., infantry began advancing to try to roll up the Buffs' line from the left. This gave the Hampshire's rifles and machine-guns the opportunity they had been awaiting, and their good use of it appreciably assisted the Buffs to repulse the attack, many Germans being shot down as they sought to enter the wood. The attack was renewed, however, after a fresh bombardment, and this time the Buffs, very much reduced, were driven back to support trenches behind Berlin Wood. On this the Germans turned their attention to the Hampshire, shelling their lines vigorously but ineffectually, and when the infantry attack at last developed C and D Companies and the machine-guns now got their real chance and profited by it most satisfactorily and effectively, the Germans being very decisively repulsed with heavy losses.[1] By 9 p.m. the bombardment had died down and the retirement, ordered earlier in the afternoon, could be started.

It was carried out by half battalions, the C.O., who had rejoined on Colonel Prowse of the Somerset L. I. taking over the brigade, started off with two companies at 10.30 p.m., leaving two under Major Palk to follow at midnight, a few picked men under Lt. Stevens [2] remaining a little longer to bluff the enemy into believing our line was still held. The German losses earlier in the day may have discouraged them ; close as they were in places to the British line, only about 50 yards away, they certainly did nothing to impede the move, which was carried out in excellent order, and, despite the crowded roads, there was no confusion. Only the very seriously wounded [3] had to be left behind, the machine-guns, entrenching tools and spare ammunition were all removed. Heavy rain made the move uncomfortable but helped to conceal it from the the enemy's aeroplanes, and by daylight the battalion was across the canal, halting near Elverdinghe about 5 a.m. to get some very welcome hot tea and a rest, which was soon disturbed, shell-fire making a move necessary. This time a well-wooded park gave shelter, a really warm day soon dried damp clothes, and nightfall found the battalion in bivouac two miles SW. of Elverdinghe, where it got a real rest, a change of clothing and a chance to wash and shave.

May 3rd added another 40 to the casualty list, Captain Twining being killed : this brought the total losses up to six officers and 116 other ranks killed and missing, among them some irreplaceable N.C.O.s, and five officers and 208 other ranks wounded. But the battalion's achievement had been one of outstanding merit, which earned it the well-deserved praise of the higher authorities from

---

[1] This attack seems to have been made mainly by the XXVIIth Reserve Corps which suffered heavily, as their regimental histories admit.

[2] He received the M.C., which was also awarded to Lt. Wyld.

[3] Captain Gwynne, the M.O., had done outstanding work during this time, always cheerful, helpful and untiring, while Corporal Turner, Lance Corporals Simms, Bone and Golding and Privates Brewer, Crawford, Cuffs, T. Smith and G. Williams all displayed great gallantry in attending to wounded men when under heavy fire.

the Commander-in-Chief downward. It could claim, as could the the whole 11th Brigade that, despite the scantiest artillery support, it had never lost a trench.[1] If the infantry attacks had not been pushed home with all the force and vigour of those it had withstood at ' Plugstreet ' Wood, the unceasing shelling had been terrible and the trials the battalion had had to face had tested discipline, endurance and training to the utmost. All who endured the ordeal could testify to the value of the example of calm and steadiness given by Colonel Hicks, ably seconded by Major Palk.

Only the briefest rest could be allowed to any unit engaged in ' Second Ypres '. The Germans, if rather cautious about following up our withdrawal, had soon brought their guns forward to renew their bombardment, and on May 8th after a tremendous shelling our new line was attacked in great force. The Fourth Division, which was on the left, having the 12th Brigade in line from Mouse Trap Farm to the junction with the French, escaped the main brunt of the attack, which fell on the Twenty-Eighth Division in the centre about Frezenberg. This was a weak spot ; our line was on a forward slope, exposed and overlooked ; the hastily dug defences were pretty well obliterated by the bombardment and the Germans, attacking in force, wrested a long stretch of our front line from the few surviving defenders. The 10th and 11th Brigades, both in reserve West of the canal, were called up to reinforce, the 10th counter-attacking with some success, while the 11th was mostly placed in second-line trenches, the Hampshire having their right at Wieltje Farm. They were heavily shelled and caught some machine-gun fire, mainly ' overs ' aimed at the front line, and had a dozen casualties, unfortunately including the C.O. who was hit when on his way to Brigade head-quarters. His wounds were very serious [2] and combined with enteric eventually proved fatal, to the great regret of the battalion. Colonel Hicks had had nearly 25 years service in the regiment and had been commanding the battalion for nearly six months, including its successful and tenacious defence in the Ypres Salient, an outstanding episode in its history and one in which his leadership and inspiring example had played a big part. He had left his mark on a battalion which owed him much.

After two days in second line the battalion, now again under Major Palk, moved up into the front line on May 10th, relieving the King's Own between Canadian (left) and Hampshire Farms. The line here faced North and, having been occupied for some days, was rather stronger than the lost trenches on the Frezenberg ridge, B Company in the centre benefitted by being on a reverse slope, with a section in an advanced post on the crest. Here the Hampshire were to have a hard week, including a really big attack on May 13th. They had been heavily shelled before that, and rifle grenades had been troublesome on May 12th till our trench-mortars, now passing beyond the experi-

---

[1] Besides the N.C.O.s and men already mentioned for good services, Sergeants Buller and Hardy were noted for their reconnaisance work, Sergeants Brown and Ley for services as platoon commanders, Sergeants Ormond and Wootten for coolness and good example under heavy fire and Sergeant Wright for taking messages under fire. Several men were also noted for repairing telephone wires under fire and for gallantry in action.

[2] His right leg was amputated above the knee.

mental stage and therefore less dangerous to those who handled them, replied effectively.

The bombardment on May 13th started with daylight. ' It *was* a shelling ' one officer wrote ' at one time the whole line of trench disappeared in a yellow cloud of smoke and the earth was absolutely rocking '. D Company on the right got the heaviest shelling, but eventually after nearly three hours the German guns lifted off the first line to the second and about 7 a.m. infantry began to advance. Before this the battalion had had to extend to its right, where the virtual annihilation of the Rifle Brigade's left platoon had left a gap near Mouse Trap Farm. No Man's Land was about 300 yards across but this was more than the attackers could cover in face of the rifles and machine-guns of the Hampshire and of the Somerset on their left flank. A few only reached the wire, to be shot down there. One forward trench held by D Company had to be abandoned after the garrison of 40 had been reduced to five, but even then Drummer Eldridge held on at a barricade across a communication trench up which Germans were trying to follow our men, refusing to retire till he had thrown all the bombs at hand, some 60. He was wounded but he kept the Germans at bay for half an hour, and then they went back.[1] Two further advances were repulsed, heavy casualties being inflicted on the attackers, and, to the disappointment of the defenders, who even stood up and challenged them to try again, the Germans abandoned the effort and let their gunners resume the bombardment, which raged on until nearly 2 p.m. when it gradually died away. After that, enemy trying to dig in on our front gave the battalion something to shoot at, but the infantry attacks were not renewed and though, away to the right, Mouse Trap Farm was for a time lost it was ultimately recovered. The day had cost the Hampshire 90 casualties, D Company being particularly hard hit, but once again the line had been maintained intact, and the German infantry attacks repulsed with loss. In the centre, where dismounted cavalry had replaced the Twenty-Eighth Division, we had again lost a long stretch of our front, but the Fourth regained such ground as it had had to evacuate, and, further to the right, the Twenty-Seventh, to which the Germans had recently transferred their attentions, was almost equally successful.

The Hampshire remained in front line until May 14th and were then back in the Divisional support line at View Farm : two drafts of 57 and 96 men respectively did something to replace the casualties, 60 killed and missing and Lt. Prendergast and 2/Lt. Holroyd and 107 men wounded, suffered since May 3rd. The battalion's next turn in front line was from May 19th to 22nd, just West of Mouse Trap Farm, but the fighting seemed to have died down and casualties only came to half-a-dozen. The battalion was back at rest near Pezelhoek when on May 24th the Germans started their final attempt to reach Ypres. This made a big dent in our centre, astride the Ypres–Roulers railway, but once again the gap was filled and a new line was patched up without the 11th Brigade doing more than move up to the Yser canal in readiness to reinforce.

---

[1] Drummer Eldridge, going out later to the evacuated trench, found it empty save for several wounded men whom he bandaged. He received the D.C.M. and the French Croix de Guerre.

May 27th found it in front line again, just East of Potijze. It had nearly a week here, the trenches were good, the weather fine and warm and the enemy had suspended his attacks and was not aggressive. The week's casualties were under 20, only three men being killed, while 2/Lt. Burge was wounded when on patrol. After three days in support at La Brique the battalion recrossed the canal again to its old billets near Poperinghe. If it had not quite finished with the Salient, ' Second Ypres ' was over.

'Second Ypres' had been a hard and exhausting trial, the brunt of which had been borne by the ' Old Army ' Divisions, the Fourth, Fifth, Twenty-Seventh and Twenty-Eighth, who suffered over 41,000 of the 59,000 British casualties. Great credit is due to the Canadians for their splendid resistance in their ' baptism of fire ' to attacks backed by gas and by an overwhelming superiority in artillery and ammunition, but it should not be allowed to obscure the much severer and more prolonged strain which the ' Old Army ' units endured. All the Canadian infantry were out of the fighting line before May 1st and their 5,500 casualties were less by nearly 2000 than those of the least hard hit of the four ' Old Army ' Divisions. Heavy as our casualties were, and the loss of ground was in comparison a minor matter, we had again and again prevented the Germans from exploiting opportunities which, against a less determined and devoted defence, might have been turned to great advantage. Whatever th German purpose may have been, they had failed to drive us out of Ypres an so establish their claim to have completed the conquest of Belgium. ' Second Ypres ' has well been likened [1] to Inkerman, as a ' soldiers' battle ', enormously to the credit of the regimental officers and men who endured the strain and the shelling for over 30 days and stood up to the terrible new weapon against which no provision had been made, until in the end they brought the enemy's advance to a standstill. ' Second Ypres ' is an episode of which the Hampshire may well be proud, perhaps the severest strain to which the 1st Battalion was subjected in the whole war, if July 1st, 1916 was to cost it even more.

One satisfactory feature of May was that for the first time discharges from hospital, 104, nearly balanced admissions, 107 : drafts amounting to 266 men joined during the month with ten officers, including one ' pre-war ' Regular, of whom the battalion was now sadly short, Captain R. D. Johnston. Another 160 men joined the battalion on its arrival at Poperinghe, where it enjoyed several days of welcome rest, during which it was inspected by General Keir, to whose newly formed Sixth Corps [2] the Division had been transferred. This Corps had taken over the left of our line in the Salient, relieving the French East of the canal.

June 11th saw the Hampshire beginning their first spell in the new line, ' no health resort ' as one account says. As with most French trenches, the line did not conform to the British standards, especially as regards sanitation, and the battalion was kept busy if the enemy were unenterprising, apart from making much use of his very efficient trench mortars. The 1st Hampshire had two

---

[1] *Official History.* 1915. I p. 356.
[2] It was virtually the old Third Corps, as it consisted of the Fourth and Sixth Divisions.

spells in front line during June, from the 11th to 16th and from the 21st to 25th. Both were fairly quiet, patrols did some effective work, locating the enemy and finding targets for our guns when they had any shells to fire, and during the second tour a new forward trench was dug close to the enemy, A, now under Captain Garsia who had rejoined after a spell on the Staff, and B (Captain K. A. Johnston) doing the work, while a black night helped to conceal the diggers, whose work was warmly commended by the authorities. Casualties were light, 4 men killed and 38 wounded, together with Major Humphery (3rd Bn.), whose cheerfulness and unfailing coolness had been a great stand-by at Gravenstafel, Lt. Gill and 2/Lt. Beatty. Nearly 140 men went to hospital during the month, only 52 being discharged, but drafts numbering nearly 100 kept the battalion at a fairly good strength.

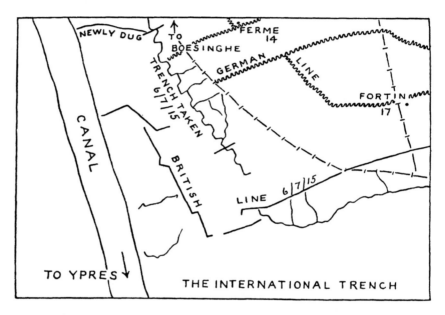

At the Western end of the British line, which here ran North and South parallel to the canal for a short time and then turned Eastward, the French had lost about 300 yards of trench, now called ' the International Trench '[1]: and the Second Army was anxious for its recovery which would improve our tactical position, while General Plumer also wanted to distract the enemy's attention from a larger operation soon to be undertaken at Hooge. The Fourth Division's commander, in view of the Division's recent losses and the shortage of really trained officers and men, was reluctant to attempt anything substantial, like the capture of the whole salient between Ferme 14 and Fortin 17, of which the ' International Trench ' formed the front. However, to meet the Army Commander's wishes he prepared an attack on this International Trench, to be

[1] At one point only a barricade separated the two sides.

carried out on July 6th by the Rifle Brigade, the Hampshire, who had just had another four days in front line (June 30th–July 4th) with 25 casualties,[1] mainly from shell-fire, being across the canal, in reserve.

The attackers, though losing heavily, carried their objective, capturing 30 prisoners, and then set to work consolidating under a heavy shell-fire, punctuated with infantry attacks, which were easily beaten off, and by bombing attacks on both ends of the line. To help deal with these the Hampshire bombing squad under 2/Lt. Stevens was sent up, while C and D Companies ' stood to ' in readiness. The Rifle Brigade, however, though hard pressed and suffering heavily from the German guns, held on stoutly to their gains with the help of the Somerset and of the Hampshire's bombers, among whom Sergeant Gledhill was prominent, while 2/Lt. Stevens as before did splendid work ; they had a very hard time, only five out of the 28 escaping unhurt, but they did not a little for the retention of the captured line, which was handed over that evening to the Lancashire Fusiliers. They in turn were hard pressed next day, when they were assisted in consolidating by working-parties from the Hampshire, whose machine-gunners also contributed effectively to repulse the most vigorous of the German efforts to recover their lost ground. But for the heavy losses inflicted on the Germans it might have been asked whether the capture of 300 yards of trenches had been worth 450 casualties. Of these nine killed and 2/Lts. Bradshaw and Stevens [2] and 25 men wounded belonged to the Hampshire.

After two more days in support the Hampshire on the night of July 8/9th relieved the Lancashire Fusiliers in the captured trenches, A and D Companies going into the front line and being heavily shelled and trench-mortared, while bombing duels went on all day. ' We had an awful time ' one officer wrote ' my company was in the worst place in the whole line and they shelled us the whole time.' But the battalion held the ground and took every chance of answering back and of improving the line. With the trenches much damaged and the parapet not bullet-proof casualties were heavy,[3] and to the general regret Captain Gwynne, who had given the battalion such devoted and efficient service as M.O. for nearly a year, was killed. He was right up in the front line and had dressed the wounds of several Lancashire Fusiliers, but hearing that a Rifle Brigade man, who had been badly wounded three days earlier, was lying out in a half-dug trench, he went forward to him and had just bandaged his wounds when he was hit in the head. ' One of the finest and bravest ' he had done splendid work and had endeared himself to all : his place was not to be easily filled.

Before being relieved next night, the Hampshire had had the satisfaction of catching and dispersing a party massing for an attack, which was thus effectively

---

[1] These included 2/Lt. d'Arcy, one of several officers recently posted to the battalion from the Artists' Rifles, now virtually an O.T.C.

[2] He died of his wounds : a particularly intrepid leader, always to the fore when a difficult job had to be tackled, he was a great loss to the battalion. He had received his commission in October, in recognition of fine work in the retreat from La Cateau. He was awarded the M.C., Gazetted after his death.

[3] 18 killed and 55 wounded.

nipped in the bud. They now went right back to comfortable billets in farms round Watou, to enjoy their first fortnight of real rest since reaching France. They were visited by the Commander-in-Chief and by General Plumer, now commanding the Second Army, who congratulated them warmly on their fine work at Ypres and at the International Trench, for which they were also thanked in emphatic terms by their Brigadier who told them he had put them in to hold the trench because they had never lost a trench and he knew they would not lose this one. Much refitting went on and several officers joined, including 2/Lts. Harding, lately R.S.M., and Diamond, lately R.Q.M.S., who both remained with the battalion though Gazetted to the Northumberland Fusiliers, while C.S.M. King now became R.S.M. Major Perkins being away sick,[1] Lt. Hume was acting as Adjutant, Lt. Sprake succeeding him as Transport Officer on Lt. Tarrant coming out to be Quartermaster.

Meanwhile the wildest rumours were rife about the battalion's next move, the Dardanelles being a hot favourite. Doubts were resolved when on July 23rd the battalion entrained for the South, where the newly-formed Third Army [2] was relieving the French on a fifteen mile frontage from Curlu on the Somme to Hebuterne. Whatever the new front might prove to be like, nobody could believe it would not be preferable to ' the Salient '.

---

[1] Captain im Thurn was also sent home sick, he had been out since August 1914 and was the last ' original ' who had served continuously.

[2] Its headquarters were formed on July 13th.

CHAPTER VI

GALLIPOLI

THE LANDING—THE ADVANCE ON ACHI BABA

THE venture for which the 2nd Hampshire were embarking was a fine example of that ' doing things by halves ' for which Sir Walter Raleigh long ago and with good reason criticized Queen Elizabeth's handling of the war with Spain and of which British ministries have so frequently been guilty. An operation which, if anything ever did, called for the properly co-ordinated efforts of Army and Navy together, was started by the Navy alone, and only after its single-handed effort had failed, possibly by the narrowest of margins, was the Army called in to attempt a now almost hopeless task and try to retrieve the initial ill-success. Between the Navy's failure in the middle of March and the Army's belated arrival on the scene, the Turks and their German advisers had over a month to profit by the warning given them, and a well-prepared defensive was to await our troops and to make doubly difficult an enterprise which even with the advantage of surprise would have been none too easy. Even had the Navy postponed its attack till troops were available, the Germans might have persuaded the Turks to make adequate preparations against a highly probable contingency, but, had we not already shown our hand in March, the defenders might have been in doubt about the destination of the troops who were being collected in Egypt : the Dardanelles, if our most likely objective, was not the only one possible. If better planned and co-ordinated, our attack on the Dardanelles should have secured important results, while its object, the opening up of direct communications with our Russian allies, was one of such immense importance as to justify the diversion of a substantial effort from France to the Mediterranean. But the premature naval attack had thrown away the inestimable advantage of surprise. Our enemies, forewarned, were well prepared.

Leaving Warwick on March 28th the 2nd Hampshire embarked that day at Avonmouth, headquarters with W and X Companies on board the H.T. *Aragon*, Y and Z in the *Manitou*, the transport and machine-gun wagons travelling separately. Colonel Carrington-Smith was in command and Major Leigh senior Major. Majors Deane (W) and Beckwith (Z) and Captains Addison (Y) and Wymer (X) commanded the companies, Captain Reid was Adjutant and Lt. A. Smith Quartermaster. The other officers were Captains[1] B. S. Parker, Penn-Gaskell, Corner, Boxall, Day (Transport Officer), and Spencer-Smith, Lts. Rosser (machine-guns), C. R. Smith, Webb, Silk, White and Pakenham, 2/Lts. Gillett,[2] C. C. Harland,[2] G. R. D. Moor,[2] Howard, Lord and H. Parker, with R.S.M. Holdway and R.Q.M.S. Tyler : the embarkation strength in other ranks being 993.

---

[1] All Lieutenants down to Lt. Spencer-Smith had been promoted to Captain before the end of 1914, all pre-war 2nd Lieutenants becoming Lieutenants.
[2] Of the 3rd Battalion.

Sailing next day the Hampshire had a rather crowded and uncomfortable but uneventful journey, with much sea-sickness and rough weather. After calling at Malta, where some sick were landed, they reached Alexandria on April 2nd and had a week ashore, while the troops were being re-allotted to ships, these not having been loaded originally with a view to the tactical requirements of a landing. The opportunity was taken to get practice in boat work,

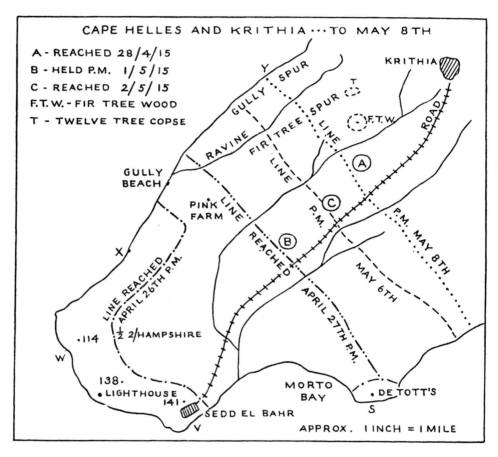

CAPE HELLES AND KRITHIA ··· TO MAY 8TH

A - REACHED 28/4/15
B - HELD P.M. 1/5/15
C - REACHED 2/5/15
F.T.W. - FIR TREE WOOD
T - TWELVE TREE COPSE

KRITHIA

GULLY SPUR
FIR TREE SPUR
RAVINE
GULLY BEACH
PINK FARM
LINE
P.M.
F.T.W.
ROAD
(A)
(C)
(B)
REACHED
LINE REACHED / APRIL 26TH P.M.
APRIL 27TH P.M.
MAY 6TH
P.M. MAY 8TH
X
·114
½ 2/HAMPSHIRE
W
138·
·LIGHTHOUSE
141·
SEDD EL BAHR
MORTO BAY
·DE TOTT'S
S
V
APPROX. I INCH = I MILE

for which more chances were given at Lemnos, the advanced base, whither the *Aragon* conveyed the battalion, arriving on April 13th.

Sir Ian Hamilton's plan of attack was rather elaborate. The Australians and New Zealanders were to land on the West coast of the Gallipoli peninsula about 14 miles from Cape Helles, where the Twenty-Ninth Division was to attempt to get ashore at five points, the most Easterly, at Morto Bay inside the mouth of the Straits, being nearly six miles by the coast from the most Westerly, Y Beach on the West coast. Meanwhile the French were landing on the Asiatic shore, mainly as a diversion. The Twenty-Ninth Division's main attack was being made at three beaches, X and W, NE. and SE. respectively of Tekke Burnu, the most Westerly point of the peninsula, and V, East of Cape Helles and close under the forts and village of Sedd el Bahr. The 86th (Fusilier) Brigade was to form a ' covering force ', to which the 2nd Hampshire, less two companies, were attached; this was to secure a line running roughly NW. from Sedd el Bahr to the cliffs above X beach, from which, after the landing of the main body, in which the remaining Hampshire companies under Major Leigh were included, an advance would be made to the dominating high ground of Achi Baba and the cliffs overlooking the Narrows.

It is easy to see now that the plan was over-optimistic; the covering force could hardly be expected both to secure the necessary foothold ashore and to play a major part in the subsequent advance; too small a reserve was left to exploit any opening that might be made; while the probability of serious casualties in getting ashore, a difficult task even in face of quite slight opposition, had hardly been appreciated; open boats crowded with men afford machine-guns and riflemen ideal targets and even a few well-placed and well-concealed defenders might do incalculable damage. These things perhaps should have been foreseen; what was less easy to foresee, without more experience, was the very limited support naval guns could give to troops ashore, that when accurate shelling of small targets like field or machine guns was needed the naval guns could not achieve it.

The covering force was making its biggest effort at V Beach. Three companies of the Dublin Fusiliers were to lead the way in ' tows ', each of four boats holding about 30 men apiece and hauled by steamboats. The Munsters, the last company of the Dublins and the headquarter wing of the Hampshire, with Y and Z Companies, were on board a collier, the *River Clyde*, which was to be run aground on the beach; ports had been cut in her sides to enable the men to get out quickly on to a steam hopper towed alongside her port side to provide a gangway ashore.

On April 24th headquarters and Y and Z Companies left Lemnos in the *Alaunia* for Tenedos, where they transferred to the *River Clyde*. The Hampshire were allotted to No. 3 hold, abaft the funnel and, as one account says, ' nicely placed to have it down on them should it get hit ', while the men were so tightly packed that movement and even sleep was impossible. Men were heavily laden, carrying 200 rounds, full packs, haversacks and three days' ' iron rations ', a total weight of 84 lbs. Shortly before midnight on April 24th the flotilla left for the peninsula, the movements being so timed that the ships and boats with the troops and their escorting warships should be off the landing places just before dawn.

At V Beach 300 yards of sand separate a steep cliff on the West, crowned by a fort, from the fort and village of Sedd el Bahr on another cliff to the East. A bank about five feet in height fringes the back of the sandy strip, beyond which the ground rises to a ridge about 100 feet up. Several lines of wire stretched across this rising ground, in which were several machine-guns and pom-poms in well-sited positions, hard to locate but covering the beach and all approaching it. These the naval bombardment, even with 12-inch guns, had been powerless to silence.

As the *River Clyde* [1] approached the shore she outstripped the tows and had to wait and let them get ahead, even so she had grounded 40 yards from the shore before the tows reached the beach. Almost immediately a devastating fire caught the crowded boats and within a few minutes terrible losses had been inflicted, many men being shot down before they could leave them, others were hit in the water, most of the wounded being drowned, and the few who survived to get ashore could only shelter behind the bank beyond the beach. Worse still, a hopper should have bridged the gap between the *River Clyde* and the shore, but it had swung away to port and failed to establish the connecting link, and the men had to jump out into shoulder-deep water and gave good targets as they slowly struggled shorewards. The *River Clyde's* captain, Commander Unwin,[2] managed to get three lighters in tow on her starboard side into position to make a bridge, giving the Munsters a chance to dash along the gangways towards the shore. So murderous and accurate was the fire, mainly machine-guns, that only a handful achieved their purpose and the gangways and lighters were soon crowded with dead and wounded, while after a sailor who was helping Commander Unwin to hold the lighters in position had been killed they drifted into deep water. A few men managed to wade ashore but after No. 9 Platoon of Y Company had lost its commander, Captain Boxall,[3] mortally wounded, and nearly 20 men in a gallant attempt to get ashore, Colonel Carrington-Smith, senior officer on board the *Clyde*, stopped further efforts as merely entailing useless sacrifice of life.

Meanwhile the battalion's machine-guns on board the *Clyde* under Lt. Rosser and some R.N.D. guns were trying hard to keep down the machine-gun fire and giving effective covering-fire to the men ashore, but the well-concealed Turkish guns were hard to locate and harder to silence.

The fleet sweepers with the bulk of the 88th Brigade were now approaching V Beach, and such few boats as had survived the first trip took off from one of them Brigadier General Napier himself, 50 men of W and X Companies of the Hampshire with Captains Wymer and Spencer-Smith and two platoons of the Worcestershire. On their coming alongside the *Clyde* they were hailed and warned that it was hopeless to try to get ashore. The Brigadier, however, would not be deterred and reached the hopper, only to be shot down along with Captain Costeker, his Brigade Major.[4] His death was a great loss: very much liked and respected, he had already gained a great hold on the brigade as a leader of great character and ability. Meanwhile the boats carrying the parties under Captains Wymer and Spencer-Smith were making a dash for the shore to starboard of the collier. A burst of fire met them, but they kept on and, jump-

---

[1] Lt. Colonel W. de L. Williams of the regiment, who was on the G.H.Q. staff, was on board and his account of the landing has been very helpful in compiling this chapter.

[2] The gallantry of the Naval officers and men who were acting as ' beach party ' here was outstanding, and all accounts from Hampshire eye-witnesses emphasize it.

[3] He was to have been the next Adjutant.

[4] This was rather before 11 a.m.

ing into fairly shallow water and scrambling along a projecting spit of rock, the two officers and two-thirds of their men [1] joined those Dublins and Munsters who were sheltering along the bank under the Sedd el Bahr cliffs. Here they were held up, and if the Turks never attempted to dislodge them they could only hang on with hardly a chance of a target: the stalemate was complete. The naval guns might pound away but they could not get at the machine-guns which dominated the situation.

It was while trying to locate the machine-guns that, about 3 p.m., Colonel Carrington-Smith was hit and killed. He was on the bridge of the *River Clyde* and had just marked down one machine-gun when he was hit. He had not been long with the 2nd Hampshire, he had won the confidence and respect of officers and men, and in him the regiment lost a most competent commander who might have gone far.

At the other beaches things had gone better: the Royal Fusiliers had landed almost unopposed at X and had eventually linked up with the Lancashire Fusiliers, who despite a far rougher passage had made good their landing at W. Reinforcements had followed the original attackers and about 10.30 Sir Ian Hamilton directed General Hunter-Weston to divert the rest of the 88th Brigade to W Beach, where accordingly the main body of W and X Companies under Major Leigh landed unopposed, pushing forward to fill a gap in the line which now stretched from the lighthouse near Cape Helles, which the Worcestershire had taken, across by Hill 138 to Hill 114, where the W Beach troops had gained touch with the Royal Fusiliers. By the time this party was ashore the two redoubts on Hill 138 had been taken and the Hampshire merely filled a gap in the extended line of the Essex, North of Hill 138. Fighting had died down, if there were still Turks close in front of the line which we were entrenching. An advance from this line might have relieved the remnants hanging on to their precarious hold on V Beach, but the urgency of their situation does not seem to have been realised; the 86th Brigade's commander had been wounded and no senior officer was present to take charge and push on.

During the afternoon the fire on V Beach slackened and the sailors hauled the lighters connecting the collier with the shore back into position, whereupon the Munsters again tried a rush, only to awaken the Turkish machine-guns into renewed activity and be checked. Rather later three battleships gave the Turkish positions a fresh pounding, under cover of which a handful of Munsters and Hampshire tried to force an entrance into the Sedd el Bahr fort but without much success, having to shelter on the seaward face without getting in. Before it was dark, however, Major Beckwith went ashore to take over command and directed Captain Spencer-Smith and the 18 men left out of his 26 to push on into the fort and secure the exit from it to the North. Accompanied by some Dublins and Munsters, the party moved some way to the right, climbed the cliff, cutting many strands of barbed wire, and dashed into the fort, the Turks bolting before them. They then established themselves on the Northern face of the fort, where most of the walls were still standing, and under cover of

---

[1] Some 15 were hit.

this party, whose occupation of the fort prevented a counter-attack on that side, the remaining fighting troops from the *Clyde* crossed the gangways quite unhindered and brought welcome help to the survivors ashore. The wounded could now be succoured and removed and the troops sorted out and reorganized. To have attempted an immediate attack would have been futile, the exhausted survivors of the earlier attempts to land wanted a rest, and Major Beckwith had to arrange with Colonels Williams and Doughty-Wylie of the G.H.Q. Staff for a fresh naval bombardment before any further advance against Sedd el Bahr and the old castle could be attempted.

The Turks at V made no effort to impede our preparations, if patrols and scouts more than once approached the line further West in which W and X Companies were stationed and disturbed their rest, already rather broken into by the need for working parties to get rations, ammunition and water ashore. Few men had had a proper night's rest on the night before landing, and their fatigue and the need for unloading supplies largely explains the scanty progress made next day by the force covering W and X Beaches. Actually very few Turks were facing them, the defenders being apparently concentrated at Sedd el Bahr to resist our renewed attacks.

At V Beach two points had to be attacked, the fort and village of Sedd el Bahr on the East and the old castle on Hill 141 to the N.W. Nearly all the Hampshire had been collected on the Sedd el Bahr side. Before dawn Captain Spencer-Smith's party, who had held the ruins during the night, were withdrawn [1] to join the rest of the Hampshire on the top of the cliff. This detachment and the machine-guns could give covering fire to the main attack, some Hampshires under Captain Penn-Gaskell working through a gap which had been cut in the wire, were to attack West of the fort, the rest, together with some Munsters, after re-occupying the fort were to press forward against the village. These preparations were difficult to make in the dark, especially as many wounded had to be got away and a tangle of wire impeded movement.

Shortly before dawn (April 26th) the supporting ships opened fire again but directed their fire more against the village than against the fort. This led to some delay but eventually the attack went in, the fort being quickly cleared. In debouching beyond it by a narrow postern gate the troops came under accurate fire from trenches on the edge of the cliff and were checked. However, Major Beckwith soon had the advance going again and, headed by Captain Addison and by Captain Walford of the G.H.Q. staff, Y Company forced their way into the village, the machine-guns covering their advance. In the village they met desperate resistance; the Turks contested every house and had to be ousted with the bayonet from one after another. Some lay quiet, concealed in cellars or ruins, till our men had passed by and then fired into their backs. Machine-gun and rifle fire from Hill 141 was troublesome and, with the snipers very hard to dislodge, it took nearly three hours before the Hampshire finished clearing the village. Major Beckwith's gallantry and inspiring leadership were outstanding and made a tremendous impression on the men. It was largely due

[1] This was to let the naval guns bombard Sedd el Bahr.

to his leading that Sedd el Bahr was taken, he exposed himself recklessly and how he escaped being hit was a marvel. Captain Addison, who vied with him in leading the attack, was less fortunate, being killed by a bomb.

The fight for Sedd el Bahr finished with a charge against some trenches beyond the village, for which every available man had been collected, including Captain Spencer-Smith's party from the right. Major Beckwith himself headed the charge, brandishing an axe with which he had just cut a cable, leading, it was thought, to Kum Kale. This charge sent the surviving Turks flying,

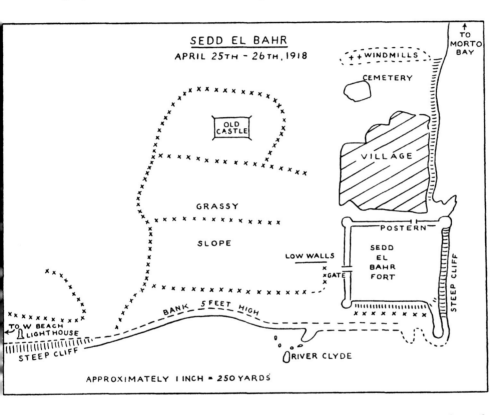

SEDD EL BAHR

APRIL 25TH – 26TH, 1918

APPROXIMATELY 1 INCH = 250 YARDS

several being shot down as they bolted. Pressing on, the Hampshire cleared a row of windmills on a hill overlooking Morto Bay and started to consolidate. Meanwhile, more to the left, where Colonel Williams had been organizing the attack, Dublins and Munsters with the two Hampshire platoons under Captain Penn-Gaskell were having hard fighting for the old castle: the enemy's resistance was obstinate and it took some time before the final attack could be launched. Enfilade fire from the village by which a Major of the Dublins was killed, had been troublesome, but about 2.30 p.m. Captain Penn-Gaskell could start the final charge which carried the position, when the surviving defenders, in making off Northward, gave good targets to the Hampshire's machine-guns with which Sergeant Jackson had been giving an effective covering fire. Touch was now gained with the troops at W. Beach and a continuous line was established from Sedd el Bahr to X Beach, Y and Z Companies being on the right on the cliff edge beyond Sedd el Bahr,[1] while W and X were well away to the left between Hills 138 and 114.

Sedd el Bahr had cost the Hampshire nearly 60 casualties, 2/Lts. Harland and Gillett being wounded. The fighting had been fierce, and if wisdom after the event suggests that the rest of the Division might have advanced at any time during the day without meeting serious opposition, the men were short of sleep and rest, water was short and the information available about the general position scanty and inaccurate.[2] The stubbornness of the opposition had concealed its weakness and, as things appeared at the time, it seemed reasonable to wait for the French, who only started to land late in the afternoon.

Fatigue and delays over landing supplies and getting the French ashore held things up on April 27th also. On enough French landing to relieve the troops at V Beach, Major Beckwith's wing moved across to rejoin the other companies, Major Leigh now taking command. Late in the afternoon an advance was begun, the troops crossing the saucer-like depression draining into Morto Bay and beginning to ascend the long slopes leading to Achi Baba. The French were on the right, the 88th Brigade in the centre, the 87th on the left and the 86th in reserve. Except for a little shell-fire the advance was unopposed, though a reconnoitring platoon of X, which carefully searched any vestige of cover, disposed of many snipers, some shamming dead.[3] After advancing about 200 yards a line was taken up running roughly Westward from the S.W.B's position at de Tott's Battery across to a point 500 yards beyond the mouth of the big ravine, later known as Gully Ravine, the Hampshire being astride the road leading to Krithia, with Z Company flung back on the left where the next battalion was some way in rear.

Once again, though no serious attack was made by the Turks during the night, several small advances, mostly against Z Company, being easily stopped, a rather disturbed night did not give the men much rest and most of them started the next day's advance hardly fit for strenuous work. However, the attack started quite well, the Turkish outposts falling back in disorder, and at first their shell-fire was negligible, if we had too few guns ashore to give really effective artillery support.

As the Essex on their left across the Krithia road had had to keep back level with the extreme left, the Hampshire had started nearly 600 yards ahead of them. Pushing straight ahead, with W and Z in the firing line and preceded by Lt. White's platoon of Z, the battalion made good progress and was soon ahead also of the Worcestershire on the right, whom the slowness of the French advance kept back. The thick scrub made the Turks hard to locate, and gullies

---

[1] The occupation of the windmill ridge meant that all the high ground overlooking V Beach was in our hands and the Turks were denied direct observation of it.

[2] Major Beckwith at Sedd el Bahr was quite unaware that the South Wales Borderers were at S Beach, a bare mile away.

[3] One account speaks of passing many dead Turks, apparently killed by the ships' fire.

and small ravines provided admirable natural cover, of which the enemy made good use. The men pressed on, however, and the leading platoon was under a mile from Krithia before the Turks were seen advancing to meet us. Lt. White's platoon now lined a low ridge and was soon reinforced by the rest of Z, W prolonging the line to the left, but with both flanks exposed to enfilade fire we could not get on.

About 11.30 a counter-attack in force checked the French, who fell back some way,[1] but the Hampshire machine-guns, well handled by Corporal Stone, helped to stop its progress. Without more artillery support, infantry could make little progress over the difficult country, but, while W and Z hung on stubbornly, Major Deane brought a party forward on the left and secured that flank, and eventually a determined advance brought the Worcestershire up level on the right, while rather later some Essex and Royal Scots got forward on the other flank. The machine-guns got some good targets at fairly long ranges and efforts to advance against the Hampshire met with little success, except where dead ground ahead of W Company gave cover. But Turkish reinforcements were arriving and ammunition began to run short. The Worcestershire in particular ran short and sent to ask the Hampshire if they could spare any. The 87th Brigade had also been checked, an effort by the much depleted 86th resulted in a handful of men reaching Fir Tree Wood, a little nearer Krithia than the Hampshire, but the general position remained unchanged. A gallant effort by W Company, led by Major Deane, reached a low crest line and our men carried two trenches, killing their occupants, but, on advancing again, they came under very heavy fire and could go no further, Major Deane being killed and half the company falling. The decisive episode was a counter-attack which drove the French right back. The Worcestershire, with their right exposed, had to give ground, and X Company had to conform. On the left also our troops were driven back and the Hampshire found themselves under fire from both flanks. With ammunition failing, despite untiring efforts by R.S.M. Holdway to replenish the pouches of the firing-line, and many men without water or rations, the position was untenable in face of the continuous Turkish pressure and their heavy fire, and eventually about 5 p.m. it was vacated by order, the troops falling back approximately to their starting line.[2] The machine-guns, assisted by those of the Royal Scots, covered the retirement effectively, but the day had been most exhausting and with everyone nearly dead beat it was not possible to get all the wounded away. The battalion's casualties had been heavy, 100 men killed and missing and 250 wounded. Besides Major Deane Lt. Pakenham had been killed. Major Beckwith, who had again led and rallied the men splendidly, was wounded, as were Captain Spencer-Smith and 2/Lts. Howard (mortally), Lord, Moor and Parker (mortally).

[1] R.S.M. Holdway, who was sent by Major Leigh with a message to the nearest French commander, expressed his opinion to that officer in no uncertain terms but without much result.

[2] On the extreme left the 87th Brigade had advanced nearly to Y Beach but had to be brought back during the night to straighten the line and avoid a salient. The line held that evening was to all intents that later known as the ' Eski ' line.

With Captain Corner sick only a dozen officers and barely 500 rank and file remained fit for duty.

The Turks did not molest the retirement; they also had lost very heavily and had indeed been very near to giving way: accordingly the troops had an almost undisturbed night and a quiet day followed, spent in entrenching,[1] while Colonel Williams assumed temporary command of the 88th Brigade. Many wounded were now brought in, the Turkish failure to follow up having allowed most of those left behind to escape capture. About mid-day on April 30th the battalion was relieved by the French and went back to Morto Bay for the briefest of rests.

The failure to exploit our success in landing was most disappointing, but what the troops had achieved was an outstanding testimony to their gallantry and devotion, the regimental officers and men had made efforts which are beyond praise. The unhappy chance which so quickly had deprived the landing force of Brigadier General Napier, Colonel Carrington-Smith and so many other senior officers had been no small factor in the result, but it is hard to resist the conclusion that too much was expected of the men, that those who had forced a landing could hardly be expected also to exploit it immediately and that the plan was too ambitious for the force actually available. What the weakened and exhausted Twenty-Ninth could not accomplish, mainly because they had reached the limits of their physical powers, a fresh Division might well have achived, and Achi Baba might have been taken on April 28th. Spent force as the Twenty-Ninth Division was on that day, it was only by a narrow margin that the Turks had stopped its advance. It seems that they had put in their last available reserves.

The 2nd Hampshire had less than a day in reserve; by 4 a.m. (May 1st) they were relieving the Essex in the front line, between the track leading to Krithia (right) and the Kirte Dere or Krithia Nullah (left), the French were on their right and the combined Dublins and Munsters of the 86th Brigade on their left. That evening about 10 p.m. a heavy bombardment started followed an hour later by an attack in force.[2] Firing steadily with great effect, the Hampshire held up the attack, but the Turks broke through the 86th Brigade and pushed on nearly to the support line. Prompt counter-attacks by the Royal Fusiliers and Royal Scots restored the situation, but a small party penetrated to the Hampshire's support trench and someone, probably an English-speaking German, raised the cry ' All officers on the left '. Hurrying to the spot, Major Leigh and Captain Reid with two R.A. officers were shot down, and if the Turks were promptly wiped out to a man, it was little consolation to the Hampshire for the loss of an officer like Major Leigh, who had been doing magnificently and had inspired his men with affection as well as admiration and respect. His example and courage had been magnificent, he had exposed himself freely, ' always in the thick of things ' where he was most wanted, inspiring calm and confidence. Captain Reid, an admirable Adjutant, was also much missed.

---

[1] The discovery of a good spring of water just behind the battalion's trenches was most welcome
[2] The Turks had been reinforced and were putting in some 20 battalions.

But for the loss of two such invaluable officers, all the more felt after that of the C.O. and Major Deane, the Hampshire, now under Captain Wymer with Lt. Rosser as Adjutant, might have congratulated themselves on the night's work: they had held firm and never let the Turks get anywhere near, though the attacks were kept up until dawn and were pushed home, while the bodies whom daylight revealed lying thickly in our front bore witness to the accuracy of the battalion's fire, at least 400 could be counted within sight of its line. Elsewhere also the attacks had been repulsed, the Worcestershire from the support line having restored a nasty position on the right where some Senegalese had given way, while on the left the 87th Brigade had counter-attacked most successfully, carrying their line well forward and taking 120 prisoners, the 88th Brigade sending in another 100.

This encouraged those in command to order another general advance and at 10 a.m. (May 2nd) the Hampshire started forward. Heavy shrapnel fire met them almost at once but did not stop them, and they had covered nearly 1200 yards, capturing a good many Turks who were sheltering in holes and hollows, pinned to the ground by our fire, before they again found themselves ahead of the general line, especially on the right. Here [1] they held on till a French retirement completely uncovered their right and compelled them to fall back to the line from which they had advanced, no ground having been gained. Their casualties had been serious, 22 killed and missing, Lts. Smith, Webb, and Silk and 87 men wounded,[2] leaving them as the weakest unit in their brigade, little over 400 all told. But the enemy had lost heavily and the brigade had taken over 300 prisoners.

Three fairly quiet days followed, one in the trenches consolidating, two in reserve near Morto Bay, when for the first time since the landing a wash and a shave were possible, then on May 6th another advance was attempted. For this two fresh brigades were available, both recently arrived from Egypt, one of the Forty-Second (East Lancashire Territorial) Division and the 29th Indian Brigade. The 88th Brigade in the left centre [3] had to advance up a spur between the Krithia Nullah and Gully Ravine which was dotted with clumps of firs and consequently christened 'Fir Tree Spur'. Its aim was to capture Krithia and then to wheel round to the right and secure a position facing Achi Baba from the West, through which the 87th and Indian Brigades would deliver the final assault.

If the troops had started tired on April 28th they were little fresher now. Few officers or men had had any real rest since April 25th, few had had a change of clothes or many chances to wash. One officer wrote that ' officers and men have lived like animals, no blankets or kits, no clothes off at night, not even boots, feeding from hand to mouth and snatching sleep when we can '. Another wrote appreciatively of a wash in an empty oil tin, another described himself

[1] The Brigade diary puts them at Point 169 B., i.e. just South of Fir Tree Wood, but the squared map at first in use proved to be inaccurate and suggests further advances both on April 28th and May 2nd than were actually achieved. Sketch 12 is copied from a plan based on this map and is probably not accurate.
[2] Captain Wymer was also hit but remained at duty.
[3] The Hampshire were well to the left (North) of the line of their advance on May 2nd.

as ' filthy and black with dust and exposure '; ' we are not fed up but only tired ' was another summary.   Luckily the weather had been fine, if cold enough at night to make men miss their blankets, though one letter speaks of being ' too sleepy to mind the cold '.   Considering everything, the losses, the exertions and the fatigue, the general cheerfulness was amazing: like the B.E.F. in the Retreat from Mons the men seemed to be going on almost automatically and unquestioning.

In this fresh attempt (May 6th) the 88th Brigade had the Worcestershire on the right, then the Hampshire, with the Royal Fusiliers [1] beyond them, reaching to Gully Ravine.   A screen of scouts headed the advance, which worked slowly forward for several hundred yards before opposition, largely from machine-guns in advanced posts, began to be serious.   On neither flank were troops coming forward, the Lancashire Territorials could make little headway over the bare ground of Gully Spur, and though the French right made some progress their centre and left failed to get far.   As before the artillery support was quite inadequate and the Turks, using the good natural cover, were hard to locate. Some of the 88th Brigade reached Fir Tree Wood but failed to clear it, and the line came to a halt about 500 yards from its starting line, with the Hampshire West of Fir Tree Wood; they and the Royal Fusiliers beyond them might have been able to get forward but that, being ahead of the troops on Gully Spur they were liable to be enfiladed from across the ravine.   They could only dig in where they were to secure what ground had been gained.   Casualties had not been heavy, the Hampshire returning six killed and 53 wounded but unluckily two more of the eight officers present were wounded, Captains B. S. Parker and Penn-Gaskell.[2]

The scanty success achieved on May 6th did not deter the higher command from renewing the attempt next day; though without more artillery support our tired infantry could hardly do much against a defence so well supplied with machine-guns.   Once again the inability of the troops on Gully Spur to gain ground held back those East of Gully Ravine; neither the Royal Fusiliers, next the Ravine, nor the Hampshire could get on far, and further to the right Fir Tree Wood remained untaken, although the 87th Brigade had reinforced the attack, while the French also suffered heavily to little purpose.

However, the New Zealand Brigade and one Australian had been brought round to Cape Helles to reinforce the attack and May 8th saw yet another attempt to reach the objectives of May 6th.   The New Zealanders, passing through the 88th Brigade, who remained in reserve, attacked up Fir Tree Spur, the 87th Brigade co-operating West of Gully Ravine.   Advancing with great gallantry and determination, the New Zealanders could make little headway against a fire our bombardment had failed to subdue and were soon checked.   After another bombardment they went forward again, with the 88th

---

[1] Attached from the temporarily broken up 86th Brigade.

[2] Those still unhit were Captains Wymer and Day, who had rejoined from the transport, and Rosser, Lt. White, the only subaltern still unhit, the Quartermaster and Captain Hodson (Reserve of Officers, attached).

in support and the Australians advancing on the right up the Krithia Spur. Once again the bombardment had been unsuccessful, the machine-guns were still unsubdued and the New Zealanders, despite another splendid effort, again came to a standstill. The 88th Brigade struggled forward some little way despite a raking fire from well-concealed machine-guns, but it also was checked somewhere NW. of the still untaken Fir Tree Wood [1] and though it held on here till well into the night, before dawn it was ordered back. The Hampshire had made another determined effort [2] which had cost them another 28, including Captain Hodson, killed and missing and Captain Day and 97 men wounded, leaving only four officers, Captains Wymer and Rosser, Lt. White and the Quartermaster, and 204 men, a remnant who badly needed the week's rest they were now given in a reserve position North of Sedd el Bahr, having been relieved by Australians. In little over a fortnight three-quarters of the battalion had become casualties [3] and the survivors were for a time completely played out. It was wonderful that their gallant effort to accomplish a task altogether beyond the scope of one Division had come within reasonable distance of success.

[1] The precise positions are hard to locate owing to the inaccuracy of the maps in use at first. The map in the brigade diary would show that the battalion was in front of the North and South line through Fir Tree Wood, which seems too far.

[2] Lance Corporal Alexander did fine work, re-forming men and leading them forward to re-force an isolated advanced party. He received the D.C.M.

[3] Up to May 14th eleven officers had been killed, twelve wounded, and one invalided ; of other ranks killed, missing and died of wounds came to 198, wounded to 507. 2/Lieutenant Richards, killed on May 13th, had just received his commission.

CHAPTER VII

GALLIPOLI (continued)

THE STRUGGLE FOR KRITHIA

THE operations of May 6th to 8th ended a definite phase in the Gallipoli venture, the attempt to rush the defences at the Southern end of the peninsula and so assist the fleet to force its way through. That object had not been achieved, though if the Australian and New Zealand Corps had hardly enlarged the slender foothold originally obtained, at Cape Helles enough elbow-room had

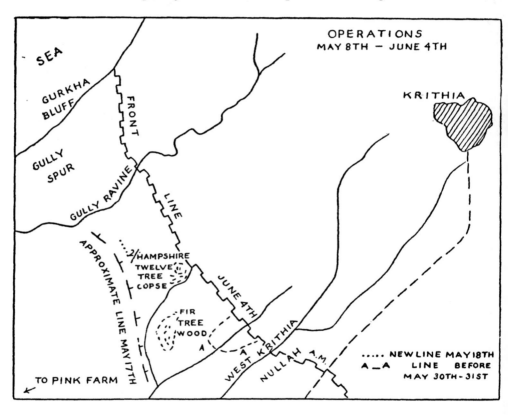

been gained to allow of making preparations for another attempt whenever sufficient artillery and ammunition and substantial reinforcements should have reached the peninsula to warrant it. Why three months passed before these were forthcoming concerns rather the general history of the war than a regimental chronicle, which can hardly examine in detail the various strategical and political considerations concerned, even if ultimately they closely affected the fortunes of regimental officers and men; it is equally beyond its province to embark on a discussion of the conflicting claims of the Western Front and this subordinate operation, begun to assist the Navy but now developing into a major military venture. What the ' M.E.F. ' might have done on May 9th with half the guns, shells and men employed in that day's gallant failure to break the German lines in France can easily be conjectured; actually during the next three months it had to do its best to gain ground by local attacks against positions daily becoming more formidable, with but little additional artillery and ammunition, with drafts which hardly sufficed to replace the losses at the landing, let alone those incurred in the subsequent attacks, and with only one Division to reinforce the three who had already found their task beyond what could be reasonably expected of them.

These months therefore the 2nd Hampshire found both strenuous and exhausting ; with the elbow-room gained quite insufficient the troops in reserve, unless at Lemnos or Imbros, were always within range of the enemy's guns, and it was urgent to enlarge our territory and improve our tactical position.

When the 2nd Hampshire went back to a brief ' rest ' on May 10th their other ranks were up to 229, some convalescents having rejoined. During this ' rest ' 2/Lt. C. Harland rejoined from hospital and R.S.M. Holdway's well-deserved promotion to 2/Lieutenant increased officers present to six, while other ranks rose to 282, more convalescents reappearing. May 16th saw the battalion back in its old trenches 200 yards NW. of Fir Tree Wood, relieving the 127th (Manchester) Brigade of the Forty-Second Division.[1] The line was being advanced by sapping forward and then joining up the saps laterally: this was done mainly by night, while by day snipers usually remained at their forward ends. Once a new line had been linked up fresh saps were started, while on the night of May 17th/18th an advance of 100 yards was made over the open and a new line dug and joined to the old front. This was followed up by more successful sapping. Advantage was taken meanwhile of any targets the Turks offered and soon after the 88th Brigade returned to the line it had their snipers well under control. The Turks were being equally busy and constructed a formidable-looking redoubt on a knoll on front of the Hampshire's left, about 150 yards away. This target was well plastered by our 60 pounders, and on May 24th the arrival of some trench mortars allowed us to bombard the enemy's front trenches very effectively. The whole Division was carrying on the same work with no small success, and May not only saw Fir Tree Wood made good but the line advanced 400 yards beyond it, while Twelve Tree Copse, some 600 yards North of it, was brought within our lines, the Hampshire's front line being within 300 yards of the Turks when they were relieved on May 25th. Further to the left a well-executed enterprise by the Indian Brigade had improved the position on Gully Spur, capturing a valuable bluff [2] above Y Beach, by which advance the flank of troops advancing up Fir Tree Spur was covered. These minor successes greatly encouraged the troops, whose determination and cheerful endurance of great discomforts was notable. When in reserve they could

[1] Captain Allen of the regiment was D.A.A. and Q.M.G. of this Division.
[2] Subsequently known as Gurkha Bluff.

indulge in excellent bathing, otherwise they were far worse off than the troops
in France, where by this time troops out of the line were fairly comfortable.
Never out of range of gun-fire, to which we could rarely reply, owing to the
shortage of ammunition, they never faltered, put a good face on a bad situation
and responded to every call.

This spell in trenches cost the 2nd Hampshire 18 killed and missing and
2/Lt. Holdway and 27 men wounded, but the Turkish accounts show clearly
that their casualties during this period were heavier than ours. To balance our
losses 46 men under 2/Lt. Lambert had arrived from the 3rd Battalion   while

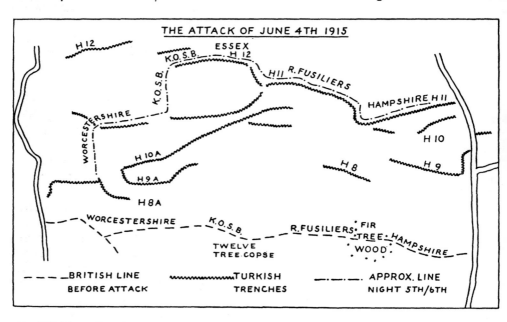

Lt. Webb, 2/Lt. G. R. D. Moor and 37 men rejoined from hospital, and by May
22nd other ranks had reached 334.

From May 25th to 30th the battalion was ' out ' at Pink Farm a mile SW.
of Fir Tree Wood. Here Captain Ford with 2/Lts. M.F. Cromie, N. Harland,
C. Moor and Reeves joined from the 3rd Battalion with 48 men, and 200 of the
10th Manchester were attached for instruction. This instruction was rather
impeded by calls for large ' fatigues ', but as Pink Farm was within half a mile
of Gully Beach bathing was possible.

May 30th saw the Hampshire back in reserve trenches about 2 miles SW.
of Krithia. Colonel Williams had that morning taken command,[1] Brigadier
General Doran having taken over the brigade. On the following evening X
and Y Companies had to be put in on the 88th Brigade's right, SE. of Fir Tree
Wood where the Forty-Second Division's advance had fallen behind the Twenty-
Ninth's. This position they greatly improved by advancing by night and digging

---

[1] He was the fifth officer to command the battalion since April 25th.

a line of rifle pits across the gap, a very useful piece of work which was accomplished with only four casualties.

Preparations were now complete for another general attack to be made on June 4th, in which the 88th Brigade, to which the Royal Fusiliers and K.O.S.B. were attached, was advancing up Fir Tree Spur, with the 2nd Hampshire on the right, with thin flank on the Krithia Nullah, beyond which was the Forty-Second Division, on whose right a brigade of the R.N.D. and the French were also attacking. Fourteen officers of ' K 4 ' battalions [1] had arrived on June 1st and been attached to the battalion, so that though other ranks were little over 300 it was strong in officers. But after all the Twenty-Ninth Division had endured at and since the landing, another big attack asked much of its surviving officers and men.

The available artillery support was still sadly scanty, only four 60 pounders and eight howitzers altogether, while the ammunition allowance was far from adequate for the destruction of substantial defences, so the bombardment, which started at 8 a.m. could only be maintained at a slow rate until the last half-hour preceeding the infantry attack, which was to start at midday. The battalion's first objective, the Turkish first line, now marked on our maps as H.8 and H.9.,[2] was to be assaulted by X (Captain Wymer) and Y (2/Lt. C. Harland), and at 12.15 p.m. W (Captain Evans) and Z (Lt. White) were to go through and attack the second line, H.10. The very minute that the bombardment stopped X and Y went forward splendidly, despite a very heavy fire, and were quickly into H.8 and H.9, capturing them with some 30 prisoners, including several officers, though both Captain Wymer and 2/Lt. Harland were hit. Sergeant Fisher, almost the first man to enter the Turkish line, seeing several Turks trying to creep away along a communication trench, pushed ahead, intercepted them and made them surrender.[3] Just before W and Z started to reinforce the leaders Lt. White was killed, but Captain Rosser took his place and, as ordered, the supporting companies went through the leaders, taking H.10 and the SE. end of H.11 beyond it. Both company commanders were wounded, but Lt. Lambert took over and led the advance to its objective. On the Hampshire's left the Royal Fusiliers and the K.O.S.B. had been checked by a redoubt facing Twelve Tree Copse and by H.9a, so that the Hampshire, being well ahead of them, had their left ' in the air '. The Forty-Second Division had also been held up, so Lt. Colonel Williams [4] decided not to press on but to consolidate what had been gained, good work being done by the machine-guns which their officer, 2/Lt. M. F. Cromie, brought forward ' in the nick of time ' as one account puts it ' to be instrumental in saving the situation '. Further to the left the Worcestershire had forged right ahead, taking part of H.12, while their leading men even reached H.14, within tantalizing

---

[1] Captain Evans of the 12th R. Warwickshire was an ex-Colour-Sergeant of the regiment.

[2] The trenches on Gully Spur were given serial numbers under J, those on Fir Tree Spur under H. and those on Krithia Spur under F.

[3] He received the D.C.M., also awarded to Sergeant Milne for conspicuous gallantry and good leading in the operations following the landing.

[4] He was wounded soon afterwards, 2/Lt. Cromie being killed.

nearness to Krithia, but unfortunately the attack up Gully Spur had not fared well and enfilade fire from across Gully Ravine prevented the Worcestershire exploiting their success. By 1.45 p.m., however, the Royal Fusiliers and K.O.S.B., having carried their redoubt despite heavy casualties and come up level with them, the Hampshire were reported as 'advancing again', and before 2.17 p.m. [1] H.12 had been secured all along the brigade's front,[2] while at 3.40 p.m. another advance was reported, the Hampshire actually reaching a fifth trench line before having to halt. If the French had failed and had thereby uncovered the R.N.D's right, the Forty-Second Division meanwhile had also got well forward, the Turks had lost heavily, few defences intervened between Krithia and our most advanced troops and, could a substantial portion of the Corps reserve [3] have now been put in to exploit the 88th Brigade's success, Krithia might have been secured. This was not done, and before long strong Turkish reinforcements were counter-attacking and exploiting their repulse of the French by driving in the R.N.D., whose retirement exposed the Forty-Second's right and in turn drove that Division back to its first objective, F.11 and the Vineyard,[4] which line it tried to maintain. The two most advanced of the five lines of trenches the Hampshire had over-run now become untenable, so at 6 p.m. they had by order to fall back to H.11, which with its continuation westward in H.12 the 88th Brigade was consolidating, and this line was successfully maintained.

The Hampshire's achievement had been notable, none the less that failures elsewhere prevented its exploitation, but the losses had been heavy. Of the battalion's own officers Lt. White and 2/Lt. M.F. Cromie had been killed, Colonel Williams, Captains Wymer and Rosser, 2/Lts. C. Harland, N. Harland and Lambert (mortally) were wounded, while those attached, Lt. Chilton (Argyll & Sutherlands) was killed, Lt. Malet was missing, Captains Evans and Bird and 2/Lt. McNair (all four R. Warwickshire) and Lts. Humbert and Phillips-Jones (both R. Berkshire) were wounded, last two mortally; of other ranks 56 were killed and missing and 95 wounded, out of about 300 in action. But the Turks had been heavily punished and the 88th Brigade could claim 250 prisoners.

Consolidation was little impeded that night or next day, though the guns did a little shooting to break up apparently impending counter-attacks. June 5th saw some small advances made on the left, and that evening the Hampshire shifted slightly to their right, keeping touch with the Forty-Second Division. Early next morning (June 6th) a heavy attack developed all along the 88th Brigade's front and beyond it to the right. Against the Hampshire the Turks made no headway, Sergeant Hanna doing most effective work with the machine-guns and breaking-up several attacks, and the battalion held firmly on, although it had to throw back its right, which the Forty-Second Division's loss of two trenches, G.11 and G.12,[5] had exposed. Confused fighting went on for some time

[1] Reported by the 88th Brigade at that hour.
[2] H.12 apparently proved to be not complete or continuous along the front attacked.
[3] The 87th Brigade and half the R.N.D.
[4] Just across the West Krithia Nullah to the right of the re-entrant marked on Sketch 14.
[5] Just across the West Krithia Nullah and in continuation of the right of H.11.

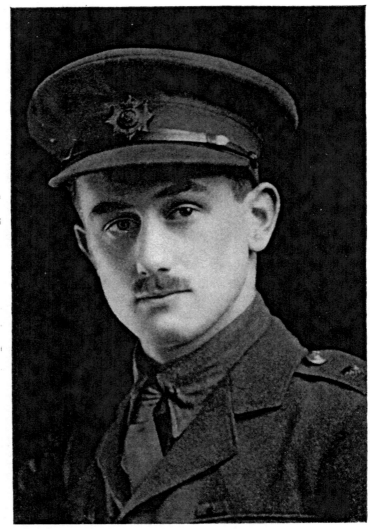

SECOND LIEUTENANT GEORGE RAYMOND DALLAS MOOR, V.C., M.C. AND BAR

Born on October 22nd, 1896 ; son of William Henry Moor (Auditor General, Transvaal, retired) and Mrs. Moor, and nephew of the late Sir Ralph Moor, formerly High Commissioner for Southern Nigeria. He was educated at Cheltenham College, commissioned into the 3rd Battalion The Hampshire Regiment in October 1914, and was granted a Regular Commission on August 1st, 1915.

After six months training in England and Egypt, he went with the 2nd Battalion to the Dardanelles, and was at the landing at V. Beach at Gallipoli.

His decoration was gazetted on July 24th, 1915, when he was only 18 years of age.

' For most conspicuous bravery and resource on June 6th, 1915, during operations South of Krithia, Dardanelles. When a detachment of a battalion on his left, which had lost all its officers, was rapidly retiring before a heavy Turkish attack, 2nd Lieutenant Moor immediately grasping the danger to the remainder of the line, dashed back some two hundred yards, stemmed the retirement, led back the men, and recaptured the lost trench. This young officer who only joined the Army in October, 1914, by his personal bravery and presence of mind saved a dangerous situation.'

He was invalided home soon afterwards suffering with dysentery. After recovering he joined the 1st Battalion, in France, and was badly wounded, in the arm. He returned to England, and —before regaining the use of his arm—was appointed A.D.C. to Major-General W. de L. Williams, C.B., C.M.G., D.S.O. (The Hampshire Regiment) in France, where he gained the M.C. and Bar. He died of influenza at Mouveaux on November 3rd, 1918.

Lieut-General Sir Beauvoir de Lisle, K.C.B., K.C.M.G., D.S.O., in a narrative of this action said: ' I have often quoted this young officer as being one of the bravest men I have met in this war.'

at this point, where our line was now a re-entrant, but the Hampshire were not shifted. On the other flank Turks outflanked the K.O.S.B's left and also broke in between them and the Royal Fusiliers, where a company of the Essex had come up into line; most of H.12 was lost and a disorganized mass of men was being pressed back against the Royal Fusiliers' left, where crowded and narrow trenches impeded any reorganization of the defence. The situation was becoming critical, officerless men were retreating in confusion when 2/Lt. G. R. D. Moor, left in temporary command of the battalion,[1] dashed across the open from the Hampshire's lines with a few men and stemmed the retirement by vigorous and forcible measures, actually shooting one or two panic-stricken fugitives. He did not stop here: having rallied and reorganized the men in a hollow, he led them back to the lost trench and cleared the Turks out, setting a magnificent example of bravery and resourcefulness which was most deservedly recognized by the battalion's first V.C.[2] since the Taku Forts.

Further to the left the Worcestershire had also held firmly on and, though no attempt was made to recover the salient formed by H.12, the line of H. 11 was secured, largely thanks to 2/Lt. Moor, and a renewed attack made about 6 p.m. was repulsed with heavy losses. In other ranks the Hampshire's losses, under 30 all told, were slight, while they had taken no small toll of the Turks, whose losses in the three days' fighting seem to have substantially exceeded the Allied casualties, though these came to over 6,000. But once again a big success had been missed, if by a narrow margin.

That evening 2/Lt. Moor had to be taken to Brigade headquarters, being completely exhausted, which left only the Quartermaster and three attached officers, Lts. Poole (Argyll & Sutherlands), who took command, Barrett (R. Warwickshire) and Manders (R. Berkshire), other ranks being down below 200. This remnant was relieved next afternoon and placed in support trenches, having its headquarters at Twelve Tree Copse. After three days here, during which Lt. Silk rejoined from hospital and took command, the battalion had four days' rest at Gully Beach. It was then in reserve trenches till June 19th, busily engaged on improving the line and digging communication trenches up to the new front in H.11 and burying the dead. On June 14th it welcomed Major Beckwith back, on whose arrival Lt. Silk took over the Adjutant's duties, and next day a draft from the 13th Battalion of 360 men with six officers [3] made its sadly attenuated ranks look quite full again.

From June 19th to 24th the battalion was 'at rest' on Y Beach, being persistently shelled by guns from across the Straits and having several casualties. The 88th Brigade then relieved the recently arrived 156th Brigade of the Fifty-

---

[1] Since June 4th Captain Mackay (A. & S. H.) and 2/Lt. Reeves had been killed and Captain Ellis (Suffolk) and 2/Lt. Cooper (Dorsets) wounded, while Captain Ford, Lt. Webb and 2/Lt. C. Moor were away sick.

[2] He was recommended for it by officers of the Royal Fusiliers who had watched his gallantry and determination. Lt. Colonel Williams, addressing the battalion before the attack, had expressed the hope that some one would win the V.C. for the battalion that day. 2/Lt. Moor was, it was said, the youngest winner of the V.C.

[3] Captains Bousfield, Pigott and Cowland, Lts. Morris, Sheffield and Luffmann.

Second (Lowland Territorial) Division who had been holding the Twenty-Ninth's right sector, the Hampshire taking over part of H.11, which they found much in need of repair. They quickly made the trench look very different and on June 25th had the satisfaction of getting good targets in wiring parties.

A fresh attack was about to be made by the 86th and 87th Brigades West of Gully Ravine and by the 156th East of it, with the 88th in support. To make room for the 156th Brigade the Hampshire moved back on June 26th to reserve trenches behind Twelve Tree Copse, where 30 recovered and wounded rejoined and with them Lt. Webb and 2/Lt. Lord, the latter taking over the Adjutant's duties.

This time more artillery support was available and when, at 11 a.m. on June 28th, the main attack went in, it was clear that West of Gully Ravine the bombardment had been most effective: the 87th Brigade carried its objectives with a fine rush, and the 86th and Indian Brigades, going through, pressed on and secured Fusilier Bluff, 1000 yards beyond the starting line, many prisoners being taken and the Turks heavily punished, while during the next few days, despite repeated efforts and heavy losses, they failed to regain any more than a very little of what had been wrested from them here. Unfortunately the ammunition had not sufficed for more than a most inadequate shelling of the H trenches, and though the Border Regiment stormed the Boomerang, a very troublesome redoubt on the Eastern edge of Gully Ravine, and the 156th Brigade's left and centre battalions took the Western half of H.12, further to the right another battalion was shot down wholesale by machine-guns on its right flank, so that, despite a gallant effort, it failed to reach its objectives. Counter-attacks were not slow to develop; the upper part of Gully Ravine provided a covered approach, and the troops in the captured Western portion of H.12 were soon hard pressed to hold on, let alone extend their gains, largely because the Turks were better off for bombs, a great asset in trench warfare, and if they lost heavily while they regained some ground, although the 88th Brigade put in the Essex and the 5th Royal Scots against the untaken Eastern half of H.12, [1] machine-guns in H.13 and H.14 to their right held them up.

Accordingly that evening the Hampshire were sent forward to take over the Western end of H.12. The trenches were terribly congested with dead and wounded, including many Turks, and about midnight, while the relief was still in progress, a sharp counter-attack developed, crowds of Turks pouring forward from Gully Ravine. This the Hampshire helped to repulse, though the Turks pressed the attack hard, only to be shot down in numbers. After this the relief could be continued and was completed before dawn, whereon the battalion set to work to consolidate and clear up the trenches and to dig a trench connecting the Eastern ends of our portions of H.12 and H.12a, these ends having been blocked by barricades.

This work the Hampshire carried on with considerable success for the next six days, besides getting some chances of killing enemy: the machine-guns for example co-operated most effectively on June 30th with the 87th Brigade

---

[1] H.12 seems to have been completed before this and another line, H.12a, dug in front of it.

in punishing a large party retreating from near Fusilier Bluff. On July 2nd W Company gained about 20 yards in H.12a. Further they could not go: rifle fire from the next trench behind and enfilade fire from a communication trench commanded a bend round which it proved impossible to advance, so a barricade was made. X also made about the same distance in H.12 and established another barricade, where also much bombing activity developed, while the battalion's machine-guns contributed very effectively to the decisive repulse of a most determined effort to recover the Fusilier Bluff position on July 2nd. ' We got two machine-guns on to them—that was quite enough ' wrote one

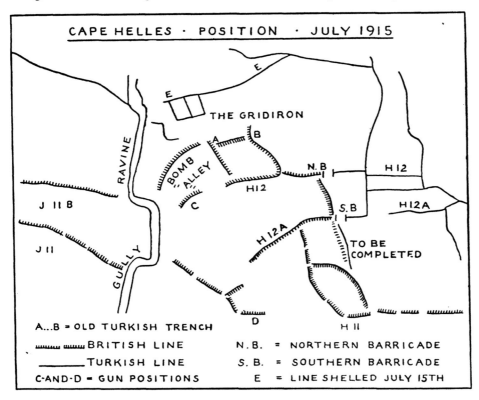

CAPE HELLES · POSITION · JULY 1915

THE GRIDIRON

A...B = OLD TURKISH TRENCH
BRITISH LINE
TURKISH LINE
C·AND·D = GUN POSITIONS

N.B. = NORTHERN BARRICADE
S.B. = SOUTHERN BARRICADE
E = LINE SHELLED JULY 15TH

officer, and these days added substantially to the Turkish casualties, once again even heavier than the British. But the Hampshire were severely shelled, six days costing them 28 killed and missing and Captains Pigott and Cowland and 76 men wounded, and the strain was great. However, only three days' ' rest ' could be given them, spent at Y Beach, where dug-outs cut into the steep face of the cliff gave good shelter from the shelling from which ' rest ' areas at Cape Helles were never immune. Splendid sea bathing was some alleviation for all that had to be endured, discomforts of every kind and, what was even worse, the stench of the unburied corpses over which dense clouds of foul dust blew to and fro, the plague of flies which descended on every article of food, the shortage of water and that mainly brought from overseas in tanks and conveyed to the troops in petrol tins, the increasing heat, the lack of shade and shelter, the monotony of the rations, which could not be supplemented at canteens as in France. Diarrhoea and dysentry were rampant, the sick-rate was high and many not actually on the sick-list were in poor condition. It was some alleviation to hear rumours of substantial reinforcements, and with the whole Fifty-Second Division now present some of the more exhausted men could be given a real rest at Lemnos. Indeed the 2nd Hampshire were under orders for a spell there, when on July 7th they were ordered to relieve the S.W.B. astride Gully Ravine, holding H.12 and the Eastern end of J.11b, about 500 yards of front. Six officers of ' K 4 ' units [1] had joined with 20 convalescents, but the battalion remained much below establishment.

Holding these trenches proved strenuous. The trench just East of the Gully, ' Bomb Alley ', ran down to a barricade in the ravine, within bombing range of the enemy; 300 yards further to the East our holdings in H.12 and H12a [2] were blocked by barricades. Turkish snipers were troublesome, and from a knoll known as the Gridiron, they would shoot down Gully Ravine. Saps were started out towards it, and the Hampshire used trench mortars against the snipers to good purpose, besides improving the line appreciably. One useful achievement was the digging of a trench on the night of July 14th/15th across the open to get rid of a re-entrant in our line. This was done within 60 yards of the Turks but was not interrupted. ' It made a vast difference to a very shaky part of our line ' one officer wrote, while our machine-guns got some good targets and by simulating an intention to attack we induced Turkish machine-guns to give away their location and waste ammunition.

One feature of this spell in the trenches was the attachment for instruction first of a company of Argyll & Sutherlands of the 157th Brigade, whose arrival had completed the Fifty-Second Division, and then, much to everyone's interest, of the first instalment of the three ' New Army ' Divisions now reinforcing the M.E.F. This was a company of the 6th Loyal North Lancashire (Thirteenth Division) who, after 48 hours in the line, were relieved by one of the 6th East Lancashire. Their appearance was encouraging, it showed that the large reinforcements needed to carry the venture through to a definite success were at last coming out and that the hard-tried Twenty-Ninth Division was to be vigorously supported, while for the moment it was to get its much-needed and well-earned rest at Lemnos.

If July found the Twenty-Ninth Division too exhausted and spent for another serious offensive, one was attempted on July 15th by the Fifty-Second Division, the R.N.D. and the French. The 2nd Hampshire co-operated by keeping the trenches in their front under machine-gun fire, and on their immediate right the 86th Brigade's bombers tried to gain ground in H.12 and H.12a

---

[1] Captain Thomas, Lts. Falcon and Harding and 2/Lts. Armitage and Pearce (11th E. Surrey) and Lt. Hearnden (9th R.W.K.): Captain Day had also rejoined from hospital.
[2] The portions of these lines secured by the attack of June 28th were in advance of the line further to our right.

without much success. The main attack, gallantly pressed, after starting well failed to fulfil its promise, heavy losses were incurred and little more than the first objective was eventually consolidated; thus, as on June 4th and 28th, the strategical situation remained unaltered; if local advantages had been secured and rather more depth obtained behind our line, Krithia and Achi Baba were untaken. Such slender gains seemed hardly worth the casualties, 12,000 British and 6,000 French, incurred in these attacks, but there seems little doubt that the Turkish losses had been very much heavier. The recklessness with which they had thrown in mass after mass in counter-attacks had exposed them to be mown down wholesale: again and again they had virtually exhausted their reserves and on each occasion it looked as if, had another fresh Division been available and rather more artillery and ammunition, the Turkish resistance might have collapsed, but, as throughout the tragic story of Gallipoli, we had not secured ' the advantage of time and place, which ' as Drake tried unsuccessfully to explain to Queen Elizabeth ' in martial actions is half the victory ', reinforcements arrived too late and chances went a-begging. When early on July 17th [1] the 2nd Hampshire embarked at V Beach to follow the other battalions of the Division to Lemnos, a notable page had been added to the regimental annals. That, handicapped as it was from the start, the Twenty-Ninth Division [2] failed to reach Achi Baba and open the Straits to the Navy is not surprising, what is remarkable is that it went so near to achieving success. Sir John Fortescue has said that Albuera has a special place among battle honours, the same may with equal justice be said of ' Cape Helles '.

[1] Casualties in a ten days' spell in the lines came to 10 killed, Lt. Sheffield and 40 men wounded, Captain Parker, 2/Lt. G.R.D. Moor and 20 men had meanwhile rejoined.

[2] Now under Major General de Lisle, General Hunter-Weston having taken command of the Eighth Corps, comprising all our troops at Cape Helles.

CHAPTER VIII

GALLIPOLI (continued)

SARI BAIR AND SUVLA

THE troops now reinforcing the M.E.F. for the effort it was hoped would carry us to Constantinople included two Divisions in which the Hampshire were represented, the Tenth and the Fifty-Fourth (East Anglian Territorial), to which last the Isle of Wight Rifles had been posted in April, joining the 4th and 5th Norfolk and the 5th Suffolk in Brigadier General Brunker's 163rd Brigade [1] and replacing the 4th Suffolk, who had been among the picked Territorial battalions sent out to France in 1914.

The 10th Battalion had had nearly two months in Hampshire before embarking at Liverpool on July 6th in the *Transylvania*. The transport under Lt. Scott was left to follow later, Lt. Lowy being placed in charge of such details as did not accompany the battalion, while several surplus subalterns went off to the 13th Battalion. The *Transylvania* was terribly crowded, the 6th R. Irish Rifles being also on board, giving little space for the exercise needed to keep men fit, while great vigilance had to be maintained on account of submarines. None appeared, and after brief calls at Gibraltar and Malta the *Transylvania* reached Alexandria on July 17th, disembarked company storemen and base kits and went on to Mudros, where the battalion landed on July 26th to make the acquaintance of the dust, the flies, the thirst—the allowance of rather tepid water was only a gallon a day—and the diarrhoea which were the chief features of residence on Lemnos. Incessant ' fatigues ' severely limited the chances of training and made it difficult to recover the condition and fitness which the cramped conditions of the voyage had naturally impaired.

With three fresh Divisions at his disposal and two more following them, Sir Ian Hamilton could at last attempt a major operation. For this the cramped space available at Cape Helles afforded nothing like enough room, apart from other unfavourable aspects of the tactical situation, but although the Australian and New Zealand Corps had been unable to enlarge appreciably its rather precarious original foothold, that quarter offered more chance of developing an attack. Now that sufficient force was available, an attempt to break out on its Northern flank in hopes of securing the dominating Sari Bair ridge could be combined with a fresh landing further North in Suvla Bay, where conditions seemed to invite a surprise attack. The Turks appeared to have only a few troops in this area, so a prompt advance might secure the ridge running from . North to South on the Eastward edge of the Suvla plain. This, it was hoped, would not only secure the new base to be established in Suvla Bay but would cover the flank of the Sari Bair attack and appreciably improve its chances. The Turks had no reinforcements within easy reach of Suvla, our persistent

---

[1] The 162nd Brigade was under Brigadier General de Winton, formerly C.O. of the 1st Hampshire.

attacks from Cape Helles had attracted their reserves to Krithia and Achi Baba, and the new venture's prospects seemed promising enough, even if its planners had been rather optimistic and had certainly underestimated the practical difficulties of negotiating the rugged and virtually unknown slopes of Sari Bair. They certainly asked rather much of the inexperienced ' New Army ' battalions in their ' baptism of fire ': while unfortunately the Australians and New Zealanders, after being so long cooped up in their cramped position, were mostly verging on ' staleness ' and lacked something of their old dash and fire, never more needed than in this new attack over such difficult ground.

For the attack on Sari Bair General Birdwood's Australians and New Zealanders were being reinforced by the 29th Brigade, the Thirteenth Division and the 29th Indian Brigade, while the Eleventh Division with the rest of the Tenth were alloted to the Suvla landing and were to be reinforced by the Fifty-Third and Fifty-Fourth Divisions. Accordingly the 10th Hampshire embarked on the afternoon of August 5th on board the small vessels which served as ferries between the islands and the peninsula and started off in time to approach the shore under cover of darkness. Major Morley, Captain Hudson, 2/Lt. Calderwood and 150 men had been left at Mudros as a 'first reinforcement', rather 'robbing Peter to pay Paul'. All ranks were wearing thin khaki drill with patches of coloured cloth sewn on their helmets as distinguishing marks, the Hampshire's patch being claret and yellow. All were heavily laden, three days' rations having been issued, and the boats were so closely packed that movement was virtually impossible. Except for occasional snipers there was no firing and the men were soon transferred to lighters, from which they landed just at daybreak (August 6th), to be hurried off up Shrapnel Gully and hidden away from Turkish observation and fire in the shelters excavated in its sides. Movement by daylight had to be carefully restricted: it was essential that the Turks should not discover that five additional brigades were being concentrated in General Birdwood's narrow area, and both Staff and troops deserve much credit for the successful accomplishment of this difficult task.

The advance against Sari Bair and the landing at Suvla were to be started after dark on August 6th. To distract the enemy's attention and keep him from reinforcing the crucial point, subsidiary attacks were to be made, by the Australians' right at Lone Pine and by the Eighth Corps at Cape Helles. The Lone Pine attack merely affected the Hampshire because it drew down heavy retaliatory shelling on the whole of General Birdwood's position which cost the 10th Battalion a dozen wounded, the Cape Helles attack was to involve the 2nd in the worst of all its experiences at Gallipoli.

The 2nd Hampshire had landed at Lemnos about 10 a.m., July 17th, to find a welcome draft of 300 men awaiting them. These came mainly from other regiments, notably the Oxford and Bucks L.I., but the officers with them, Captain Popham, Lt. Pigott and 2/Lts. Gawn and Nalder, came from the 3rd and 13th Battalions. 2/Lt. C. Moor also rejoined from hospital, and companies could now be reorganized with four platoons apiece, each platoon having an officer: Captains B. S. Parker (W) and Day (Z) and Lts. Webb (X) and Lord (Y), commanded the companies, while Lt. Poole acted as Adjutant. Other ranks now stood at 732 and officers, including the M.O., Captain Levi, an Australian, at 24.

The 2nd should have had a full fortnight at Lemnos, where, if conditions were far from ideal, a dusty camp site, no canteen or means of supplementing the monotonous rations, except by purchase at exorbitant rates from the inhabitants, and few amenities, they were out even of sound of shelling. However, an alarm of an intended Turkish attack cut the Division's rest short, and on July 28th the 2nd Hampshire were back at Cape Helles, being in brigade

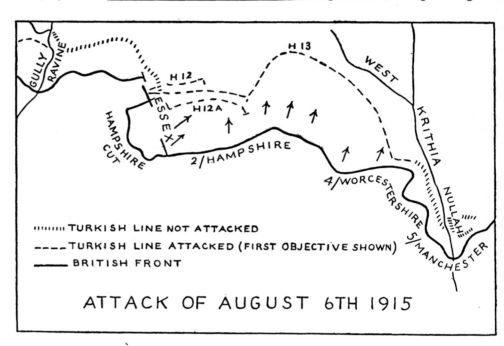

reserve at Gully Beach, mainly occupied in road making. Two officers [1] and 110 men now joined, and with Captain C. B. Pigott, Lt. Sheffield and 16 men returning from hospital the battalion was stronger than it had been since the landing. Unluckily on August 1st Colonel Beckwith was nastily wounded in the hand, and while he was in the C.C.S. having a shattered finger amputated, a shell, hitting the cliff above, brought down a lot of it, burying him just as he had come round from the anaesthetic. He was nearly suffocated and very badly hurt and had to be shipped off to hospital, Captain Parker taking command.

After five days in the reserve line the 88th Brigade took over the right sub-section of the Divisional line, East of Gully Ravine, in readiness for another

[1] Lt. Mercer and 2/Lt Mann.

attempt on its old objectives, H.12a, H.12 and H.13, on August 6th, the Forty-
Second Division being ready to exploit any success by attacking next day
beyond the Krithia Nullah. The Turkish position had been considerably
strengthened since our last attack, and the Hampshire had the nastiest piece
of the work, for their left had to tackle a formidable redoubt while their right
and centre had nearly 300 yards of open to cross to reach H.13, here a re-
entrant, whereas on their flanks the Worcestershire (right) and the Essex (left)
had shorter distances to cover and the Essex could also attack from the flank,
from Hampshire Cut.

The assaulting troops were in position by 8 a.m. (August 6th) but had to
wait for six hours before the bombardment started. As again the artillery
support was utterly inadequate: General Davies, who had just arrived from
France to take over the Eighth Corps [1] from General Hunter-Weston, invalided,
was quite horrified to see how very far it fell short of the Western Front standard, low as that was in 1915, and the volume and vigour of the Turkish reply
showed that they were unpleasantly ready for the attack and augured ill for its
chances. After an hour's deliberate bombardment by a handful of heavy guns,
the field guns took up the tale and for 30 minutes plastered the objective as
vigorously as their scanty ammunition would allow: then at 3.50 p.m. the
infantry went forward with the utmost dash and gallantry, the Hampshire
attacking in four waves. A low crest fifty yards from our line was crossed
almost without loss but then machine-guns opened up on all sides and mowed
the attackers down wholesale before many of them had got any way across No
Man's Land, some guns across the Krithia Nullah on our right being particularly
deadly. Our guns could do nothing to subdue their fire and under it the attack
soon withered away. The Hampshire suffered terribly, above all in losing
Captain Parker, who fell in leading the advance of the second line, and with
him two other ' originals ', Captain Day and Lt. Webb, both previously wounded
but back at duty, and 2/Lt. Gawn, who had won the D.C.M. in Somaliland,
while 2/Lt. C. Moor fell on the Turkish parapet, which a very few of the
leading waves seem to have reached. The supports lost as heavily as the
leaders but pressed forward with equal determination, and some men, among
them Lt. Morris and some of Z Company's second wave, entered the Turkish
lines and established themselves in H.12a, some apparently even reaching
H.13. Too few to maintain their foothold, they were overcome by numbers,
though Sergeant Sinsbury held on for some time to a sap with a few men and,
when they were bombed out, he covered their retirement with great skill and
resource.[2] Rather more Worcestershire got in and held out till dark, while a
fair number of Essex from Hampshire Cut established themselves in H.12
and eventually managed to retain a tiny corner, but within a few minutes
the attack had come to a complete standstill, the unhit survivors lying out
among the dead and wounded, pinned to the ground by the machine-guns and

[1] The troops at Cape Helles, those at Suvla forming a Ninth.
[2] He was awarded the D.C.M., which was also given to Private Hampton for carrying a message
across ground swept by heavy fire.

unable to move until darkness let them and the more slightly wounded crawl back. It had been the worst day in the whole story of Cape Helles.

Inadequate artillery support had once again led to a heavy sacrifice of lives to little purpose. Nothing had been gained locally and even if the Turks had been distracted from the main attack at Suvla, its unavailing gallantry had left the 88th Brigade a wreck, the Hampshire having lost eighteen officers and 224 other ranks [1] killed and missing. Of their own officers, besides those already mentioned, Captain Popham, Lts. Sheffield and L. B. Piggott, 2/Lts. Derry [2] and Nalder were killed and of those attached Captain Thomas, Lts. Barrett, Falcon, Harding and Hearnden and 2/Lts. Armitage and Pearce also fell, an eloquent testimony to the devoted gallantry with which the attack had been led. The M.O., Captain Levi, after working strenuously all night, was killed next morning by a shell which hit the dressing station and also killed C.Q.M.S. Fisher and wounded R.Q.M.S. Smith, C.Q.M.S. Giles and several men, Captain Pigott and 2/Lt. F. R. Mann and 210 men were wounded. This left the battalion with only the Quartermaster, Lts. Lord, Manders (R. Berkshire) and Poole (A. & S.H.), and 2/Lt. G. R. D. Moor and about 400 other ranks. [3] *Photograph   Page 11. Jan 16*

During the night any wounded who could be reached were brought in, [4] and then the 86th Brigade relieved the 88th and the surviving Hampshires made their way back to Gully Beach, where they were warmly congratulated on their gallantry by General de Lisle and reorganized in two companies. Little rest could be given to the brigade: shattered as it was, it had on August 14th to take over the line again from the 86th. Things had gone wrong at Suvla, and though Sir Ian Hamilton had deliberately refrained from using the Twenty-Ninth Division in that attack because he had already asked so much of it and wished, if possible, to spare it, [5] he had now to employ the 'Old Guard' of the M.E.F. in a last-minute effort to retrieve the situation.

Before this both the 8th and 10th Hampshire had been heavily engaged, though neither actually went into action till the situation had been jeopardised beyond recall. The plan for the attack on Sari Bair involved the preliminary seizure of covering positions by flanking columns to protect the main advance in the centre, but in the intricate and difficult country to be traversed, virtually a terra incognita to all concerned, delays and loss of direction, with some want of determination and enterprise in the handling of one assaulting column, meant that Chunuk Bair, which should have been secured, was not occupied, and though next day, (August 8th) a belated lodgement was made on this all-important point, sufficient Turkish reinforcements had arrived to prevent our consolidating, let alone expanding, our precarious foothold. On the left of the line errors over the positions reached and the fatigue of the troops equally pre-

---

[1] Corrected figures. The Worcestershire's losses were even heavier.
[2] Just joined from the Ceylon Planters Rifle Corps.
[3] Lt. Mercer had gone sick.
[4] A party of volunteers went up next day to make a fresh search of No Man's Land, but by then all survivors had been brought in.
[5] I had this from Sir Ian Hamilton himself.

vented our securing the positions we wanted, and the plans for August 8th had to be modified. Even then the 2/6th Gurkhas established themselves on Hill Q, beyond Chunuk Bair, and had they been supported promptly and in force their achievement might have been exploited. Most of the Thirteenth Division had before this been thrown in to support or relieve the Australians and New Zealanders who had opened the move, and the evening of August 8th found only four battalions, two of Brigadier General Baldwin's 38th Brigade with the 10th Hampshire and the 6th R. Irish Rifles, available for a last effort to gain the ridge. These were now to advance up the Chailak Dere, one of the many gullies leading up to Chunuk Bair, and to come in on the left of the New Zealanders and the other troops who were clinging on at Chunuk Bair.

The 10th Hampshire meanwhile had spent the early hours of August 7th in a futile move up another gully North of Russell's Top, only to be sent back again to Shrapnel Gully and to spend the day there inactively, hearing all sorts of rumours. Starting off again about 10 a.m. next day they filed along the great sap running Northward up the coast to the Fisherman's Hut, where they remained until evening. Advancing again, they found the seaward end of the Chailak Dere being shelled and so had to rush across in small parties and then to struggle in single file along the narrow gully, choked with wounded making their way down it. Progress was slow and tiring, touch was hard to keep, halts and delays were frequent, and the column had barely settled down in a bivouac before, about 10 p.m., orders were received to push on. The guides then went wrong and led the column to the foot of a precipice. This meant turning round and retracing the route, doubly difficult in the dark and in the congested narrow space, and though General Baldwin eventually found a track leading across to the left into the Aghyl Dere, by 5 a.m. (August 9th), when the troops on Chunuk Bair (right) and on Hill Q (left) should have started an advance, his column was not up in its place to join in. Accordingly no advance was attempted on the right, and though the Gurkhas pressed forward and even established themselves on the crest of Hill Q, for want of support they were driven back, to hang on just below.

By the time (6 a.m.) that Baldwin's battalions could start their advance, moving just North of Rhododendron Spur, the main approach to Chunuk Bair, the Turks were ready and well placed. The East Lancashire, who were leading, were soon checked and the Irish Rifles could not get any further, The Hampshire accordingly halted about 600 yards West of ' the Farm ' [1], a building in a patch of cultivation, and stayed there till, about 9 a.m., Colonel Bewsher was ordered to fill a gap between the Irish Rifles and the New Zealanders on Chunuk Bair and Rhododendron Spur. For this purpose Major Pilleau, with A Company and half D, now went forward up a gully SW. of the Farm;[2] at its head, however, they came under heavy fire, mainly machine-guns with some shrapnel, and could advance no further. Accordingly they established themselves in the best positions to be found and before long obtained touch with the New Zealanders on their right. Major Pilleau was wounded but, after being bandaged, rejoined the detachment.

[1] About 80 D. 6 on plan. [2] 80. F. 7.

Meanwhile Lts. Grellier and Williams had taken another party to support the East Lancashire nearer the Farm, and about 2 p.m. Captain Hicks took half B Company to reinforce the New Zealanders on Rhododendron Spur but was sent back as the Brigadier was unable to use the party, which thus incurred a good many casualties and was quite exhausted to no purpose before it got back to battalion head-quarters. Eventually after dark half B [1] was placed on the left of Major Pilleau's men, who were digging in along the ridge at the head of their gully, while C Company also moved forward and linked up with the Irish Rifles.[2] This left only a small reserve with battalion head-quarters, one machine-gun being put in front and the other well forward up the hill. Further to the left a vigorous counter-attack against our troops on Damakjelik Bair had been repulsed with heavy losses, but no forward move could be developed on that flank to assist the troops on the bare slopes of Chunuk Bair. They had to lie out, exposed without shelter to a scorching sun, with a mere mouthful of water, while every attempt to advance or move instantly drew fire, and as the troops had little to fire at, their own casualties, though not heavy, were the more noticeable.

No more counter-attacks were attempted during the night, but with dawn (August 10th) the Turks came forward in great force, pressing hardest against the troops on Chunuk Bair and driving them back upon Rhododendron Spur. One attack on the Irish Rifles was caught in flank by the Hampshire's fire and stopped, but the attack soon spread to Major Pilleau's men, who found their right flank exposed but held on stoutly for some time [3] until a specially vigorous attack dislodged No. 1 platoon and drove them back down hill, Lt. Cheesman being killed. The survivors rallied on B Company, who had been getting good targets in Turks moving across a cornfield below them, but meanwhile other Turks had got in between the New Zealanders and D Company, outflanking D and driving it back. However, as the Turks did not follow up their success, Captain Shone took two platoons [4] forward to try to regain D.s trenches. They reached them, but in insufficient strength to maintain the ground, and were forced back, Captain Shone being wounded and Sergeant Barber killed, while about 8.45 a.m. Captain Hicks, finding B's advanced position untenable, had also to fall back towards battalion head-quarters; A Company, with Lt. Hellyer the only officer unhit, had likewise to quit its now exposed forward position. Before this Captain Black-Hawkins had taken the reserve [5] forward to reinforce the left, which also was being hard pressed, where he was before long hit and killed, setting his men a fine example, and Colonel Bewsher himself had been wounded. He had been bandaged up and was starting off for the beach when a wounded N.C.O. came in, declaring that no officers were left unhurt in the firing line. The Colonel therefore went forward, to find that General Baldwin had

---

[1] Two platoons, VI and VII, were away on fatigue.

[2] Some of A seem to have become detached and were further to the left, but the exact localities are hard to fix accurately. The Irish Rifles seem to have been to the left (North) of the Farm.

[3] Major Pilleau was apparently killed about this time, leading a counter-attack : he had already been wounded again.

[4] Apparently Nos. VI and VII platoons, who had rejoined.   [5] Apparently the rest of D.

been killed, that General Cooper, who had reached 38th Brigade headquarters, had been wounded and that he was the senior officer left. He therefore remained near the Farm, where the line was now held by C Company with some Irish Rifles on the left and a few of the 38th Brigade. Only one machine-gun was left but the line was holding on, though the enemy were pressing hard. Their attacks had now extended further to the left and after the survivors of Major Pilleau's party and Captain Hicks and the remnant of his men had been driven in, it was clear that the Farm plateau could not be held without grave risk of its defenders being surrounded, so Colonel Bewsher now ordered them to fall back and re-form on the next ridge, Cheshire Ridge.[1] This was done and the

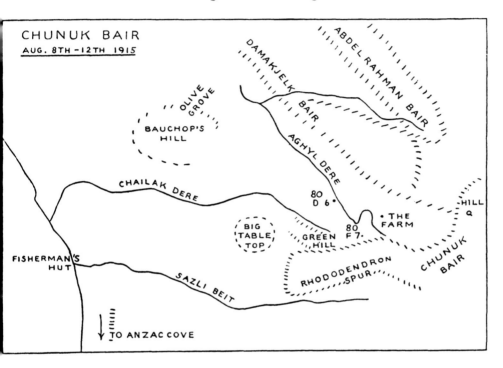

men were rallied and actually made a gallant but hopeless attempt to advance. However, Cheshire Ridge was held and the Turks checked. Not only was this position secured, touch was eventually obtained with the troops still holding on to the slopes of Rhododendron Spur. Further to the left also the Turks were held and a line maintained running North down the Damakjelik Spur. Colonel Bewsher [2] had now been ordered back to hospital by a senior Staff officer and, with Captain Hicks also wounded, only Lt. Hellyer and the Quartermaster were left unhurt. As far as could be ascertained Major Pilleau, Captains Savage, Black-Hawkins and Hayes, Lts. Bell, Cheesman and Williams and 2/Lts. S. A. Smith, Whalley and Morse were killed or missing. Other ranks killed and

---

[1] Marked on some maps as Green Hill.　　　[2] He subsequently received the D.S.O.

missing came to 155, with 276 wounded. Besides the C.O. and Captain Hicks, Captains Faith and Shone, Lts. Clement, Griffiths and Tanner and 2/Lts. de Gaury, Dupree, German, Parry, Grellier and Whittome had been wounded.[1]

The fight which the battalion had put up was greatly to its credit: its Brigadier wrote that its resistance had saved the situation on the right and enabled the next brigade to withstand the pressure: he had always, he said, had a high opinion of the battalion and its fighting had fully justified him.

To so depleted a battalion the arrival on August 10th of the ' first reinforcement ' was very welcome. This party had left Lemnos on the previous evening, arrived at Anzac Cove about 1 a.m., landed and moved by the Anzac Sap to the Fisherman's Hut, to find the beach crowded with wounded. They were then sent on up the Chailak Dere to 29th Brigade H.Q. on Cheshire Ridge, which they reached about 4 p.m. after a tiring march. Here Major Morley got orders to collect the battalion, two parties being eventually discovered still in line, one of 80 under Sergeant Lewis and a smaller one further to the front under Lt. Hellyer. All told some 280 were present, but the battalion was very short not only of officers but of N.C.O's, nearly all the seniors having been hit. It was now ordered back to a small valley in rear, where the only available water was a well, which was under continuous rifle and machine-gun fire, so directly it was dark the men were turned to construct a covered approach to it. Rocky ground and the exhaustion of all ranks made this very difficult and with 100 men required as a burial party, few got any rest. Here the battalion remained for three days, working away at the sap despite all difficulties and several casualties. Some stragglers[2] had turned up and some re-organization was now possible, Lt. Saunders, a tower of strength in this emergency, indefatigable and resourceful, combined the Adjutant's duties with his own, and the men were sorted out into four weak companies.

August 14th brought a move, not into reserve to rest, but back in the firing line to relieve Gurkhas at the upper end of Damakjelik Bair, the spur beyond the Aghyl Dere. It was a bad position, being enfiladed and overlooked from Abdelrahman Bair, a spur of the Chunuk Bair ridge, while our line formed a salient; moreover in that hard and rocky soil trench-digging had been difficult and the trenches in places were under 3 feet deep; to obtain any cover breastworks and sangars had to be built up and the battalion had many casualties before it could subdue the enemy's snipers. It held this line for six days, improving the defences and communications and burying the nearest of the many dead who littered the ground in front. The position was always under fire, mainly machine-gun, which at times developed into a regular ' hate ' of considerable intensity, and between sickness and casualties the battalion was nearly 80 weaker before it was relieved on August 20th and given its first night's real rest for nearly a fortnight. This merely meant that another effort was to be demanded of it, part of an eleventh hour snatch at the success which had eluded us at Suvla.

[1] Captain Waddington, the Brigade machine-gun officer, was also wounded.
[2] In that intricate and little-known country many men had naturally got detached.

If the failure at Sari Bair may partly be put down to the poor physical state of such experienced soldiers as were employed, many of the inexperienced men who landed here and at Suvla were suffering from the diarrhoea and similar complaints which had fastened on them soon after reaching the Eastern Mediterranean. An equally serious handicap was that while these new troops ' knew what they ought to do, they did not know how to do it ',[1] they were being required to race on their trial trip, but at Suvla the root of the failure to develope a splendid opening and to exploit surprise must lie at the door of Corps and Divisional headquarters; where energy, initiative and promptitude in appreciating the situation and the urgent value of time were so conspicuously lacking. By the time the Fifty-Fourth Division's infantry were ashore the chance of success was already almost lost. The vital Anafarta hills and the ridge running Northward from them to the Kiretch Tepe ridge along the coast were firmly held by the Turks in some strength, and the artillery ashore was quite insufficient support for an attack on their position, strong in itself and already partially entrenched.

The Isle of Wight Rifles, on joining the Fifty-Fourth Division in April, had first found quarters at Bury St. Edmunds but soon moved to Watford, round which the Division was being concentrated. Here they spent two months, largely notable for the arrival of some fine and very lively transport mules from South America, and in July the Division started for Gallipoli, the battalion [2] being among the 8,000 troops carried by the great Cunarder *Aquitania* which sailed from Liverpool on July 30th and reached Lemnos inside a week. The 8th did not land but were transferred almost at once to smaller vessels for transport to Suvla Bay, where they disembarked on August 9th. A ' first reinforcement ' of four officers and 180 men under Captain Fardell having been left at Mudros, only 25 officers and 750 other ranks were present.

Sir Ian Hamilton was intending to keep the Fifty-Fourth Division together and not throw it into action piece-meal, as other reinforcements had been, but when its first battalions landed they found Ninth Corps head-quarters greatly agitated about a gap between the Tenth Division's right on the Kiretch Tepe Ridge and the left of the Eleventh and Fifty-Third, now much intermingled, which did not extend much beyond Sulajik in the plain. Accordingly, despite G.H.Q's intentions, several units of the Fifty-Fourth Division were hurried forward into this gap and among them the 8th Hampshire, who found themselves on outpost [3] with the very vaguest idea of the ground, of the situation and of what was expected of them.

Being uninformed of this G.H.Q. sent orders next morning (August 11th) that the Fifty-Fourth Division should push forward that evening to the foot-

[1] A company commander of the Eleventh Division.
[2] Colonel Rhodes was in command and had with him Majors Lewes and Veasey (Adjt.), Captains C. and D. W. Ratsey, Ellery, Holmes-Gore, Fardell, Marsh and Loader, Lts. Read, Pittis, Young-James, Seeley and Curtis, 2/Lts. Bartlett, Brannon, Sutton, S. G. Ratsey, Kingdom, Murphy, Shelton, Latham, Watson, Fox, F. C. Raymond and Weeding and Lt. and Quartermaster Giddens. Captain G. Raymond (R.A.M.C.) was M.O.
[3] Apparently just East of Point 28.

hills of the Tekke Tepe ridge in readiness to attack at dawn. Against this the Ninth Corps protested, but the operation was merely postponed 24 hours and on the afternoon of August 12th the 163rd Brigade started forward, its objective being some huts about a mile ahead of its outpost line..

Since August 10th the troops had been sorted out and brigades got together, but little opportunity had offered for becoming better acquainted with the lie of the land and the enemy's dispositions. Immediately ahead lay open grazing land, dotted with a few scattered trees and patches of cultivation, with some ditches and hedges. Beyond this scrub extended to the foothills, which it covered.

The 163rd Brigade had three battalions in front line, the Isle of Wight Rifles being in the centre between the 5th Norfolk (right) and 5th Suffolk (left) with the 4th Norfolk in support behind the left. An 18 pounder battery, two mountain batteries and some naval guns were to provide artillery support, but, like the infantry, the gunners had little idea of the enemy's dispositions and without more definite targets could give little help.

Starting off at 4.40 p.m. the brigade at first made fair progress, though directly it moved machine-guns from the left inflicted many casualties, while from the other flank came shrapnel fire. The troops pushed on, however, meeting no very great opposition,[1] but casualties mounted up, the supporting artillery being quite unable to subdue the flanking fire, and before long the battalions were losing touch and the brigade's line had become disconnected. Most of the 5th Norfolk, carrying with them some Hampshire, diverged to the right and lost touch, many of them penetrating deep through the scrub into the Turkish position, where they were overwhelmed, their bodies being discovered half a mile beyond the front line, after the armistice.[2] The Hampshire, with their flank uncovered, pushed on about 1000 yards over ground which grew worse with scrub as they got further on, until the machine-guns on the left eventually halted them near the Anafarta Ova wells. Here along a ditch the leading men established themselves: but being only a handful they could not maintain their ground and had to retire, rallying in a sunken track some way back, where about 800 of all units of the brigade were eventually collected, with others further back on the left, where the 4th Norfolk were entrenching. Here they hung on until the evening of August 14th, consolidating the position as far as possible when short of tools and in rather hard ground, despite persistent sniping, to which the men endeavoured to reply. On the right touch had been gained with the Fifty-Third Division, but the left was open. An attempted Turkish advance on August 14th gave the 8th Hampshire's machine-guns under Lt. Pittis a chance to do some effective shooting in repulsing an effort to outflank the left, and that evening the 5th Essex arrived to relieve the battalion, which withdrew to its original position near Point 28.[3] It had been a hard trial

---

[1] The rifle fire was mainly from long range, if there were snipers in the scrub, whom the brigade pushed back as it went forward.

[2] Some Hampshire were among them.

[3] Major Veasey (Adjutant), Lieutenant Pittis and R.S.M. Bryant were mentioned in dispatches, Lieutenant Pittis being subsequently awarded the M.C., while Captain Raymond, the Medical Officer, who had worked untiringly, was also ' mentioned '.

for inexperienced troops, especially when so little artillery support was available. Casualties now proved to have amounted to nearly half those in action, Major Lewes, Captains Holmes-Gore, C and D. W. Ratsey and Loader, Lts. Young-James and 2/Lts. Raymond and Watson and 150 men had been killed or were missing, Lt. Sutton and 140 men being wounded. Practically all those returned as ' missing ' must have been killed, though about 20 turned up later among the wounded in hospital, having got detached and been rescued by other units. The 5th Norfolk had suffered even more heavily, but the brigade, though for the moment incapable of another offensive, was on the evening of August 16th ordered to take over trenches on the Kiretch Tepe Sirt ridge behind the Tenth Division. That Division had on the previous day attempted to advance along that ridge, while on its right the 162nd Brigade had attacked Kidney Hill, from which had come the flanking fire which had been mainly responsible for checking the 163rd Brigade's attack. In directing this attack Brigadier General de Winton had been very seriously wounded and though, thanks largely to his leadership and example,[1] some ground had been gained, it had been impossible to retain it and these days' operations had added another 2,000 to our casualties without any appreciable improvement in our position, even if the Turkish losses may have been nearly as heavy.

By August 15th the great attack had virtually failed: if the British had extended substantially the area they occupied they were no nearer to having attained their objective, tactically or strategically; the ground gained was not worth a fraction of their heavy casualties and even at Suvla their reserve positions were, as at Helles, still within range of the Turkish guns. The great reinforcement had shot its bolt, and the question now arose whether more troops should be thrown in, if they could be found, or whether failure should be admitted and the enterprise abandoned, if indeed the troops could be re-embarked without disastrous losses.

However, Sir Ian Hamilton's optimism was not quite quenched. He had given General de Lisle command of the Ninth Corps and, as already mentioned he now decided after all to call on the Twenty-Ninth Division to snatch success out of failure at the eleventh hour. Accordingly on August 17th the 87th Brigade reached Suvla, being followed in turn by the 86th and 88th.

After two days in the H trenches the 2nd Hampshire had moved across Gully Ravine on August 16th to take over the front line beyond Fusilier Bluff. Lts. Silk and C. Harland had rejoined from hospital, Lt. Silk taking command, but 250 men from the 3rd and 13th Battalions who should have reinforced the 2nd had most unfortunately been lost through the torpedoing on August 13th of their transport, the *Royal Edward*, only about 30 surviving. Then, late on August 19th, the battalion was relieved and moved back down Gully Ravine, to go on next day to V Beach and embark there, only arriving at Suvla after day-break (August 21st) and having to disembark under shell-fire, which fortunately proved innocuous.

[1] He subsequently received the C.M.G.

This new attack involved an attempt by the Twenty-Ninth Division, advancing from Chocolate Hill, to capture Scimitar Hill and Hill 112 South of it, while the Eleventh on their right advanced by Hetman Chair and Aire Kavak against the ' W Hills ', with the Tenth, in which dismounted Yeomanry just arrived from Egypt had replaced the 29th Brigade, forming a reserve.   Simultaneously, a composite force from General Birdwood's Corps under the New Zealanders' Brigadier, General Russell, was to assault the strongly held Hill 60, at the seaward end of the spur facing Damakjelik Bair.   Could this hill be carried it was hoped to push forward to Susak Kuyu wells NW. of it and gain touch with the Eleventh Division further North.   This composite force included the 10th Hampshire, now up to five officers and 330 men,[1] who were to cross the Kaiajik Dere [2] to our right of Hill 60 and nearer the inland end of the spur.

The main attack started at 3 p.m. on August 21st, but once again the utterly inadequate artillery support proved the decisive factor.   The Turks were well dug in, and their numerous and well-sited machine-guns could not be subdued by the British guns, too few and including naval guns whose armour-piercing projectiles were ill-suited for bombarding trenches which were none too accurately located.   Both Eleventh and Twenty-Ninth Divisions attacked with great determination, but while on both flanks a little ground was gained, by the 34th Brigade at Azmak Dere and by the 87th on Scimitar Hill, in the main the attack was held up and, during the night, even the slender gains had to be relinquished, a proposal to put in the 88th Brigade being fortunately rejected.   It could have achieved nothing except add to our losses.

The Hampshire meanwhile had merely advanced in open order across the Salt Lake, now virtually dry, to reserve trenches behind Chocolate Hill. Though shelled during this advance, they escaped with one casualty, Lt. C. Harland being hit in the leg, but while digging in they caught more shell-fire and had over 20 more casualties.   On the following evening the battalion shifted to its left to One Tree Gully, the 88th Brigade having relieved the Fifty-Fourth Division and taken over the line just South of Kiretch Tepe Sirt.   The battalion now welcomed back Captain Spencer-Smith, who took command with the rank of Major, and with him came 180 men and four officers, including Captain Lane and Lt. Collett of the 3rd Battalion, followed shortly by another 40 men under Lt. Swayne (13th Battalion).   Lts. Silk and Poole now had to go to hospital, Lt. Lord taking over duty as Adjutant.   After a week here, during which snipers on the higher ground in front and on the left flank proved troublesome but did not cause many casualties, while a bad line was much improved, the brigade was relieved and went off to Imbros for a well-earned rest.

Unlike the 2nd Battalion, the 10th Hampshire had been heavily engaged on August 21st.   The position they had to attack was unpleasantly strong and where they were crossing the ravine it could be enfiladed from higher up on Abdelrahman Bair.   Hill 60 itself was being attacked by the 5th Connaught Rangers and some New Zealand Mounted Rifles, the Hampshire being in support,

---

[1] More details had rejoined.   [2] Between the Hill 60 spur and Damakjelik Bair.

while on the right two Australian battalions were attacking. The assault was timed for 3.30 p.m., but, as always at Gallipoli, too little artillery was available for a really effective preparation and the half an hour's bombardment only served to give warning of the coming attack.

Consequently, when the Australians went forward, they met so fierce a fire that they were soon brought to a standstill, their leading lines being nearly

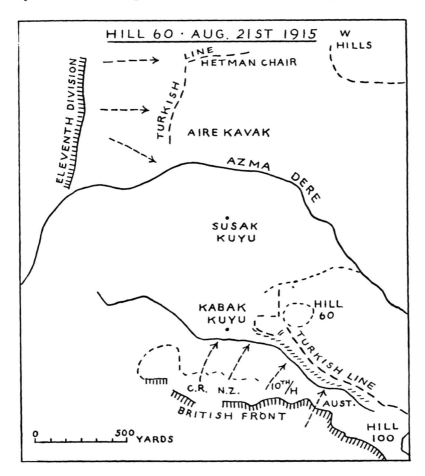

wiped out; though the New Zealanders fared better, making a lodgement in the enemy's lines. Major Morley, bringing the Hampshire forward in support[1] found that the danger point was the passage of a flat-topped ridge which was completely exposed to artillery and machine-gun fire from our right. However, it was essential to support the few New Zealanders visible in the Turkish trenches, who were trying to extend their hold by bombing, and accordingly he sent C

[1] They were in four lines C (Captain Hudson) in front, then D (Lt. Calderwood), then A and B (Captain Hellyer).

Company forward. They had to cross one gully and then the flat-topped ridge before reaching some shelter at the foot of the rise to the Turkish line. On the flat ridge a hail of fire bowled most of them over, hardly any getting across or reaching the captured position. D followed, only to fare as badly, Lt. Calderwood being killed, while to make matters worse the scrub took fire, though luckily the wind blew the flames away from where most of the wounded were lying. Advancing in their turn A Company met as fierce a fire and were checked, Captain Hellyer being very badly wounded.[1] Coming forward with B Company, Major Morley himself was hit and, realizing the hopelessness of crossing the ridge at this point, on handing over to Lt. Saunders, he told him to take B down the gully and try to cross at a less exposed spot. Meanwhile the Connaught Rangers had reached Hill 60, and though its summit remained in Turkish hands they had secured two valuable wells at Kabak Kuyu at its foot. On reporting to General Russell Lt. Saunders was ordered to bring his men up on the left of the position gained. Taking advantage of the cover of a sunken road, they reached the point indicated and got touch with the Gurkhas on the left who had secured the wells at Susak Kuyu to the North West. Here Captain Hudson and the survivors of the other companies rejoined them after dark and eventually, on being relieved by the Indian Brigade, the Hampshire went back to 29th Brigade head-quarters in S.W.B. Gully on Damakjelik Bair.

The attack had hit them hard, with another 43 killed and missing and 110 wounded. This reduced the battalion to well under 200 all told, Captain Hudson and Lt. Saunders being the only officers, and left it quite unfit for the moment for anything more than finding various fatigues for Brigade Head-quarters.[2]

The unsuccessful attack of August 21st was the last offensive effort of the Gallipoli venture, after that only local attacks were made for the improvement of the line. Before another advance could be attempted substantial reinforcements must be provided, over and above the drafts needed to bring the existing forces up to establishment and to relieve the many men who were carrying on though debilitated and really unfit for hard work. Moreover without far more artillery and ammunition it would be futile to send more troops, and even then the slender foothold already gained would hardly provide enough space for the artillery and reinforcements needed. Reluctant as were the higher authorities, both on the spot and at home, to admit it, the necessity of evacuation was making itself increasingly clear as the weeks passed on. Over four months were to elapse before that evacuation was to be successfully completed and, if long before that one Hampshire battalion had left Gallipoli, the other two had still much to endure there.

---

[1] He died of his wounds.

[2] Lt. Saunders was 'mentioned' in Sir Ian Hamilton's dispatches describing the Suvla and Anzac operations and received a well-deserved M.C. Captain Hudson was also 'mentioned', as were C.S.M. Sturges, Lance Sergeant Bowers, Privates Biddlecombe, Dyer, Moxham and Shaw, Sturges, Bowers and Biddlecombe received the D.C.M.

CHAPTER IX

GALLIPOLI

THE FINAL STAGES—THE EVACUATION

REGIMENTAL officers and men serving on the Gallipoli peninsula in the autumn of 1915 were naturally not aware of the course of the discussions about the future of the expedition which followed the check of August 21st., still they could hardly fail to realize that sooner or later something must be done to break down the existing stalemate, and they could form their own opinions as to the prospects, about which few can have been very optimistic. If the majority were quite ready to deal with a Turkish offensive, which would have given them a chance of getting their own back, there could be little question that tactically the Turks had the advantage, that conditions on the peninsula were most unpleasant and trying and largely responsible for a high sick-rate, with dysentery and diarrhoea as substantial contributors, that such amenities as troops in France enjoyed when ' resting ' were unknown even on the islands, whose one attraction was being out of range of the Turkish guns, that merely to maintain our position meant hard and monotonous work with little tangible result, while an ascendancy over the enemy in sniping, in bombing, in patrolling and in other activities of trench warfare, took some establishing. It was impossible not to be depressed by the failure of the great effort from which so much had been hoped: if those chiefly responsible for the miscarriage at Suvla had been replaced by more energetic and more inspiring commanders, the harm they had done was not easily eradicated and some of the more inexperienced and less well-trained units were slow to recover their former standards. Hardly a battalion in the M.E.F. but had suffered heavily and lost most of those who had made and trained it, many indeed needed to be virtually re-made. If the Twenty-Ninth Division, despite all it had endured, was quick to give others a lead and morally had little lee-way to make up, even it was weak and terribly short of experienced officers and N.C.O.s, so that the return of any ' original ', was an event of note and a good draft from a 3rd Battalion, imbued with the regimental traditions and spirit, worth much more than its mere numbers. The War Office, more perhaps from accident and necessity than from design, was terribly apt to reinforce battalions with officers and men from other regiments, though few of these had been long enough with their proper unit to feel themselves strangers in another.

The three Hampshire battalions in the M.E.F. were to go their own individual ways without meeting. The Twenty-Ninth Division had just taken over, at the end of August, the sector North of Sulajik, the left centre of the Suvla position, the spot where a Turkish counter-attack had fewest natural obstacles to meet and could most easily penetrate to the vital beach area. The Tenth Division, which had moved down off Kiretch Tepe Sirt for the attack on August 21st, remained in the Chocolate Hill sector until transferred to Salonica early in

October, while the Fifty-Fourth, which had replaced the Tenth astride Kiretch Tepe Sirt, moved to General Birdwood's command early in September to allow of the Thirteenth Division joining the Ninth Corps, to which it properly belonged. This brought the 8th Hampshire to the Rhododendron Spur—Damakjelik Bair sector, where the 10th had undergone its strenuous initiation to active service. Thus the paths of the three battalions did not cross.

The Twenty-Ninth Division's sector offered more opportunities than the others for minor tactical enterprises. The line here needed much improving, detached posts and trenches had to be joined up, communications improved and the line made habitable as well as defensible, and after that a wide and uneven No Man's Land, with many gullies, nullahs and hillocks, challenged our troops to push forward and establish advanced posts out of which a new line could be constructed. It gave chances also to snipers and the Twenty-Ninth Division had no intention of leaving the enemy alone.

The 2nd Hampshire had just a week at Imbros, really resting. The weather was good, the men got plenty of bathing and were refitted. Returning to Suvla on September 7th, they found 34 men from the 3rd Battalion awaiting them and next day took over from the Munster Fusiliers some excellent trenches on the Division's right, some two miles West of Anafarta Sagir. Saps were now pushed forward and, when far enough out, were joined up as an advanced line and meanwhile served as good sniping posts. Patrols were active; one which ran into a Turkish outpost on the night of September 17/18th had four men wounded, but thanks to good work and resourcefulness all four were brought safely in to our lines; on another occasion Corporal Nunn distinguished himself greatly by skilful handling of a covering party when a ditch in front of our line was being cleared, while other patrols located Turkish posts accurately so that our machine-guns could be turned on to them. One feature of the month was the attachment to the battalion for instruction of parties of the Royal Newfoundland Regiment and of the 2/1st London (T.F.), both these battalions having been attached to the 88th Brigade. Our snipers on balance had much the best of the exchanges, the month's casualties despite much shelling only coming to 20, five being killed. Diarrhoea, dysentery and other ailments sent three officers [1] and 133 other ranks to hospital, and although 80 men under 2/Lt. Bircham joined on September 29th, the battalion ended the month with only 12 officers and 564 other ranks.

After nearly four weeks in front line the 2nd Hampshire went back on October 4th to a reserve line, a mile in rear, consisting chiefly of dug-outs. This did not take them beyond the range of the Turkish guns, which did their best to discourage cleanliness by persistently shelling bathing parties. However, a week here, mainly spent in working on communication trenches, only cost the battalion one killed and two wounded. It then took over the Division's extreme left, on the rocky lower slopes of Kiretch Tepe Sirt, where digging was very difficult, indeed blasting was needed to get down any depth, so that sand-

[1] Captain Lane (3rd Battalion), 2/Lts. G. R. D. Moor and N. R. Gill.

bags had to be extensively used. It was as bad a piece of line as the battalion had yet met, and with the snipers opposite very active and enjoying the advantage of higher ground, hard work was needed to establish a satisfactory ascendancy. This was done, rifle grenades being also used effectively, while the battalion's patrols scored several successes and the month's casualties only came to eight killed and 32 wounded, though once again sickness caused many admissions to hospital, 137, including four officers. Against that drafts amounting to 138 men joined, another 80 returning from hospital, with ten officers, four attached from the 5th Royal Scots, who now had to leave the brigade [1] as their reserve unit could not produce the drafts they needed. Of these Lt. Kingsley Darling took over Z Company. From October 30th to November 6th the battalion was again in brigade reserve and then relieved the Essex in the right of the brigade sector. Here a ruined cottage, converted into a bullet-proof blockhouse, was a great centre of activity, Turkish bombers were inclined to be active, but the Hampshire replied effectively with rifle-grenades and with bombs from a catapult [2] with a range of 170 yards, besides dispersing wiring and working parties with rifle fire or rifle grenades. In common with the rest of the Twenty-Ninth Division they were not going to let the Turks have the best of things, and they effectively discouraged any attempt to attack our lines.

The weather was now turning colder and bathing had been given up, but the sudden change which produced the terrible blizzard of November 28th to 30th was hardly expected. Luckily for the 2nd Hampshire they had gone into reserve on the 20th, their occupations now including the removal to the beach of all surplus trench stores, a step distinctly suggestive of evacuation. Being on rather higher ground they escaped the worst of the blizzard, though even so they suffered considerably from the combination of the torrents of rain, the piercing wind and the intense cold, and three officers and over 100 men had to be sent to hospital in three days. They now had to find parties to occupy the key points in the 86th Brigade's line, among them the block-house, ' Dublin Castle '. The 86th had suffered particularly severely, its trenches being submerged by the flood of icy-cold water which poured down from the higher slopes, filling every depression, drowning several men and carrying away arms, equipment and food. After the flood had subsided, the Hampshire found many corpses [3] in the trenches, men who had been drowned or frozen, with any amount of material to be salvaged. The battalions in front line were virtually out of action, but fortunately the Turks, if on higher ground, were worse clothed and worse fed than our men and suffered even more from exposure to the bitter cold. At one time 170 Hampshires were holding the 86th Brigade's entire front, some 1,200 yards long, but the Turks were incapable of attacking, and in moving about behind their wrecked trenches they gave good targets to the Hampshires' rifles and machine-guns, not to mention the bomb-throwing

---

[1] The Newfoundland Regiment replaced them.
[2] One, accurately directed by the Adjutant, pitched within a yard of one sniper's loophole from which there was no more firing.
[3] Some Turks as well as British, washed down from their lines.

catapult. But the main need was to get the mud out of the trenches, recover the arms and equipment submerged under it, repair the parapet and clear the communication trenches. A return to fine weather early in December was very welcome and not only cheered up the troops after the bitter cold and wet of the previous week but allowed much of the preliminary work before evacuation to be pushed on, while the arrival within five days of four drafts amounting in all to 270 restored the battalion to a good strength, more than balancing the 207 admissions to hospital of November, and provided additional labour for working parties.

The evacuation was a triumph of care, forethought and organization. Intermediate lines of defence were prepared between the front line and the beach, the routes to be taken by the different parties were most carefully selected and marked out: all trench stores and weapons that could be got off were taken down to the beach and embarked, and yet all the while no hint of what was in preparation had to be given to the Turks. The front line had therefore to appear to be fully manned, snipers and machine-gunners continued to harass the enemy and all evacuating was done under cover of darkness.

For the 2nd Hampshire the first big step was their occupation on December 13th of the 86th Brigade's whole firing line. Three companies took over, X remaining behind at Hill 10, a key point in the line to be held after the evacuation of the front line, as it provided an upper tier of trenches from which men could fire over the front line. Next day the 86th Brigade embarked.[1] Then on the 16th packs, officers' valises and everything removable were sent down to the beach. Meanwhile normal activities were pursued in the front line, damaged parapets were repaired and trenches drained, snipers continued to be active, and any patrols which ventured to approach our line were promptly received with rifle-fire and driven back. If any suspicions had been aroused by the assembly of more ships than usual at Imbros, they were assuaged by the appearance of our lines and the activity of our trench garrisons.[2] At 6.45 p.m. on December 18th five officers and over 300 men [3] moved out of line and quietly filed back to the beach, leaving 275 of all ranks behind. These carried on as usual, except that all sniping was stopped for three hours and then suddenly resumed, a move calculated to make the Turks think that a cessation of sniping was a trap to lure him into an unwise advance. Another 100 of all ranks left the front line at 5 a.m. (Dec. 19th) for Essex Ravine, 1000 yards back, where they spent the day in readiness to reinforce the second line, 30 men and two machine-guns taking post at Hill 10. This left under 150 men to hold the 1200 yards frontage. These made as much show as possible, moving about and firing from different points: it was an anxious time, had the Turks realized what was happening and attacked, the tiny parties still on shore would have stood little chance. But the precautions had been sufficient, the Turks, deceived perhaps by the activity of our snipers, evinced no suspicion of anything unusual being afoot, gradually the day wore uneventfully on, and with evening the Essex Ravine

---

[1] The 87th had been sent round in October to reinforce the three weak Divisions at Cape Helles.
[2] Cf. *Gallipoli*, II. 459.   [3] These included X Company from Hill 10.

party could embark, followed about 11.15 p.m. by battalion head-quarters, who had left the front at 7.45 p.m. Another 20 moved off at 10.15 p.m. picking up the Hill 10 party on their way. Forty picked men under Lt. Cuddon [1], one to every thirty yards, were left in the front line but moved at 1.30 a.m. (December 20th), having first lighted candles which had been prepared with fuses and detonators so as to let off fixed rifles to imitate snipers, even after the line had been evacuated. As this last party made its way towards the beach they could hear these shots and the Turks replying, while sounds of wiring suggested that the Turk was improving his defences in anticipation of attack. Not a shell was fired as these rear parties filed down the communication trenches, all being aboard by 3 a.m. The night had been wonderfully still, the sea was quite smooth and the moon if anything too bright, and the actual embarkation went off quite quietly and quickly, motor lighters taking the men out to the larger ships. The Turk had been magnificently and completely hood-winked, and a difficult task,[2] which even the optimistic had calculated must involve at least 25% of casualties, had been accomplished without loss of life and with less sacrifice of stores and guns than had been expected, thanks to careful planning and well-disciplined execution. German critics have themselves hailed it as a ' masterpiece ', something till then quite unprecedented.

Neither the 8th nor the 10th Hampshire had seen anything of the evacuation: the 10th having quitted the peninsula at the end of September and the 8th early in December.

The 10th, a mere remnant after their fight for Hill 60 and the wells, had spent nearly all September on beach duties. Lt. Dupree, the first wounded officer to return, had rejoined on August 23rd, Lt. Clement soon following, and the arrival on September 9th of 134 men from the 3rd Battalion, many of them old Regulars, including a sprinkling of transfers from the cavalry, was very welcome as it increased the number available for the numerous ' fatigues '. A few officers also joined, Major Colquhoun of the Leinsters assuming command on September 25th. Shell-fire caused a dozen casualties, including four killed, while Captain Hudson and over 80 men had to go to hospital, dysentery and other bowel complaints being prevalent, and when on September 30th, the battalion embarked for Mudros, ' other ranks ' barely mustered 300, very few recovered sick and wounded having rejoined. At Mudros it found drafts from the 3rd and 13th Battalions, amounting to 117, with whom was Lt. Nicholson of the 1st Battalion, who relieved Lt. Saunders of the Adjutant's duties he had been discharging in addition to his own labours as Quartermaster.

This move proved to be no ordinary relief to give the battalion a chance to get rested and refitted, though it needed both. The changed situation in the Balkans had led to the decision to dispatch British and French troops, among them the Tenth Division, to assist the hard-pressed Servians.

[1] 7th Queen's, he had joined in November, being given a regular commission in the Regiment in June 1916.
[2] The evacuation of the ' Anzac ' position had been equally successful.

The 10th Hampshire who left Gallipoli for this new venture were very different from the battalion which had embarked in July so full of hope and promise.   To have made so fine a unit in so brief a time had been an achievement greatly to the credit both of instructors and instructed.   It was one of the worst features of the tragedy of Gallipoli that so many units of that great company, the ' First Hundred Thousand ', should have been shattered and broken in an attempt to accomplish a task which, as can be seen now, was from the first fraught with the greatest difficulties.   The 10th Hampshire had been put into the fight when the chances of success had all but vanished: they had made a fine effort and had shown themselves worthy members of the regiment, to whose record their effort had added no mean page, even if the phrase to be applied to it is that in which every stage of the Gallipoli campaign from April 25th onward may be summarized, ' too late '.[1]

The 8th Hampshire had had two days on the Kiretch Tepe Ridge, being persistently sniped from the slopes above them and finding the snipers hard to subdue.   Their losses here included Lts. Bartlett and Latham and though the ' first reinforcements ' had rejoined, nearly 100 men had gone to hospital besides their 300 casualties.   A spell at Lala Baba, in reserve, which allowed of bathing, was a welcome change and from there the battalion shifted to its new sector.

When the Fifty-Fourth Division reached ' Anzac ' its battalions were all much below establishment, several having suffered heavy casualties, while sickness had hit its unacclimatized men hard.   Fortunately, if a renewal of our offensive was out of the question, the Turks also had suffered too heavily to be anxious to risk incurring more losses in trying to recover their lost ground, and the Fifty-Fourth found its new positions fairly well consolidated.   Consequently the three months the 8th Hampshire spent in this sector passed uneventfully, though maintaining and improving their line kept them fully occupied. They were at first posted on Hill 60, where the smell of the unburied bodies between the lines was very offensive.   There was some activity here, bombing and sniping, but the position remained unchanged.   From the middle of September, being very weak, little over 400 strong, they were attached to the 161st (Essex) Brigade, in exchange for the stronger 7th Essex, as their own brigade, who were holding the Hill 60 sector, needed reinforcing and a fresh effort to secure the rest of that important tactical feature was under contemplation.   The 161st Brigade's sector was further to the right, on the Southern side of the Kaiajik Dere and opposite Hill 100, another post which Turkish industry had converted into a veritable fortress.   Few drafts appeared and a steady drain of sick to hospital left the brigade so weak that the mere maintenance of the line put a considerable strain on those present   A man who got one full night's sleep a week could reckon himself lucky, and with rations monotonous, water hardly sufficient for washing and shaving, no real rest even when in reserve and constant hard work with many ' fatigues ', the troops were

---

[1] In Sir Ian Hamilton's dispatches, published on January 6th, 1916, Lt. Colonel Bewsher, Captain Hicks, R.S.M. Smith and C.S.M. Groves (killed in action) were ' mentioned '.

not well off.   Most of the brigade's line was beyond bombing range of the enemy and despite occasional shelling, casualties were few, the 30 which the 8th recorded in September being mostly suffered at Hill 60 [1] early in the month, while in October and November, hardly any are recorded, though in November 2/Lts. Pavey and Reeve were wounded when out on patrol.

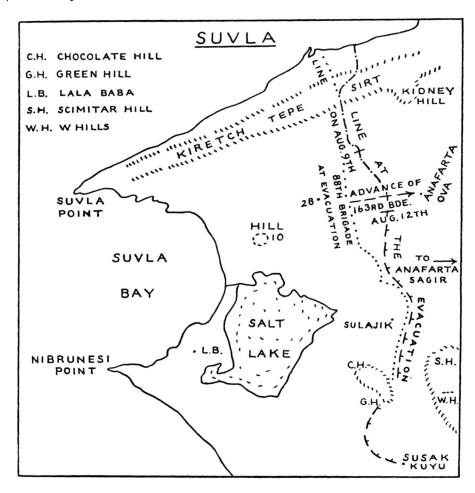

An issue of serge clothing in the middle of October was welcome, as the weather was getting colder and the khaki drill shirts and shorts, appropriate enough in August, were no longer adequate, but little occurred to vary the regular routine.

Colonel Rhodes had to go to hospital on September 10th, Captain Ellery taking command, but he also went sick in the middle of October when Captain

---

[1] 2/Lt. Fox, who remained at Hill 60 as bombing officer, did excellent work until wounded on October 21st and eventually received the M.C.

Marsh took over. A dozen subalterns, mostly from the 8th Wiltshire, reported for duty and 40 men rejoined from hospital, Lt. Brannon also returning. Clashes with the enemy were infrequent: our snipers, though constantly on the look-out, got few chances, though Sergeant Halsey scored several successes, for which and for good work on patrol he was awarded the D.C.M., while a catapult bomb-thrower was occasionally used to good effect. Incidents of note were few, the enemy were unenterprising and, with evacuation becoming daily more probable, nothing was to be gained by an attack, which, even if it might improve the tactical situation, could not affect the strategical deadlock.

The great November blizzard was perhaps less felt at Anzac than at Suvla. Being high up in the hills the 161st Brigade escaped the flooding from which troops in the lower ground suffered so severely, and if the cold and the wet produced several cases of frost-bite the Division's sick rate did not leap up so alarmingly after it, as did that of some Divisions at Suvla.

The Fifty-Fourth Division had indeed received orders to move before the blizzard, which found the 8th Hampshire in reserve at ' Hatfield Park ', expecting orders to embark. These were cancelled and not until December 3rd did the battalion leave the peninsula, reaching Mudros next day and rejoining its own brigade when that in turn reached the islands. After ten days in camp it embarked on December 15th in H.M.S. *Victorious* for Alexandria, where it arrived on December 19th, going to Sidi Bishr camp. The infantry of the Division had left the peninsula nearly 60% below establishment, but its artillery and other units which had not accompanied it to Gallipoli were now to rejoin, and the whole Division was to be re-united and its infantry brought up to establishment.

Suvla and Anzac had been evacuated: would it be possible to repeat the feat at Cape Helles with the Turk and his German mentor on the look-out for its repetition. Now that the factor of surprise had been eliminated the difficulties would be greater, but there was also the consideration that after all the British might retain possession of Cape Helles. Naval reasons made it desirable, to assist the fleet to maintain a blockade of the Straits, while some believed that evacuation would be so difficult that retention would be the lesser evil. The Turk might well be in doubt, but evacuation here was clearly going to be even more difficult than getting away from Anzac and Suvla and it would require the best troops at General Birdwood's [1] disposal. The Divisions composing the Eighth Corps were much below establishment and in urgent need of relief, and once again it was to the Twenty-Ninth Division that those in command turned to carry out the second evacuation. [2]

Much to their surprise therefore the 2nd Hampshire had hardly landed at Imbros before they had to re-embark and on the evening of December 22nd they found themselves landing at W Beach. Only the later parties to embark were with battalion head-quarters, the first and larger detachment having gone

[1] He was now in command, Sir Charles Monro, who had succeeded Sir Ian Hamilton in October, having returned to France.
[2] The Thirteenth Division was also sent to Cape Helles.

on to Mudros and not rejoining till December 25th. The 86th Brigade, now commanded by Brigadier General Williams [1], had already joined the 87th, and the Division was holding the line between Gully Ravine and the Krithia Nullahs, ground only too familiar to the survivors of August 6th. A new firing line had been formed between the barricades in H.12 and H.12a and the front trenches were dry, if some of the communication trenches were nearly knee-deep in mud.

Their first few days at Cape Helles the 2nd Hampshire spent in reserve, fully occupied in clearing the communication trenches and improving the Eski Line, now the line to be held to cover the evacuation. This line they took over on December 31st, sending their machine-gunners and picked bombers up to reinforce the Essex in front line between the two branches of the Krithia Nullah, to the right of their old position. Major Spencer-Smith was still in command, with Captain Lord as Adjutant and Captain Jones (Y), Lts. Cuddon (W) and Darling (X) and 2/Lt. Bircham (Z), commanding companies, Lt. Smith, the Quartermaster, had gone to hospital in November, he had long out-stayed all the others present on April 25th, if some had rejoined.

These bombers had a lively time. The front line had been captured in a recent local attack by the Fifty-Second Division and, being much knocked about, wanted much consolidating, while three saps, really parts of Turkish communication trenches, were to be connected into a new firing line. This work had to be carried on within bombing range, the enemy being in places only ten yards off and bombing away vigorously, though our reply seemed much more effective; his guns also were active, though luckily their fire was not very accurate. It was the more important to push on with the new firing line in order to conceal from the Turk our approaching withdrawal, preparations for which were being steadily pushed forward. Altogether the battalion's last turn in the Cape Helles trenches was distinctly 'lively' and it was lucky to escape with many fewer casualties than the volume and vigour of the enemy's bombing and bombarding might have caused. These included 2/Lt. Lambourne, mortally wounded on January 5th, the last of the many officers [2] the 2nd Hampshire had lost at Gallipoli.

It was really rather remarkable that the Turks, who can hardly have failed realize that we were likely to evacuate Cape Helles also, should not have tried to catch us in the act and drive us into the sea. Their abstention perhaps indicated a reluctance to risk the reception we should give. Their one tentative attempt was certainly not encouraging to them. Heavy shelling on January 7th seemed to indicate a coming attack, for which Turks could be seen to be collecting, but opposite the Hampshire they could not be induced to leave their trenches, and a rather feeble attempt against the Thirteenth Division on our left was speedily and effectively discouraged.

Next day (January 8th) was 'Z' day for the final evacuation. The programme adopted at Suvla was repeated: parties withdrawing according to a carefully arranged schedule. Of the Hampshire Z Company from the Eski Line

---

[1] He commanded it until promoted in April 1917 to command the Thirtieth Division.
[2] In all 26, apart from 13 attached officers: the 8th Battalion lost ten and the 10th twelve.

led off directly it was dark, followed by X from the Redoubt Line. At 8 p.m. 160 of all ranks, including battalion headquarters, left the firing line for W Beach, leaving 80 men, mainly bombers, under Captain Jones to hold the firing line for another four hours. Just before this party was due to leave the Turks started bombing our sap-heads and our men had to return bomb for bomb. This they did so successfully that the Turks stopped bombing in time for this rear-guard to quit the firing line just before midnight as arranged.

The actual embarkation was more difficult than at Suvla: the sea was getting up, one lighter in which the Hampshire should have embarked was damaged and could not be used and it was touch and go whether the last parties could get away. However, once again good discipline, careful arrangements and a strict adherence to programme surmounted the difficulties, and eventually all were on board, the last Hampshire embarking in a destroyer, already uncomfortably crowded, which carried them to Imbros. Luckily the Turks had never realized what was happening, their shelling, though fairly heavy, was desultory and only when all were on board was our departure announced by a big ammunition dump blowing up, followed by other explosions which set fire to all the stores which had been left behind. Then their guns opened up in style and blazed away, merely wasting their ammunition on destroying stores which might have been very useful to them. As from Suvla and Anzac we had got away from Cape Helles almost without losing a man: once again a stupendous task had been accomplished with amazing success. As at Suvla the 2nd Hampshire had been selected for the most difficult and dangerous part of the operation and had carried it out most successfully.

' Wars are not won by evacuations ', however successful, and highly satis-factory as was the M.E.F's safe extrication from the Gallipoli peninsula, the abandonment of the enterprise was an admission of failure. In that enterprise the regimental officers and men of the Twenty-Ninth Division had made a name for their Division which stands high in the records of our Army, and ' Landing at Helles ' and ' Suvla ' very properly appear among the ten battle-honours for 1914–1918 on the regiment's King's Colours. In the story of the Sixty-Seventh ' Landing at Helles ' may well rank with ' Barrosa '.

CHAPTER X

THE TERRITORIALS IN INDIA—MESOPOTAMIA—1915

THE seven Hampshire Territorial battalions who had gone out to India all started with much the same experiences: they had to become acclimatized, to accommodate themselves to the very unfamiliar conditions of Indian service and to complete their training. Of this last the three Second Line units naturally were most in need, but the others had been somewhat disorganized by the changes of personnel caused by the reorganization into Foreign Service and Home Service units and they contained many recruits, even if many ex-Territorials and old Volunteers had rejoined. All were short of equipment, being issued with anything but the latest pattern of rifle, and the officers and senior N.C.O's had a task of much difficulty, especially as the subalterns were mainly newly commissioned. Some battalions were fortunate in going to Frontier stations like Quetta, to which the 2/4th were posted, and Rawal Pindi, whither the 1/4th moved from Poona in January, where they found themselves alongside some of the few Regular battalions remaining in India. Others were lucky to have detachments from those units attached to them as instructors [1] and benefitted enormously from their help, while nearly all battalions included some sprinkling of ex-Regulars of the regiment who had served in India and from whose knowledge of the country and its ways the uninitiated benefitted greatly. All soon settled down to the new conditions and duties,[2] but training was impeded by the need to make substantial detachments, the 1/6th sent several companies from Dinapore to Dum Dum and the 1/5th at Allahabad had to find detachments for duty at Benares and Cawnpore, while before long battalions were having to find men for the multifarious 'employments' for which skilled men were needed, and another and, in the end quite substantial, drain developed in the commissioning of many N.C.O's and men, some in the Indian Reserve of Officers, whose demands were continually increasing, others going home to take 'New Army' commissions. Many men quite suitable for commissions but lacking the qualifications for selection for the earliest formed 'Service' battalions, which could not at once absorb all those who came forward, had enlisted rather than wait about until further additions to the Army found them vacancies, and it was not long before many of these were wanted for bigger responsibilities than those of a Private or Lance Corporal. On the whole the health of the Territorials was better than might have been expected from as large a body of unacclimatized [3] and inexperienced men, many of them young, though some time elapsed before drafts from home were forthcoming to balance the wastage.

[1] The 2/5th at Secunderabad, for example, owed much to a most helpful party of the 1st Royal Sussex, the 2/7th to the 2nd North Staffordshire and the 2/4th at Quetta to the Somerset L. I.

[2] Captain Bacon's *Wanderings of a Temporary Warrior* gives a most interesting account of the experiences of the Territorials in India. It has been most helpful.

[3] At one time nearly 100 of the 2/4th were suffering from defective heart action, caused by hard work in an atmosphere as rarified as that of Quetta, but these men soon became fit again.

Before long another substantial drain developed, drafts being wanted for the British units in Mesopotamia, whither the Sixth Indian Division had been sent in October. In the major campaign into which the operations in that country were to develope, several Hampshire battalions saw some very varied active service, extending as far afield as Persia and the Trans-Caspian, while the 1/4th had the distinction of being the first Territorial battalion to be selected for service there.

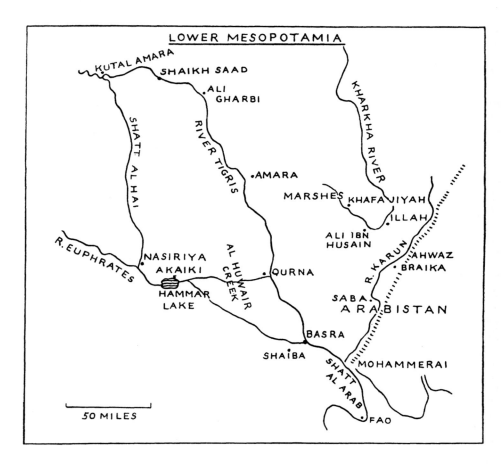

The campaigns in Mesopotamia provide an excellent example of the difficulties of confining a 'side-show' to its original purpose, even if that has been purely defensive and indeed necessary to prevent an enemy from attacking some vulnerable point. Once Turkey had come into the war we could not ignore the danger of her developing, under German guidance, an attack from Mesopotamia upon the Persian oil-fields, all-important to our oil-burning Navy, or fomenting trouble on the inflammable North West Frontier, and it is hard to criticize the dispatch of a force to the Persian Gulf to secure the oil supplies.

But, once Basra and Qurna had been occupied, the local tactical and strategical advantages of a further advance, first to Amara, then to the junction of the Tigris and the Shatt al Hai at Kut, even to Baghdad, began to be urged. It could be argued that to halt at Qurna would allow the Turks to counter-attack, at their own time and convenience, that our adoption of a defensive attitude would discourage those Arabs who might otherwise be inclined to take our side. It was easier to lay down the principle that our object was merely to achieve security than to agree upon the exact method of attaining that end and no more. Anyhow in January another brigade had been ordered to reinforce the original Division, and hardly had it arrived before the development of trouble in Arabistan threatened the pipe-line from the Ahwaz oil-fields and made further reinforcements necessary, whereupon a 33rd Brigade was mobilized with the 1/4th Hampshire as its British battalion.

The 1/4th had had not quite two months with the Second Indian Division at Pindi, when they received on March 7th orders to mobilize at once. No mobilization scheme had been worked out, but with welcome help from the Adjutant and staff of the 2nd North Staffordshire all was soon in train. Machine-guns were received from the 114th Mahrattas at Jhelum, new rifles were issued, the necessary stores and equipment drawn: by 6 p.m. on March 9th mobilization could be reported as virtually complete, and next evening 31 officers and 790 other ranks entrained for Karachi.[1]

Four days took the battalion to Basra, where it was established in camp at Makina Masus, in a palm grove cut up into small islands by deep ditches. For the moment the ground was dry and conditions not unpleasant, the days being not unbearably hot and the nights cool. The duty here consisted mainly of finding many guards, picquets and night outposts, with occasional escorts to convoys going out to Shaiba, five miles West of Basra, where a substantial force was posted in readiness to meet an advance down the Euphrates. This meant hard work, toiling through mud and water, but before long much of the intervening country became flooded and supplies had to be sent up in ' bellums '[2], the escort also travelling by water. One party engaged in this duty under 2/Lts. E. A. Burrell and Rutherford had a miniature naval battle, being attacked by Turks in bellums, but it soon drove the attackers off by rifle-fire, without suffering any casualties.

The first detachment more actively employed was one of 25 men under Lt. Forbes detailed to man the *Sulimi*, one of the steamers employed in the ' Euphrates Blockade ' and operating against the communications of the Turkish force which was concentrating on that river and evidently intending to attack. A machine-gun section under Sergeant Raynbird on board the *Shushan*, another of the flotilla, was also very active and had several encounters with the enemy.

[1] Lt. Colonel Bowker was in command, the other officers being Majors Footner and W. B. Stilwell, Captains Barton (Adjutant), Brandon, G. P. Burrell, Foster, Page-Roberts, Parsons, Reeks, Simmons and Spinney, Lts. Cooper, Forbes, Harris, Lester-Garland, Macrae, Naish, Osborne and J. G. Stilwell 2/Lts. Andrews, Bucknill, G. A. Burrell, H. A. Burrelll, Capes, Chitty, Cowan, Lacey, and Rutherford and Lt. and Qr. Mr. Buckingham with Captain Jones, R.A.M.C.

[2] Country sailing boats which might be as large as 75 tons.

In April the Turkish counter-attack developed and was effectively defeated in a hard-fought engagement at Shaiba (April 12th–14th). The Hampshire had no part in this, though held in readiness to reinforce, but they were busy after the battle in helping to get our wounded down from Shaiba and in guarding the numerous prisoners captured, while the *Shushan* took part in pursuing the enemy, capturing and destroying many mahailas [1] and other country sailing craft which formed their transport. Several hostile Arab villages were destroyed and an effective control of the water-way was established, while valuable information was acquired about its navigation. Lt. Forbes' party was away till the middle of May, the machine-gunners remaining on board the *Shushan* for another three weeks. [2]

With this attack defeated, General Nixon, now commanding in Mesopotamia, could resume the offensive and undertake operations in Arabistan against the forces menacing the pipe-line, and on April 25th the 4th Hampshire were ordered to embark for Ahwaz. Disembarking at Saba on the Karun river on the evening of April 27th, the battalion marched upstream to Braika, 16 miles below Ahwaz. It had now been transferred to the 30th Brigade under Major-General Melliss, which moved forward NW. on May 1st to Ali Ibn Husain on the old bed of the Kharkha river. The heat was now great, frequent dust storms were a great inconvenience, while occasional heavy rain slowed down the marching over the loose soil and impeded operations. Advancing again on May 6th, in hopes of bringing the enemy to action and assisting the operations General Nixon was now developing from Qurna, the troops reached the Kharkha at Illah next day. Here the river was 250 yards wide and in full flood, [3] and its passage was no easy matter, as the bridging material available was quite insufficient. It was effected, however, the Hampshire manning pontoons and rowing them across, and then, on May 13th, the main body moved forward NW., leaving the Hampshire and other troops to protect the crossing place, assist to construct a flying-bridge and cover the arrival of supplies. They were kept busy and with the heat increasing, supplies short—it was an unattractive country, bare where not swamp and marsh—the sick rate soon began rising. On May 15th half the battalion had a long and trying march escorting a convoy to Khafajiyah, 15 miles down the Kharkha, to which the main body had advanced, engaging and punishing the enemy very successfully. Various punitive operations were now undertaken against the local Arabs, the Hampshire providing an escort for the guns during the burning of one big village.

By May 17th the battalion was concentrated at Illah, whence it moved back on the 19th to Ahwaz, marching 18 miles in great heat, to embark there next day and regain Basra on May 21st. Some very fatiguing operations involving much hard work with little shelter and scanty rations without the satisfaction of a fight had sent 60 men to hospital. But they had achieved their object, most of the troops employed could now return to Basra and Qurna, and General

---

[1] Another type of country river craft.   [2] They had two casualties.
[3] Private Woods distinguished himself by a gallant effort to rescue two sepoys who were in danger of drowning.

Nixon could undertake the attack, generally known as ' Townshend's Regatta ' on the Turkish positions North of Qurna. In these, largely conducted by water, the troops advancing through the marshes in bellums, Lt. Macrae and 16 men of the Hampshire joined Sergeant Raynbird and the machine-gun section already aboard the *Shushan*, and Lt. Osborne and 30 men were on board the river steamer *P.7*, the battalion itself remaining at Basra. It was feeling the effects of its hard work in Arabistan and of the increasing heat, many more men going sick, while several died.

In the highly successful attack of May 31st the *Shushan* and another steamer were detailed to advance by the Al Huwain creek, which joins the Euphrates above Qurna, and to demonstrate against the enemy's right flank, but some ' friendly ' Arabs, who should have co-operated, did not prove too eager to fight, while difficulties over navigation prevented the steamers getting into really effective range. Still the attack diverted the attention of the Arabs who might otherwise have seriously impeded the main attack. This was completely successful, the Turkish advanced positions were captured with very few casualties and next morning's advance found the main position behind evacuated, the Turks having retired in disorder upstream. Thereupon the river flotilla started off in pursuit, half-a-dozen Hampshire in H.M.S. *Comet* [1] sharing in the amazing adventure which culminated in the unopposed occupation of Amara (June 4th) by some 40 men. This handful not only received the surrender of several hundreds of Turks, but disarmed them, put them on board boats for conveyance downstream and policed the town, discouraging looting by shooting down any Arabs seen making off with plunder. Early on June 4th the arrival of the leading party of the 16th Brigade made the situation secure.

The party on board the *P.7* had had less excitement, merely escorting captured Turks downstream to Basra. They made two journeys on this errand and one upstream to Amara to bring back more prisoners and sick, before rejoining the battalion on June 9th. By this time the climate and particularly the moist heat was making itself felt, sick in hospital were up to 180 by June 16th, half a dozen men had died, mainly from heat-stroke, and on June 17th 84 men were invalided to India. With others detailed for various employments, under 300 other ranks and 16 officers were available when on June 24th the battalion was detailed to join the force about to advance up the Euphrates to Nasiriya.

This advance was aimed at securing the greater part of the Basra vilayet (district) against another counter-attack down the Euphrates and at making an impression on the local Arabs. As a first step it was essential to secure the navigation of the channels leading into the Hammar Lake from Sukash Shuyukh where the main stream of the Euphrates divides into several branches. The most navigable, the Akaika channel, was known to be blocked by a dam just above the lake, but no other channel could be used by vessels of any draught and there was no alternative to forcing its passage.

For this expedition the 30th Brigade, still including the 4th Hampshire, had

[1] General Townshend himself was also on board.

been selected, two batteries, half the 48th Pioneers and other details being attached to it. The force was carried in a most miscellaneous flotilla, stern-wheelers like the *Shushan*, armed launches, tugs, rafts, mahailas and bellums. The larger vessels could not cross the shallow Hammar Lake and this reduced considerably the artillery support available.

Contrary to expectations, no opposition was offered at the dam, through which a passage, large enough for the stern-wheelers, was blasted, though such was the force of the water rushing through the narrow opening that large parties had to haul on hawsers to get the vessels through, 150 men on one hawser, and

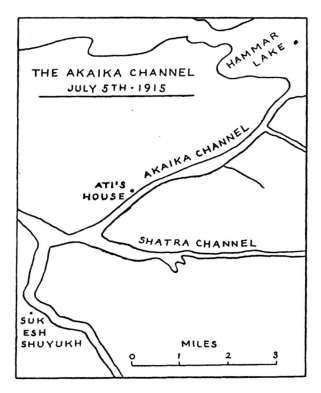

THE AKAIKA CHANNEL
JULY 5TH · 1915

HAMMAR LAKE

AKAIKA CHANNEL

ATI'S HOUSE

SHATRA CHANNEL

SUK ESH SHUYUKH

MILES
0   1   2   3

even then it was difficult enough. The *Blosse Lynch*, in which the 4th Hampshire had embarked, only got through on July 2nd after one failure, and not till July 4th was the whole flotilla through, so that an advance could be made.

The enemy were posted on both banks of the Akaika channel above a tower, known as Ati's House, on the left bank. They were hard to locate in the thick date-plantations, themselves no small obstacle, even when not intersected by ditches and channels. Landings were made on both banks on July 4th, but little progress was made and before daybreak (July 5th) the Hampshire, till then held in reserve, were landed on the right bank to reinforce the 2/7th Gurkhas, who were held up along the Shatra channel, which leaves the Akaika some way above Ati's House. After crossing this Shatra channel they were to advance towards the main stream of the Euphrates, while another column advanced on the left bank of the Akaika channel. The Shatra channel, however, was deep and broad, while the Arabs were well posted and too well concealed to give many targets and, like the Gurkhas, the Hampshire could not get across but had to hang on for several hours, taking advantage of any targets they got [1] until, the left bank advance having proved successful, some 48th Pioneers could be sent over to cross the Shatra some way to the left of the Hampshire. The Hampshire were then withdrawn from the firing line to follow them, and, crossing the creek in small boats, which took them two hours, worked along it to take in flank the stockade from behind which the enemy had been holding them up. On their advance it was evacuated, and by this time the troops beyond the Akaika had not only cleared the enemy out but had crossed the Euphrates and captured two guns, so that the flotilla could push on up the river.

This success had cost the British 100 casualties, the Hampshire losing Lt. Macrae, a pre-war subaltern, and three men killed and Lt. Lester-Garland and four men wounded, but with all units so much below establishment it was clear that reinforcements would be required if Nasiriya was to be taken. Accordingly at the Asani Bend, ten miles below that town, General Gorringe [2] decided to halt and await reinforcements before pushing on. Careful reconnaissances, including one in a ' masheuf ' (native boat) over the flooded area on the Turkish right, now showed that the enemy were strongly posted some way upstream, at the Majinina creek on the right bank and between the Atabiya and Maiyadiya creeks on the left, having several guns. During the next fortnight gradual advances up the right bank took us nearly to the Umm as Sabiyan creek, where on July 13th the Hampshire took over from the 24th Punjabis. They had moved upstream in a barge, which got stuck on the mud, attracting a heavy fire as soon as daylight revealed it to the Turks. It was set on fire, but the fire was promptly put out by a small guard who had been left on board. The battalion's trenches were also heavily shelled, but they had been well dug and its casualties only came to half-a-dozen. Meanwhile the 76th Punjabis had pushed forward another 1,200 yards and had their right on the river at Sixteen Palms. This line the Hampshire took over next evening and held for 24 hours, improving and consolidating it despite heavy fire and so intense a heat that 15 men collapsed with heat-stroke, one dying. From July 16th to 23rd the battalion was back in support trenches near Umm as Sabiyan and then moved up to Sixteen Palms in readiness to attack next day (July 24th), when it and the 2/7th Gurkhas were to assault the Majinina creek trenches as soon as the left bank attack came up level with their positions.

The artillery opened fire at 5 a.m. and half an hour later the left bank attack started and, going well, gradually captured the trenches below the Maiyadiya creek. Thereupon, at 7.8 a.m., General Melliss ordered the Hampshire and 2/7th Gurkhas forward, Nos. 2 and 4 forming the Hampshire's firing line under

---

[1] Private Elkins got the D.C.M. for returning to the steamer under heavy fire for ammunition.
[2] G.O.C. Twelfth Division to which the 30th Brigade belonged, who was in command.

Captain Burrell, with No. 1 (Major Stillwell) in support and the 2/7th Gurkhas on the left, No. 3 (Captain Parsons) being on board a barge carrying material for bridging the Majinina creek, which was believed to be unfordable.

Directly the advance started a heavy fire was opened, but the men pushed forward well and covered about 200 yards before halting to return the fire. High grass made it difficult to fire while lying down, so the troops pressed on and by 7.30 a.m. had reached the creek. Here they halted to let the barge be got into place, which was eventually accomplished about 8 a.m., when the survivors of No. 3, who had had 20 casualties among 35 men, landed on the far bank and took up position to cover the construction of the bridges. Before this Lt. Colonel Bowker had been hit and disabled, Major Stilwell taking over, and the battalion had suffered a grievous loss, the Adjutant, Captain Barton, being killed.

By this time the Gurkhas and Hampshires were all mixed up in the firing line, and as the creek had unexpectedly proved fordable the men waded across, formed under cover of the far bank and, dashing forward across a second and smaller creek, were quickly into the enemy's front trenches. Privates Hill, Verrall and Player were much to the fore in the assault, Hill and Player being first into the trenches, while Verrall fell just before reaching them. Lance Corporal Snow also used his machine-gun effectively throughout the attack, firing steadily and carefully and continuing in action although wounded till a shell disabled his gun.[1] A few Turks held out on the flanks of the position carried, but they were quickly dislodged by enfilade fire and went off at top speed, pursued by the Gurkhas, the Hampshire halting by order to consolidate the position captured and to cover a machine-gun battery now in position there. Five guns had been taken in these trenches with 100 prisoners and, with the left bank attack also a complete success, the Turks were soon in flight, Nasiriya being occupied without further opposition.

Reduced, mainly by sickness, to 150 of all ranks before the attack, the 4th Hampshire had really suffered very severely in losing Captains Barton and Simmons and nine men killed and Colonel Bowker, Captain Parsons, Lt. Osborne[2] and 34 men wounded, leaving Major Stilwell, Captain Burrell, Lt. Forbes, who took over as Adjutant, and 2/Lt. Bucknill as the only officers unhit. But the battalion's work was warmly praised by General Melliss and the D.S.O. awarded to Major Stilwell, the M.C's given to Captain Burrell, Lt. Forbes and 2/Lt. Bucknill and the four D.C.M's[3] were some indication of the approval of the authorities. Captain Barton, a most popular and efficient Adjutant, had done much for the battalion and was greatly missed.

Beyond Nasiriya there was no intention of advancing, the Turks had been well and truly beaten, nearly 1,000 being taken with 15 guns, and with another 2,000 casualties there was nothing much left of them, while the Arabs had been given reason to be respectful. Only a small force was required up the Euphrates, but though the rest of the 30th Brigade returned downstream, the mere handful

---

[1] All four received the D.C.M.   [2] He died of his wounds.
[3] Besides these Lt. Colonel Bowker and Lt. Osborne were mentioned in dispatches.

left of the 4th Hampshire remained at Nasiriya till the middle of August. They were encamped in a date plantation which gave some shelter but was rather airless; plenty of vegetables and fresh meat could be obtained and as little work was required, the men got some relief after their strenuous exertions. On July 26th they took part in a ceremonial parade when the Union Jack was hoisted over the Turkish barracks, after which the battalion was congratulated by General Melliss for its assault on the Turkish defences. The battalion was then

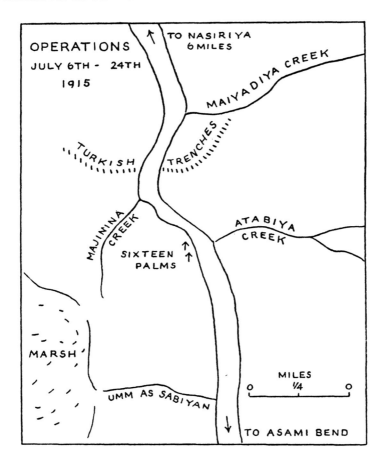

sent back to Qurna, one large barge accommodating all present. The voyage downstream was adventurous, the steamer which was towing the barge lost the channel and grounded, remaining firmly fixed. However, another steamer which was aground nearby was eventually got off and took the battalion's barge in tow. Passing down the Akaika channel the steamer had to cross the bar leading to the Hammar Lake stern first, as steering bow first, was impossible. Lt. Forbes, knowing the lake, successfully piloted the steamer across its shallows, a task quite beyond her Arab captain, and on August 23rd Qurna was reached. Here the battalion transhipped to the steamer *Malamir*, which carried it up the bending Tigris to Amara, where eight officers and 167 men landed, another 25 having been left sick at Qurna. Captain Floyd of the Norfolk had joined and taken over the Adjutant's duties.

Too weak for active employment, the 4th Hampshire now began a spell of ' line of communication ' duties at Amara, which kept it out of both Townshend's success at Kut (September 28th) and his ill-fated advance on Baghdad, which took him and the Sixth Division to the Pyrrhic victory at Ctesiphon (November 22nd). Not till nearly the end of November did any Hampshire quit Amara, the headquarters wing being then ordered up to Kut. Before this the battalion's scanty numbers had been substantially replenished by the arrival on September 1st of 200 men from Hampshire Territorial battalions in India. With these were Lts. Needham (5th), Palmer (6th) and Padmore (1/7th), and 2/Lt. Vernon (2/7th); 2/Lt. Bucknill and 25 of the battalion's own men also rejoined, and the battalion could be reorganized as four companies and more machine-gunners and signallers trained. The new arrivals were a fine lot, their healthy appearance contrasting notably with that of those who had endured a summer in Mesopotamia, and with the increased numbers the camp and garrison duties were not too heavy. It was getting cooler now, at nights ' British warms ' and jerseys were being worn and it was possible to play football. Rations were good, the Tigris teemed with fish, eggs could be got and milk, if poor, was plentiful. The men's health was in consequence much improved.

The battalion had been inspected both by General Nixon, G.O.C. ' Force D ', and by General Townshend, under whose command it had been at Rawal Pindi, both being very complimentary about its achievements.

Another substantial reinforcement arrived at the end of October, when Captains Brandon and Reeks, Lt. E. A. Burrell and 2/Lts. Andrews and Lacy and 82 men rejoined from sick leave in India,[1] and Captain North, Lts. Butler, Elton and Jensen and 2/Lts. Fine and Wyles of the 2/4th joined with 237 men from that battalion. Thanks to this, when on November 24th headquarters and two companies were ordered to embark at once for Kut, they could produce 14 officers and 302 other ranks. Major Footner was in command and with him were the Adjutant, Captains Foster and Reeks and the M.O., Captain Jones. Major Stilwell remained in command of B and C Companies at Amara.

The battalions in India had meanwhile carried on their routine of duties without having anything very special to chronicle.[2] The ordinary routine gave most men a turn at hill stations during the ' hot weather ', the four-company organization was adopted and training went steadily on. The 2/4th had some lifelike training in Frontier warfare with the Quetta Division, now under General Grover, which was to stand them in good stead later on, in Palestine,

---

[1] Major Footner and Captain Foster rejoined a little later.

[2] Without the Part II Records it is impossible to check the many changes in personnel which occurred, or to note many other details they would have supplied. ' War Diaries ' were only begun when battalions were ordered on active service.

and most battalions were put through strenuous ' Kitchener tests ', though some suffered from being split up, having to make detachments for ' internal security ' purposes, particularly the 2/5th and 1/6th, while the 2/5th had to find a company for duty at Fort St. George at Madras. Numbers available for duty were considerably reduced by the drafts required for Mesopotamia, the 2/4th having to send off 250 of their best men to the 1/4th in October, but before the end of 1915 wastage was being replaced from the ' Third Line ' units which had been formed at home. Thus the 1/5th got a good draft in November and 50 men joined the 1/7th about the same time. Less wastage was caused by sickness than might have been expected, but skilled men were always being taken away for employments of different characters, from munition making to driving motors, and the claims did not decline. One change occurred among the C.O's, Lord Montagu becoming Director of Motor Transport in India in April 1915, whereon Major Gott took command of the 2/7th.

CHAPTER XI
FROM SECOND YPRES TO THE SOMME

THE formation of a British Third Army in the summer of 1915 had been made possible by the arrival of substantial reinforcements. By the end of January the original six Divisions had been doubled by the addition of the Indian Corps and of the Seventh, Eighth, Twenty-Seventh and Twenty-Eighth Divisions. Six Territorial Divisions and the Canadians had followed during the spring, allowing a third Division to be added to each Corps, and in May ' K 1 ' had begun to appear, though the Tenth Division's diversion to the Dardanelles and the replacement in ' K 2 ' of the Sixteenth Division by the Thirty-Seventh postponed the appearance in France of any Hampshire Service battalion till ' K 3 ' came out in September, and as even then within five weeks the Twenty-Sixth Division was transferred to Salonica, and with it the 12th Hampshire, the 1st Battalion remained as the regiment's sole representative on the Western Front until nearly the end of the year, as it was late in December before the Sixteenth and with it the 11th Hampshire appeared. Moreover, as the Fourth Division's new front lay outside the area of the ' Loos ' offensive and remained ' quiet ' throughout the winter and spring, even the 1st Battalion had only minor activities to record for nearly a year.

This new front[1] lay NE. of Amiens and stretched from the Ancre near Hamel Northward. The 1st Hampshire made the acquaintance of its extreme right after dark on July 29th, when they relieved the 62me Infanterie in trenches just North of Hamel. They had detrained at Doullens on July 24th, had been inspected next day by their new Army Commander, General Monro, and had then moved forward to Engelbelmer in readiness to take over. A small draft with three officers had just arrived from the 3rd Battalion and the battalion was fairly strong in officers. The relief was easily accomplished, despite some difficulties over language, without any interference from the enemy, and the battalion could take stock of its new surroundings. These were very different from the damp and breastworks of ' Plugstreet ' Wood and free from the unattractive features of the Salient. The front line was on a ridge, from which the ground sloped down forward towards the enemy's line and on the right to the Ancre, though it was overlooked from high ground across the river, near Thiepval. The trenches were cut deep into chalk and loam, which in fine weather required little revetting and had allowed deep and capacious dugouts to be constructed, in which bunks and even arm-chairs were available. From the fighting point of view the trenches left more to be desired, in places the parapet was hardly bullet-proof, evidently neither side here had been inclined to disturb their opponents into unnecessary activity, but this was soon put right. Good communication trenches permitted access to the front line by day, and to the battalion's satisfaction hot meals could be supplied even in that line, as the ' cookers ' could be safely brought far enough forward to allow of this. Battalion head-

[1] Cf. Sketch 24 (p. 181).

quarters were comfortably housed in Hamel, with good swimming within easy reach, and officers and men could congratulate themselves on a degree of comfort never encountered ' in the line ' anywhere else. If the French standards of cleanliness and sanitation were hardly satisfactory, the battalion put in a lot of work on its billets and did much to clean them and clear things up.

Apart from having better trenches and more amenities behind the line, the battalion found itself faced across a ' No Man's Land ' about 250 yards wide with an unobtrusive enemy, who might indulge in a little shelling on most days but did not do much sniping and rarely patrolled. The area had seen heavy fighting in 1914, during the ' Race for the Sea ', but since then neither side had attempted to alter the situation and both had very much left their opposite numbers alone. If the British were slightly more active than either allies or enemies, especially about patrolling, the serious shell shortage so acutely felt both by the B.E.F. and in the Mediterranean precluded major activities, though if the enemy started a bombardment our guns were usually prompt in retaliating and as effective as the limits of the ammunition supply allowed.

However, the 1st Hampshire were hardly idle. The 11th Brigade promptly started digging a new line along a railway embankment, 150 yards nearer the enemy, but the large working parties employed were not seriously impeded. Our patrols were active and the Hampshire's, which were quick to find their way about No Man's Land, showed considerable enterprise in locating the enemy and indicating targets for our guns' none too plentiful ammunition, while the battalion's snipers gradually established a definite ascendancy over their opposite numbers and made the most of the occasional targets offered them. The Ancre's banks were swampy and it took some time to discover the best line to follow in these marshes.[1] Several encounters occurred near a large ruined mill, which both sides were in the habit of visiting but which neither tried to occupy permanently. On August 28th 2/Lt. May and two men, one a gamekeeper in civil life, who had waded and swum through the marshes to avoid approaching the mill by the only track, reached the buildings and were examining them when they were attacked by a German patrol of several times their numbers. However, they promptly attacked the enemy, apparently inflicting some casualties, under cover of which they made good their escape.[2] Another patrol had captured two prisoners a few days earlier, while some unusually inquisitive Germans had ventured near enough to our line to be fired at and dispersed, so that the battalion could congratulate itself on the situation ' between the lines '.

Occasionally the German guns became active. On August 28th trench-mortars and howitzers bombarded one of our posts vigorously until the 37th Battery R.F.A. retaliated so effectively that they stopped firing, while our trench-mortars also helped to ' give the Germans back all we had got '. Two other ' hates ' caused several casualties, and between August 26th and September 2nd the battalion had six killed, including an excellent N.C.O., Sergeant

---

[1] 2/Lt. May, who had come home from Canada to serve, found the mosquitos of these marshes quite as active as the Canadian.
[2] Their enterprise was warmly praised by the Brigadier, B. General Brown.

Jackson, and 20 wounded. This was much above the average; if the August casualties reached 35, including nine killed and 2/Lt. Dale wounded, the next four months only saw nine men killed and 27 wounded; nearly all by artillery fire. In the colder winter months men did three nights in front line, followed by three in close support, so that the amount of night work was reduced and with it the sick-rate, but even so admissions to hospital caused a considerable drain, 240 in five months, while various 'employments' absorbed a substantial number so that, though nearly 100 reinforcements arrived and about as many men returned from hospital, those available for duty tended to decline. Still the end of December found the battalion with just over 800 other ranks available. Among the officers who joined or re-joined were Majors Middleton [1] and Moore, who became Brigade M.G. officer, Captain Edsell and Lt. Westmorland, but Major Perkins was posted to the staff of the Mediterranean Expeditionary Force, Major Middleton replacing him as second in command. During most of the autumn Captains R. D. and K. A. Johnston, Smythe and Wyld were commanding the companies.

Outstanding incidents were few. Parties of 'New Army' Divisions were attached for instruction, notably some from the Thirty-Sixth (Ulster) Division. During 'Loos' our bombers were active and we frequently opened rapid fire as if we were going to attack. Something more might have been attempted had it seemed that the Germans had substantially weakened their trench garrisons to meet the Loos offensive, but their reply showed that this had not happened. Moreover their position was too strong to warrant any local attack without far more artillery support than was available. Occasional 'hates', in which trench-mortars were largely used, did some damage to our trenches without inflicting much loss, and we retaliated effectively, making good use of rifle-grenades, while some excitement was caused in September by two deserters, Alsatians, coming over to give themselves up. The autumn was wet, heavy rain brought new problems of maintenance, especially in draining the trenches, which tended to dissolve into liquid mud and 'went like a lump of sugar in a cup of warm water', so that much revetting was necessary and an issue of 'waders' had to be made, while the fall of the leaves exposed things which the foliage had concealed, whereupon brushwood screens had to be put up. During October patrols from A and D Companies met and scattered German patrols very successfully and Lt. Hillis [2] twice penetrated well beyond the Mill and obtained useful information, while Lts. Goodford and May, Sergeants New and Squibb, Lance Corporals Dollery and Morris and Privates Levy, Simcock and Upson were also 'brought to notice' for patrol activities. An advanced post had been established quite close to the Mill, so that that spot was much easier to approach and at night we usually had men posted in the gateway to wait for

[1] He had been relieved as Adjutant of the 3rd Battalion by Captain Aitchison, the latter having recovered from his wounds. In September all Captains of 15 years service and upward were promoted to Major, the promotion extending to Captain Symes, who was still with the Egyptian Army, as was also Captain Mills. 'Pre-war' subalterns, if not already promoted to temporary rank, as had several Gazetted since the outbreak of war.

[2] Transferred to a Service battalion of the Irish Rifles as Adjutant in December.

any inquisitive Germans. One misty morning in November gave the battalion a chance: the mist suddenly cleared, exposing to view some 20 Germans on the top of their parapet, and the good target thus offered before they realized their peril was not missed. If the very wet weather made life in the trenches most unpleasant, parcels with every variety of comforts and extra food were arriving regularly from home and were very welcome, and when out of the line men could reckon on being able to get cleaned and to be really very comfortable. Things were better than they had been at ' Plugstreet '.

Meanwhile another battalion of the regiment had reached France. The 12th had spent the summer at Sutton Veney, where its Division was completing its training despite considerable difficulties over equipment, a matter of ' first formed, first equipped '; if the reserve supplies had hardly sufficed for ' K 1 ', ' K 2 ' and ' K 3 ' fared progressively worse, and for many months they had to put up with makeshifts and improvisations, the R.A. being especially handicapped. Many changes, both in officers and other ranks occurred: several veterans who had done good service in helping to form the battalion and in inculcating in its ex-civilians the ideas and standards of disciplined soldiers could not meet the medical requirements for active service and had to be replaced, mainly from the 13th Battalion. Despite all its difficulties before going overseas the 12th had reached a good level all round, though it was a bare twelve months since its formation had been authorized.

Leaving Sutton Veney early on September 20th the 12th Hampshire [1] had an uneventful passage from Southampton to Havre, landing early on the 26th and entraining for Longeau, whence three marches took them to Gentelles near Amiens. On the way they were inspected by Sir Charles Monro, to whose Third Army their Division had been allotted, and again, just as they reached Gentelles, by their Corps commander, Lt. General H. F. M. Wilson,[2] G.O.C. Twelfth Corps. After ten days training and route-marching at Gentelles, the battalion moved to Cachy on October 8th to be initiated into trench warfare by the Twenty-Seventh Division,[3] head-quarters with C and D Companies being instructed by the 3rd/60th, A and B, under the second in command, Major Bazalgette, by the 2nd K.S.L.I. No casualties were suffered during this ' inoculation ', after which the battalion returned to Gentelles for further training, including a strenuous two days' tactical exercise (October 15th/16th) which tested fitness severely, the battalion's mere handful of stragglers testifying to its fitness. Just before this Lt. Colonel Majendie of the 60th had replaced Colonel Walker, who had done so much to make the battalion and train it on sound lines but, like other officers of his seniority, could hardly be expected to be physically equal to the exacting strain of trench-warfare, especially in winter, severe enough even for much younger men.

[1] 30 officers and 883 other ranks. Unfortunately the battalion's diary does not detail the officers and the destruction of the Part II Orders makes it impossible to give their names.
[2] Formerly G.O.C. Fourth Division.
[3] Then in line South of the Somme, the Third Army having taken over more line.

A move to Cardonette on October 21st brought no change in occupations and after a week the battalion moved on to Chipilly, for further instruction under the Fifth Division, in line just North of the Somme. Before it could go into the line its Division was selected for transfer to Salonica, and accordingly the 12th marched back to Beaucourt, where they spent a week, preparing for the move, which involved some re-equipment, the transport exchanging its horses for mules, and then, on November 11th, 29 officers and 845 men entrained at Longeau for Marseilles. There the battalion embarked in the S.S. *Canada* along with the 79th Brigade head-quarters, sailing for Alexandria on November 15th.

The 12th Battalion's departure for Salonica left the 1st as again the only Hampshires in France, but just before the end of 1915 the 11th arrived and doubled the regiment's representation. The Sixteenth Division's training had been much retarded, not till late in August could it leave Kilworth Camp for Aldershot and the final stages of its preparation. Eventually December found the Division reported as fit to go overseas, and on December 18th the 11th Hampshire, who had been quartered at Pirbright, crossed from Southampton to Havre, going on by train to Chocques, whence they marched to Noeux les Mines. Lt. Colonel Crockett now had Major G. H. Earle [1] as his second in command, Captain Berkeley as Adjutant and Lt. Davies as Quartermaster. Majors Palmer and Bell [2] and Captains Hazard [3] and Andrews commanded the companies, with Captains Stacke, Bland, Powell and Thyne under them and no less than 21 subalterns.

The 11th's first work was to erect huts for other units of the Division, with some road-making and boring wells, while though the Division did not go into the trenches till well into the New Year, parties of the 11th were sent up before that to assist the Forty-Seventh Division in wiring and entrenching.

Shortly before the end of 1915 Sir John French's final dispatch had been published, which ' mentioned ' Captains Wyld and and Hume, 2/Lts. Dale, Goodford, Harding, May, Rodocanachi (3rd Battalion, attached O.B.L.I.), M.T. Smith, Stevens and Ward (attached M.G. School) C.Q.M.S. Wheeler and Sergeants Ley and Price, together with Lt. General Haking, Brigadier General Nicholson and Captain Garsia, all three on the staff. The ' New Year Honours ' brought General Haking the K.C.B., Brigadier Generals Nicholson and de Winton the C.B. and C.M.G. respectively, Captains Garsia, Hume and Wyld and 2/Lts. Goodford, Harding and M. T. Smith the M.C., while Colour Sergeant Shearing, Sergeants Budden and Ley and Privates Eldridge and Harden were awarded the D.C.M.

The New Year, which saw the 11th Hampshire start their apprenticeship

---

[1] From the 3rd Battalion, which he had rejoined early in 1914 after serving in the Inniskilling Dragoons.
[2] A Winchester master and an O.T.C. officer.
[3] One of several former officers of the Volunteer battalions who had rejoined.

to war, brought little change to the 1st Battalion, but before the end of the first quarter of 1916 two more battalions of the regiment had reached France, the 2nd arriving from Egypt in March, in which month the 14th also came out, while the 15th followed in May, so that when ' the Somme ' started on July 1st five Hampshire battalions were on the Western Front, a number never exceeded during the war.

The 1st Battalion continued on the Hamel front all January, but being ' out ' on January 4th it escaped one heavy bombardment which almost obliterated the right company's usual trenches. These it had to re-dig when next in the line and in doing so dug out an East Lancashire private, who had survived under a pile of debris for six days and was not seriously damaged. Much attention was now being paid to instruction in bombing, and another feature of the period was the issue of ' tin hats ', shrapnel-proof steel helmets, with which all ranks were soon provided. In an encounter on January 21st near the Mill in the Ancre marshes [1] the battalion had the misfortune to lose 2/Lt. Wilde, who had been very successful in patrolling, another of his party being reported as missing, though two others who were wounded succeeded in escaping, but several successes for the battalion's snipers afforded some compensation, while its patrols continued their activities with good results, one under 2/Lt. May [2] having a satisfactory brush near ' the Ravine ' on January 23rd, using a rifle grenade most effectively. Several fresh subalterns were warmly welcomed, the battalion being so short of officers that ' duties ' were becoming rather burdensome.

February 5th saw the battalion beginning its first long rest since reaching France. This was in billets at Beauval, far enough back to be merely reminded of the war by the sound of distant gunfire. After ten days here it moved to Lucheux, having to cover twelve miles in heavy rain. Here the billets were good and the people cordial, and the battalion could settle down to a programme of training, which was about equally impeded by bad weather, ' real winter ' with much snow and very cold, and by the difficulty of finding ground not under cultivation which could be used for field exercises and for football and athletic sports. A move to Beaudicourt followed early in March, a month marked by a Brigade Assault at Arms and a Horse Show, the battalion winning the former and doing quite well in the Horse Show. Several drafts joined, with Captain Bonham Carter of the 3rd Battalion who had served in South Africa with the 1st Volunteer Service Company and had more recently seen more fighting in East Africa,[3] but Colonel Palk had to go to hospital, Major Middleton taking over command. Towards the end of March the Fourth Division went into the line again South of Arras [4] where the battalion was at first employed

---

[1] The Third Army's frontage had been reduced since the departure of the Twelfth Corps to Salonica but now extended Eastward across the Ancre to the Somme.

[2] He was awarded the M.C. in June, primarily for his good work on patrol.

[3] He was well over 40 but stood the strain better than some younger men.

[4] On the frontage recently taken over from the French, to set troops free to reinforce the defenders of Verdun.

on second-line trenches (A Company), road-mending (B and C) and wood-cutting and hurdle-making (D). This seemed to many hardly the best use for a fine fighting battalion, but labour for such work was scarce and the state of the roads a serious handicap to the development of offensive plans. Several officers now took the chance to visit the 2nd Battalion, recently arrived from Egypt and in billets nearby at Louvencourt. Then in the last week of April the battalion returned to the front line, this time East of Fonquevillers, where it found that heavy rain had turned the trenches into a mass of sticky yellow mud, while the enemy were inclined to be busy, using rifle-grenades and trench-mortars freely, to which our machine-guns replied, often very effectively. The rain had reduced some communication trenches to mere drains and the line needed a lot of work. Casualties were not numerous, barely a dozen, but the officers were very unlucky, Captain Westmorland was hit by a sniper on April 29th when taking ranges and in the same week three, Lt. V. C. Smith and 2/Lts. Sims and Swettenham, were wounded by shell-fire.

This spell in trenches was very short, the Division being ' out ' nearly all May, training. The Hampshire were constantly on the move, once or twice in great heat,[1] and sampled a great variety of places, Auteuil (May 3rd–6th), Longuevilliers (May 6th–14th), Yvrencheux (14th–21st), where the brigade rehearsed its part in the coming attack over ground similar to its intended objective, and finally Bertrancourt (May 23rd–June 10th), where the battalion was employed in digging assembly trenches. On May 18th Lt. Colonel Palk rejoined, Lt. Colonel Middleton transferring to the 2nd Battalion.

On June 11th the battalion left Bertrancourt for Beauval, had three days rest there and then moved to Beausant and Mailly, putting in some final work on the assembly trenches, mainly carried on at night, and practising the attack. From June 26th to 29th it was in front line NW. of Beaumont Hamel and then, after a very brief spell ' out ' for final preparations, moved up again on the evening of June 30th in readiness for the assault. It had been a little dis-couraging that, despite the deluge of shell to which the German lines had been subjected, the discharge of smoke on the Division's front, after four days' bombardment, aimed at drawing the German fire, had produced so vigorous a reply from machine-guns and artillery as to make it doubtful if, after all, the bombardment had been as effective as the higher authorities calculated.

Meanwhile the 11th Battalion had come in for some fairly lively times. The Loos sector, behind which their Division was concentrated, was far from ' quiet ', the Forty-Seventh Division, though much below establishment, was holding a long frontage and welcomed the 11th's assistance, C and D Companies under Major Earle going up on January 11th to relieve its Pioneers. This party had plenty of hard work and suffered several casualties, and on January 22nd the battalion undertook its first minor operation, a detachment under 2/Lt. Donni-thorne assisting to consolidate a new crater near the Double Crassier, SE. of

---

[1] On one march of 15 miles some men of other regiments died, but the Hampshire came through well, with the least number of men falling out in the brigade.

Loos. Directly our mine went up the Pioneers dashed forward and started work, though under heavy fire, redoubled when German flares went up and the men showed up clearly against the white chalk thrown up by the explosion. They stuck to their task, however, encouraged and directed effectively by 2/Lt. Donnithorne who, though wounded, refused to go back till all the other wounded had been succoured and the work had been done.[1]

The 11th's total casualties for January came to three killed and 44 wounded, including shell-shock cases, while their work was much commended by the Forty-Seventh Division, whose G.O.C., on the battalion being relieved on January 10th, warmly praised its steadiness under fire, its good discipline and its hard work.

Until the middle of March the battalion was ' out ', mainly working in quarries or under the Forest Control. An epidemic of measles sent many men and several subalterns to hospital, but the February casualties were little over 20, including 2/Lt. Tollemache wounded. A spell in March at Mazingarbe under the Fifteenth Division was chiefly notable for snow and generally bad weather, but good work was done and the line much improved.

Early in April the Sixteenth Division took over the Northern portion of the Loos salient and the 11th Hampshire reverted to its command. But under whatever Division they were the Pioneers were always busy, some in the front line, others on communication trenches and rear areas. One piece of work which earned special praise was the virtual reconstruction of Railway Alley, a communication trench running North of Loos to the front near Chalk Pit Wood. Casualties, though frequent, were never heavy, and some small drafts with several officers from the 13th Battalion filled up the gaps, caused more by sickness and various ' employments ' than in action. April 27th brought an intense bombardment of our Hulluch and Chalk Pit Wood sectors, followed up by the release of gas and an attack in some force. Several parties entered our lines only to be promptly counter-attacked and driven out, while the corpses visible in No Man's Land testified to the efficiency of our counter-bombardment and rifle and machine-gun fire, but repairing the badly damaged trenches gave the 11th strenuous work. A renewed gas-attack two days later caused heavy casualties, but this time the Germans never reached our trenches, while they suffered severely from their own weapon when a shift of wind carried the gas back over their lines. This gave the 11th more damage to repair under harassing machine-gun fire, while on the night of May 1st/2nd bombers who had forced an entrance into our lines gave a wiring-party under Captain Hazard the chance to help in driving them out, Captain Hazard's successful leading of his bombers and recovery of the lost ground earning him the M.C., the second awarded to the 11th.

The middle of May brought the battalion a shift, into the defences of Loos, from which detachments went forward to work in the front line. Outstanding incidents were few, though both sides did some raiding, but in this quarter no major operations were projected and we merely sought to keep our line intact

[1] He was awarded the battalion's first M.C.

and harass the enemy, so as to prevent him thinning his line. Casualties, seven killed and missing and 2/Lt. Pearce and 21 men wounded, were not heavy, considering how much was done and the enemy's increasing activity with rifle-grenades and aerial torpedoes.

June the 11th spent in the Loos salient. Thunderstorms and heavy rain produced much mud and impeded work and casualties were heavier than in May, Captain Wellsted, the first officer of the 11th to lose his life, being killed on June 29th when the Germans bombarded our lines and back areas vigorously, the Quartermaster, Lt. Davies, being slightly wounded. This may have been in retaliation for a successful raid two days previously by the 7th Leinster, following mine explosions at Harrison's and Hart's Craters near the Double Crassier. Consolidating the new craters gave the 11th plenty of work, and then, on June 30th, the First Division attacked near the Double Crassier to distract the enemy's attention from the opening of our offensive on the Somme, and the 11th stood to, ready to help consolidate any gains, while their machine-guns supported the attack, whose failure left the 11th with nothing to consolidate.

The 2nd Battalion meanwhile had reached Alexandria on January 13th and on landing was dispatched to Suez. Under 600 all told had left Gallipoli, but reinforcements amounting to over 450, including nearly 200 of the battalion's own convalescents, brought numbers up to establishment, so that companies could be re-formed with four platoons. Sixteen new officers appeared, among them Lt. Arnell, who had left the battalion in South Africa in 1910 as a Sergeant to join the Rhodesian Police and had recently seen active service in German South West Africa. At Suez much-needed refitting and re-equipping was possible, with some company training, and nearly 160 men were given instruction as ' grenadiers '. The last week of February saw the battalion employed on the Shaluffa defences across the Canal, but by then the threat of a Turkish attack in force on Egypt and the Canal had virtually vanished. If the Turks had held us at Gallipoli, the achievement had fairly crippled them and their heavy losses had left them incapable of developing their expected counter-offensive. If they managed to reinforce Mesopotamia and clinched their hold on the beleagured Kut, against Egypt they were impotent, and it was soon evident that the large force available there could be safely reduced, the Twenty-Ninth Division being among the first formations to be transferred to France, where German pressure on Verdun was making it urgent that the British Armies should take over more line to allow of the French troops thus set free reinforcing the hard pressed defence. March 15th found the 2nd Hampshire at sea again, Marseilles being reached on March 21st. Several attached officers had rejoined their own units, among them Captain Kingsley-Darling and Lt. Cowan. Major Spencer-Smith was still in command and Captain Lord Adjutant, Lt. Cornish was Machine-gun officer, Captain Cardy Transport officer, 2/Lt. Miller was officiating as Quartermaster and Captains Cuddon (W), Arnell (X), Jones (Y), and Field (Z) commanded the companies. R.S.M. Tyler and R.Q.M.S. Sumner were among the very few present at ' the landing ' who had never been away from the battalion, others being Orderly Room Sergeant Thompson, Sergeant-Cook Holman, Sergeant-Shoemaker Crease, Sergeant-Drummer Holman, C.S.M's Bird and Salmon, C.Q.M.S. Penney and Sergeants Norris, Ghell and Woolford.

The Twenty-Ninth Division was now allotted to the Third Army, joining the Fourth Division in the Eighth Corps [1] under its old G.O.C., General Hunter-Weston, so that both Regular Hampshire battalions were close together, though by March 1916 ' pre-wars ' still with either battalion were but a handful, if many others who had enlisted since August 1914 had already served in both battalions. The 2nd Battalion's first quarters were at Vauchelles les Quesnoy, whence it moved early in April to Louvencourt. Much re-equipping was necessary, with instruction in gas-drill, a new feature to troops from Gallipoli, and other training. Leave to England was given as freely as possible and the battalion welcomed back the Quartermaster, in time to be present along with Major Spencer-Smith and the Adjutant at a dinner given by General Hunter-Weston on April 25th to the officers who had been at ' the landing '.

The 2nd Hampshire were in Divisional reserve at Mailly-Maillet from April 13th to 23rd and then took over the line opposite Beaumont-Hamel. The trenches were in bad condition after heavy rain, but things were generally ' quiet ' and less rifle ammunition was expended than at Gallipoli, though opportunities of hampering and harassing the enemy with rifle and machine-gun fire were not neglected, several German working parties being dispersed.[2] while their ' minenwerfer ' were successfully discouraged. An attempted raid under 2/Lt. Saunders on April 29th near Mary Redan found the enemy on the alert and lining their parapet in strength: the raiders nevertheless, using a Bangalore torpedo and finishing off the last two feet of the wire with hand-cutters, got within bombing range, but they could not force their way in and had to retire after throwing their bombs. An effort to cut them off was checked by our machine-guns and by Corporal Lark, who covered the retirement most effectively, while some Germans who started crawling forward as though to counter-attack were caught by Lewis gun fire and driven back. Our casualties were one man killed and two wounded, both of whom 2/Lt. Saunders brought in to our line, going back into No Man's Land for the second man. Two nights later a raid on one of our saps was beaten back, and when, after a sharp but brief bombardment, the Germans collected for another attempt, they were effectively dispersed by our fire, our casualties being only three killed and five wounded. Much useful information about the enemy's defences and the work in progress was obtained by our patrols and passed on to the artillery.

From May 3rd to 18th the battalion was out of the line and had ten days in Corps reserve before going back to the firing line at Mary Redan on May 18th. Lt. Colonel Middleton joined on the 21st and took command and a dozen officers

---

[1] Holding the frontage from the Ancre Northward.

[2] Thus on the night of April 25th enemy were heard hammering stakes into some ' dead ground near one of our sap heads, so a Lewis gun was taken forward to the end of our sap and the work came to a quick conclusion.

arrived, mainly from the 3rd Battalion, while drafts amounting to 120 filled up the ranks. Until May 28th the 2nd remained in front line, having a quiet time though our patrols were active; our snipers now scored several successes, reducing the German snipers almost to inactivity, while good work was done on communication trenches. From May 28th to June 6th the battalion was in Divisional support at Mailly-Maillet and then had a week at Louvencourt, practising the attack over ground marked out to resemble the trenches to be assaulted. Eight quiet days on its old front opposite Mary Redan followed, after which it went back to Louvencourt for final preparations. Seven officers and about 100 men joined during June and, with only 30 casualties, 40 officers [1] and 950 other ranks were available for the big attack, in which the 88th Brigade was to be in reserve.

As late-formed a Division as the Thirty-Ninth had naturally had to wait for weapons and equipment, and in consequence its training had been much retarded. The Division had not been brought together until October 1915 when it was assembled round Winchester, and even after that one infantry brigade had been reconstituted.[2] A move to Witley followed in November, and there the Division remained till ordered in February 1916 to mobilize. Shortly before this the infantry had fired their musketry course at Aldershot, having only just previously received Service rifles. Many changes had occurred among the personnel [3] and the 14th Hampshire who went overseas differed considerably from the original battalion. Lt. Colonel Hickie (Royal Fusiliers), who had taken over from Colonel Ramsbottom-Isherwood in January, was in command, with Major Furley as senior Major and Captain Finlay [4] as Adjutant.

Leaving Witley on March 5th, the battalion crossed that night from Southampton to Havre and went on up country by train to a concentration area round Blaringhen. Its Division had been allotted to the First Army and received its initiation to war under the 23rd Brigade in a sector which no Hampshires had yet visited, at Laventie, opposite the Aubers ridge.

The 14th Hampshire were unlucky in their first experience in the trenches, as all C Company's kit and rations was destroyed by a heavy bombardment and 2/Lt. Langdon was mortally wounded. After undergoing the usual introductory process the battalion was first put into the line on its own at Givenchy on April 14th, and for several months it did duty here or South of the La Bassée Canal at Cuinchy or further North at Festubert, going usually to Riez du Vinage or Annequin when 'out'. This part of the front was less unattractive in the spring and early summer than when autumn and winter rains reduced much of it to swamps, in which flooded trenches had to be replaced by breast-

[1] Captains Cuddon (W), Arnell (X), Jones (Y) and Massey (Z) were commanding the companies, none of which had less than six subalterns : orders had, however, been issued that only 25 officers were to take part in any attack.

[2] Eventually one brigade was left behind and replaced by four Territorial battalions already in France. The composition of the 116th Brigade was not changed.

[3] Here also the loss of the Part II Orders is much to be regretted. The diary does not detail the officers who went out with the battalion.

[4] Formerly of the Leinster.

works and isolated ' island ' posts.[1] Mining activity had left the drier ground at Givenchy a tangle of craters and was still going on, the 14th losing Lt. ~~G. L.~~ Y. L Ellis and C.S.M. Graham in a mine explosion on May 28th. The battalion made its first raid at Cuinchy on June 7th, when a party under Lt. Ashmore, effectively covered by another under 2/Lt. Fairlie-Cunninghame, got into the German trenches and did some useful bombing, driving the trench garrison back some way and inflicting several casualties, only five of the 20 raiders being wounded. Before this Lts. Moxley, ~~Y. P.~~ Ellis and Ashmore had all carried out patrols with considerable success and several N.C.O.s and men were commended by the Brigadier [2] for good work on patrol and in wiring. Several drafts from the 13th and 16th [3] Battalions kept the ranks fairly full, though casualties were rather heavy for a ' quiet ' part of the front, the total up to June 30th coming to 24 killed and 42 wounded, including 2/Lt. F. C. H. Gilbert, killed in April on his first day in the trenches, apart from those suffered on June 30th, when the 12th and 13th Royal Sussex attacked the Boar's Head, a salient East of Richebourg St. Vaast, A Company of the Hampshire holding part of our original front, while the other three were in readiness to exploit success.

This attack was another of the diversionary operations undertaken to assist the opening of the ' Somme '. The attackers carried their first objective, but their losses were heavy and the attack provoked an immediate retaliation which prevented consolidation, let alone exploitation, and eventually drove the survivors of the assaulting battalions back to our lines, which meanwhile had been heavily bombarded, the 14th having early 50 casualties, including Lt. Allen and 2/Lt. Sangster wounded and eight men killed. Several men did good work in bringing in the wounded, Sergeants Byrne, Gibbons and Lee and Corporal Midlam making rescues in broad daylight.

The 15th Battalion reached France two months after the 14th. Like the Thirty-Ninth, the Forty-First Division had had to contend against many difficulties in training, and not till it was collected in the Aldershot area in October [4] 1915 and received short Lee Enfields, Mark III, with proper equipment for training signallers and other specialists, could very serious progress be made. In Major General Lawford, formerly a brigadier in the Seventh Division, the Forty-First was fortunate in its G.O.C.: he worked it hard but developed no small degree of efficiency, and after the Division was concentrated during February in Aldershot itself for final training, progress was rapid. Lt. Colonel Malone, who had taken command in September 1915, when Colonel O'Farrell went to the 16th Battalion, vacated command in February, being succeeded by

---

[1] Corporal King distinguished himself by crossing over in broad daylight to one of these islands ' to bandage two wounded men.

[2] Brigadier General M. L. Hornby.

[3] Formed in September 1915 from the reserves of the 14th and 15th, Lt. Colonel O'Farrell taking command : like the 13th it was a draft-finding unit, becoming part of the Training Reserve early in 1917.

[4] The battalion had spent most of 1915 at Portsmouth, moving first to Witley in Surrey and then into barracks at Aldershot.

Lt. Colonel Harvey, formerly of the O.B.L.I., but in April he also retired, being replaced by Lt. Colonel Cary-Bernard of the Wiltshire who had gone out with the B.E.F. in August 1914. A most competent and efficient commander, he did much to ' make ' the 15th, which was to earn a fine reputation under his command.

Before the end of April the Division[1] was ready for service overseas, and after an inspection by the King on April 26th departure was not long delayed, the 122nd Brigade crossing to Havre on May 1st. Its destination was the Hazebrouck area, the 15th Hampshire going first to Meteren. From May 10th to 27th parties were sent to the Ninth Division for their preliminary dose of trench warfare, one party which was attached to the 11th Royal Scots coming in for a violent bombardment. This was followed by a raid, some enemy entering our line to be promptly expelled without reaching their apparent objective, the shaft of one of our mines. The Hampshire party took its share in repulsing this attack, Captain Amery and 2/Lts. Afriat and Pearse being commended for their coolness and resource, and was lucky in escaping with under a dozen casualties.

After a short spell in reserve the brigade took over on May 30th trenches in ' Plugstreet Wood ' of which the 1st Hampshire had seen so much in the ' first winter '. Its line turned West at the NE. angle of the wood and in places had been pushed slightly forward since 1915. The Division promptly started to harass the enemy, using rifle-grenades fairly freely and being active in patrolling and small raids. Lts. Gates and Peterson, who were soon prominent in patrolling, had one narrow escape from capture but got back all right, and the battalion had the best of several minor encounters, notably on June 23rd when a patrol under Sergeant Learey met ten Germans close to the enemy's wire, knocked out several with bombs and brought in all its own wounded. The battalion's snipers and machine-gunners scored several successes, and then on June 30th the 15th tried its first raid; three parties under Lts. James and Gates and Sergeant Green leaving our trenches after the enemy's lines had been drenched with gas. One party got within bombing range and threw its bombs, apparently with good effect, but the others were hampered by our own gas and could not get in, and eventually the raiders had to return, having had eight casualties. Lt. Gates, after seeing his men back into our trenches, returned into No Man's Land with Corporal Murden and Private Parris to bring back Sergeant Green's body from close to the enemy's wire and, despite heavy machine-gun fire, recovered it.[2] The raid provoked violent retaliation and the day's casualties came to nearly 40, including ten killed, but still it had apparently achieved its purpose in drawing the enemy's attention and making them apprehensive of an attack and the Divisional commander congratulated the battalion warmly on its spirited effort.

[1] The 15th was in the 122nd Brigade (B. General Towsey) along with the 12th E. Surrey, 16th R. W. Kent and 18th K. R. R. C.
[2] Lt. Gates received the M.C. and the two men the M.M.

CHAPTER XII

SALONICA, 1915–1916

To the decision to abandon the Gallipoli enterprise the development of a new drain on the Allies' military resources had contributed appreciably: assistance had to be sent to Servia. The transfer to Salonica of the Tenth Division and nearly half the French contingent may not have materially affected the tactical situation at Gallipoli, but any chance of the substantial reinforcement necessary for a renewed effort to force the Straits was rendered most unlikely when a big effort was required to succour the junior partner in the alliance, who had done so well in beating off the first attacks of the Austrians in the autumn of 1914 but was now threatened with an attack in greater force, directed by Germans and combined with a flank attack in strength from Bulgaria.

The renewed offensive against Servia had been made possible by the Austro-German successes in Poland against Russia, which, together with our failure to achieve a real success at the Dardanelles, had decided Bulgaria to join the Central Powers. The Servians had been quite unable to resist the double attack, while the Bulgarian advance not only took them in flank and rear but interposed between them and the Allied troops who landed at Salonica early in October, too late, as it proved, to gain touch with them. Overwhelmed and outnumbered, the Servian armies were pressed Southward and Westward and driven to the desperate expedient of crossing the mountains of Albania and Montenegro in the hope of being taken off by Allied vessels should they reach the shores of the Adriatic. This object a substantial portion eventually achieved after desperate efforts and great sufferings, while the Allied advance from Salonica had distracted the Bulgarians sufficiently to prevent their cutting off the Southern wing of the retreating Servians. This work, however, fell mainly on the French, who were able to push three Divisions up the Vardar, where during November they had quite heavy fighting.

Into the tangled story of the Allied relations with Greece and Servia and of the projects and counter-projects for additional Allied action in the Mediterranean, a regimental chronicle need not plunge. Whatever the verdict on the political and strategical considerations which decided the British government to send troops to Salonica, they affected the Hampshire Regiment because not only was the 10th Hampshire transferred from Gallipoli to Macedonia but the four British Divisions sent from France to the new theatre of operations included the Twenty-Sixth and with it the 12th Hampshire. That Division, however, did not reach Macedonia till the Servians were nearing the Adriatic, while what with the trouble caused by the very doubtful Allied relations with Greece and delays over providing transport and equipment, the Tenth Division never reached the front until the French had been driven back down the Vardar. All it could do was to take over a line from the NW. corner of Lake Doiran to Kosturino, on the right of that of which the French were seeking to stand.

The 10th Hampshire had reached Mudros barely 300 strong, and even the reinforcements awaiting them there had not brought them within 50% of establishment, but on October 4th no less than 520 men appeared, mainly transfers from the Bedfordshire and the East Surrey. With them came ten subalterns, including Lt. Lowy left behind with the details when the 10th started for Gallipoli, and when, on October 5th, the battalion embarked again, sharing the H.T. *Clan Macgillivry* with the Royal Irish and the Connaught Rangers, it mustered 19 officers and 947 other ranks. Major Colquhoun had rejoined the Leinster but Captain Lyster of that regiment had replaced him.

The *Clan Macgillivry* was terribly overcrowded, carrying 2,000 men when intended for 1,200, but the voyage was soon over and the evening of October

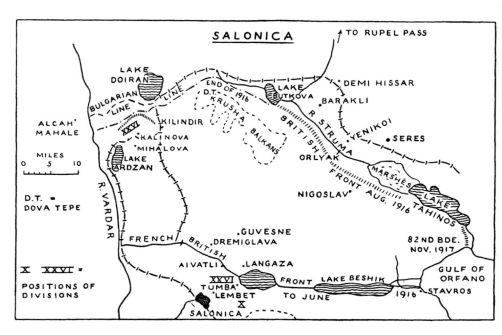

6th found the 10th encamping 2½ miles outside Salonica. Only a few tents were available: heavy rain had turned the clay soil into mud, and the constant fatigues impeded training and made it difficult for officers to get their companies and platoons into shape. Moreover as the Division's transport had been left in England it had to make shift with that of another Division: its own artillery had been likewise replaced by any brigades available in Egypt: great shortages of essential equipment existed and could not be quickly made good, and when at last the Division advanced it was far from ready for service, being still short of numbers and equipment. Meanwhile route marches were attempted, with a brigade field day and other instruction in open warfare, the bare and rocky hills, intersected by gullies and with steep gradients, providing useful preparation for what was actually in store. Bad weather did not make things easier and many men went sick, the ' effective strength ' on October 31st being down to 860, though 35 men under Lt. Scott had rejoined with the battalion transport on October 25th. Early in November Major Scully of the Royal Irish replaced Captain Lyster, while on November 14th 2/Lt. Grellier rejoined on recovery from his Sari Bair wounds. The next day brought orders to move and, that afternoon, 20 officers and 859 other ranks entrained for Doiran, where the battalion arrived early next morning, to encamp SE. of Doiran Town, across the Servian–Greek frontier and near enough to the lake to let the men wash in it.

Two days later the 10th moved forward by Causli to Tatarli, where they were in Divisional reserve, finding two companies to prepare a defensive line on Crete Simonet, a ridge North of Tatarli. They remained here until November 29th, during which time Major Beckett arrived from England and took over command, having recovered from the wounds he had received at Ypres. The weather had turned very cold, with much snow and rain, and the troops in front line, many of them none too well off for clothes and others still affected by their experiences at Gallipoli, went sick in such numbers that the Hampshire and Connaught Rangers had to be lent to the 30th Brigade to allow its two most depleted units to be brought back into reserve and given a chance to recover.

The battalion now found itself on the Dorsale des Cinq Arbres, a rocky ridge North of Kajarli, formerly occupied by the French, whose siting of the trenches excited much criticism. ' So badly sited originally that little could be made of them ' is one account.[1] The line was on a forward slope, exposed to the enemy on higher ground across a valley, and rocky ground made satisfactory defences hard to construct, especially as work had to be carried on in full view of the enemy and under fire. The wiring of the line was very imperfect, but no more wire was available, while not enough tools were to be had. Snow and frost increased the strain on officers and men, to provide hot food was almost impossible, everything had to be carried up to the line by hand over steep ground slippery with ice, and the men were very severely tried. On December 2nd 20 men went sick with frost-bite and, when it thawed, the trenches filled with slush, while foggy weather concealed the enemy's movements and meant that extra vigilance in patrolling was necessary. The Bulgarians, who were collecting in force opposite the Division, contented themselves at first with shelling our line, sometimes quite heavily, while their snipers tried to draw our fire and make our men disclose our positions, without much success, though our artillery replied, apparently to some good purpose, while advantage was taken of any targets the enemy might present; thus on the evening of December 4th parties were seen collecting in front of the Connaught Rangers' right, as if to attack, but a heavy and accurate fire soon discouraged this.[2]

---

[1] *The History of the Connaught Rangers* by Colonel H. F. N. Jourdain, which gives the best and fullest account of these operations and of the hardships endured.

[2] It was intended to evacuate the position on December 12th, and as the 10th and the Rangers had already had a week on end in the line it was proposed to relieve them on the 6th for two days but to bring them back for the evacuation. In view of the exertions involved in the journey to and fro, including a stiff climb on the return, Colonel Beckett and the Rangers' C.O. preferred to stick it out.

The 30th Brigade's line was none too satisfactory, its right formed a salient, being liable to be enfiladed. The key to the position was Rocky Peak, a detached hill SW. of Ormanli, held by two companies of the 31st Brigade, who continued the Division's line to the Hampshire's right, facing almost East. This Rocky Peak was attacked in force on December 6th, when the enemy entered our trenches but was driven out by a counter-attack. This attack was not pressed home on the 30th Brigade's front, though the line had been subjected to heavy shelling and rifle fire, but our rifles got targets in parties which pushed forward and tried to collect in the gullies and ravines in our front. Here dead ground gave them cover, but beyond this cover they failed to advance and during the night our patrols found plenty of evidence of the effectiveness of the 30th Brigade's reply.[1]

Early on December 7th the attack was resumed and in greater force. The shelling was very heavy and before long infantry were pressing forward also. The fog helped them considerably, and they made good use of the dead ground in which they were collecting and which prevented the British guns from giving the infantry really effective support, though our men were able to use their rifles to good effect and kept the enemy at bay. The Bulgarian guns proved very effective, gradually demolishing the ill-sited trenches of the Hampshire and of the Rangers and making their position untenable, while the loss of Rocky Peak, which this time was not retaken, allowed mountain guns and machine-guns to enfilade the position from the right. Up till then the Rangers had been inflicting very heavy casualties on the enemy, and if the Hampshire were rather less favoured by opportunities, they did not neglect what they got. An artillery officer in describing the action wrote with enthusiasm of the battalion's stubborn resistance. Some 7th R.D.F. had reinforced the Hampshire's right and were soon absorbed into the firing line, but the pressure steadily increased, the Bulgarians were in great force and their heavy losses did not deter their efforts to advance. Eventually about 2 p.m. the Hampshire's left company and, according to one account, the Rangers' right company also had to be withdrawn from their virtually demolished forward trenches to get some shelter behind the crest. This move was unfortunately mistaken by the next company of the Hampshire for the beginning of an ordered retirement, to which it conformed, going right back to Crete Simonet, where the 6th R.D.F. of the Divisional reserve were manning the rear position.[2] Here the company rallied but its retirement had left a gap in the line, which could not be re-established, and the Bulgarians pressed forward, coming to close quarters. A general retirement now became necessary and, covered by Colonel Beckett [3] and a party mainly from battalion head-quarters, it was effected in fairly good order, first to Crete Rivet, where the battalion took post on the right of the 7th R.D.F., and then

[1] The Connaught Rangers' *History* speaks of Bulgarian prisoners admitting to heavy losses on December 6th.

[2] What exactly happened is obscure : the accounts are most conflicting.

[3] The Brigadier's report emphasizes his good work in getting the bulk of the battalion back. Major Scully, 2/Lt. Grellier and Privates Flaxman and Payne were also brought to notice ' for good services '.

back to Crete Simonet. Meanwhile some of the left company had not gone back any further and along with the Rangers held on for some considerable time longer, until eventually they could not maintain their now quite isolated position. On the Crete Simonet line the Hampshire and the 6th and 7th R.D.F. made a successful stand, with the 31st and 29th Brigades on their right prolonging the line North of Tatarli towards Lake Doiran. On the left were

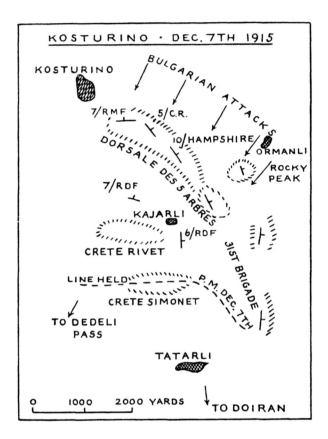

the Rangers, with whom were some 40 Hampshires,[1] and the 7th R.M.F. were covering the Dedeli Pass, with the French beyond them.

If the front line had been lost its capture had evidently cost the Bulgarians dear, as they showed no disposition to press our retreating troops: indeed by daybreak next morning they had not even advanced to Crete Rivet, which two companies of the 6th R.D.F. reoccupied and held for several hours, repulsing several advances, while the troops on Crete Simonet maintained their position until dark. They might have held on longer but that the enemy broke in between two battalions of the 31st Brigade further to the right, and to its

[1] From the left company.

retirement the 30th had to conform, though just as it started to go its rear-guard had the satisfaction of beating off a Bulgarian advance by rapid fire. The evening's retirement, which was unmolested, took the Division no further back than the Kara Bail ridge, which the 29th Brigade and a recently arrived brigade of the Twenty-Second Division were holding, the 10th Hampshire, still under the 30th Brigade, being placed on the left, towards the Dedeli Pass. All ranks were very tired, having had no food for two days, while most men had lost packs and great-coats, but Colonel Beckett had the battalion well in hand and an issue of rations helped to put a better complection on the situation, especially as the Bulgarians made no attempt to follow up their success or to try another attack, rather to the disappointment of the Tenth Division, the Hampshire being reported as in excellent spirits despite all their difficulties and the bad weather. It was intensely cold and the men's cheerfulness and behaviour deserved the greatest praise.

After two bitterly cold but quiet days, practically untroubled by the enemy, a fresh retirement was ordered on December 10th, the Hampshire being directed to Doiran station. One officer and 20 men from each battalion remained behind to conceal the move from the enemy, should he prove more inquisitive than of late. Before daybreak on December 11th the battalion started off. The move was unmolested, though much delayed by the roads being crowded with French troops and transport, who should have been further West, but before midday the Hampshire were South of Doiran station and once more under their own Brigadier. The losses could now be ascertained, killed and missing, mainly the latter, came to 183,[1] wounded to two officers[2] and 86 men, which with those already evacuated sick reduced officers to 16 and other ranks to 480.

As before the enemy had not pressed the retreat. The little rear parties had only seen a few scouts and had got safely away. It seemed as though the Bulgarians did not mean to cross the Greek frontier, behind which the Allies had now withdrawn, and though positions were taken up in readiness to deal with an advance, the 29th Brigade being West of Doiran station, the force was to be withdrawn to Salonica as soon as possible. The brigade had to spend two more cold and trying days on outpost, many were in rags, what clothes they had were soaked with rain and mist and all ranks were nearly exhausted. However, the 30th Brigade started the entraining, the 29th following on December 15th, when the 10th Hampshire marched back to Kilindir, to entrain there, and reached Salonica next morning.

Despite the failure to assist the Servians the Allies had no intention of quitting Macedonia, if they were content to adopt a defensive position covering Salonica. Of this the British took the Eastern portion, extending from just West of Salonica to Stavros on the Gulf of Orfano. Of their 50 miles of front two lakes, Langaza and Beshik, accounted for nearly half, and while three Divisions were allotted to the thirteen miles West of Lake Langaza, one was

---

[1] Of the missing 44 were known to have been wounded. A good many were later reported as prisoners of war.
[2] 2/Lts. Lowy and White.

considered enough for the eight between the lakes together with the four at their seaward end. The Tenth Division was selected to hold these two sectors, the Twenty-Sixth being originally posted just West of Lake Langaza, from Tumba to Aivatli.

The Tenth Division had got back to Salonica much weakened, by sickness even more than by battle casualties, and in great need of refitting. It could be given only ten days for this before having to take up its new line, the 29th

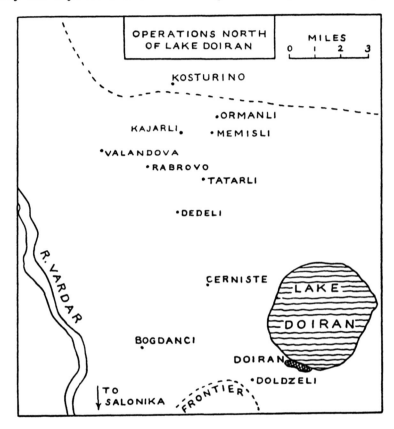

OPERATIONS NORTH OF LAKE DOIRAN

Brigade being sent by sea to take over the portion between Lake Beshik and Stavros, where it landed on December 29th, the Hampshire having their left flank on the lake. They were here just over a month, improving the defences as much as a shortage of tools and their scanty numbers would permit. This last defect was to some extent remedied by the arrival of seven subalterns and 145 men on January 12th, while some stragglers re-appeared, and with returns from hospital, among them Lt. Dupree, other ranks reached 680 by the end of the month. The weather was none too good, with snow and the piercing ' Vardar ' wind, which penetrated even goatskins, but the men worked well and before long the defences were far enough advanced to be held by reduced garrisons.

Accordingly, early in February the Division could be relieved by the Twenty-Seventh and brought back to Salonica, where it was placed in reserve on the Ortiach plateau, SE. of Salonica, and could settle down to a programme of training, varied by quarrying, road-making and preparing a second line of defence. This was to occupy it for the next four months, during which Captains Faith and Hicks rejoined. Captain Davies of the Royal Warwickshire had joined in February as second in command, Major Scully having transferred to the Connaught Rangers. Several other officers joined, including Captain Cowland, who had been in France with the 1st Battalion and at Gallipoli with the 2nd, while drafts brought its numbers well up above 700, though as the weather warmed up the climate began to take its toll of the unacclimatized. In April the battalion was converted to pack-transport, which caused many men to make the better acquaintance of the mule, while slouch hats were issued, giving the battalion something of the appearance of Australians. Some quite strenuous brigade manoeuvres during April included much picqueting of hills and other training in hill warfare.

The 12th Hampshire, who had reached Salonica on November 25th, after ten days at sea, were undergoing very similar experiences meanwhile, digging, wiring, road-making and training keeping them busy enough, with more training and route marching and less digging as the defences grew stronger. Incidents were few. The battalion was at Lembet Camp most of December, moved forward on the 20th to take over Langaza village as an advanced post and thereafter until June was either forward at Langaza or back in support or reserve in the Lembet valley. The work on the defences was heavy, the ground was rocky, and with hardly any explosives to assist the men's picks and shovels what they accomplished when so ill-equipped did them no little credit. The War Diary makes rather monotonous reading. The usual record runs ' Work on trenches —musketry—various fatigues ' with an occasional ' Battalion exercise in hills —picqueting in advance '.

Various changes occurred, mainly through invalidings, with some promotions and transfers. Lt. Colonel Majendie returned to the 60th in June to command the 4th Battalion, being replaced by Major Baker of the Royal Fusiliers, who soon returned to his own regiment, when Major Tweedie of the Gloucestershire took over but transferred to the 12th Lancashire Fusiliers in July, command then passing to Major Koebel of the North Staffordshire. Before this the battalion had shifted early in June to Dremiglava, NW. of Langaza, moving after a fortnight to another camp at Summerhill but without much change in its occupations. With the weather getting hotter sickness increased, though only in the Struma valley was malaria much in evidence.

The first half of 1916, eventful enough on other fronts, passed uneventfully at Salonica. If an Allied offensive in this quarter had ever been contemplated ' Verdun ' put an end to it. Most of the troops evacuated from Gallipoli had to be hurried from Egypt to France, one Division was rushed off to Mesopotamia to succour the beleaguered garrison of Kut, and though the expected Turkish offensive against the Suez Canal never developed Egypt could not be denuded of troops, and those at Salonica remained too few for a major offensive but uneconomically numerous when immobilized by merely facing an enemy who showed no inclination to attack. General Sarrail, the French Commander-in-Chief at Salonica, may have entertained ideas of an offensive; all that happened was that the French established an outpost line on the near side of the Greco-Servian frontier, two British brigades, the 7th Mounted and one of the Twenty-Second Division, being sent forward in April to assist in watching the enemy. The French then brought their main forces forward, taking post from the Vardar Eastward, South of Lake Doiran and into the Struma valley, but though the Twenty-Second Division moved forward (May) to assist them neither the Tenth nor Twenty-Sixth left the Salonica defences.

If it was not desirable to have so many troops idle in Macedonia, at best giving occupation only to Bulgarians who were unlikely to be used anywhere else, many considerations, tactical, administrative and strategical, were against an Allied offensive from Salonica. Still the French would never have agreed to withdraw the troops for use elsewhere or that the British should withdraw and leave the campaign to France to run, even if such a proposal would have been politically acceptable.

At the end of May, Germans and Bulgarians suddenly advanced into the Struma valley, quite unopposed by the Greeks, and thereby, to some extent, forced the hand of the British Commander-in-Chief, General Milne, who now used the Tenth Division to relieve the Twenty-Sixth between Tumba and Aivatli, the Twenty-Sixth moving West and forming an Army Reserve. General Sarrail now announced his intention to adopt an offensive, whatever the British did, and this led to General Milne's agreeing to take over the Allied line from the mouth of the Struma virtually to Lake Doiran. The Tenth Division accordingly advanced to the Struma, early in June, the Twenty-Sixth remaining in the old defence line until the end of July. It then took over the left of the Twelfth Corps' front from Kilindir to just North of Lake Ardzan, the whole British force having now come forward, though East of Lake Doiran French troops interposed between the Twelfth Corps and the Sixteenth in the Struma valley. Roumania seemed now on the point of joining the Allies, in which event the forces at Salonica would be undertaking offensive operations to assist their new ally.

When eventually, towards the end of August, Roumania did take up arms, the Allied offensive was delivered West of the Vardar, with the re-fitted Servian army having the hardest fighting: the British, both on the Doiran and Struma fronts, confined themselves to distracting the enemy by raids and local attacks, some quite considerable affairs, which involved no small aggregate of casualties besides inflicting heavy losses on the Bulgarians. Neither 10th nor 12th Hampshire, however, was required to undertake anything substantial.

When in June its long inactivity had ended, the Tenth Division had advanced from the Ortiach plateau towards the Struma, taking the Seres road. The weather was very hot and the heavily-laden men, still on winter-scale equipment, suffered severely, many falling out exhausted and one dying. On the Division relieving the French between Lakes Tahinos and Butkova (June 11th) the Hampshire were at first in reserve but then took over the Orlyak Bridge defences from the Connaught Rangers. Much work was required here, particularly in wiring, and with the river falling the banks had to be patrolled and posts established at the fords. Fruit, vegetables and eggs could be obtained and the countryside was still green and more attractive than Gallipoli, while the river gave good bathing and shelters of branches covered with waterproof sheets and blankets kept off the sun. Mosquitoes were rampant, so quinine was now a regular daily issue, but nevertheless admissions to hospital were increasing and

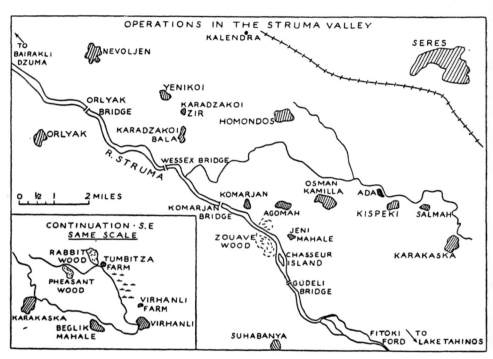

when, after four weeks in this position, the 10th moved back into reserve (July 19th), other ranks fit for duty were down to 440, a fall of over 100 men in three weeks. The battalion now moved back by Aivatli to Dremiglava, the whole Division having been withdrawn into reserve, much reduced in numbers by its brief sojourn in the malaria-infested Struma valley. Major Garsia, who had been attached to the Servian army, now joined, becoming second in command, while any remaining wheeled transport was exchanged for pack. With no drafts and returns from hospital far below admissions, the battalion could only produce one company of reasonable size, after finding all the specialists required,[1] and

[1] These were given on June 4th as bombers 9, Lewis gunners 32, scouts 16, signallers 16, transport 110.

though it had 604 other ranks nominally effective it could only parade 349 when inspected on August 9th by the Divisional Commander, Major General Longley. The other units of the brigade being no stronger, a 29th Composite Battalion was formed on August 21st, each battalion contributing one company, the Hampshire finding the head-quarters under Lt. Colonel Beckett with Major Garsia as second in command and Captain Nicholson as Adjutant, Major Davies commanding the Hampshire company [1] with Captain Clement as his second in command.

This battalion now moved forward again to the Struma [2] and on August 27th relieved the French between Komarjan Bridge and Zouave Wood, three miles downstream. An attack being expected, great vigilance was maintained and many patrols were sent out, one having a successful brush with the enemy near Komarjan, while much useful information about the enemy's dispositions was obtained. The Bulgarians did not attack, and it was the British who took the offensive, the Sixteenth Corps undertaking several raids and local attacks aimed at keeping its opposite numbers from reinforcing the front further West which was being more seriously attacked.

These actions gave the Hampshire their first real clash with the enemy since Kosturino, as the 29th Composite Battalion was to attack the villages of Komarjan and Jeni Mahale on September 15th. On the right two and a half companies under Major Garsia, crossing in rafts to Chasseur Island, made for Jeni Mahale and, well supported by the artillery, worked steadily forward despite the enemy's fire. Having got within 100 yards of the village they assaulted and carried it, the enemy offering a poor resistance and being quickly ousted, to open a heavy fire from Agomah, North of the village. A line was taken up just outside Jeni Mahale in readiness for a counter-attack; none was attempted and, after holding on for about an hour, the detachment withdrew quite unimpeded and in good order, bringing away all its few wounded.

Meanwhile the rest of the battalion under Lt. Colonel Beckett had been equally successful at Komarjan. Assisted by a good barrage from field guns and the brigade machine-gun company, the attackers pressed forward despite heavy fire from front and flanks and cleared the village, taking over 20 prisoners. Here also no counter-attack followed, though heavy fire was maintained on the captured position and the right flank had to be reinforced by Lewis guns from the left. At 7 p.m., as arranged, the troops began falling back and duly recrossed the river at Zouave Ford. The total casualties came to just over 20. less than the prisoners alone, Lt. Tanner, who was among the half-dozen killed, being the only Hampshire casualty.

The Composite Battalion was now in camp for several days, during which the Irish Rifles and Leinster companies were withdrawn, sufficient reinforcements having arrived to allow their battalions to provide independent wings, while on the arrival of seven officers and 112 men from the details at Dremiglava

---

[1] Details not required for the battalion remained at Dremiglava under Captain Faith, who, however, left in September to become Camp Commandant on the L of C, being promoted to Major.

[2] The Tenth Division was coming into line again.

the Hampshire formed a second company, under Captain Grellier, as did the Rangers also. Major Garsia now left the battalion to join the staff of the Twenty-Sixth Division.

To improve his position and to distract the enemy General Briggs [1] was now preparing a really substantial operation, aiming at securing possession of the villages of Karadzakoi Bala, Karadzakoi Zir and Yenikoi, opposite Orlyak. The first two were to be attacked by the 81st Brigade (Twenty-Seventh Division), after which the 30th was to tackle Yenikoi. The 29th Brigade was to cover the flanks, the Composite Battalion protecting the 81st Brigade's right rear by crossing at Wessex Bridge downstream of the main passage and working forward along a nullah which entered the Struma rather lower down.

The attack was delivered early on September 30th, a foggy night having helped to cover the passage and assembly. The bombardment started at 5.45 a.m., half an hour later the infantry advanced and despite stubborn opposition carried Karadzakoi Bala, taking nearly 100 prisoners. The Composite Battalion, which had already crossed the river and collected in a wood, then pushed forward along a sunken road and, having got touch with the 81st Brigade, began to consolidate a line facing SE. and leading back to the river. Beyond a little shelling the enemy did not interfere with the work and by the early afternoon a good line had been dug. Meanwhile Karadzakoi Zir had given more trouble and was only taken after a first effort had been checked. Violent counter-attacks followed, the Bulgarians displaying great determination, coming on again after their first repulse and being only beaten off with some difficulty and after suffering very heavily. The counter-attacks, which went on at intervals for three days, did not extend to the Composite Battalion's front, and it merely continued its consolidation despite the shelling and some rather wild and innocuous rifle fire. It was relieved on October 2nd and moved over to the left, to be in reserve to the 30th Brigade, who next day (October 3rd) attacked and with some difficulty mastered and held Yenikoi against determined counter-attacks. The Composite Battalion had merely found carrying parties and afterwards entrenched a line running back from Yenikoi to the Struma, again being shelled but escaping almost without casualties.

This line was not attacked. The Bulgarians, whose repeated attacks had been heavily punished,[2] had to leave us in possession of the captured villages along with Nevoljen, NW. of Yenikoi, and now retired on a wide front, going back nearly four miles to the foot of the hills. The action had certainly left them depressed and not disposed to try conclusions with the British again.

The Composite Battalion was next placed in line between Yenikoi and Karadzakoi Zir, where it reverted to the orders of its own brigade, and on October 10th on more details coming up from Dremiglava the Rangers and Hampshire resumed their independent formations, though only two companies,

[1] G.O.C. Sixteenth Corps.
[2] Apart from 350 prisoners the dead actually buried considerably exceeded the 1150 British casualties.

Y (Captain Grellier) and X (Captain Clement) could be formed.[1] For the next fortnight the 10th continued in the same line, finding a strong outpost to occupy Kalendra Wood across the Doiran–Constantinople railway, beyond which line the Bulgarians had been drawn back. With the enemy some way off, things had quietened down, apart from some shelling and occasional patrol encounters, and though on October 31st the Twenty-Eighth Division attacked Barakli Dzuma with great success, the 29th Brigade merely covered its right flank and the Hampshire were not seriously engaged, being in reserve until the attacking troops fell back, when the battalion occupied Kalendra Wood and found advanced posts along the railway. Altogether the battalion had had only half a dozen casualties before it was relieved on November 2nd. Both Colonel Beckett and the Adjutant had now to go to hospital, 2/Lt. Harfield taking over the latter's duties.

The lack of recruits from Ireland, to which compulsory service had not been extended, was leaving Irish units much below establishment and several battalions in the Tenth Division had to be amalgamated, whereupon the three Irish Regular battalions in the Twenty-Seventh Division were transferred to the Tenth, the 10th Hampshire in exchange being posted to the 82nd Brigade under Brigadier General Brooke, now in line between the Karadajakois and Komarjan, in which they found the 2nd Gloucestershire, the 2nd D.C.L.I. and the 10th Camerons.[2]

Both General Longley and Brigadier General Vandeleur were warm in their praise of all the 10th had done in the Tenth Division and expressed their regret at losing Lt. Colonel Beckett and his fine battalion. As it turned out the transfer meant that the 10th were to see the war out in Macedonia instead of in Palestine, whither the Tenth Division moved in 1917 in time for General Allenby's penetration of the Gaza–Beersheba line and other subsequent successes, though its Service battalions were broken up or transferred to France before the final victory at Megiddo.

Meanwhile the Allied attacks West of the Vardar were continuing, the Servians making good progress towards Monastir, and though autumn rains were swelling the Struma and its tributaries, so that the valley was getting waterlogged, an active attitude had still to be maintained on the Struma to keep the enemy occupied. The 10th Hampshire thus came in for the last operations attempted that autumn by the Sixteenth Corps, an effort to secure two large farms across the Virhanli stream, which enters Lake Tahinos from the NW. These were attacked on November 16th by the D.C.L.I., the Hampshire taking post in Pheasant Wood, just short of the objective, to cover their left. The D.C.L.I. found the stream unfordable and, after failing to force the passage of a foot-bridge, had to remain out all day, pinned to the ground by the enemy's fire, before darkness allowed them to regain Pheasant Wood, where the Hampshire had spent the day under a steady fire which only caused one casualty.

The battalion was then posted at Karakaska, SW. of Tumbitza Farm, where it

---

[1] Other ranks mustered 420. The rest of the details under Captain Cowland rejoined before the end of October.
[2] A battalion formed from Lovat's Scouts.

had a long line to hold and, being none too strong, might have been hard pressed by a vigorous attack. However, though the battalion was much on the alert no attack came: after the handling they had received at the Karadajakois and Barakli Dzuma, the Bulgars were not feeling aggressive and the weakly-held defences were not tested before, on November 20th, the 10th moved back to Jeni Mahale in reserve. Here they had fairly good quarters and for a time life was a peaceful discharge of routine. Lt. Colonel Beckett and a few convalescents had before this returned from hospital, and the battalion had been re-formed as four companies (November 15th), but it was still very weak, a big draft on its way out having been held up by an outbreak of German measles.

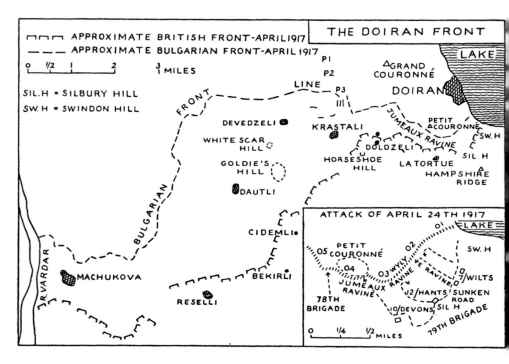

December 4th brought another attempt upon Tumbitza and Virhanli Farms. This time the 10th Hampshire with a Greek battalion acting under Lt. Colonel Beckett's orders moved out towards Beglik Mahale, opposite Virhanli Farm, in readiness to advance against Virhanli Farm and Virhanli in co-operation with an attack from the North by two other battalions who were to cross the stream above Tumbitza Farm. The battalion remained here for two days, its patrols' efforts to reconnoitre Virhanli Farm being checked by heavy fire. It was shelled at intervals and cooking was impossible as the smoke attracted the enemy's gun-fire, but casualties were very few. Then as the main attack had had to be abandoned, the stream again proving unfordable and the passage of the bridge being checked, it went back to Beglik Mahale, where it held on until

December 10th, sending out several patrols, and then recrossed the Struma to Suhabanja to take over the watch between Gudeli Bridge and Fitoki Ford. Here it found quite comfortable quarters in well-built houses with fire-places, which were acceptable when it turned cold and snowed, and for the time could get some rest. All offensive activity had now been suspended and the main occupation was improving the defence line.

The 12th Hampshire's part of the front had seen less activity than had fallen to the 10th in the Struma valley, where the lie of the land had offered more scope for operations than on the Twenty-Sixth Division's frontage near Lake Doiran, West and SW. of which the Bulgarians were strongly entrenched on some forbidding-looking hills behind the deep and narrow Jumeaux Ravine. Of these the Petit Couronné lay South of Doiran, with the lofty Grand Couronné, due West of Doiran, NW. of it. South of the Jumeaux Ravine we were holding part of a lower ridge, running about SW. from the lake, the main features in it being Hampshire Ridge, La Tortue and Horseshoe Hill. Horseshoe Hill, South of the ruins of Dolzeli and S.E. of a rather larger village, Krastali, had been secured by the Twenty-Sixth Division in August, and thereafter a series of minor activities had gradually secured a line running SW. from Horseshoe Hill towards Reselli. A wide No Man's Land invited patrol activities and even raids, several villages in front of the main Bulgarian line being believed to be held as outposts.

The 12th Hampshire had come forward at the end of July to Mihalova, NE. of Lake Ardzan, where they spent the next three weeks in reserve, training and ' on fatigues '. The alarm of an attack then brought them up to support the forward battalions, and though this never developed they remained encamped in a ravine near Kalinova, finding large parties at night to assist the Devons and Wiltshire in entrenching. Their first turn in the front line began on September 2nd, when they relieved the Wiltshire at Cidemli. Things were not very active, except for artillery exchanges, which did little damage and only inflicted three casualties in eight days, two more being incurred by patrols, one fatal, the battalion's first loss in action. From September 10th to 17th the battalion was in support near Kalinova: ' digging and wiring as usual '. It was then back in front line for a week, during which patrols which penetrated to Goldie's Hill near Dautli found it very strongly held. Here one patrol ran into trouble; Lts. M. L. Pearce and W. C. Williams were badly hit and could not get back,[1] but Private Hinley, himself slightly wounded, brought in Corporal West, who had been more severely hit. In its next turn in front line, from October 2nd to 9th, the 12th's patrols did very useful work, Lt. Roberton and 2/Lts. Hale and Frampton bringing in excellent information. This bore fruit when, on the evening of October 11th, D Company raided Goldie's Hill with C in support and A and B as flank guards. D pushed forward behind an admirable barrage, but the enemy did not await the charge and bolted, though one prisoner was secured. On the enemy starting to shell the hill a retirement was duly

[1] They were never heard of again and must have died of wounds.

carried out with only one casualty. Another turn in front line, October 18th to 27th, led to another patrol encounter near Goldie's Hill, and then the Twenty-Second Division took over the sector to let the Twenty-Sixth relieve the French nearer the Lake. Here the 79th Brigade took over the line from the Lake Westward, the Hampshire and Wiltshire sharing the right trenches on Hampshire Ridge, the Devons and D.C.L.I. relieving each other on La Tortue on the left. Eight days ' in ' and eight ' out ' was the routine and little occurred to vary it. With the enemy's line only just across the Jumeaux Ravine, there was no scope for the patrolling which the wide No Man's Land further West had invited. The enemy usually did a little shelling each day, our guns replying, with occasional exchanges of rifle and machine-gun fire, but neither side was inclined to attack strong positions which were steadily being strengthened. Two drafts, one of 100, another of 170, arrived during November and did something to balance the wastage from sickness and other causes. Casualties were low and altogether half a dozen men were killed before the end of the year, though Lt. Reavell was killed in December when a reserve camp was shelled. Major Bazalgette had left in September to take up an appointment in England, Major Barry of the West Somerset Yeomanry replacing him. Major Bazalgette, an old officer of the 3rd Battalion, had done valuable work in helping to make the 12th.

CHAPTER XIII

MESOPOTAMIA, 1916

THE 1/4th Hampshire's head-quarters were being hurried to Kut al Amara because of the collapse of General Townshend's advance upon Baghdad. The great collection of stores and supplies at Kut was in some danger of attack by Turkish irregulars and Arabs, in whom the news of our retreat had excited hopes of plunder, and on reaching Kut on November 29th the Hampshire were promptly set to work to strengthen the defences. Apart from this immediate need, General Townshend had decided to stand at Kut, even at the cost of being invested there, and even half a battalion would be a useful addition to his much reduced British bayonets, the sheet anchor as they were to prove of the defence. Actually only one company of the 4th Hampshire was to share in that defence, for when General Nixon, who reached Kut from upstream on November 28th, tried to go on downstream, he was held up near Sheikh Saad by Arabs and Turks on the river banks and had to return to Kut. Starting off again on December 1st with as many sick and wounded as the available vessels could embark, he succeeded in forcing his way through, thanks to good work by his escort, which included D Company of the Hampshire under Captain Foster. Landing above Orah and working along the bank, keeping level with the gun-boats and the barges carrying the wounded, they thrust the enemy aside and cleared the way. The Arabs were taught to keep their distance by effective rifle fire and Sheikh Saad was safely reached. The company was then sent back upstream to escort another convoy and on its return downstream had a sharp fire-fight at Orah, without disembarking again, but merely firing from the steamer,[1] apparently with good effect as it got the convoy through. Trying again to make its way back to Kut, D found the enemy in too great force on both banks at Orah for a passage to be possible; it had therefore to retire to Ali Gharbi, 50 miles below Kut, where it entrenched a position covering Amara, ten miles further downstream.

The detachment left at Kut[2] now came under the 30th Brigade, which included a wing of the Queen's Own Royal West Kent and the 24th and 76th Punjabis,[3] with whom the 1/4th had co-operated at Nasiriya. This brigade and the 16th were detailed to hold the NW. section of the defences across the neck of the Kut peninsula, being alternatively in front line and in a ' Middle Line ' behind.

In the earlier stages of the siege the Turks pressed the garrison hard, presumably hoping to overcome its resistance before the relieving forces gathering downstream could intervene. They pressed hardest against a fort in the Eastern half of the front and against the 30th Brigade confined themselves almost entirely to fire attacks and to persistent sniping. To this the 30th

---

[1] The G.H.Q. staff joined in the shooting, for once getting a chance in action.
[2] Ten officers and 163 other ranks under Major Footner.
[3] After 1922 4/14th and 3/1st Punjab.

replied vigorously and effectively, there was no shortage of rifle ammunition, and if the Turks managed to push their trenches well forward, in places almost to within bombing range, it cost them not a little. Their efforts against the fort culminated on December 25th, when its garrison's determined resistance ultimately prevailed against particularly violent attacks, the Hampshire and Queen's Own, who worked as a provisional battalion under Major Nelson of the Queen's Own, using their rifles so effectively that on their front West of the main attack the Turkish efforts to advance were not allowed to develope.

The Turk was not the garrison's only enemy; the rising Tigris had also to be feared, and hard as the troops in reserve worked at the ' bunds ' along the

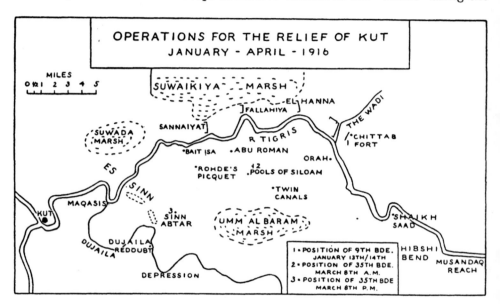

river in hopes of preventing the water breaking through, before the end of January much of our front line and immediate support trenches had been flooded, forcing the defenders to fall back to our Middle Line. As the communication trenches could not be used, they had to retire across the open under heavy fire and had several casualties, but from the Middle Line they retaliated most effectively, the Turks, themselves flooded out of their front line, having to expose themselves in the open. After this, instead of the Turks being only 50 yards away, nearly 1,000 yards separated the main lines, though the Turks occupied some sand-hills in the floods as advanced posts. The defenders did some long-range sniping, but the Turks, whose attacks had cost them very heavy losses, now abandoned any idea of capturing Kut by assault and devoted themselves to keeping the relievers at bay, leaving the garrison to be worn down by starvation.

After the New Year the all-important question was how long the food would last. At first full-scale rations were issued, partly to let the exhausted survivors of Ctesiphon recover condition. The first cut was in the tea ration, reduced by a half on January 20th, four days later half-rations of bread and meat were issued, with only half an ounce of sugar a day. The battery bullocks were the first animals sacrificed, but horse and mule meat soon made an appearance, the officers' chargers and the artillery horses being spared till after the relievers' failure in the Dujaila redoubt operations early in March, after which all ideas of the garrison's co-operating with the relievers had to be dropped. All sorts of expedients were tried to supplement the diminishing rations, fish were caught in the Tigris, weeds and grasses were used as vegetables, some proving poisonous, one officer even used a shot-gun to good effect against the flocks of starlings. Where even necessities were short, all ' comforts ' had long ago disappeared or were reserved for the hospitals.

Naturally on these scanty rations men got steadily weaker and less capable of any hard work, though guards had to be maintained and some work on the trenches could not be avoided. The sick-rate inevitably rose, dysentery affected almost everybody and deaths steadily increased, especially among the wounded. Slowly the siege dragged on, communication was maintained with the outer world by wireless, but the news of the relievers' progress was a succession of disappointments and the efforts to drop food from aeroplanes could do nothing to avert the exhaustion of the garrison and its supplies. When the end came on April 29th over 700 men had already succumbed and few of the remainder were fit for anything—let alone for the awful sufferings they were to undergo in captivity, for which Turkish incompetence and carelessness as well as sheer brutality and cruelty were responsible.

Of the 4th Hampshire in Kut all ten[1] officers survived the siege, of other ranks one return shows 154 ' believed to be prisoners of war ', nine had already died. Of these hardly 40[2] survived the trials of their two and a half years' captivity. Many perished in the terrible march to Asia Minor, which would have tried fit and fresh men severely enough but was a death sentence to men utterly enfeebled by the privations of the siege. Of those who survived to reach the prison camps of Asia Minor most succumbed to the hardships endured there, hard labour under brutal masters on a meagre diet. If the Turks may possibly be acquitted of the deliberate and calculated cruelty of the Japanese, those so unfortunate as to fall into Turkish hands fared little better than the prisoners of another generation.

When the whole situation in Mesopotamia was so radically altered for the worse by Townshend's enforced retreat to Kut, the two Indian Divisions in France were under orders for Mesopotamia, but the transfer was necessarily a lengthy affair, the leading units were not due at Basra till December, and even

---

[1] Major Footner, Captains Floyd, Reeks and Jones (R.A.M.C.), Lts. Forbes, Harris, Patmore, Lacy, Elton and Chitty. R.S.M. Leach, who was also among the prisoners of war, died in captivity after doing outstanding work for his fellow captives. Lt. (later Captain) Harris was awarded the M.C. for his courageous efforts to escape.

[2] 37 attended a dinner organized in their honour at Winchester n February 1919, and a few more were prevented from attending.

before Ctesiphon nearly another Division had been ordered from India to Mesopotamia, where the troops not engaged in the advance on Baghdad only came
to two weak brigades.

The Turks had fortunately been too hard hit at Ctesiphon to press the
retiring troops very effectively, and at first General Townshend's decision to
stand at Kut seemed likely to be justified, the Turkish advance promised to be
held up there till an adequate relieving force could be collected. But to collect
it and even more to provide transport was not easy. The Divisions from France
arrived piece-meal,[1] brigades were mixed up, several had to be changed in composition, and when eventually an advance was begun it was very much a
'scratch' force which went forward, with improvised formations with commanders and troops who did not know each other, short of artillery and transport and shorter of medical staff and equipment.

As reinforcements reached Basra they were promptly sent on to Ali Gharbi,
where the relieving force was concentrating. The bulk of the 1/4th meanwhile
remained at Amara, busy with garrison duties, which fell heavily on a half
battalion. Lt. Colonel Bowker returned from sick leave in India on December
11th and resumed command, and then on December 31st the two companies,
14 officers and 350 other ranks, left Amara by boat for Ali Gharbi, which they
reached next day, rejoining D Company, who had been busy with outpost duties
and fatigues and had been much worried by Arab snipers.

January 4th saw the Seventh (Meerut) Division start the advance, the 1/4th
Hampshire following two days later. They had been allotted to an incomplete
9th Brigade, with half the 2nd Rajputs and the 107th Pioneers. The brigade
was in reserve when, on January 7th, the Turks were found strongly entrenched
astride the Tigris at Sheikh Saad and were only dislodged after heavy and costly
fighting. The Hampshire had reached the Musandaq reach of the river late on
January 6th, having covered over 28 miles in the day. Advancing again next
morning to the Hibshi Bend, where a boat-bridge had been erected, they
waited in reserve, with a tremendous battle raging in front; till, about 2 p.m.,
they were sent across the river to reinforce our right, which was being counter-
attacked. They came under heavy shrapnel fire but were not actively engaged,
as the attack had not developed into anything serious and they therefore
escaped with only a few casualties, while after dark they were withdrawn
to the bridge, to spend a miserable night in cold and wet, the ground being
soaked. Besides the Turks who had counter-attacked our right, others were
believed to be working Southward some way inland from the river to strike in
behind us, so early next day (January 8th) the 9th Brigade was sent off downstream to deal with the threat. It covered several miles over difficult ground
cut up by ditches, but without encountering any enemy, and then returned to
the bridge to take up a position on our right rear where more hostile movements
were reported. Meanwhile, though held up on the left bank, we had carried the
main position on the right, and this decided the Turks to clear out during the
night of January 8th/9th and retire to the Wadi, six miles upstream. On find-

[1] One was still in France in the middle of December.

ing them gone the relievers advanced again, leaving the Hampshire to help clear up the battlefield, collect rifles and equipment, bury the dead and bring in any wounded who had been overlooked. That evening they moved forward to rejoin the main body, now preparing to attack the Wadi position.

This the Tigris Corps [1] could not attack until January 13th. With its transport so inadequate, supplies and ammunition could not be promptly replenished or satisfactory arrangements made for the numerous wounded, while the arrival of drafts and reinforcements was impeded and, in general, the difficulties of organization, already bad enough with the improvisations necessitated by what was believed to be the urgent need of reaching Kut, were hopelessly complicated. Unfortunately General Townshend, not having undertaken soon enough a careful survey of the food actually available in Kut, originally greatly underestimated the endurance of his garrison. Had it been known in January that Kut could hold out into April the hurry of the original hasty advance with all its disadvantages might have been avoided. Where improvisations and hurry were among the chief causes of failure, a systematically organized advance might well have succeeded.

The position behind the Wadi stretched about two miles inland and while the 28th Brigade, attacking frontally, sought to hold and distract the defence, three other brigades crossed the Wadi some way higher up to outflank the Turkish left. The 9th Brigade meanwhile was held in reserve near Sheikh Saad.

The attack, delivered early on Janauary 13th, started well enough; the outflanking force crossed the Wadi without meeting any opposition, though the nullah, 30 to 40 yards wide, with steep sandy banks 30 feet high, proved a more serious obstacle than was expected. However, when the three brigades wheeled round SW. and South, they soon came up against a strongly-held line thrown back almost at right angles to the Wadi and facing North, against which, despite determined efforts, little progress could be made without more artillery support. On this the 9th Brigade was ordered up to reinforce the 28th, which had driven in the Turkish outposts and advanced some way towards the Wadi before being held up. Unluckily the orders were slow to reach it, and the 9th only arrived at Chittab Fort, from which the 28th had started its attack, long after dark and was then used to throw out an outpost line behind which the 28th Brigade was withdrawn. Here the Hampshire spent another bitterly cold night, digging in under occasional bursts of heavy firing, mainly innocuous.

Moving forward before daybreak (January 14th) to renew the frontal attack, the Hampshire soon discovered that the Turkish trenches were empty: the defenders, threatened with being cut off by a renewal of the flank attack, had evacuated them and had gone back to El Hanna, at the lower end of that flankless defile between the river and the marshes [2] which formed an even more formidable position than those they had defended so tenaciously and whose capture had already cost the Tigris Corps over 6,000 casualties. These positions had been formidable enough, approached over bare and fairly level ground,

---

[1] The relieving force was known by this title.

[2] With so little land transport a move round the marshes was out of the question.

L   H.R. II.

devoid of cover, while dry water-courses had provided the defence with ready-made trenches, hard to locate even if the scanty British artillery had been assisted by the aeroplanes whose help was so conspicuously absent. But there was not even the chance of outflanking the El Hanna positions which the Wadi had offered: only a frontal attack could be made.

After clearing the Wadi battle-field and having a short rest, the 9th Brigade moved up on January 19th towards the El Hanna trenches. Persistent bad weather with much heavy rain had greatly increased the attackers' difficulties, a boat bridge had been swept away, breaking just as the Hampshire were about

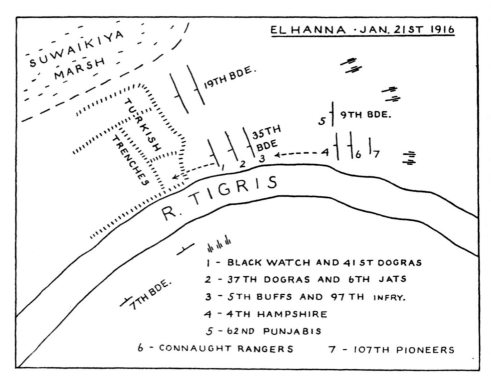

EL HANNA · JAN. 21ST 1916

1 - BLACK WATCH AND 41 ST DOGRAS
2 - 37TH DOGRAS AND 6TH JATS
3 - 5TH BUFFS AND 97 TH INFRY.
4 - 4TH HAMPSHIRE
5 - 62ND PUNJABIS
6 - CONNAUGHT RANGERS   7 - 107TH PIONEERS

to cross it, and communication between the banks was with difficulty maintained by ferry, all ranks had had to contend against cold and wet and the all-pervading mud, ankle-deep everywhere, and the sufferings of the sick and wounded had been much increased. However, despite the bad weather, by January 20th the British trenches were within 300 yards of the Turkish position, which had been as heavily bombarded as the limited artillery and ammunition allowed, and though Skeikh Saad and the Wadi had greatly reduced the striking power of the Tigris Corps there was no thought of suspending the attack. Townshend's need was believed to be too acute.

' Zero ' on January 21st was fixed for 6.30 a.m., but a mirage prevented the gunners from seeing their targets, so the attack had to be postponed till 7.45

a.m. by which time the Turks had fully realized what was coming. However, the 19th (right) and 35th (left) Brigades pushed gallantly forward, and ten minutes after the 35th Brigade had advanced, the 9th Brigade followed in its steps, with the 4th Hampshire on its left next the river: the Hampshire had been under fairly heavy long-range rifle fire even before ' Zero ' and had had a few men hit. The 9th Brigade pressed ahead resolutely, ' as steady and determined as if on parade ' one officer wrote, but directly the advance had begun rifles, machine-guns and field-guns had opened a heavy fire, and with the ground flat and affording no cover casualties quickly mounted up, the supports also soon being caught by the shells and suffering almost as severely from the fire as the leading brigades. Nevertheless on the 35th Brigade's left a fair number of the Black Watch effected a lodgement and besides them some Dogras also got in. Of the brigade's second and third lines some Jats entered the Turkish line and joined the Black Watch, but only a few, and those who had got in were soon hard pressed to maintain their hold.

Meanwhile the Hampshire were coming up, B Company (Lt. Needham) leading, C (Captain Page-Roberts), with which was Major Stilwell, following and D (Captain North) in support. The fire was heavy, and the battalion had a long stretch to cover even to gain our old front trench. Before reaching it Colonel Bowker, following with the third line, had been hit, but pushed on nevertheless, to be hit again and killed. The Adjutant, Captain Brandon, now joined Major Stilwell in the leading line to inform him that he was in command, but in advancing again from our old line Captain Brandon also was hit and killed and, with no support coming up and casualties heavy, the advance was held up short of the Turkish line. On the extreme left next the river, however, some men under Lts. Stilwell and Palmer managed to join the Black Watch in the Turkish trenches and lend a hand in the gallant struggle which they maintained for over an hour against heavy odds, though no more support reached them. Eventually, with their left attacked down a communication trench and their right from the uncaptured line beyond their lodgement, they were overwhelmed, only a few survivors regaining our lines. Lts. Stillwell and Palmer, wounded and disabled, were left behind. Meanwhile the rest of the battalion could merely hang on behind such cover as they could scrape together with their entrenching tools and wait till darkness allowed them to move and to try to assist the many wounded. A pelting rain and bitter cold added to the trials to be endured and stamina and endurance were severely taxed.

No better success had attended the 19th Brigade on the 35th's right and, despite a renewed bombardment, a belated advance by the 28th Brigade made no headway. Losses had been terribly heavy, and we had not even the modified success of the Sheik Saad and Wadi attacks to set against them. This time our defeat was unequivocal. Well over half the attacking infantry were casualties, even the 4th Hampshire in losing 13 officers and 230 men out of 16 and 339 in action were not actually the hardest hit battalion. Lt. Colonel Bowker, Captains North and Brandon, Lts. Needham, Bucknill, Stilwell [1] and Palmer

---

[1] Later reported as alive but a prisoner, Lt. Palmer died of his wounds in Turkish hands.

and 106 men were killed or missing, Captain Page-Roberts, Lts. Andrews, E. A. Burrell, and Jensen and 2/Lts. Pirie and Wyles and 124 men were wounded, Of the handful who were left Lt. Lester-Garland now took command, as Major Stilwell, though unhit, had collapsed from exposure and exhaustion [1] and was sent to hospital, Captain Foster having previously gone sick. Colonel Bowker's loss was much regretted: he had done much for the battalion, winning universal confidence and respect, and was greatly missed.

Nearly a month elapsed before another major attack was attempted. It was now known that the supplies in Kut would allow the garrison to hold out, if on much reduced rations, for some time longer and that the headlong attacks of January had not really been necessary, so that a more systematic and better supported attack could be prepared and reinforcements and drafts brought up.

A mere fragment like the 4th Hampshire was fit for nothing beyond camp duties and guards, and even the arrival from England on February 13th of 420 men with 13 officers [2] left it little over half its establishment. Of these men 135 came from the regiment, from the 2/6th, 3/5th and the 3/7th Battalions, 160 were from the 3/4th D.C.L.I., the rest from the Somerset L.I. and the Wiltshire. This draft had left England on December 10th, reaching Basra on January 7th, and an exhausting march up country in bad weather had reduced its original strength by over 100 through sickness.

Meanwhile the Third (Lahore) Division had been re-formed and in February the 4th Hampshire were transferred to the 35th Brigade under Brigadier General Rice, where they were combined with the 5th Buffs, also sadly reduced, as the ' Composite Territorial Battalion ', which was nick-named ' the Huffs '. It was indeed a ' composite ' unit, the Buffs' reinforcements being mostly from the Gloucestershire and Worcestershire with officers from many other regiments, while Major Thorne, who took command on February 15th, came from the 1st Royal Sussex. This battalion's [3] first active duty was finding picquets on the right bank. Here our lines had been pushed well forward upstream of the Hanna trenches, reaching the Abu Roman mounds, but though we could fire across the Tigris into the flanks and rear of the Turkish front lines, most elaborate defences had been constructed along the river bank and the Turk held on unshaken.

By the beginning of March all was in train for another attempt. This time we were to advance up the right bank to outflank the line running Southward from Es Sinn to a redoubt on the Dujaila depression.[4] To cover the concentration near the Pools of Siloam of the attacking force, the 35th Brigade, which was allotted to the Corps reserve, spent March 7th holding a line running Southward from the river towards the Umm al Baram marsh. The Turks made no attempt to interfere with the assembly of the attacking force, which apparently

[1] The cold and wet, added to their exertions and some shortage of rations, sent many unwounded men to hospital from all units.
[2] All subalterns and, with the exception of Lt. Beavis (2/6th) and 2/Lts. Brine, D. A. Hamley, E.A. Hamley and Weatherall (3/4th), all from other regiments.
[3] On March 7th it was returned as 33 officers and 970 other ranks.
[4] Probably an old bed of the Tigris.

they had never detected, and, early on March 8th, after the advance had started, the brigade formed up at the rendezvous and moved forward to escort the great mass of second-line transport to the point, about two miles East of Sinn Abtar, where the two attacking columns had diverged, the left crossing the Dujaila depression to attack the trenches running SW. from the redoubt towards the Shatt el Hai, the right attacking between the redoubt and Sinn Abtar. Here the brigade remained halted from midday onwards in readiness to meet the counter-attack which it was thought the Turks might attempt from their left. None developed and meanwhile, for one reason and another, the chances of a decisive success were slipping away. After a most admirably guided and conducted night march had completely surprised the enemy and brought the relief of Kut within reach, a really splendid opportunity was lamentably thrown away, and another day ended in failure and bitter disappointment.

That night the 35th Brigade spent dug in on the right flank of the force, for whose retirement orders were issued early next morning, the 35th, who were detailed as rear-guard, remaining in position till, early in the afternoon, the long train of transport and guns was all under way. When at last the brigade moved off the Turks at first seemed inclined to press the retreat and the rear-guard looked to be in for a difficult time, but the timely intervention of some British guns discouraged the pursuers most effectively, and but for shell fire, which caused a few casualties, the ' Composite Territorial Battalion ' was unmolested, regaining the starting-point shortly before midnight.

After three days in camp near the Wadi the battalion held our trenches opposite the El Hanna line from March 13th to 22nd, sapping forward to bring our front line within assaulting range of the enemy's trenches, work which cost it only trifling casualties. It was then back at the Wadi camp or at Orah across the river for a fortnight. At Orah it found outposts and had some brushes with Arabs, always on the alert to pounce on stragglers or stray animals or even to attempt to surprise a picquet.

By the first week in April the Thirteenth Division had arrived from Egypt, and on April 5th it attacked and carried the El Hanna trenches, now only lightly held, and, pushing on, also carried the Fallahiya position, three miles upstream. But the next trenches, at Sannaiyat, another three miles ahead, checked the advance, and this decided General Gorringe, now commanding the Tigris Corps, to transfer his effort to the right bank. Here again an initial success was achieved (April 17th), but violent counter-attacks coupled with the floods checked our progress and robbed us of decisive success. A final desperate effort to storm the Sannaiyat lines (April 21st) was no more fortunate, and after the gallant failure of the steamer *Julnar* to run supplies through (April 24th) the end came and Kut had to surrender.

April had given the ' Huffs ' little fighting but plenty of hard work, first in clearing the battlefield after the capture of the Hanna lines, when, among others, Lt. Bucknill's body was found and buried. Then after four days (April 8th–11th) at Falahiya, finding guards and picquets to protect the rear of the attacking force, the battalion was similarly employed across the river until April 20th, while it was in support during the last attack on Sannaiyat and then recrossed the river to take over picquet duty on the left of our front line near Rohde's Picquet, SE. of Bait Isa.

The fall of Kut after so tenacious a defence and the heavy losses incurred in the relievers' gallant efforts forms the low-water mark of our fortunes in Mesopotamia. It had been a sheer gamble to try to rush Baghdad with a force which, even had luck been with it instead of mainly against it, was unequal to its task and without any preparation for retrieving a reverse, and, as at Gallipoli, the initial error of expecting the force originally available to accomplish more than was reasonable had never been made good. Had the original advance been postponed until substantial reserves were available, the check at Ctesiphon might not have been decisive, while had the capacity of Kut to hold out been correctly estimated and unnecessary haste subsequently avoided, the 4th Hampshire might not have been cut to pieces so unavailingly.

A prolonged inactivity followed the fall of Kut. The Turks made no effort to improve their success by driving the baffled relieving force downstream and thereby allowed us to retain our advanced positions unchallenged. This may have contributed to minimize the ill-effects of our defeat. The Arabs on the whole did not stir, contenting themselves with minor activities against our outposts, communications, convoys and foraging parties. The North-West Frontier, where trouble had been feared, remained quiet, the battered Tigris Corps could gradually be brought back to strength and to full efficiency, so that before the year was out it could start the operations which were to recover Kut and carry the British flag to Baghdad.

But to the units who had to spend an unusually hot and exhausting summer far up the Tigris, at the end of an over-worked line of communications, without amenities and comforts, in an exceptionally trying climate, the time passed slowly and painfully. The daily routine was both strenuous and terribly monotonous; weakened units found themselves hardly equal to all their duties, the sick-rate was very high, rations were none too plentiful or palatable, nor did things improve until the careful and strenuous reorganization of the Basra base and of the lines of communication at last began to yield fruit upstream. Meanwhile trenches had to be held and kept in repair and picquets found, with escorts to convoys between our forward position and the camps further downstream, as the Arabs were always on the alert to descend upon any ill-guarded quarry.

During May the Hampshire were mainly at Twin Canals, occasionally holding the forward trenches, which were advanced in the middle of the month to Es Sinn, the Turks having very unexpectedly vacated that position. An outbreak of cholera cost them several lives, including those of Lt. Corser (2/6th) and of the Brigadier, but it never became an epidemic. A draft of 140 men from the 2/4th joined at the end of May, and on June 19th the Composite Territorial Battalion was broken up, the 4th Hampshire resuming their independent formation under Major Matthews of the Durham L.I., while Captain

Gribbon joined from the 6th Devons, to which he had been attached, to become Adjutant. Before this the 35th, 36th and 37th Brigades, hitherto independent, had been organized as a Fourteenth Indian Division under Major General Egerton.

July the battalion spent in the Sinn area, carrying on as before with finding escorts, guards and picquets and digging trenches. The weather was terribly hot, conditions most uncomfortable and the sick-rate naturally very high, but Colonel Matthews proved an able and inspiring commander and did much for the efficiency and welfare of the battalion. During August it was for a time at the Northern end of the Es Sinn line and found sniping picquets to look out for targets across the Tigris. The light railway from Orah had now reached Twin Canals and was creeping forward towards Es Sinn and needed guarding, block houses being established at intervals and usually held by picquets of about a a dozen men to keep the Arabs at a distance.

In September the battalion was ordered back to Sheikh Saad to be transferred to duty on the line of communications; it had marched back to railhead on September 13th, when its orders were cancelled and it was posted to the 37th Brigade under Brigadier General Walton, in which it found the 26th, 62nd and 82nd Punjabis.[1] This brigade the Hampshire joined at the Dujaila Redoubt [2] where it was employed on the usual routine, varied in October by ten days in reserve for intensive company and battalion training, after which the brigade moved up to the front and took over the line about Magasis, holding the river front. Here an advanced picquet line was being dug: No Man's Land was wide and we were gradually pushing forward our posts to bring us nearer the enemy, who had now gone well back.

November brought substantial drafts from India, seven officers and 571 men altogether from the 2/4th, 1/6th, 1/7th and 2/7th Battalions, with an officer and 28 men rejoining from hospital. The draft-finding battalions had sent good men, well trained and fit, and the opening in December of General Maude's operations for the recapture of Kut found the 4th Hampshire strong and efficient and ready for the chance to get their own back on the Turks.

Meanwhile the battalions in India had been following the usual routine of training and duties, sending ' hot weather ' detachments to ' the Hills ', and were steadily becoming both acclimatized and highly trained, the Second Line units in particular, with more lee-way to make up, improving greatly. The 2/4th, who remained at Quetta, lost Lt. Colonel Naish, invalided home in April 1916, Major J. B. L. Stilwell replacing him. They had been joined by the depot left behind by the 1/4th and had at one time 1500 men in barracks. They benefitted greatly from strenuous training in quite a good climate and had by now become quite expert in mountain warfare. The 1/5th, who had been much split up, having detachments at Benares, Cawnpore and Jhansi, were concentrated at Lucknow and moved in March to Fyzabad. Their signallers being

---

[1] Afterwards 2/15th, 1/1st and 5/1st Punjab.
[2] Evacuated by the Turks in May.

taken away for service on the Frontier a new section had to be trained, but numbers were maintained by over 200 arrivals from England, and despite large drafts to Mesopotamia and the departure of men to take commissions or for various employments the battalion ended 1916 nearly 1,000 strong, having only lost nine men by disease in two years and had 20 invalided. It lost one of its 'pre-war' subalterns when Lt. Needham was killed at El Hanna.

The 2/5th in like manner got large drafts, over 450 in all, and could send several officers and many men to Mesopotamia. Lt. Jenner took over the Adjutancy from Captain Archdale and several officers left for Staff appointments. The men's health was good and the hot weather less extreme and less trying than in 1915.

The 1/6th, who moved from Agra to Ambala in March 1916, had two companies at Solon during the hot weather, companies exchanging stations in July: by October the battalion was concentrated again at Ambala, going into camp later for cold weather training. Drafts to Mesopotamia, where one of its officers, Lieutenant Palmer, was killed at El Hanna, were replaced from home.

The 1/7th lost Lt. Colonel Parke, invalided home in February 1916; Major Roberts-Thomson succeeding him, on which Captain Rebbeck went up to Major. The battalion moved from Meerut to Ambala in March, sent 'hot weather' detachments to Dagshai and Kasauli and received drafts amounting to nearly 450 with several officers, itself sending drafts to the 1/4th, with whom Captain Allen was killed early in 1917 at the recapture of Kut.

The 2/7th got a change of station in March, from Secunderabad to Jubbulpore. Major Gott went home on leave in February and was replaced in command by Major Maturin, Captain Boucher becoming second in command. Captain Gribbon left in February to join the 6th Devons in Mesopotamia, Lt. W. A. de Geijer becoming Adjutant. Drafts from the 3/7th kept the battalion's numbers up, despite the drain to Mesopotamia and other wastage.

Meanwhile another Hampshire battalion had reached India, the 1/9th, who, after much work on their coastal duties, had been converted into ordinary infantry in November 1915, when they had joined a brigade of other ex-cyclist battalions. This was in turn detailed for East Africa, for Egypt and for France, but was finally sent off in February 1916 to India: the 1/9th going to Bangalore and remaining there until December 1916, when they were ordered up to the NW. Frontier. They were still under their original C.O., Lt. Colonel R. A. Johnson.

CHAPTER XIV

THE SOMME

THE OPENING PHASES [1]

THE great attack which opened on July 1st 1916 on a 25 mile front astride the Somme was undertaken at a time and in a locality dictated rather by French interests and considerations than by British. Left to himself Sir Douglas Haig would have deferred attacking till his preparations and the training of some of his troops were more complete, possibly till he could use the new weapon, the ' tank ', of which so much was expected by those in the secret of it: he would certainly have chosen a different front.[2] On the open downland of the Somme area, over and above certain tactical disadvantages and the lack of roads, railways and housing, our intentions had been impossible to conceal, the manifold administrative measures involved in the assembly of so large a force had been obvious, the construction of camps and the improvement of the communications and of the very inadequate water supply could not be hidden to the degree of which other areas might have allowed. Consequently surprise, so essential to the success of an offensive, had been lacking, except on the British right and where the French attacked, and there surprise had much to do with the success achieved: between Fricourt and Serre, where the British centre and left attacked, the Germans were expecting an attack; they were fully prepared and, effective as our bombardment had on the whole been, their counter-measures were ready; if any element of surprise came in, it was the efficacy of the deep dug-outs in which most of their trench garrisons had found safety and shelter during the bombardment.

North of the Ancre the Fourth and Twenty-Ninth Divisions were facing defences as strong or stronger than anywhere else and the task before these Divisions was difficult and formidable in the extreme. For many months the Germans had been in position here and had benefitted by the natural difficulties of the ground to construct a veritable fortress, almost warranting the epithet ' impregnable '.

The German lines here ran Northward along a ridge from which spurs projected SE. towards the Ancre, shallow valleys between them giving cover for supports and reserves. Here the key to the position was the strongly fortified Beaumont Hamel. That village confronted the Twenty-Ninth Division's left brigade, the 86th, which had to advance along a spur known as Hawthorn Ridge, while its right brigade, the 87th, faced the Southern side of a salient round the head of the deep depression known as Y Ravine, the 88th Brigade being in reserve. Beyond the Division's left was the Fourth Division, whose

---

[1] See Sketch 31 (p. 181).
[2] The late hour chosen for the attack, 7.30 a.m., was also insisted upon by the French. Sir Douglas Haig would have attacked before it was light enough for the enemy's machine gunners to see their targets clearly, a plan to be adopted with good results on July 14th.

11th Brigade, reinforced by two battalions of the Forty-Eighth Division, was attacking North of Beaumont Hamel, where two redoubts, Ridge Redoubt and the Quadrilateral, were particularly strong. It was hoped that the brigade would reach Munich Trench, 1,000 yards behind the front line, where the supporting brigades, the 10th and 12th, would go through it. On the Fourth Division's left the Thirty-First, also part of the Eighth Corps, had the village of Serre as its objective. No Man's Land, 500 yards wide South of Beaumont Hamel, was half that width further North, but it was bare of cover and the German defences were well-sited and constructed, while in places the slope of the ground had made it very difficult for our guns, and particularly the heavier pieces, to bring their fire to bear on them. Observation of our fire had not been easy and our bombardment, despite its volume, had not fulfilled expectations. It had neither silenced the enemy's batteries, subdued his machine-guns nor shattered his defences, if his wire had been well cut.[1] If hopes were high, those who had had a close view could not avoid some misgivings after the volume of machine-gun fire provoked by a discharge of smoke after the fourth day of the bombardment.

The Fourth Division had had no serious fighting since moving to the Somme and, thanks to this respite from heavy casualties and the changes consequent on them, its battalions had fully recovered from their losses and shattering experiences in ' Second Ypres '. They had had ample time to assimilate their drafts and to recover their cohesion. It has been well said [2] that the Division was as ' fighting fit as at any time in its existence ', and the 1st Hampshire had never been as near again to their August 1914 standard. It was the more unfortunate that the task set to the Division proved to be more than any infantry could have accomplished.

It had unfortunately been decided to fire a big mine under the German redoubt on Hawthorn Ridge at 7.20 a.m., ten minutes before ' Zero '. This gave away completely the one thing the Germans did not know, the exact time of our attack, and as simultaneously our heavy guns ' lifted ' off the front line, the defenders had ample time to swarm up from the safety of their undamaged deep dug-outs, to get their machine-guns into place and to man their parapets just as our heavily-laden infantry began crossing No Man's Land, while their barrage came crashing down, many batteries hitherto deliberately silent and therefore unlocated and undamaged joining in.

The 1st Hampshire,[3] following the East Lancashire on the 11th Brigade's right, went forward at 7.40 a.m., before which the East Lancashire had already been almost wiped out, less by the barrage than by the deadlier machine-guns in Ridge Redoubt, which swept both No Man's Land and the British front trenches, mowing the attackers down wholesale. Hardly any East Lancashire reached the German trenches and they were too few to achieve anything. The

---

[1] The full stength of the German defences at this point, in particular of their deep dug-outs was not revealed till the capture of Beaumont Hamel in November.

[2] *Official History*, 1916, I. 426.

[3] Even before the attack started our own ' shorts ' had buried a section of one platoon and it took nearly an hour to dig them out.

Hampshire had A, B and half C Companies in front line, the rest of C being detailed to deal with a trench on the right flank, while D was in reserve. Plunging forward into the deadly hail of fire they fared no better than their predecessors, gallantly as they advanced; Colonel Palk [1] being among the many who fell before they could get half-way across. A few bombers are reported to have got into the enemy's line, but the majority of the Hampshire were brought down at or short of the wire, only a few reaching it, and the survivors could only seek the poor shelter of the shell-holes which pitted No Man's Land. Here they had to lie for hours, mixed up with the East Lancashire, pinned to the ground, unable to move and with little chance to hit back. Captain Fawkes, though badly wounded and unable to get on, did great work in encouraging his men, while 2/Lt. Money and C.S.M. Palmer also showed conspicuous gallantry, keeping their men together and setting a fine example [2] during this long and trying ordeal.

Better fortune had attended the left of the 11th Brigade, who got rather more shelter from the ground, and despite heavy losses a fair number entered the German lines, carried the Quadrilateral and even reached the back trenches of the front system. Some of the 10th and 12th Brigades also got across and in places pushed on still further and for the moment a lodgement seemed to have been made which might be developed, heavy though losses had been. However, nothing could be done to shift those defenders who were facing the survivors of the Hampshire and both flanks of the lodgement were exposed; on the left the handfuls of the Thirty-First Division who had succeeded in entering the German lines had been speedily overwhelmed, while not only had the 11th Brigade's right been checked but hardly any of the Twenty-Ninth Division's left brigade had got in, though the mine crater at the Hawthorn Redoubt was in our hands. The Germans could therefore concentrate their attention on dislodging those of the Fourth Division who had penetrated into their position.

Of the Twenty-Ninth Division not only had both attacking brigades been engaged without avail, the 88th's leading battalions, the Essex and the Newfoundland Regiment, had also gone forward, with equally disastrous results. However, their fate had caused the Divisional commander to stop the 2nd Hampshire and the Worcestershire from advancing beyond our own lines, where they came under artillery fire but escaped serious exposure to the machine-guns. To support the Fourth Division it was now proposed to utilize these two battalions in a fresh attack upon Beaumont Hamel, while such of the 10th Brigade as was still in hand advanced on their left. Terribly congested trenches prevented this attack from being started at the time ordered, 12.30 p.m.; indeed, the orders never reached the 2nd Hampshire till long after that hour, and eventually the plan was abandoned and further fruitless sacrifice avoided. The 2nd Hampshire remained therefore in our own lines.

---

[1] He went forward carrying only a stick and was very soon hit : he was brought in but died in the C.C.S. that morning.
[2] All three received the M.C.

Our artillery did their best to help the Fourth Division to hang on, but the pressure on those across No Man's Land steadily increased, to reinforce them and to get ammunition and bombs across to them proved almost impossible in face of the barrage and the machine-guns, and after a stubborn resistance they were gradually forced back till at midnight we only retained the Quadrilateral. Elsewhere on the Eighth Corps' front the Germans contented themselves with having held their positions and did not attempt anything against the survivors lying out in No Man's Land. Indeed for some time our stretcher-bearers were able to go out unhindered into the open to bring in the wounded, in which work Sergeant Bone and Private Pidgeley [1] were conspicuous, carrying on even when the Germans resumed shelling in response to our renewing our bombardment.

With darkness the survivors [2] from No Man's Land could get back to our line, bringing with them many of the wounded, and what remained of the attacking battalions could be collected and to some degree reorganized. The 2nd Hampshire and the Worcestershire took over the Division's frontage, much damaged by the counter-bombardment and needing much reconstruction. During the night parties were hard at work bringing in the wounded, Privates Barton, Morgan and Parkinson displaying the greatest devotion,[3] while Pte. Mildenhall was constantly out in No Man's Land, bandaging and assisting the wounded, the Germans making little effort to interfere, even next morning, though they would not let our stretcher-bearers bring in those close to their wire.[4]

The Eighth Corps' losses had been terrible, heavier than any other Corps suffered, nearly 6000 in the Fourth Division, well over 5000 in the Twenty-Ninth and 3600 in the Thirty-First; and in the end it had nothing to show for them, as the untenable lodgement in the Quadrilateral was evacuated by order early on July 2nd. The 1st Hampshire indeed had had their worst experience of the war, comparable to the 2nd Battalion's ordeal at Cape Helles on August 6th, 1915: Second Ypres had hit them hard, July 1st 1916 had cost them eleven officers and 310 men killed and missing, 15 officers and 250 men wounded. Colonel Palk's loss was very deeply regretted. A tower of strength from Le Cateau onwards, where his coolness and calm had been an inspiration to many who were enduring their ' baptism of fire ', he had taken over after Colonel Hicks had been wounded on May 8th and had been in command in the closing stages of Second Ypres and at the International Trench, where he and his men had earned the warmest praise from all above them. An officer has written of him: ' He was a great character. He used to read Gibbon to his junior officers and spoke French and German fluently. The first time I met him he said, " There are three things I will never have said to me: ' it always 'as been done, Sir '; ' never 'as been done, Sir ' and ' I thought '. It is your business to know and to act ' ". He was often a thorn in the side of the Division and the senior

---

[1] Of the 1st Hampshire. Both received the D.C.M.
[2] Soon after 10 p.m. it was dark enough for this, and though the Germans had put down a barrage about 9.45 p.m. this had stopped after half an hour.
[3] They received the M.M.
[4] These were mostly made prisoners.

Staff officers did not like him. He was utterly outspoken and feared nobody.
He was a magnificent regimental officer, fresh and amusing, and was revered by
the men '. A shrewd judge of men, kindly but firm, he was one who could ill be
spared: ' the men would have followed him anywhere '. A battalion which
had had two such C.O's as Colonels Hicks and Palk had been fortunate. With
him had fallen Captain Bonham-Carter, the only other officer with the South
African war medals, Lts. Adams and Price, 2/Lts. H. Alexander, N. H. Bell,
Bramble, Cane, Goodford, Nixon,[1] F. P. Thompson and Westmore. The officers
wounded were Captains K. A. Johnston, Hume, Wyld[2] and Fawkes, Lt. Shearer,
2/Lts. D. Day, Doyle, P. J. Hall, Harding, Hiddingh, Jacob, Newnham, Sims,
Sweetenham and Welhams.

The 2nd Battalion had got off with trifling loss, two killed and 2/Lt. Riggs
and twenty men wounded, but during the next ten days 2/Lt. Counsell and 13
men were killed and 2/Lts. Black and Tilley and 84 men wounded. These days
were spent in front line at Mary Redan, repairing much damaged trenches under
persistent shell fire. Large quantities of arms and equipment were recovered
from No Man's Land and many dead buried, while another 60 wounded were
brought in, all at night.

The battalion went out of the line on July 10th but sent 28 men under Captain Arnell up to try a raid near Y Ravine on July 14th. The raiders reached
the wire and were making their way through when they came under heavy fire
and bombing. They replied vigorously with rifles and bombs for 15 minutes
but then had to fall back. Two wounded were brought in, but Captain Arnell
and three others were missing, believed killed, while next day a party carrying
a gas cylinder up to the line was caught by a H.E. shell in Auchonvillers and
had 25 casualties, seven fatal, so that the month's casualties came to 150.

July 17th brought the 2nd a move back, to Acheux Wood, and after several
days devoted to company training the battalion went still further back, to
Beauval, to entrain on July 29th for the North. It was now to make its first
acquaintance with the Ypres Salient where its Division was relieving the Sixth,
the 2nd Hampshire taking over front line trenches on July 30th opposite St.
Julien with one company in reserve at Potijze.

The Fourth Division had also reached the Salient and had relieved the
Guards SW. of Pilkem, on the extreme British left. The 1st Hampshire had
been back at Mailly Maillet and then at Bertrancourt till July 9th and had then
had five days in line at Beaumont Hamel, though only six officers were available
for duty. They were in line here when early on July 14th smoke was discharged
all along the Divisional front and a heavy bombardment maintained for an hour
to distract the enemy's attention and make him expect an attack here also,
while away to the right the Fourth Army was making its highly successful dawn
attack which took the Bazentins and reached Longueval and Delville and High
Woods. Captain Lockhart and Lts. Smythe and Collett now rejoined and over 20

[1] With the Brigade Trench Mortar Battery.   [2] He lost a leg.

other officers arrived, of whom Lts. German and de Gaury had been at Gallipoli with the 10th Battalion, while over 300 men arrived, mainly from the 13th and 16th Battalions, though, unfortunately, some were of very poor physique. After a week at Mailly Maillet in support, the battalion went back, on July 23rd, to entrain for Ypres at Doullens, reaching Poperinghe on July 25th and relieving the 4th Grenadiers in front line SW. of Pilkem on the night of the 27th/28th. It was thus back near the International Trench, if not many were left to renew the acquaintance of that locality, nor were these particularly delighted to do so. Next day (July 28th) Major Armitage of the West Yorkshire arrived to assume command.

The Eighth Corps' failure on July 1st had been to some extent balanced by the success of the British right from Fricourt Eastward and of the French beyond Montauban. These gains Sir Douglas Haig did succeed in developing, and gradually and slowly the British line was pushed forward until the German defences between Thiepval and Delville Wood were mastered piecemeal in chequered and costly fighting, with the balance just in our favour; the Germans fought skilfully and stubbornly, again and again they counter-attacked in force and only by determined efforts were they held and pushed back. All through July and August the struggle raged without another Hampshire battalion being engaged: the 1st and 2nd were recuperating in the comparative ' quiet ' of the Ypres Salient, while the 11th remained at Loos, the 14th in the Neuve Chapelle area and the 15th at Ploegsteert.

Still these battalions were far from inactive. If the British attacks on the Somme gave the enemy all he could do to hold them and soon substantially relieved the pressure on Verdun, while all chance of a major counter-attack on the British front promptly disappeared, the Germans were not precluded from trying local counter-attacks to keep us occupied and to interfere with our systematic relief of exhausted Divisions by fresh troops from ' quiet ' sectors, while we with much the same end tried raids and even occasionally something more extensive.

The 1st Hampshire had two months in the Salient before returning to the Somme. They found the trenches fairly dry, but in need of repair, and at first snipers were troublesome while at night machine-guns were often active. Returning to the line on August 4th after a few days ' out ' at Elverdinghe, where a lake in the Chateau grounds provided good bathing, they came in on the evening of August 8th for the enemy's one use of gas on any substantial scale during this month, gas being released on nearly the whole front of the Eighth Corps [1] On the 1st Hampshire's front the discharge lasted ten minutes and meanwhile the trenches were heavily shelled, the S.O.S. rockets, being mostly damp, failed to go off, and some minutes elapsed before our barrage came down to co-operate effectively with our rifles in driving back Germans who attempted

---

[1] This Corps headquarters had been transferred from the Beaumont Hamel front to Ypres at the end of July.

to reach our lines, none managing to get in, though some came within bombing range. But the Hampshire had nearly 70 casualties, 14 killed or died of gas or missing, as many wounded and nearly 40 gassed, 2/Lt. Love being wounded.

From August 11th to 21st the battalion was ' out ' again, after which it relieved the Canadians South of the Menin Road, a nasty piece of line which seemed to be overlooked from all around. Here the enemy were active, and on August 26th a heavy bombardment caused 20 casualties in C Company, both Captain Smythe and 2/Lt. Prynn being buried for a time but dug out without serious injury. During the shelling about a dozen Germans started working down a trench towards A Company's bombing post, where Sergeant Clark dealt with them most effectively; well backed up by two men, he drove them off with bombs,[1] while another advance was repulsed by our fire, the Germans, big men and apparently Prussian Guardsmen, running back to the shelter of a wood.[2]

After another turn in the line East of Zillebeke early in September, the battalion was in camp at Vlamertinghe and then near Dunkirk, where it was practised in embarking. This aimed at making it appear that we intended landing on the Belgian coast, and it seems that coupled with naval activities in the Thames and elsewhere the threat did arouse German apprehensions and lead to their devoting men and materials to strengthening the coast defences. The battalion then found itself under orders to return to the Somme, and after entraining for Amiens on September 17th it spent the rest of the month training, first at Cardonette, three miles NE. of Amiens, and then at Corbie. Casualties for September only came to a dozen, but over 110 admissions to hospital considerably exceeded returns from hospital, 49, and drafts, 27. Four officers joined, including Lt. Newnham wounded on July 1st, but Lt. Sprake after a long spell as Transport Officer was detailed for a turn of home duty.

The 2nd Battalion had also been caught by the gas on August 8th but with far more disastrous results. It had gone into trenches East of Potijze on July 30th and had had ten fairly quiet days, working on defences which required much improvement, a new mine crater needing consolidation, before the gas alarm was sounded and a gas cloud was seen approaching slowly from the NE. The wind was light and the gas, moving slowly, was the more efficacious, and between it and the German barrage the battalion suffered terribly, having nearly 240 casualties, more than half fatal; Captain Hall (Buffs), 2/Lts. McCurdy, Scoggin and E. W. C. Turner[3] and no less than 125 men died, while 2/Lts. Churcher, Foster, Graham, Miller, M. T. Smith and Tollemache were incapacitated. Sergeant Graham, though gassed, stuck to his post and gave his officers valuable help in keeping the men steady while Pte. Osbourne displayed great

---

[1] He received an ' immediate ' M.M.

[2] The total casualties for August were 25 killed and missing, including deaths from gas, 38 wounded and 46 gassed. Captain Lockhart and 90 men were admitted to hospital, from which 36 men were discharged.

[3] He had only joined a week earlier.

devotion to duty in maintaining communications and repairing wires and Corporal Hopgood kept his Lewis gun in use and did much to reconstruct a damaged trench. Here no attempt was made by the Germans to exploit what seemed to offer them a very favourable opportunity and attack: the gas, which was phosgene and particularly deadly, killing birds and rats for some distance in rear and corroding metal, had been sufficiently effective. Luckily two large drafts, 98 men on August 12th and 125 five days later, nearly replaced the losses and for the rest of the month casualties were low, 2/Lt.Manlove and four men killed and 2/Lt. Tilley and a dozen men wounded. With 60 admissions to hospital the battalion could produce 36 officers [1] and 773 other ranks on August 31st, ten new officers having joined.

Ten days in brigade reserve and as many in Divisional reserve had followed this gas attack, after which the battalion was in brigade reserve at Ypres for ten days, finding working parties under R.E. supervision to improve the defences behind Railway Wood. It then had another ten in front line at Potijze, during which it came in for heavy retaliation for a raid by the 4th Worcestershire from Railway Wood on its right (September 15th). It was again heavily bombarded on September 18th but again escaped with trifling casualties. Chances of hitting back were few but were not neglected. While in Divisional reserve from September 19th to 28th the battalion was inspected by General Hunter-Weston and by the Army Commander, General Plumer. Another short spell in trenches followed, and then October 5th found it at Poperinghe in readiness to entrain for the South. Since September 1st casualties had only just come to 20, including 2/Lt. Hayward killed, though over 80 admissions to hospital had just exceeded drafts.

Of the Service battalions the 11th and 14th reached the Somme about the same time, to be employed at the opposite ends of the fighting front, the Sixteenth Division against Guillemont and Ginchy and the Thirty-Ninth on the right bank of the Ancre, just South of the frontage of the Twenty-Ninth Division on July 1st. The 15th came in slightly later, for the big attack of September 15th, which ushered in a new phase in the struggle.

The 11th had found the Loos salient fairly lively during July. We were using trench-mortars against the wire and were harassing the enemy energetically to keep him from thinning his force on this front. He retaliated fairly vigorously and parties working in back areas suffered rather severely, two officers were wounded by a shell which hit the Officers' Club at Mazingarbe, while Captain Powell was killed in the High Street at Loos on July 2nd. The Division made several raids and a party of the 11th helped to consolidate two new craters formed by a mine explosion near Seaforth Crater on July 15th. Otherwise its work continued as usual. At the end of July the battalion was relieved by the Pioneers of the Thirty-Ninth Division, head-quarters going back to Philosophe but moving early in August to Mazingarbe, though such changes did not mean any less work. The Division was then (August 23rd) with-

[1] All battalions had now 16 Lewis guns, the heavier machine guns having been withdrawn.

drawn from the line to move Southward, the 11th Hampshire arriving at Daours on the 28th and being sent forward on September 1st to Meaulté to work under the Fifth Division. That Division had just taken over the extreme right of our line opposite Falfemont Farm and Wedge Wood, SW. of Combles: on its left was a brigade of the Sixteenth Division which had been placed under the Twentieth to assist to capture Guillemont.

After the 116th Brigade's repulse at the Boar's Head the 14th Hampshire had a brief time out of the line, but they were soon in again at Cuinchy, where mining was going on vigorously and rifle-grenades were freely used. They were then in trenches in the Ferme du Bois and Festubert sectors. At Festubert also things were active, our snipers claimed several victims and our trench mortars did some effective work, while the battalion had the satisfaction of repulsing a patrol which tried to get in between two of our posts, a wounded prisoner being brought in; it was twice heavily shelled in retaliation for raids by other battalions, having over 30 casualties in two days, and then on July 30th it tried a large raid on its own, three officers and 103 men taking part. The party detailed to get a Bangalore torpedo into place failed to do so, and thick and uncut wire held the raiders up, so they could only engage in some brisk bombing in which they threw about 200 bombs before retiring. Five men were killed, but ten wounded, including 2/Lts. Marshall and Meade,[1] were brought safely in. After another turn in front line, at Givenchy from August 6th to 11th, in which one shell, landing on their company's H.Q. dug-out, wounded three subalterns, the battalion went back by Allouagne to Magnicourt, the Division being in Army reserve. Here it had ten days training and got a useful draft of 54 men before moving South by rail on August 24th. Detraining at Le Souich, it marched to Bertrancourt, where it encamped. Here Colonel Hickie left it (August 30th) on promotion to command a brigade of the Thirty-Eighth Division, leaving Captain Skinner in command, as Majors Childe-Thomas and Finlay were both away, the former having joined the Brigade staff in July.

The 15th Hampshire were not far behind the 11th and 14th, arriving at Dernancourt on September 5th. Their Divison had been ' out ' for nearly a month, having quitted ' Plugstreet ' on August 9th and moved back to Fletre, where it entrained for Longprè on August 24th, to have a week at Villers sous Ailly, training. Its last weeks at ' Plugstreet ' had been fairly active; on July 12th rescue parties had helped to bring in wounded after an unsuccessful raid by another battalion. The work was carried out under heavy fire and 2/Lt. W. Morgan was killed, while 2/Lt. Challis and Sergeant Dugan [2] were specially commended for their gallantry and good work. In a gas attack a few days later 2/Lt. Challis was killed, and several men were gassed next day through the drifting back into our trenches of pockets of gas. Between August 3rd and 9th the battalion was active with rifle grenades, sending over nearly 100 a day without exciting much reply. Trench mortars co-operated effectively and the battalion's

[1] C.S.M. Duffin brought this officer in.   [2] Received the M.M.

M   H.R. II.

patrols were active.   One under 2/Lt. Menzies-Calder ran into enemy and after a brief encounter scattered to make its way back. The subaltern, who was making his first patrol, being unable to find his way, managed to lie in hiding until next evening, apparently behind the enemy's line, and got back with useful information.   Casualties during July and August had come to about 30, well below those for June.

CHAPTER XV

THE SOMME (continued)

WHEN, early in September, a Hampshire battalion was again in action on the Somme the situation there had altered considerably since the 1st and 2nd Battalions had faced Beaumont Hamel. There, indeed, the position remained unchanged, but just East of the Ancre we had advanced to the outskirts of Thiepval and, beyond that, were well past Pozieres and the Bazentins, while if we had not yet completely mastered Delville Wood and Longueval or taken Ginchy or Guillemont, our right also had gained ground, and beyond it nearer the Somme the French had made good progress. It had been ' hard pounding ' and costly, but despite the vigour, skill and determination of the German resistance the Allies had made substantial gains, while German Divisions were being used up in the struggle even faster than the Allied units [1] and were coming out reduced to a fraction of their former strength, usually with even heavier losses than their opponents. The break-through for which Sir Douglas Haig had hoped had eluded us, and the battle had developed into the attrition which Generals Joffre and Foch had all along looked upon as inevitable, reckoning, as they did, that victory must be unattainable until the hard core of German resistance had been worn down by the killing or disabling of their pre-war trained officers and men. Till the Somme German units had retained a high proportion of their trained personnel, ours had largely perished in the devoted efforts of 1914 to win time for the developement of our unready resources or in the abortive offensives of 1915; if an invaluable leaven of the ' Old Army ' still remained, in the main the British troops of 1916, if fully a match to the Germans in courage and determination, were hardly their equals in training and experience or equipment. We had to make our Armies in the field and the process was proving expensive. However, by the beginning of September the contest of endurance was turning slowly in our favour, our advance had reached a point at which our prospects were becoming more promising. If few regimental officers or men had any suspicion of the secret weapon we were about to use, they could not but realize that we were gaining ground, if but gradually, and were punishing our enemy fully as hard as he was hitting us.

The objective of our next big effort included the veritable ' fortress ' of Thiepval, and as a preliminary the Reserve Army [2] was on September 3rd to renew the attack beyond the Ancre, where it had been suspended since July 1st. In this attack the Thirty-Ninth Division, now in General Fanshawe's Fifth Corps which was holding the front from Hébuterne Southward, was to be employed, and late on September 2nd therefore the 14th Hampshire moved up through Englebelmer for their first battle. On the extreme right next the Ancre

---

[1] German regimental histories make this abundantly clear.
[2] Formed in July out of the left of the Fourth Army and commanded by General Gough. It later (October 30th) became the Fifth Army.

was a battalion of the 118th Brigade, with the 11th R. Sussex next and the 14th Hampshire beyond them, the 117th Brigade being on the left of the 116th. Across the Ancre the Forty-Ninth Division, was attacking with St. Pierre Divion and a line running down from the Schwaben Redoubt [1] on the crest of the ridge as objectives. The Thirty-Ninth Division was covering the flank of this attack which, if successful, would have established us in a good position for the big task of capturing Thiepval and the redoubts behind it.

The Thirty-Ninth Division's infantry was now much below establishment: drafts had been few and had not kept pace with casualties and other wastage, and though the Hampshire and the 11th Royal Sussex could produce about 550 rifles apiece, the supporting battalions were much weaker. The British line here,[2] NE. of Hamel, ran South of the spur stretching down from Beaumont Hamel to the Ancre and was overlooked from the German trenches, but at Zero, 5.10 a.m., the attacking battalions went forward well; a machine-gun barrage fired over their heads mowed down Germans who stood up on their parapet to fire, and the attackers were soon in possession of the front line and could press on against the next, which also was carried, 2/Lt. Leach being conspicuous for leading his men with great initiative and gallantry. Opposition then stiffened; C Company's advance towards the final objective met heavy rifle and machine-gun fire and, despite gallant efforts, it failed to penetrate the wire. Of the 11th Sussex some had even gained their final objective, but the 117th Brigade had been less successful and its failure uncovered the Hampshire's left flank. However, a determined effort was made to consolidate the ground gained, and when the 117th Brigade attempted another advance, Captain Skinner and the Adjutant, Lt. Goldsmith, collected all the men they could and went forward, almost to the wire in front of the final objective where the attack was checked, Captain Skinner being killed. Even after this failure the surviving officers, especially Lt. Goldsmith, though he was wounded, did much to hold on to the German second line and keep up a defence which was soon hard pressed, bombers assailing it on the flanks, while heavy guns bombarded the captured position steadily, inflicting heavy losses and impeding consolidation and the advance of reinforcements. The attack across the Ancre had failed and from the steeper slopes above St. Pierre Divion the enemy had good observation.

However, the 14th hung on stoutly, blocking the ends of the captured trenches, beating back several advances and using bombs, Lewis guns and rifles to good purpose. But the enemy's shell-fire prevented reinforcements and the much-needed fresh ammunition from reaching the front and made it impossible for the Pioneers to open up communications. Thus, when bombs and cartridges ran short, the Hampshire were gradually thrust back, though the second line captured was held till about 1 p.m., while after that small parties maintained themselves in the old German front line for some time. 2/Lt. Tew was conspicuous in this effort, controlling his men's fire and shooting

---

[1] North by East of Thiepval. See Sketch 37 (p. 198).

[2] It had been pushed forward since July 1st and No Man's Land was barely half as wide as on that day.

many Germans himself, Lt. Goldsmith, despite his wound, worked hard to organize the defenders and 2/Lts. Ball and Bearn also did much to maintain our

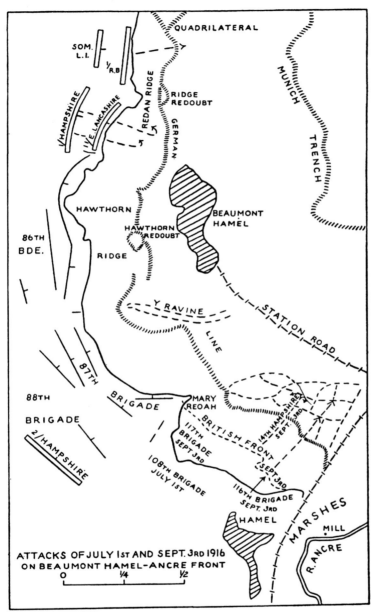

ATTACKS OF JULY IST AND SEPT. 3RD 1916
ON BEAUMONT HAMEL-ANCRE FRONT

hold. One party under 2/Lt. Bartlett held out till late in the afternoon before, having finished off all their ammunition, they had to get back. In retiring 2/Lt. Bartlett was hit for a second time and fell into a shell-hole, where he remained

till the night of September 4th/5th, then managing to regain our lines. After
dark any men still holding out in the enemy's lines were ordered to retire, and
the fragment that remained of the 14th went right back to Mailly Maillet to
reorganize. Of the 570 in action, 17 officers and 440 other ranks were casualties.[1]
The only consolation was that the men had fought splendidly, hanging on most
stubbornly after a good attack, while the enemy's losses must have been very

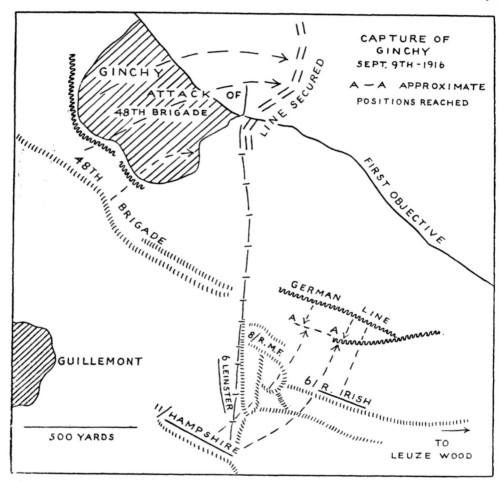

heavy, the battered trenches captured showed how effective our bombardment
had been, many dug-outs having had ' direct ' hits, while our riflemen had found

[1] Those killed included Captains Green and Rowsell and 2/Lts. Ash, Ball, Bearn, W. G. May,
Peel and Rodger ; 2/Lts. Haydon and Tew were missing and subsequently reported as prisoners of
war. Captain E. C. Freeman now assumed command. Lts. Goldsmith, Bartlett and Leach were
awarded the M.C. The account in the battalion diary is distinctly meagre and gives little detail,
not even naming the officers killed and wounded, having apparently been written up later. The
Brigade's diary supplies more of the story.

and used satisfactory targets. The Germans had had to pay high for the success of their counter-attacks.

Despite this repulse, the Thirty-Ninth Division was not relieved but had on September 10th to extend its frontage, so that only it and one other were holding the whole front from the Ancre to Hébuterne. Luckily the Germans were too well occupied to think of a counter-attack, thinly as our line was held.

With the Division so hard pressed the 14th had come into line again on September 14th, in the Auchonvillers sector and almost at the point from which the 1st had attacked on July 1st. A new C.O. arrived, Major Harman of the Leinster, who relieved Captain Freeman on September 21st, when a large batch of officers also arrived, mainly of the 3rd Battalion, while drafts nearly 300 strong had appeared. These, however, came mainly from the Suffolk or the Essex, the War Office having a peculiar capacity for sending drafts to strange regiments. All three brigades were in the line, with orders to be active so as to detain as many Germans as possible while the big thrust was being made elsewhere, and accordingly trench mortars and rifle grenades were freely used, to which the enemy retaliated fairly vigorously, his minenwerfer being unpleasantly in evidence.

Meanwhile on the British right the 11th Hampshire also were having the 'liveliest' times they had yet gone through. Our line now turned sharply Southward at Delville Wood to face Ginchy and Guillemont, localities which were proving stones of stumbling. Their capture was essential to securing a good starting line for the next big attack; several Divisions had incurred heavy losses in attempts to master them, and it was to a 'sticky' point that the Sixteenth Division had found itself directed at the end of August, becoming Corps reserve to the Fourteenth Corps.

Pioneers were not allowed to be idle even in Corps reserve. Two companies of the 11th Hampshire were promptly placed under the Fifth Division to help in consolidating some hard-won gains on our extreme right. After September 4th the 11th reverted to their own Division, now about to tackle Ginchy, for Guillemont, after resisting so many attacks, had at last been captured on September 3rd. Command on this front had then passed to the Sixteenth Division and the 11th Hampshire, who now moved up to Bernafay Wood, were soon busy on the defences and in finding carrying parties for the 48th Brigade, now on the Division's left, facing North towards Ginchy, an even nastier obstacle than Guillemont. The next three days gave the 11th hard work under heavy fire, digging new trenches and helping to consolidate. On September 6th Major Hazard was badly wounded when reconnoitring along with Lt. Cade. Encountering a patrol they challenged, were answered in English and coming forward were shot, Lt. Cade being killed. Major Hazard, after lying helpless in a shell hole, was eventually found by Corporal Snelling, who went back for help and, aided by Captains Stack and Thyne, brought him safely in. September 7th brought orders to take over the defences of Guillemont from the Irish Rifles, but the 'defences' were hard to discover, the trenches being almost obliterated, while shell-holes and a few dug-outs provided only a scanty shelter, so that the battalion, which had two days of severe shelling here, was really lucky to escape with under 40 casualties.

A fresh attack on Ginchy was fixed for September 9th, and as battalions were weak, recruits from Ireland being few, A and B Companies with four extra Lewis guns under Captain Stack were attached to the 47th Brigade, the rest of the 11th going back to Bernafay Wood.

A and B had during the night to dig themselves in 300 yards behind the front line, held by the 6th Royal Irish, who were to lead the attack. It was timed for 4.45 p.m., and during a long day of waiting the two companies had to endure a good deal of shelling. Casualties fortunately were not numerous, but Captain Stack was sniped when crossing the open to report to the O.C. of the 6th Connaught Rangers, under whose orders A and B had been placed.

A heavy machine-gun fire met the Royal Irish directly their first wave went forward; it seemed that the German first line had escaped our bombardment, for many machine-guns remained in action in it; the Hampshire, following the leaders, were also mown down in numbers; Captain Bland and three subalterns were hit at once, and to avoid annihilation the men could only seek what shelter they could in shell-holes. Lt. Shaw, however, helped by Lt. Durrant, brought small parties of the second wave forward by short rushes and reached a trench just short of the German line, in which he found many Royal Irish were sheltering. Here they remained till about 7 p.m., pinned down by shell-fire, and then, as the light failed, a fresh rush carried the surviving attackers into the enemy's front line. This they held for some time till a strong counter-attack forced them back to the trench where Lt. Shaw's party had sheltered and here they checked the enemy. But if itself unsuccessful, the 47th Brigade's attack had distracted the enemy's attention from the 48th on its left, who had meanwhile mastered and held Ginchy, repulsing several counter-attacks.[1]

After dark the Guards relieved the 47th Brigade and the survivors of A and B rejoined head-quarters in Bernafay Wood, C and D meanwhile making a fruitless journey to Ginchy to construct strong points, the sites selected proving not to be in our possession. Next day (September 10th) the battalion went back to Morlancourt and thence to Corbie. Here it remained till the 18th, then going by bus to Airaines, to entrain on September 21st for Flanders and the Second Army, which was using its division to relieve some of the Canadians, now under orders for the Somme, in the line NW. of Wytschaete.[2]

With Ginchy and Guillemont taken and useful gains of ground made in Delville Wood and on our right, preparations for the big attack, now fixed for September 15th, could go forward. Several fresh Divisions were now available, among them the Forty-First, which was to attack from Delville Wood, having

---

[1] Lts. Durrant and Shaw received the M.C.

[2] The battalion diary does not give the casualties for the attack of September 9th or for the whole month. 2/Lts. Chubb and Jeffries were killed on that day along with Captain Bland.

on its flanks the Fourteenth Division (right) and the New Zealanders (left); eighteen of the new secret weapons, later known as 'tanks', were to work with it.

The 122nd Brigade was on the Division's left with the 15th Hampshire (right) and 18th K.R.R.C. (left) in the leading line, their objective being Flers Trench, just South of Flers, where the supporting battalions, the 11th R.W.K. and 12th E. Surrey, would go through them and tackle Flers itself. In moving up over-night into its assembly position the battalion had been heavily shelled, and before Zero (6.20 a.m.) it had lost Captain Carrington of C Company and two platoon commanders, 2/Lts. Baddeley and Parry, while ration parties had suffered severely on the way up to the line. Advancing at Zero behind an excellent barrage, with seven tanks to help them, the Hampshire were quickly into the German front line, Tea Support, which was badly damaged, though its defenders fought hard before they were overpowered. Unluckily machine-guns on the left had done considerable damage before they were silenced, two more company commanders, Captains Stapleton and S. Thompson, being killed. One troublesome machine-gun was put out of action by a private who worked along a trench until close up and then shot down the whole team, and Lance Corporals Heath and Steer each rushed a machine-gun and disposed of it and its crew. Some dug-outs had to be cleared, but smoke bombs were used to good effect. Pushing on again, the Hampshire mastered the Switch Line also, where they met more opposition, which they soon overcame, taking many prisoners,[1] though casualties were mounting up. Here several dug-outs had to be cleared but the advance to Flers Trench went forward according to schedule, the 11th R.W.K. now reinforcing and going forward with the Hampshire. Flers Trench was full of Germans, but they were readier to bolt or surrender than to fight, being evidently terrified by the tanks, whose machine-guns had proved very effective, though most of them were already out of action, owing mainly to engine-trouble and other mishaps.

From Flers Trench a much disorganized advance was made into Flers, most of the officers had already fallen,[2] and few were left to control the men or to keep the 15th Hampshire in hand to consolidate their proper objective, and Hampshires and R.W. Kent went forward together with all formations broken up. On the outskirts of Flers a field gun in a house at a cross-roads gave trouble, till a tank arrived, ' spitting fire from its guns ', and disposed of it, Germans who tried to meet the tank with bombs finding to their surprise that the bombs did more harm to the throwers, fragments rebounding from it. Three tanks were already out of action, but this one now headed the entry into Flers, while three others worked along its Eastern edge. The sight of them was too much for the Germans, Flers was quickly cleared, and parties, pressing on beyond the village, reached the third objective, some of the 15th under 2/Lt. Menzies-Calder collecting over 20 prisoners on their way. But, when it came to consolidating

---

[1] These were sent back under the escort of some ' walking wounded '. They were Bavarians, two battalions of the 9th Bavarian Regiment being almost completely wiped out on this front.

[2] The last company commander, Captain Bailey, was killed in taking Flers Trench.

beyond the village, the lack of officers and senior N.C.O's [1] proved a serious trouble : with hardly anyone to take charge few men had any idea what to do, and when the Germans began to shell the captured positions some men drifted back into Flers and for a time the situation was critical, though parties of all battalions hung on North of the village and dug themselves in. Colonel Cary-Barnard and battalion head-quarters had by now come forward to Flers Trench, where a defensive position was consolidated and stragglers rallied, captured machine-guns being placed in position to strengthen the defence. Little news came back,[2] and that most confused, reports that Flers had been evacuated conflicting with others that the third objective was still occupied. 2/Lt. Hall and Corporal Murdin were indefatigable in obtaining accurate information, and eventually about 30 men under 2/Lts. Smith and Menzies-Calder [3] were discovered digging in beyond the village, as was also a separate party under 2/Lt. Tollemache, who had been wounded, while 2/Lt. Hall, having collected some men, took them forward to the third objective and dug in there. C.S.M. Smith also, though wounded, collected another party and consolidated a post, holding on all day until relieved at dark.[4]

Heavily as Flers and all our advanced positions were being bombarded the Germans never succeeded in regaining ground here, though they brought up large reserves and during the forenoon made several efforts to advance on Flers without success. Some of the 124th Brigade had come up into line East of Flers and secured the right flank, on the left touch was obtained with the New Zealanders,[5] while the Brigade Major of the 122nd Brigade, Major Gwyn Thomas, did much to organize the line North of the village, where Box and Cox and the Hog's Head, some trenches used for bombing practice, were occupied and consolidated, and towards evening two quite substantial counter-attacks, mainly against the 124th Brigade, were repulsed by rifle fire.

After dark the 123rd Brigade took over at Flers and the 15th Hampshire, considerably reduced in numbers, could get back to York Trench in reserve. Eight officers [6] and 97 men were killed and missing and three officers and 197 men wounded, out of the 18 officers and 557 other ranks in action, but hard as it had been hit the battalion could congratulate itself on its first battle, the capture of Flers was much to its credit, the advance here, of over 2,000 yards, being the furthest made anywhere along the front.

Elsewhere also substantial success had been achieved: we had at last cleared High Wood, Martinpuich and Courcelette had been taken and heavy punishment inflicted on the enemy. Unluckily our right had been checked, beyond it the French had done nothing, and this had helped to prevent further advances

[1] Three C.S.M's had been hit as well as nearly all the officers. The C.O. of the 11th R. West Kent was killed trying to organize the defence North of Flers.

[2] Three runners from C Company were killed within a space of 200 yards.

[3] 2/Lts. A. G. Smith and A. R. Hall subsequently received the M.C., C.S.M. Smith, Corporals Heath and Steer the D.C.M. and 12 men the M.M.

[4] Subsequently died of wounds.

[5] Their attack had gone very well and they were established NW. of Flers and beyond the road to Eaucourt l'Abbaye.

[6] Besides those mentioned 2/Lt. Stopford was killed.

in the centre and left and baulked us of the ' break-through ' for which the
' higher authorities ' had again hoped.[1] What the ' tanks ' had contributed

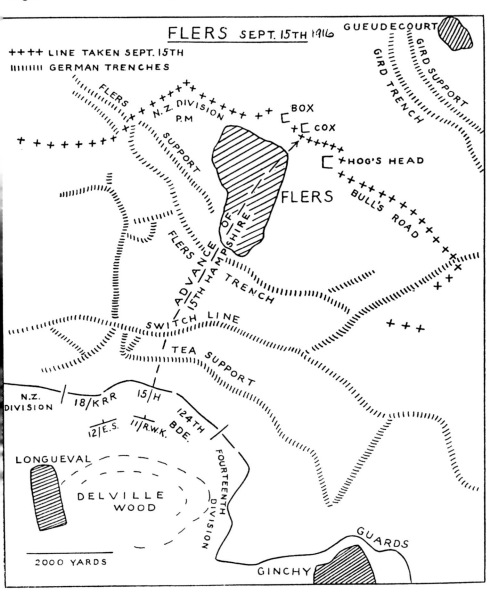

to the day's success had largely been by their influence on German morale :
their actual performances in action had fallen far short of those prophesied, very

[1] The Forty-First Division's final objective had been the Gird Trenches and Gueudecourt
behind them.

few had got far, many through developing defects and putting themselves out of action. Critics who condemn their employment in September 1916 as premature would do well to examine in detail their achievements on September 15th and reflect how much worse a disappointment might have resulted from the employment at a later date of much larger numbers, if there had been no opportunity of testing them in action and there discovering their defects and the points where improvements in design were necessary; moreover if full benefit was to be reaped from their employment infantry and guns had to learn by experience how to co-operate with them. The 15th Hampshire had learnt something from what this involved but nothing to encourage extravagant ideas of what the existing model might be expected to achieve.

In the extension and consolidation of the gains made on September 15th and in the renewed attack of September 25th no Hampshires were concerned : the 15th were too much reduced to be employed again so soon and, though the Second Army had released the Fourth Division in the middle of September, it was not in action till October 7th and then the 11th Brigade was in reserve. Indeed, though they had remained a fortnight longer in Flanders, the 2nd Hampshire, were actually in action again before the 1st Battalion, as their brigade was sent on ahead of the rest of the Twenty-Ninth Division, now also returning to the Somme. With the Thirty-Ninth Division stretched out on the long inactive front from the Ancre Northward, the Hampshire had no share in the hard fighting on both flanks which filled the last days of September.

Those days which saw Lesboeufs and Morval and Gueudecourt taken on our right also saw the Fourth Army's left brought up to Le Sars, while the Reserve Army mastered the almost impregnable Thiepval, taken by the Eighteenth Division on September 26th, and broke into the lines running Eastward along the crest of the ridge towards Courcelette. Here three redoubts, the Schwaben, North of Thiepval, and Stuff and Zollern, farther East, were particularly nasty obstacles, and even after Thiepval had been taken some weeks passed before the Thirty-Ninth Division, whose 117th and 118th Brigades relieved the Eighteenth Division at the beginning of October, had really mastered them. But even then the 14th Hampshire remained North of the Ancre, holding first the Redan sector and then that opposite Y Ravine, and did not become acquainted with the Schwaben Redoubt until October 16th. They had been as active as conditions would permit and had carried out one elaborate feint attack, ' doing everything except go over the top ' one officer wrote. Casualties for September, apart from those in the attack of September 3rd, came to about 50, including Captain Gunner (Hampshire Carabiniers) wounded.

Meanwhile the 15th Battalion had had another dose of the Somme. Flers had deprived that battalion of many competent and experienced officers and N.C.O.s, but it still had its C.O. and its Adjutant, Lt. Wilkinson,[1] and the practice, now regularly followed, of leaving out of any attack a proportion of officers,

[1] He had recently taken over from Captain Carrington.

N.C.O.s and specialists made the rebuilding of weakened battalions much easier. ' Second Line ' Yeomanry units and Cyclist Battalions, hitherto earmarked for Home Defence, were now being utilized to provide drafts and afforded some excellent material of good physique and better trained than the raw recruits so prominent in recent drafts, and when the 15th moved up to Mametz on October 2nd, after a fortnight's rest and training at Dernancourt, if none too strong they were ready again to give a good account of themselves. They came into line just to the left of their former position, relieving the New Zealanders, who had made substantial progress West of Gueudecourt, having driven the Germans a long way back up [1] the Gird and Gird Support Trenches, which the Forty-First Division had failed to reach on September 15th. The line the Forty-First were taking over ran from the Flers-Ligny Thilloy road to the Eaucourt l'Abbaye-La Barque road, NE. of Eaucourt. Gird Support here formed our front trench, but only the Eastern portions of this trench and of Gird Trench were as yet in our hands.

The 15th had hardly taken over before, about 5 a.m. on October 4th, they were attacked in force, Germans trying to break in between C and D Companies in the left centre of the front line in Gird Support. The attack was pressed with great determination, especially on the right, where some rather higher ground was evidently their objective, but the 15th offered a stubborn resistance, using bombs and machine-guns with excellent effect and doing considerable execution. 2/Lts. Gorman and Trevett gave their men a fine lead, heading bombing attacks with great success, and 2/Lt. Gorman not only drove some intruding Germans out of our line but pushed forward along a sap and established a block 25 yards down it. New Zealand machine-gunners who had remained behind did splendid service, all but one man were hit but the survivor went on working his gun till it too was disabled, while bombers from the 18th K.R.R.C. gave useful help. The enemy pressed hardest against C Company, but they could not overcome its resistance, and after over an hour's hard fighting they withdrew, having suffered heavily, while the 15th's casualties only came to a dozen.

After their repulse the Germans did not renew the attack, contenting themselves with shelling the position vigorously, but this did not prevent our bombers pushing forward 60 yards next day ; having reached a point where the trench was blown in, they waited till a German advance to this gap gave them good targets and after holding on for an hour they withdrew, having sniped successfully and done some useful reconnoitring, while it was satisfactory to find the trenches full of German dead. That evening the battalion was reported as 'short of rations but in good spirits' : it had again inflicted many more than its own dozen casualties. Next morning (October 6th) another but much less determined bombing attack was easily repulsed, the enemy being pushed back nearly 70 yards along Gird Support till a machine-gun checked our further progress. Then early on October 7th our bombers advanced about 60 yards along both Gird Trench and Gird Support and, though driven right back by a counter-

[1] i.e. NW.

attack, attacked again and eventually secured about half the ground previously taken. Stokes guns which enfiladed the enemy's trenches were used with good results and Sergeant Murdin handled a machine-gun most effectively.

That afternoon a fresh attack was attempted all along the Fourth Army's line. It was stubbornly opposed everywhere, machine-guns which our bombardment had failed to silence preventing much progress. The Forty-First Division's objective included the near ends of Gird Trench and Gird Support still in German hands and the Westward continuation of Bayonet Trench beyond the Flers-Ligny Thilloy road. On the 122nd Brigade's [1] right, the right of the 15th Hampshire carried the near ends of Gird Trench and Gird Support East of the High Wood-Ligny Thilloy road, but, after advancing about 200 yards, the left company was stopped by machine-guns which had been got into position because our barrage had gone ahead too soon.[2] They dug in here, beating back a rather feeble counter-attack, while our Lewis guns kept the enemy's infantry down under cover and allowed our men to dig. Here Lt. Foster and C.S.M. Smith were conspicuous for rallying men and re-organizing them, helping greatly towards maintaining and consolidating the line reached. Meanwhile German bombers working down Gird Trench were pressing our men hard, some of the ground gained was lost and the German advance threatened to cut off those of our men who had established themselves in Gird Support. A determined stand by a mixed party of Hampshire and 18th K.R.R.C., who were supporting the 15th, averted this danger, and eventually the Germans were bombed back nearly 90 yards, where a block was made and our gains secured. Meanwhile touch had been gained on the right with the 26th R. Fusiliers, who[3] also were consolidating short of Bayonet Trench but some way ahead of their starting line, and trenches were dug back to our old line. If in the main the attack had failed, some ground had been gained and the Germans had not escaped too lightly. Then on October 9th the battalion was relieved by the 123rd Brigade and went back into support, moving back again after two days to Mametz Wood and then to Meaulté. It had had nine officers [4] and 190 men hit out of the 17 officers and 319 men in action and sorely needed the drafts, nearly 400 in all and from a vast admixture of regiments, which it now received. After four days at Meaulte it entrained for the Abbeville area, whence it entrained again almost immediately, this time for the Ypres Salient.[5] Together with the rest of the Forty-First Division it had achieved not a little in its first major efforts.

At this stage in the operations the weather was beginning to take an increasingly important and unsatisfactory hand in affairs. Not only were

[1] This brigade was holding the left of the Division's frontage.
[2] The battalion on their left, who had much further to go to reach Gird Trench, also advanced some way before being forced to halt and dig in short of the objective.
[3] 124th Brigade.
[4] Captains James and Lacy and 2/Lt. Breslau were killed and 2/Lt. Philip died of wounds. Captain Amery was among the wounded, as was also 2/Lt. Gorman.
[5] Lt. Foster, 2/Lt. Gorman and C.S.M. Smith received the M.C. and Sergeant Murdin the D.C.M., while 10 M.M.s were awarded to men of the battalion.

frequent and heavy rain-storms making life in the trenches miserable and very exhausting, but reliefs were becoming increasingly slow and difficult, and the forwarding of ammunition, provisions and water to the troops in front, never easy, was now a most strenuous toil. In heavy rain the chalk of this area soon developed a glutinous stickiness over which heavily-laden men could hardly move. Communication trenches became knee-deep in sticky mud, in places they could hardly be used; movement across the open was little faster and by day was prohibitively costly. To attack in these conditions was almost to

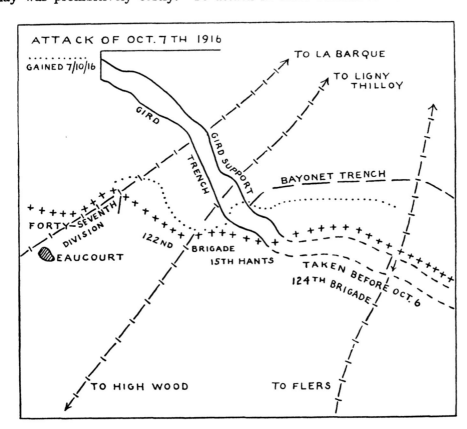

invite failure ; to achieve success bordered on the miraculous, and yet, with the Germans hard put to maintain their positions even when the weather and ground were so much in their favour, the arguments for maintaining our pressure as far as possible were weighty ; moreover, if Sir Douglas Haig showed any inclination to suspend his attacks, General Joffre would not hear of it and was prompt to urge him to continue them and even pressed him to extend their scope and frontage. Urgent French needs and strong French pressure must not be overlooked, even if the difficulties against which the four Hampshire battalions contended in their attacks of October 1916 may seem to have exceeded

what it was reasonable to ask troops to tackle. It is tantalizing to speculate on
what might have happened had the abnormally wet autumn of 1916 only been
as fine as that of 1918.

The Twelfth Division, to which the 88th Brigade was now attached, was
facing a very nasty proposition when called on to tackle the German lines just
beyond Gueudecourt in the mud and wet of October. The German front line

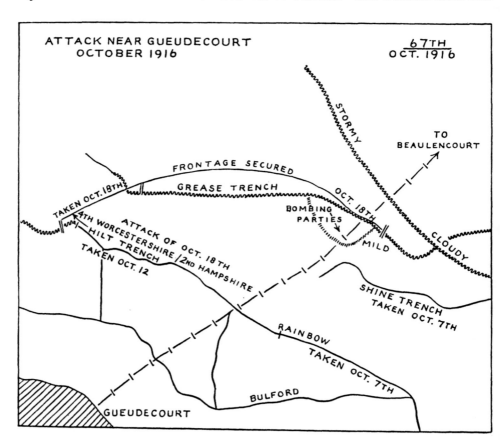

here, Hilt Trench opposite the Division's right, the Eastern part of Bayonet
Trench opposite the left, was nearly 400 yards away. Attacking on October
7th the Division had been repulsed with heavy loss, the few men who got into
the enemy's lines being overwhelmed. It was therefore decided to reinforce it
with the 88th Brigade, who were rushed down from Flanders, reaching Longeau
on October 8th and moving up by Pommiers Redoubt to reserve trenches a mile
and a half short of Gueudecourt. Before leaving Flanders the 2nd Hampshire
had been inspected by General Hunter-Weston, who had an encouraging
word with the few remaining Gallipoli men, Captain Lord, still Adjutant, and

the Quartermaster being the only officers still present who had been at the landing.

Attacking on October 12th, the Newfoundlanders and the Essex carried Hilt Trench [1] after a hard struggle, while on the left some of the Essex reached their second objective, Grease Trench. Further to the left uncut wire in front of Bayonet Trench had checked the 35th Brigade, and the Essex, with their left uncovered, were not only driven back from Grease Trench but from Hilt Trench also. The Newfoundlanders, however, held on, and, being reinforced by Y Company (Lt. Corke), not only maintained their ground but recovered some of the lost portion of Hilt Trench.

That evening, X (Lt. Borough) joined Y in Hilt Trench, relieving the Newfoundlanders, with W (Captain Cuddon) and Z (Captain Massey) in support. Their left was ' in the air ', with Germans holding the continuation NW. of Hilt Trench, while some were actually established to the left rear, near enough to ply our open flank with rifle grenades. To this an effective reply was made and great work was done in consolidating the line, despite heavy shelling, from which the companies in support suffered almost more than those in Hilt Trench itself. Three days here cost the battalion 150 casualties, 2/Lts. Amos (Buffs) and Haly being killed with 32 men, while Colonel Middleton was wounded but continued at duty, but its hard work had made the position secure and thereby assisted the Sixth Division [2] on the right to make good the ground gained on October 7th and 12th across the Beaulencourt Road, while another dozen prisoners had been added to the 150 taken in the original attack.

After two more days in support at Gueudecourt, where more heavy shelling caused another 20 casualties, the battalion moved up into Hilt Trench on the evening of October 17th for a fresh attack on Grease Trench ; on the left the 4th Worcestershire were also attacking, while beyond them the 35th Brigade were making another attempt on Bayonet Trench. On the Hampshire's immediate right the Sixth Division was attacking with Mild Trench, and a portion of Cloudy Trench as objectives.

' Zero ' was at 3.40 a.m. October 18th, but before that the leading companies Y and Z, had formed up in No Man's Land. This drew the enemy's fire but it had little effect, and at ' Zero ' the attackers went forward well and, despite heavy fire, both Hampshire and Worcestershire, keeping close to the barrage, were quickly into Grease Trench and overpowering its defenders, of whom nearly 200 were taken by the two battalions. Grease Trench was not quite continuous and in the dark some Hampshire pushed on to Stormy Trench, 200 yards further on, but, being too far ahead, had to be brought back to Grease Trench, which was being consolidated. Unfortunately the 35th Brigade had again failed against Bayonet Trench, but the Worcestershire were constructing a block at the left end of Grease Trench, while to get touch with the Sixth Division the Hampshire began pushing along the line to the right, getting into Mild Trench and by clearing nearly 200 yards of it gave great help

[1] West of the Beaulencourt road, just East of which part of Rainbow Trench was also taken on Oct. 12th, most of it having been taken by the Twentieth Division on Oct. 7th.
[2] It had replaced the Twentieth.

N

to the battalion whose objective it was. Captain Cornish [1] and 2/Lt. Harrod,[2] who had led the attack well, now did great work in directing the consolidation, in which C.S.M. Lund [3] was most helpful, while Lance Corporals Fiford and Gray[4] and Privates Johnson [4] and Wilkens [4] carried messages back across the open, despite very heavy shelling, and Privates Bowring [4] and Staples,[4] having salvaged a Lewis gun lying in No Man's Land, cleaned it and got it into action. Twice the enemy were seen gathering for a counter attack, but each time they were quickly and very effectively discouraged by our rapid fire. It had been intended to construct some strong points 80 yards out to the front, but heavy fire from Stormy Trench and the steady shelling put this out of the question, though the fire did not shift the Hampshire, who held on stoutly, repulsing all attempts to dislodge them. Captain Cornish, well backed up by 2/Lt. Harrod, was conspicuous for his cheerfulness and confidence, which greatly encouraged his men to maintain their grip on their captures despite the weather and the shelling, and, as the Brigadier [5] said, their determination and endurance were as noticeable as their dash and vigour in the attack. Their left had been secured by the Worcestershire's success in attack and tenacity in defence, but at one moment the position on the right seemed critical. The 71st Brigade's left in Mild Trench was very hard pressed, some ground being lost, and strong bombing attacks developed against the Hampshire's exposed right flank. These the battalion's bombers and Lewis gunners checked, Corporal Stockly,[6] Lance Corporal Whitcher [6] and Private Wood [6] all being prominent in repulsing them, while 2/Lt. Harrod followed up this repulse by taking a Lewis gun across the Beaulencourt road and thereby helped the 71st Brigade to hang on in Mild Trench, of which the Hampshire eventually consolidated 200 yards outside their own brigade's frontage. But to hold the captured position taxed the Hampshire's endurance severely, as the Brigadier very warmly acknowledged : the shelling was very heavy, the weather atrocious, with pelting rain, and to get supplies up to those in front required real energy and determination from the carrying parties. Useful assistance was given by our guns and by machine-guns in Gueudecourt firing overhead, and the machine-guns in the position captured were very effectively used. The stretcher bearers were very hard worked, and among them Private Bone [6] stood out, he went from shell-hole to shell-hole getting men into the comparative safety they afforded, bandaging them and even getting some men hot tea : not a few wounded owed him their lives.

The battalion should have been relieved on the night of October 19th/20th, but with the communication trenches so deep in mud and even the open so slippery and sticky that movement was terribly slow, the relieving battalion, one from the 87th Brigade, could not complete the relief in time for the Hampshire to get away before daylight : they had therefore to remain in double-manned trenches until evening. Since October 17th 2/Lts. Aitcheson, Cain,

---

[1] His orderly, Private Adams, saved his life by shooting a German who was covering him and also was most useful in the consolidation.

[2] Both officers received the M.C.   [3] Received the D.C.M.

[4] Received the M.M.   [5] Brigadier General D. E. Cayley.

[6] These four and another stretcher bearer, Private Gibbs, received the M.M.

Elton and Hailstone had been killed or were missing, with 31 men, 2/Lts. Corke, Darracott, Gilman, (E. Surrey) Graham (E. Surrey), Gravely and Rutherford were wounded with 106 men, while Captains Cuddon and Massey had to go to hospital, along with 2/Lts. Todd and Treble and 30 men. The battalion now received many congratulations on its gallantry and tenacity : the position it and the 4th Worcestershire had captured and consolidated, despite so many difficulties and stiff opposition, was a very useful gain, and the commanders of both the Sixth and Twelfth Divisions sent them special messages of thanks for their assistance. October 18th ranks among the 2nd Hampshire's most notable achievements. Success at that stage in the Somme was never easily obtained and needed dash and determination to no small degree.

Before this the Fourth Division had taken over the extreme British right [1] and were experiencing the difficulties inherent in co-operating with allies whose methods were not ours. Attacking on October 12th just East of Lesboeufs, the 10th Brigade had made a small advance, securing Antelope Trench. The 11th Brigade had been back in reserve at Montauban that day and did not take over the front line until October 17th. Even then the 1st Hampshire were in brigade reserve near Guillemont and merely supplied carrying and working parties on October 18th, when the Rifle Brigade and East Lancashire attacked with very scanty success. From October 19th to 22nd, the battalion was digging assembly and communication trenches behind Lesboeufs under great handicaps from wet and mud. It then took over the front from the Somerset L.I. who had pushed forward after dark on October 19th and secured Frosty Trench, to the left of Antelope Trench and not continuous with it.

A fresh attack was to be made on October 23rd, despite the difficulties of ground and weather, the 1st Hampshire, with the Rifle Brigade in support, seeking to capture Boritska Trench. A (left) and C (right) companies were leading, B in support having to form a defensive flank on the right. On the left the Dublins of the 10th Brigade were tackling Hazy Trench and beyond them the 12th Brigade was confronted by Rainy and Dewdrop Trenches. On our right the French were attacking.

Starting at 2.30 p.m., from Antelope and Frosty Trenches, the attack had first to clear a low ridge in No Man's Land, and directly it crossed this it met a heavy fire, both from Boritska Trench and from machine-guns further back, and C Company were soon driven to shelter in shell-holes short of the objective. The French had failed completely and our right flank was therefore exposed. A Company fared better, entering and taking the Northern end of Boritska, down which they began bombing, at first with some success. Meanwhile the Dublins had not carried Hazy Trench but had taken some gun-pits NW. of Frosty Trench and with them several machine-guns. The Rifle Brigade, coming forward in support, were checked by machine-guns in the untaken part of Boritska Trench and only about half a company of Riflemen, working

---

[1] The 1st Hampshire came up to Meaulte on October 7th and moved forward to Montauban five days later.

forward from shell-hole to shell-hole, reinforced the hard-pressed Hampshire in Boritska Trench. Lt. Icke,[1] who had led his company admirably in the attack, recrossed No Man's Land under heavy fire to collect bombers and bring them up to reinforce the men in Boritska. These made a stout fight ; 2/Lt. Gullick leading several bombing attacks, though himself wounded. As long as bombs and ammunition lasted the defence held, though the enemy were pressing them from both flanks, but after keeping the Germans at bay till well after dark the survivors, without reinforcements or supplies, had to fall back some to Frosty Trench, some to Antelope. But the fight they had made had helped the Dublins to make good the gun-pits, from which a trench was dug back to Frosty Trench, which another trench linked up with Antelope Trench, so that the attack had resulted in some improvement in our line,[2] which, with the ground in so bad a state, was no small achievement. But it had cost the 1st Hampshire over 200 casualties, Captains Cromie and Le Marchant [3] and 2/Lts. C. J. Girling and Harrison were killed, 2/Lt. Wood was missing and 2/Lts. Gullick, Hodgkins, Lapthorne, Line and Masterman wounded. Of other ranks 86 were killed and missing and 137 wounded.[4] But the Germans had not escaped lightly.

After holding on all next day and doing all they could to consolidate their position and rescue their wounded, the 1st Hampshire were relieved in the small hours of October 25th, by the 2nd R.W.F. whose Division, the Thirty-Third, was now replacing the Fourth. They now went right back, eventually finding good billets at Ramburelles, 12 miles SW. of Abbeville, where six weeks out of trenches enabled them to rest, refit and assimilate their drafts.

The 1st Battalion had thus finished with ' the Somme ', rather sooner than the 2nd, who after a week in reserve were back in front trenches North of Flers for two days at the end of October. They had returned to their own Division, which was then relieved, and before having to go back into trenches got a fortnight's rest, the 2nd Hampshire being at Mericourt. The 2nd then took over support trenches at Bernafay Wood and were there four days before taking over the front line NE. of Les boeufs on November 21st. By this time the effort to push our right further forward, over the slippery slime of the battle area, had been abandoned and the sector was ' quiet ', if nothing else could be said for it.

Beyond the Ancre, however, a last ' push ' had been made, with some success, on November 13th, Beaumont Hamel being taken, and here fighting was still raging. This final attack had completed the work on which the Fifth, the re-named Reserve, Army had been engaged since its success at Thiepval on September 26th. Gradually and only after hard fighting our lodgements in the Schwaben Redoubt had been extended and consolidated, the 117th and 118th Brigades assisting to complete its reduction during the first half of October.

[1] Received the M.C.   [2] Further to the left also rather bigger gains had been made.
[3] Both sons of old officers of the regiment.
[4] A few of these casualties occurred between October 17th and 23rd, 2/Lt. Currie also being wounded on October 20th.

The 116th, however, was left in its old line across the Ancre, strung out in a wide front which was but thinly held. The 14th Hampshire had four days ' out ' from October 6th to 10th after a spell of 16 days on end in the trenches, but they were back again in line facing Y Ravine for six days before being relieved by the Sixty-Third Division on October 16th and thus set free to rejoin the other brigades on the Thiepval front. If had been a trying time, if devoid of special incident, but casualties had fortunately been few.

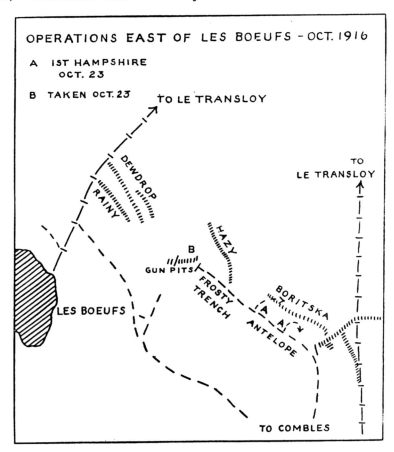

By the time the 116th Brigade were across the Ancre Stuff Redoubt also had been taken, and the next objective was formed by Stuff Trench and its Eastward continuation, Regina Trench, whose capture would complete the work already begun of driving the Germans down the reverse slope of the ridge and depriving them of the crest line and its facilities for observation.

The 14th Hampshire after a good night's rest at Engelbelmer (October 16th/17th) relieved the 12th R. Sussex in the Schwaben Redoubt next morning, to come in for as hard a time as they had yet known. The much battered and contested defences offered little protection against persistent heavy shelling and even less shelter from the constant rain and bitter cold. At one point Germans were established in a continuation of a trench which we were holding and they more than once tried to attack along it. These attempts the 14th quickly repulsed, but bombing and rifle-grenading continued intermittently, while the shelling went on steadily, causing many casualties until by hard work the defenders had done something to improve the cover. To lessen the effects of the concussion men at times sat with their backs braced up against one side of a trench and their feet pressing into the other. But the wet and cold were even worse than the shelling ; men got so stuck in the mud that their extrication took hours, at ' stand to ' some were so stiff with cold that they had to be lifted to their feet. This rain and mud doubled the difficulties of the

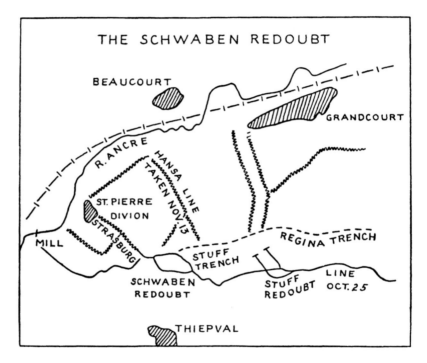

THE SCHWABEN REDOUBT

BEAUCOURT

GRANDCOURT

R. ANCRE

HANSA LINE

TAKEN NOV 13

STRASBURG

ST. PIERRE DIVION

MILL

REGINA TRENCH

STUFF TRENCH

SCHWABEN REDOUBT

STUFF REDOUBT

LINE OCT. 25

THIEPVAL

carrying parties in bringing up ammunition and rations, but fortunately the German dead who filled the trenches, in themselves an encouraging factor, had ample rations on them by which the Hampshire profited, as well as by the large quantities of excellent equipment lying about. A large parcel of cigars and tobacco, obviously lately arrived from Germany, was quickly disposed of and, as one officer wrote, ' we wore German overcoats till they were wet through and then put on others, we used their waterproof capes, we dug with German spades, in fact we made full use of all Mr. Bosche's gear, and jolly good it was.'

Even with these alleviations the 14th had four very hard days, which they endured in a manner enormously to their credit. One officer wrote in warm admiration of his men's unflinching steadfastness ; soaked to the skin, without a chance to get dry or to get food cooked, they ' stuck it ' without a murmur, took every chance to hit back and held on until, late on October 20th, the 17th K.R.R.C. turned up to relieve them, but by then casualties had come to nearly 100, including 2/Lt. C. D. F. Pearce and 20 men killed.

As the K.R.R.C. were very weak and an attack was to be made next day, D Company under Captain Warren were left behind to reinforce them, together with some details, largely men who had not been able to get away in darkness, the difficulty of getting exhausted men out of the mud and helping them along having caused many delays. Not long after the relief had been completed a heavy barrage was put down on the redoubt, under cover of which a strong body of Germans advanced to the attack and, using flammenwerfers, established two lodgements in the the Northern face, some of the defenders being almost too cold to be able to fire. However, they rose to the occasion splendidly ; chilled and dead-beat as most of the Hampshire were, once the fight began they warmed up and ' were as fresh as paint in one minute ', as one combatant put it. Counter-attacking vigorously they and the 60th hurled themselves on the intruders, many of whom surrendered almost without a fight, while the rest were driven headlong out of the redoubt, in which they left behind many dead and more prisoners. They were apparently picked men from three regiments, but the fight they made hardly suggested it ; one account says that the Hampshire hardly knew what to do with so many prisoners, and there were officers among them.

More was to be required of D Company than merely to repulse attacks. That afternoon the 116th Brigade took part in a big attack on Stuff and Regina Trenches, three other Divisions co-operating on a frontage of 5,000 yards. D Company, who had the 11th R. Sussex on their right, were on the left of the attackers. Well led by Captain Warren, who fell at the head of his men, they attacked with great dash and were quickly successful, mastering all their objectives after sharp fighting, in which 2/Lt. Green [1] distinguished himself in the capture of a bombing post, leading his bombers with great courage and determination, and, though wounded, remaining at duty to assist in the con-solidation until relieved. 2/Lt. Boustead [1] also, taking command when Captain Warren was killed, himself disposed of several Germans and directed the consolidation most effectively. Elsewhere the attack had gone well, practically the whole objective was taken, and though later on the alarm of a counter-attack caused the rest of the Hampshire to be sent up in readiness to rein-force, they were not needed and next day the whole battalion went back to a good camp at Senlis for a well-earned rest. The day's casualties had been heavy, besides Captain Warren 45 men were killed or missing, while 2/Lts. Boustead, Green and Hole and 95 men were wounded but the Germans had lost heavily and many prisoners had been taken. The 14th's achievement had been the more creditable after all they had had to endure from the shelling and the dreadful conditions : no small credit for enabling them to hold on was due to

[1] 2/Lts. Boustead and Green were awarded the M.C.

the carrying-parties, of which 2/Lt. Wallis-Wilson, the battalion's 40-year old veteran, was in charge : his unfailing energy and determination were largely responsible for the arrival of these parties with food, water and ammunition, despite all the difficulties of the approach, the mud, the lack of landmarks and the shelling ; again and again he had a nasty barrage to negotiate, but he always got his men through and ' delivered the goods '.

The weather was now making it hard to maintain the attack, but the Fifth Army had not relinquished its designs on Beaumont Hamel and of simultaneously advancing its line on the Ancre heights, and so for the next three weeks the Thirty-Ninth Division had to be retained in the fighting line in the Thiepval sector. Conditions were too bad here for battalions to stand more than 48 hours on end in the front line, but when in reserve at Thiepval German dug-outs provided almost luxurious quarters and were full of rations and all varieties of gear and equipment. by which all ranks profited. Rats were much in evidence, and as one company of the 14th could produce a ' company ferret ' some excellent rat-hunting was much enjoyed. Things were fairly quiet, a German attack on Stuff Trench on October 26th fizzled out completely, nearly 50 Germans surrendering quite tamely, eight officers among them. More rain made holding the front line very unpleasant and increased the work of the carrying-parties, but casualties were few, though Lt. Harris was killed on November 6th and the M.O. badly wounded. From November 10th to 12th the battalion was in the Schwaben Redoubt, holding a bombing-block at one point with the Germans 30 yards away, just too far to throw their ' stick ' bombs effectively but within range of our Mills bombs, while a ' plum ' bomb they were using proved too small to be very effective.

By this time the weather had improved enough to allow of the Fifth Army making its projected attack on November 13th, and on being relieved on the previous afternoon the Hampshire had merely gone back to the shelter of the Thiepval dug-outs, to be called out early next morning to move up to the Schwaben. Here they were in reserve to the 118th Brigade who, with the 117th on their left nearer the Ancre, were making for St. Pierre Divion and the Hansa Line, which ran down from the Thiepval ridge to the Ancre near Beaucourt.

The Hampshire had no easy advance up to the Schwaben : when they went forward at 5.45 a.m., 'Zero' hour, it was pitch dark, a mist did not help matters, and the tape they were to follow had been shot away, but they managed to reach the redoubt without many casualties and there they waited for orders. Prisoners were soon streaming back in numbers, but patrols sent out to keep touch with the attack reported that ' 63 ', the bombing block already familiar to the 14th, had been missed by the attackers and was causing trouble by firing into the rear of the attacking waves. Captain May accordingly organized an attack upon it and was successful in overcoming its resistance, 20 prisoners, a machine-gun, two automatic rifles and some trench-mortars being captured with it. Meanwhile the attack had gone very well, having apparently taken the Germans by surprise, but here and there pockets of Germans were holding out and about 9.30 a.m. the Hampshire were ordered forward to assist in mopping up and securing the Strassburg Line, running down from the Schwaben Redoubt to St. Pierre Divion. They promptly pushed forward, Captain Bircham, who had done fine work in holding the Schwaben Redoubt in October, again distinguished himself by gallantry and good leading, reinforcing the attackers effectively and helping to secure the objective. Everywhere the advance swept forward, reaching St. Pierre Divion, collecting many prisoners and finding many German wounded, while other battalions, pushing Eastward, secured the Hansa Line half way to Grandcourt. Casualties had been negligible and the readiness of the Germans to surrender was an encouraging thing, ' the majority hardly offered any resistance ; their tails are right between their legs ' one officer wrote. Consolidation was promptly pushed on, Captain Bircham and 2/Lt. Wallis-Wilson doing valuable work, but no counter-attack developed. Elsewhere the attack had been successful, the formidable Beaumont Hamel had been taken, if all our objectives had not been reached, and the day's work was a fine ending to the Somme as far as the 14th Hampshire were concerned. Fighting continued a little longer, mainly exploiting the success of November 13th, but the 14th Hampshire had been relieved that afternoon and with the rest of their Division were soon on their way to Flanders, entraining at Doullens on November 18th and reaching Poperinghe about midnight.

If the simultaneous capture of Beaumont Hamel rather overshadowed the Thirty-Ninth Division's work on November 13th, the 14th Hampshire could congratulate themselves on a share in a notable exploit. ' The Schwaben ' had given them the chance to get their own back for September 3rd, and if their casualties had been again heavy [1] they came out encouraged by their success, by the ample evidence of the state to which quite good German units had been reduced, of which their readiness to surrender had been the outstanding proof. To the rewards gained earlier the 14th could now add the bar to the M.C. awarded to Captain May and the M.C's given to Captain Bircham and 2/Lt. Wallis-Wilson, whose good work at the Schwaben and good leading on November 15th were fittingly recognized.

[1] Not far short of 300 all told from the time of their first occupying the Schwaben Redoubt.

CHAPTER XVI
THE THIRD WINTER

WHEN ' Meredith's ' had wintered in Ghent in Marlborough's days or ' Stuart's ' in Münster in the Seven Years' War, they had enjoyed a real suspension of hostilities and repose, with only ' peace-time ' guards and duties to perform. ' Western Front ' winters between 1914 and 1918 brought no such repose and relaxation : if by 1916 the British forces were large enough to allow whole Divisions to be out of the line together, a ' resting ' Division was usually busy training reinforcements, most of whom had still much to learn. They were lucky if this training was not seriously interrupted by demands for the working parties which the preparations for another great ' push ' made increasingly insistent. Better communications, road, tramway and rail, were essential to this great effort, and better communications meant hard work for fighting units, as the various labour forces which were gradually being developed were as yet quite unequal to the requirements.

But if Divisions nominally ' resting ' were worked quite hard, holding the line during the bitter winter of 1916–1917 was arduous in the extreme. As often, the very wet autumn was followed by a hard winter, frost and snow making existence in trenches miserably uncomfortable, except so far as it banished mud and made movement easier, if the frozen ground made work on trenches almost impossible. Occasional spasms of mild weather were really almost worse than the cold, the mud was quick to re-assert itself, and the Fourth Army, above all the others, found conditions always bad, if sometimes worse. With five miles of slippery devastation, largely water-logged shell-holes, between its front and the old line of July 1st, supports and reserves, if far enough forward to be useful, were almost as exposed and unsheltered as those in front ; merely to keep the forward troops supplied threw a never-ending strain on roads, transport and men, and the trench-garrisons had to endure greater hardships than in the previous winter, when the front line had been nearer to good billets with the manifold amenities so greatly developed since the winter of 1914–1915. Moreover, while the British had had to take over from the French twenty additional miles of frontage, behind which the whole rearward organisation had to be built up from nothing, the higher command was insistent that opportunities of harassing the enemy or gaining ground should not be neglected. The Germans could not be allowed to improve and consolidate unmolested the indifferent line to which they had been pushed back, but if cogent strategical reasons supported this policy, it demanded much of those who carried it out and troops who had endured the Somme were hampered in recovering from its strain.

The 1st Hampshire were fortunate in being out of the line from November 2nd to December 7th, in good billets near Abbeville, mainly occupied with company training, route marching and other exercises, including brigade and Divisional competitions, while leave was fairly generously given. Reinforcements amounting to 168 men joined, with 30 from hospital, to which 54 were admitted, while the officers who joined included Captain K. A. Johnston and three subalterns who had also been wounded on July 1st. December 7th started a return to the front, the battalion having a week in a muddy camp near Bray before moving up on December 15th to Priez Farm near Combles, a sector just taken over from the French and hardly conforming to British standards of what a front should be. Here it spent four days in brigade reserve and then (December 19th) relieved the East Lancashire opposite St. Pierre Vaast Wood, the enemy's front line being about 500 yards away. The ' line ' here was in shell-holes,[1] not continuous trenches, and the ground was extremely muddy, but apart from some German artillery activity the time was uneventful. The battalion had three days in line, four in reserve, three in line again and then on December 29th went back to Bray. Casualties came to 15 killed and missing, with 2/Lt. R. A. B. Hall and 11 men wounded, while so bad were conditions that seven officers and 77 men were admitted to hospital, from which 20 returned, drafts amounting to 280.

The first few weeks of January were spent at Bray, encamped in a pathless sea of mud which needed any amount of work, but nevertheless much training, largely elementary, proved possible and left everyone much smartened up. The New Year's Honours List brought promotion to Captain to the Quartermaster, Lt. Tarrant, the M.S.M. to Sergeant Catley, the Orderly Room Clerk, and ' mentions ' for Captain Wyld and Lt. Flint.

January 16th brought a move to Curlu, where four peaceful days were spent in a good hutted camp, before the battalion moved up over the snow-covered ground to relieve the East Lancashire in the Bouchavesnes sector, three miles North of Peronne. The line here was continuous but too shallow to provide much cover, especially as the Germans overlooked it from higher ground. Luckily mine-shafts abounded and accommodated most of the front line garrison, and such work as the frost allowed was done at night, though a bright moon interfered with wiring, 2/Lt. Jacob being hit while directing a wiring party. Rations and ammunition had to be brought up from five miles away, which absorbed so many of the carrying parties that it left few free to carry up the materials so badly wanted in the front line. During two turns in front line two men were killed and 2/Lt. Jacob and four men wounded, but admissions to hospital came to 93, three times the discharges. A dozen officers joined, including Major Earle[2] and Lt. N. Harland, who had been at Gallipoli with the 2nd Battalion. During a fortnight in camp near Bray, fatigues greatly impeded training : 270 men under Captain Hudson[3] having to make gun emplacements near Rancourt, where another 170 under Captain German assisted a Tunnelling Company. A very unpleasant but uneventful week at Bouchavesnes followed, a thaw filled the trenches with water and they could hardly be kept passable. Then on February 22nd the Eighth Division took over and the 1st Hampshire went

---

[1] Only one company was actually in front line.
[2] Adjutant of the 5th Battalion on mobilization, he had accompanied the 1/5th to India, where he had been on the Staff for some time.   [3] He had returned from a ' course ' at Aldershot.

back West of Corbie, where they spent a week training before moving North to join the Third Army, now being reinforced for its Spring 'push'. February had cost the 1st three men killed and Lt. Harland and ten wounded, with 150 admissions to hospital, from which 35 men had rejoined. Four officers, among them Captain Prendergast, who had already been wounded twice, had joined with 11 men.

Starting on March 4th, the 1st Hampshire reached Buire au Bois, 11 miles NW. of Doullens, on the 7th, having covered 48 miles in four marches ; only 20 men had fallen out, not bad over such roads and after trying times in the trenches. They were 'out' all March, training and being for some time at the disposal of the Army Training School for demonstration purposes. A move to Bajus near Houdain on March 21st did not interrupt the training, which included a rehearsal over ground marked out to represent the battalion's intended objective in the coming attack. Then on April 7th the battalion started for Arras, reaching Maroeuil next day. Six officers, all new-comers, and 116 men had joined in March, with another 44 from hospital, to which three officers and 85 men had been admitted, and the battalion was both strong and fit.

Like the 1st Battalion the 2nd Hampshire got through the winter without heavy casualties, having only 24 killed and 79 wounded between November 1st and March 31st, for though the Twenty-Ninth Division twice carried out minor offensives during the winter, with considerable success, the 88th Brigade was not employed in either, and if at times the German shell-fire was heavy, especially in retaliation for raids or bombardments, it did not do much damage. Most of the battalion's 400 admissions to hospital occurred in November and the first half of December, when they saw a good deal of the front line NE. of Lesboeufs, in trenches which heavy rain had reduced to a deplorable state, after which four weeks 'out' in the Cavillon area followed.

The 2nd Battalion ended the year with 37 officers and 903 other ranks ; of the officers only Colonel Beckwith, who had rejoined on December 1st, and Captains Lord (Adjutant), Cuddon (O.C. 'W' Company), and Jones (X), had been with the battalion in Gallipoli, the Quartermaster being away sick and R.S.M. Tyler acting for him.

The New Year brought Captain Lord and 2/Lt. Saunders the M.C. and Sergeant Taylor the D.C.M., Major Middleton, R.S.M. Tyler and Private Bone being 'mentioned'.

January 11th found the battalion at Hangest trying to entrain for Corbie, much hampered by snow, quantities of slush, no lights and a train which was six hours late. At Corbie it had good billets but more slush and no means of removing it. It then moved up on January 20th by Carnoy and Guillemont to take over trenches nearly two miles NE. of Morval. Ice-coated duckboards made carrying very difficult, the ground was frozen hard and the line a mere chain of isolated posts,[1] but the Germans were clearly no better off and lay quiet,

---

[1] Braziers were taken up to the front and did something to alleviate conditions there.

and three days in line only produced 15 admissions to hospital and two men killed. The battalion was ' in ' again from January 25th to 27th, when the 87th Brigade celebrated the Kaiser's birthday by a most successful attack, capturing 350 prisoners, which provoked a vigorous retaliation without causing the Hampshire any casualties. After two turns at Morval early in February, where casualties were heavier than usual, 11 in the first, 13 in the second, they were ' out ' at Raineville from the 10th to 20th and then had three days in trenches at Saillisel. Despite many admissions to hospital drafts kept the strength well up.

Both the Fourth and Twenty-Ninth Divisions were ' out ' when on March 17th the Fourth Army found the Germans beginning to retreat to the Hindenburg Line, the Fifth's opponents having already evacuated the nasty salient astride the Ancre in which the autumn fighting had left them. The 2nd Hampshire, having been relieved at Saillisel on March 3rd, were back at Meaulté, where they remained till March 19th, then moving to Vignacourt in the lower Somme area, where the Division was to go through the intensive training which its energetic commander organized and superintended so assiduously. The leading of junior officers during the Somme had frequently been severely criticised, they did not know how to utilise opportunities, much less develop them, and courage without knowledge or grasp of tactical principles was more likely to cause avoidable casualties than to achieve success. Special attention was therefore paid to their instruction and to musketry, in which our standard had declined disastrously through excessive concentration on the bomb. The Division was soon to show how much it had profited by the energetic and systematic instruction now provided.

Fifty men having joined with several officers, the 2nd mustered 44 officers and 883 other ranks on March 31st, companies having usually seven subalterns, though many fewer were normally present, mainly owing to ' courses '. Two marches of 12 miles each, in snow and bitter weather, took them to Mondicourt by April 2nd. A ' battle nucleus '[1] was detailed to go back to the Corps depot, and then on April 7th the battalion advanced to Humbercourt, its Division being under the Eighteenth Corps, in Army reserve to the Third Army, now about to attack in force.

All three Hampshire ' Service battalions ' in France being in the Second Army, they also saw nothing of the advance towards the Hindenburg Line with its numerous actions. On the Second Army's front the winter had seen no major activities. Its mines under the Messines Ridge were dug and ready for the offensive in Flanders which Sir Douglas Haig had so long projected, but most Divisions now under General Plumer had needed time to recuperate and re-build themselves after heavy losses on the Somme, while winter conditions in the Salient hardly encouraged attacking.

The 11th Hampshire, who had taken over De Zon Camp[2] before the end of

---

[1] This included the second in command, Major Middleton, one company commander and at least one subaltern per company with some ' specialist ' N.C.O's and men.

[2] Near Vierstraat.

September, remained there for six months, despite a change of the Divisional front in December, when the Sixteenth Division took over the Spanbroekmolen sector, but eventually moved at the end of March to a new camp, Moore Park, Divisional H.Q. having shifted to Locre.   Duties and occupations during this time varied little : roads, camps and the maintenance and improvement of the line kept any Pioneers amply occupied.   In the line ' strong points ' and trench-mortar emplacements had to be constructed, new trenches dug, infantry work-ing parties supervised and assisted in draining, revetting and repairing ; in back areas more hutted camps were needed and extensive drainage schemes were being carried out, while baths, drying-rooms and wash-houses were built and roads kept in repair, with miscellaneous tasks like erecting a chaff-cutting shed and engine house, while the transport horses found peaceful employment in ploughing up ground near the camp in which to plant potatoes.

Casualties among the working parties in the line were not infrequent but in the aggregate not heavy ; Lt. Hytton, hit in November when supervising work on a ' strong point ', was the only officer killed before the Messines attack of June 6th opened the Flanders offensive of 1917, though 2/Lt. T. E. Hall was wounded in March.   Changes among the officers, however, were numerous : ill-health compelled Captain Windle to relinquish his commission, Lt. Sulman taking over as Adjutant.   Captain Saye went to the R.E. and Captain Bedford to the Sudan, but Major Hazard rejoined.   The New Year brought Colonel Crockett and Major Bell the D.S.O. and ' mentions ', Captain Stack, Corporal Adnams and Pioneer Beck being also ' mentioned '.

Occasionally Lewis gun teams were attached to battalions in the line and came in for some activity, but incidents were few, if work was continuous and strenuous.   The move to Moore Park was made in extremely bad weather, heavy snow and then a thaw, and when the Arras attack started (April 9th) activity on the Divisional front increased, several raids being made, which provoked retaliation and more work for the Pioneers, whose main activities were directed towards completing the elaborate preparations for the attack on Messines.

The Thirty-Ninth Division, after reaching Flanders late in November, enjoyed nearly three weeks welcome respite from the line. This time the 14th Hampshire spent quietly at Poperinghe, mostly in good wooden huts, training, route-marching, finding many working parties, but getting a fair amount of recreation, especially football.   The Division then took over the Northern sector of the Salient, the 14th Hampshire, after four days in support on the Canal Bank, relieving the 12th Sussex at Hill Top Farm on December 16th. This quarter was very different from the Somme, the defences were mainly breastworks, to dig deeper than two feet was to reach water, both the French Territorials whom the Division relieved and their opponents seemed to have forgotten all about the war and had abstained from hostilities.   This state of affairs was quickly altered and for a time the Divisional snipers enjoyed them-selves, while despite some shelling only three men were wounded in four days, which were mainly devoted to repairing the trenches and reclaiming a disused line. The battalion next sampled the Boesinghe sub-sector from December 30th to January 16th, where it had the Germans within 50 yards across the Yser canal. It was now doing four days in support and four in reserve. Here again things were fairly quiet, though on January 6th the line was bombarded for forty minutes, fortunately without any casualties being inflicted. The battalion's snipers claimed several hits but bright moon-light hampered wiring parties. The weather was mainly cold with some snow and sleet and life in the line was far from pleasant. Colonel Harman being away ill, Major Finlay was commanding. A move into billets at Ypres then followed, the next sector taken over, on January 20th, being at Railway Wood East of Ypres. Here rather greater activity prevailed, guns and ' minenwerfer ' being much in evidence, and a second turn in front line from January 29th to February 1st caused the battalion nearly 40 casualties. This turn ended with a violent bombardment which seemed to show that an attack was coming. One trench-mortar bomb landed among B Company's officers, badly wounding Captain Bircham and killing 2/Lts. Colebrook and Humphrey-Davy. Despite this and heavy shelling and several casualties,[1] B and C stuck unflinchingly to their posts, and when Germans came forward in force on B's frontage a hot reception discouraged them, no Germans getting into our line. The defenders were effectively helped by the support company, which Captain Goldsmith [2] promptly brought up through a barrage. Unable to effect an entrance the enemy now fell back, whereupon Captain Goldsmith followed their retreat up with a party, capturing a prisoner and obtaining identifications. This repulse of a formidable attack was warmly commended by the Divisional commander, Major General Cuthbert, who emphasized the battalion's steadiness in defence and energy in counter-attacking.

After this the 14th were in camp West of Ypres till February 25th, training and resting, then taking over the Observatory Ridge sector, SE. of Ypres. Major Childe Thomas had rejoined and taken over from Major Finlay (February 12th).[3] In this Observatory Ridge sector the battalion continued till well into April, being usually at Zillebeke when in support or brigade reserve or back at Kruisstraat or Toronto Camp when its brigade was ' out ', being in huts and not in billets, which might have been preferable in the cold weather. Things were brisker now. Life was quite strenuous : one officer wrote in March of not having had his boots or clothes off fourteen days. Both sides' guns were more active and machine-gunners, rifle grenadiers, trench-mortar detachments and snipers were all in evidence, if casualties were few. A good deal of wiring was required and patrols were active, more so than the enemy's, one left a notice on the German wire to tell them of their retreat from Bapaume and Peronne. Colonel Harman returned on March 24th, and after being relieved at Zillebeke

---

[1] Nine men were killed and 14 wounded.   [2] He received a bar to his M.C.

[3] On February 1st of the officers with the battalion three were Regulars, four Special Reservists, three including the acting second in command, Captain Trevor Roper of the 8th Battalion, were Territorials and nine of the 14th or 15th Battalions, among them the Adjutant, Lt. Gammon.

on April 15th the battalion shifted back with its Division to the NE. side of the Salient to take over the Hill Top sector.

The Forty-First Division had been back in the Salient before the end of October, being in the front line at St. Eloi by October 29th. Here the tactical advantages lay with the Germans, to whom higher and rather drier ground gave better opportunities for observation, while a shell-pitted and mine-cratered No Man's Land, mainly water-logged, effectively discouraged any offensive or even much patrol activity. One piece of the line was significantly known as ' the Mud Patch ' and much work was needed to keep the trenches in some repair. Merely to maintain the line and the approaches to it in winter weather taxed the energies and resourcefulness of the troops, and if the autumn and winter months passed without any major incidents they were not times of idleness. Luckily enough troops were available to reduce the time actually spent in trenches in 1916–1917 well below that in either previous winter,[1] even if the successive extensions of the British front South of the Somme to relieve the French involved our having to put into the trenches troops who could have done with more rest and more training.

Like other battalions the 15th Hampshire found life more strenuous the further back from the line they were : even in support or brigade reserve working and carrying parties were always being wanted, and when ' out ' working parties were even more in demand, the improvement of the communications alone requiring almost all the labour available and meanwhile training, especially of the reinforcements, had to be kept up. Drafts were largely coming now from the Training Reserve Battalions, into which the former ' K 4 ' battalions like the 13th Hampshire or ' Local Reserve ' units like the 16th had recently been converted.[2]

The change had many arguments in its favour : it had proved very difficult to refill with recruits from their own areas all battalions which had suffered heavily, already men were constantly being posted to any regiment but their own, more often probably than might have been avoided had the authorities really considered the regimental sentiments and traditions to which they so freely rendered lip-service. The change therefore rather stabilized an existing practice, but it meant that the drafts who joined a Hampshire battalion usually knew little of Hampshire or the regiment. To assimilate them and imbue them with the proper esprit de corps was therefore all the harder, while if the training staffs at home were generally allowed to retain their regimental badges and

---

[1] From November 1st to March 31st the 15th Hampshire had just over 40 days in front line.

[2] The 13th became the 34th Training Reserve and the 16th ranked as the 97th. Most of the senior officers and N.C.O's of both battalions remained with them for some time longer. A Garrison Battalion had come into existence in April 1916 and did duty in back areas in France, its first C.O. being Sir A. Griffith Boscawen of the 3rd Royal West Kent, and early in 1917 an 18th (Home Service) Battalion was formed under Lt. Colonel Ellicombe of the Devons. This, however, was broken up in January 1918, whereupon the Garrison Battalion was re-numbered 18th, the Provisional Territorial Battalion, for some time numbered as the 84th Provisional Battalion, being reckoned as the 17th Hampshire. It was still under Colonel Peters and was employed in Home Defence duties.

other connections, this was slender compensation for knowing that their own regiment was about the least likely of any to profit by their devotion and hard work.

One of the more notable incidents of the winter occurred when the 15th were in reserve at Dickebusch in November : a company of another battalion on its way up to the trenches was badly shelled and had heavy casualties, whom the 15th's stretcher bearers promptly and effectively succoured, assistance which was cordially acknowledged. When in front line the 15th usually found the enemy's guns troublesome, but we now had enough ammunition to respond, sometimes with compound interest. Casualties were not numerous : the battalion diary only records four in November and nine in December, including 2/Lt. Merrett killed in the Mud Patch and Captain Mee wounded, but with many officers away on 'courses' and various employments only twelve were available for duty on December 31st.

One relief in January was 'spotted' by the enemy and brought heavy fire down on the communication trenches, cutting off two platoons whose relief had to be postponed until evening, but the battalion very fortunately escaped without casualties. Incidents of importance were not numerous, but the mere maintenance of the line in a bitter winter with constant snow, sharp frosts and intervals of thaw to reduce everything to slime and mud was a fearful strain, and the cheerful endurance of hardships was really remarkable. The frequent falls of snow hampered work and training when out of the line and, if possible, increased the demands for working parties, but both January and February passed without much to vary the usual routine 'in' or 'out'. The battalion was 'in' from February 17th to 22nd in dull and misty weather without having a single casualty, and between February 27th and March 5th only seven men were wounded, despite increased artillery and mortar activity on both sides. To divert the enemy's attention from a raid on March 14th by another battalion, 2/Lt. Fowler and ten men placed two Bangalore torpedoes in his wire, as if the 15th were about to raid : one only exploded, but the whole party got back unhurt. Another turn in trenches in the last week of March brought increased activity and a dozen casualties, including three killed, but up to the Third Army's attack at Arras on April 9th no special effort had been required of the 15th Hampshire and the battalion had had ample time to assimilate some very large drafts. If the Second Army was not to start its offensive for another two months, its three Hampshire battalions were fit and ready to strike.

CHAPTER XVII

ARRAS

THE winter of 1916–1917 had brought the Hampshire few outstanding incidents. Politically and strategically, however, changes had taken place which were to affect them and the whole course of the war profoundly. Mr. Asquith's resignation and his replacement by Mr. Lloyd George brought to the head of affairs in England a man whose great energy and driving power were unfortunately largely nullified by his impatience, his ignorance of war and his utter inability to understand the practical obstacles to the superficially attractive 'short cuts to victory' which suggested themselves to him. Impulsive and self-confident,

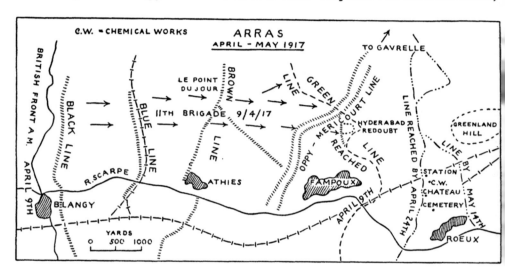

he could not realise the extent or the consequences of his own ignorance or that his military advisers knew what they were talking about, if he did not. Moreover the supersession of General Joffre and his replacement by General Nivelle, whose ideas for the coming offensive differed so profoundly from his predecessor's, might have mattered less had not Mr. Lloyd George virtually subordinated the British Armies in France to an almost untried French Commander in Chief. The consequent changes in the British part in the projected Spring offensive, notably the wide extensions of our frontage and the consequent reduction in the force available for our attack, were of profound importance : they threw away much of the moral and practical advantages our remorseless, if expensive, wearing down of the Germans on the Somme had secured, advantages not to be measured by the relatively small gains of ground as marked on a map, especially by those who read the map without seeing below the surface. If the Germans had not been pushed back very far, they had been ousted from their really prepared defences, and the weakness of their position in March, even after some respite from serious pressure, suggests how much might have been achieved by another ' push ' had a dry October allowed Sir Douglas Haig to repeat the blows of September 15th and 25th.

The very bad winter must in any case have interfered seriously with the programme arranged at Chantilly by Sir Douglas Haig and General Joffre, while the German withdrawal to the Hindenburg Line, though an unequivocal admission that they had been worsted on the Somme, must have further thrown it out of gear.   Still, both British and French might have been much better placed to impede and profit by that withdrawal had not General Nivelle's scheme been substituted for General Joffre's.

By the beginning of April the Germans were back behind the Hindenburg Line, defended as much by the belt of systematically devastated country they had left in front of it as by its own well-sited trenches and gun positions.   Weeks must elapse before we could hope to attempt to breach it.   On the Third Army's front, however, our preparations were virtually complete, and as the retreat had only affected the Southern extremity of the front to be attacked our plans did not need drastic re-adjustment.

This front extended Northward from across the Cojeul on our right to the Vimy Ridge, nearly 12 miles.   It was being attacked by four Corps, the Hampshire being only represented in the Seventeenth, in the left centre, whose right lay on the Scarpe.   The Seventeenth Corps was employing three Divisions to capture the first three of the four trench systems which confronted us, the ' Black ', ' Blue ' and ' Brown ' Lines, after which the Fourth Division, till then in reserve, would pass through the Ninth, the right Division of the Corps, and tackle a fourth system, the Oppy-Mericourt line, and then a final objective, the ' Green Line ', lying yet another 1400 yards further East, beyond Fampoux. This objective was over 6000 yards from our front line and reaching it would involve a much bigger advance than any previous attack had accomplished.

When the great attack was delivered, on April 9th, in cold and even snowy weather, the Ninth (Scottish) Division, carried out its programme most successfully and well up to time, smashing down all opposition, its prisoners alone exceeded its 2000 casualties, and thus gave a fine opening which the Fourth did not fail to exploit.   April 9th had found the Fourth at Mareouil, 3½ miles NW. of Arras, whence it had advanced very early to an assembly position North of Arras, with the 12th (right) and 11th (left) Brigades in front and the 10th in support.   Rain and snow wetted and chilled the waiting troops, but the ' cookers ' produced a hot meal and everyone was soon in good spirits over the good news which came back and was soon confirmed by the crowds of Germans making for the prisoners' cages.   At 10 a.m. the advance to the Blue Line was begun, being made in column.   One of the few German shells caused B Company of the Hampshire nearly 20 casualties, but the Blue Line was reached 30 minutes before schedule.   ' Artillery formation ' was now adopted, the Hampshire, who had the Somerset L.I. on their right, having B and D Companies in front and A in support, C being detailed a carriers.   On their left the East Lancashire were to form a defensive flank facing NE., and the Rifle Brigade followed, having to pass through the Hampshire and tackle the Hyderabad Redoubt, a strong position beyond the Hampshire's objective, Haggard and Hazard Trenches.

Advancing to the Brown Line almost without meeting any shelling, the Hampshire could see troops pushing ahead across the Scarpe, where the Sixth Corps was also doing magnificently. After an hour's pause on the Brown Line the 11th and 12th Brigades started their own attack at 3 p.m. behind a satisfactory barrage, some batteries having meanwhile been brought well forward. They now met some rather wild rifle fire and a few shells but were soon up to the wire of the Oppy-Mericourt Line. This was thick and practically uncut, though the Germans had failed to block their passages through it, and while some men were using wire-cutters, others, firing over their heads, prevented the enemy from manning the parapet to impede them. Before long the Hampshire were through the wire, D Company on the right capturing Heron Trench and B its Northward continuation, Hudson Trench. Pressing on, they also carried the rear line of this system, Haggard and Hazard Trenches, while A ' mopped up ' behind them. All opposition was quickly overcome, 80 prisoners and three 8-inch howitzers were taken and many Germans shot down as they fled Eastward, offering excellent targets, while bombers worked their way Northward along Hudson and Hazard Trenches, extending our gains. Soon after 4 p.m. all three companies could report that their objectives had been secured.

Casualties in the assault had been trifling, only 2/Lts. Hobson, who died of wounds, Man and Soward and six men wounded. The Somerset had been equally successful and though the Rifle Brigade, who duly passed through the Hampshire, suffered considerably in getting through uncut wire, they too mastered their objective, the Hyderabad Redoubt, B Company assisting them by fire. The captured line gave good observation to the East and NE. with a fair field of fire in front, and touch having been obtained with the East Lancashire on the left, the Hampshire could settle down to consolidation, despite intermittent shelling which caused more casualties, bringing the battalion's total for the day up to nearly 60, while those of the brigade, barely 300, were exceeded by its prisoners. Meanwhile the 12th Brigade had taken Fampoux, but machine-guns behind a railway embankment had prevented its reaching the Green Line, 500 yards on, though it also was consolidating a good line.

If this fine result was due even more to the Ninth Division and the guns, which had broken the back of the resistance before the Fourth got into action, the Fourth had carried out its task admirably and had played a big part in the greatest success yet achieved on the Western Front in a single day. The other Divisions of the Seventeenth Corps, if less successful than the Fourth and Ninth, had also made big advances, and beyond them the Canadians and the Fifth Division had mastered most of Vimy Ridge. South of the Scarpe the Sixth Corps had done very well, even if it had not secured its final objective. Our right Corps, the Seventh, had also gained ground, though its right had been checked. Moreover this very substantial achievement had cost only some

12,000 casualties, whereas there was ample evidence that the enemy, who had lost 100 guns and at least 7000 prisoners, had been very hard hit.

Various hindrances impeded the exploitation of this brilliant opening blow : squalls of sleet and snow had fallen at intervals all day and continued through the succeeding days, inflicting considerable hardships on the troops and greatly increasing the difficulties, bad enough anyhow, of repairing and improving communications. Moreover, it impeded the advance of our guns, most of them now too far back to reach their distant new targets. As usual, information was so slow in getting back that orders based upon it rarely fitted the situation by

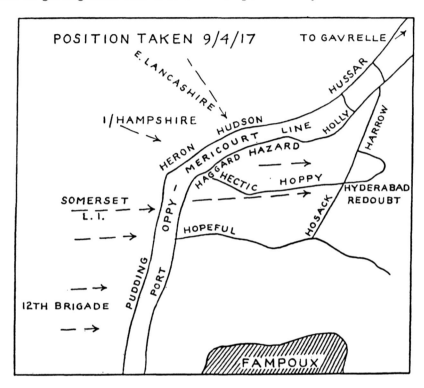

the time they reached the troops, and promising openings were therefore missed. Moreover, the Germans had half a dozen Divisions detailed for counter-attacking, which, if too far back to influence the first day's fighting, were near enough to the battle area to intervene on the days following it.

The 11th Brigade, while consolidating, was somewhat troubled by snipers, but in return got some fair targets for rifles and machine-guns, the Rifle Brigade indeed ran short of ammunition, but it had only one attempt at a counter-attack to repulse. About dusk Germans could be seen collecting in sufficient numbers to give good targets, and as it grew dark they came forward opposite the Hampshire, to wilt away under our rifle and machine-gun fire, while during the night the battalion's patrols were active and gathered in several more prisoners. Next day, though the enemy were clearly moving guns and transport back, opposition stiffened, the 12th Brigade's efforts to complete its task by capturing the Green Line were quickly checked and machine-guns held up patrols which the Hampshire and Somerset pushed out towards the Roeux-Gavrelle road. Eventually, late in the evening, another counter-attack developed, mainly against our left. One of our posts was severely pressed, but 2/Lt. Love, going forward under heavy fire, rallied the men and maintained the defence, while elsewhere the attackers were soon halted by our fire and lost heavily, the Hampshire having another 15 casualties during the day, mainly from artillery fire, Captain Prendergast being wounded.[1]

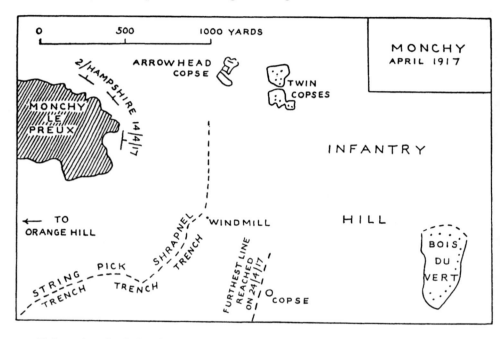

Being ahead of the flanking Divisions, before attempting a big advance the Fourth must in any case have waited till they came up level, and though on both its flanks some ground was gained, the Sixth Corps advancing nearly to Monchy le Preux, further South we were less successful and meanwhile the German reserves were arriving. The troops in front moreover, being without blankets or great-coats, were suffering greatly from more snow and sleet, the cold being bitter.

April 11th brought the Fourth Division orders to secure the road running North from Roeux to Gavrelle, 1600 yards ahead. For this the 10th (left) and 12th (right) Brigades were detailed, the 11th having to form a defensive flank on the left, but while the 12th Brigade secured part of their original objective of April 9th the 10th were held up and lost heavily. Reinforcements had now

[1] For the third time.

replaced the survivors of the original defenders, and we had not got enough guns forward to give our infantry the magnificent support which had contributed so much to our original success. The check to the other brigades left the 11th with little to do, but B Company on the Hampshire's left, bombing Northward along the Oppy-Mericourt Line, gained about 150 yards in both front and support trenches. This success they owed largely to Lt. de Gaury's fine example and skilful leading,[1] which was mainly instrumental in taking one important ' strong point ', but 2/Lt. J. P. Gilbert was killed leading his platoon gallantly and the battalion had another 30 casualties. D Company meanwhile had taken over the Hyderabad Redoubt.

Little more success attended the next day's attempt on this front, the Ninth Division, though hardly fresh, coming forward again and attacking through the Fourth, whose right and centre it subsequently relieved, leaving the 11th Brigade in line facing NE. to the left of the Hyderabad Redoubt. Meanwhile B Company's bombers had again tried to gain ground, but with little success and at the cost of nearly another 30 casualties,[2] the enemy having by now strengthened his defences.

For three more days the 1st Hampshire remained in front line. No further advance was attempted here, though our bombers made another effort on April 15th which failed, largely because our guns had almost obliterated the trenches so that our men had no cover and were exposed to machine-gun fire. The enemy's artillery fire had increased, the bad weather continued and it was a very weary battalion which was at last relieved early[3] on April 16th by the Irish Fusiliers and placed in Divisional reserve in the former German second line, where shelters in a railway cutting provided fair accommodation. The week's casualties had come to 2/Lts. Gilbert, Hobson and Seeley (died of wounds) and 48 men killed and missing, Captain Prendergast, 2/Lts. R. C. Foster, A. James, Man and Soward and 115 men wounded,[4] and all ranks badly needed the well-earned fortnight's rest they were now to get. But they could feel they had achieved a big thing and left their mark on the enemy.

Before the 1st Hampshire was relieved the 2nd had joined in the fighting. The Twenty-Ninth Division, which had moved forward from Beauval on April 1st and had spent the 9th just West of Arras in reserve, was ordered up on April 12th to take over Monchy le Preux. This village the Sixth Corps had with much difficulty succeeded in capturing and all its Divisions were now exhausted and needing relief. Monchy, as yet but little damaged, stood on a knoll at the Eastward end of a spur projecting into the plain of Douai, over which it provided fine observation, but our advance here had left us in a pronounced salient, almost inviting counter-attack.

[1] He was awarded the M.C., as was 2/Lt. Love also.
[2] 2/Lt. F.R. Seeley was wounded.
[3] D Company could not get clear of the Hyderabad Redoubt before daylight and had to remain there all day.
[4] Out of about 600 n action, so many men being employed in the manifold administratrative requirements of a big attack that few battalions ' went over the top ' much stronger.

The 2nd Hampshire had struggled forward on April 12th along the terribly congested Cambrai road to Orange Hill, a mile West of Monchy, where they bivouacked and remained in brigade reserve, going up after dark on April 13th to dig an assembly trench just East of Monchy, from which the Essex and the Newfoundlanders were next morning to attack Infantry Hill, a slight rise East of Monchy. Though heavily shelled the battalion escaped lightly, though its 20 casualties included 2/Lts. Burrage, Manton and Watson wounded, and before dawn (April 14th) it was back at Orange Hill, having left three platoons of X Company in cellars in Monchy.

For only two battalions to try to advance by half a mile an already fairly sharp salient, seemed to be asking for trouble, but Infantry Hill offered concealment to counter-attacks and its retention would have improved the position. Attacking at 5.30 a.m. the Essex and Newfoundland carried the objective, taking some prisoners. Before they could do much to consolidate they were counter-attacked in great force, in front and on both flanks. Despite an obstinate resistance both battalions had before long been overwhelmed and the Germans, a fresh Bavarian Division, seemed to have Monchy at their mercy. Apart from the head-quarters of the attacking battalions, the only troops in Monchy were the three platoons of X Company, who hastened to take up positions for its defence and helped to keep the enemy from exploiting their success, while a handful from the Newfoundland's head-quarters under Lt. Colonel Forbes Robertson, manned a bank SE. of the village and did great execution at close range, besides sending warning to the Hampshire of the critical situation.

Lt. Colonel Beckwith had already sent Y Company up to Monchy and now started forward with his remaining men. A heavy barrage was falling behind Monchy, but Colonel Beckwith noticed that this was coming down in two parallel lines with a gap between them and, utilising this skilfully, he got his men through with only 20 casualties and brought timely assistance to the hard-pressed defenders. He now disposed his men on the Northern and Eastern outskirts and several attacks were beaten off, Captain Cuddon doing outstanding work in keeping the enemy at bay and maintaining the position. Private Ferry also did well in getting an important message through at a critical moment, which led to a weak point being reinforced in time. He had to go through a heavy barrage, in which a fellow ' runner ' had been hit, but he managed it. Eventually touch was gained both with the Seventeenth Division on the left and with the 4th Worcestershire, South of Monchy, who meanwhile had been holding firmly on and doing some effective shooting, and before long the Germans abandoned further efforts to advance and fell back to their original line. The battalion's good service in securing this all-important position [1] was much commended, General de Lisle declaring that it had been ' the means of saving Monchy'; it was lucky to escape with 50 casualties, including 2/Lt. Baxter and seven men killed.

---

[1] Colonel Beckwith, in passing on this message, added his own special congratulations to the battalion's runners and stretcher-bearers. It is unfortunate that the battalion's important share in saving Monchy should be almost ignored in the *Official History* (1917. Vol. I. 291).

Next evening the 2nd Hampshire were relieved by the 86th Brigade and went back to Arras for three days' rest, after which (April 19th) they took over trenches between Monchy and the Cambrai road. These they held for three days, being heavily shelled, gas shells being much used. The four men killed unfortunately included a mainstay of the battalion in C.S.M. Lund, while 2/Lts. Rhodes and Saunders and 14 men were wounded.

Meanwhile the whole situation had been adversely affected by the failure of General Nivelle's offensive on the Aisne to accomplish anything approaching the decisive results that he had prophesied. If much ground was gained, with 20,000 prisoners and 150 guns, the anticipated break-through was not achieved, and the heavy casualties were aggravated by the break-down of the French medical services and were largely responsible for the disastrous moral effects of this disappointment on Army and country. For the rest of 1917 the British Armies in France had to attack and continue attacking, despite many disadvantages and difficulties, so as to maintain the initiative and prevent the Germans from recovering it and exploiting the demoralisation which before long spread through the French Armies and left them quite unfit to meet a serious attack, let alone continue their offensive. Had General Nivelle's attack fulfilled anticipations or even had less been expected from it, so that its result had been less of a disappointment, Sir Douglas Haig need not have continued his attacks at Arras after the Germans had had time to prepare to meet them. In these later attacks, largely improvised, carried out by Divisions who had not been properly reinforced or rested since April 9th,[1] not supported by the full weight of artillery then available and confronted with defences that had not been adequately ' softened ', the Third Army was to incur heavy casualties and achieve no commensurate direct results, though it is easy to conjecture what might have happened had the Germans been allowed to recover the initiative.

By April 14th as much had been achieved as was needed locally to improve our positions, so but for his ally's requirements, to which he never turned a deaf ear, Sir Douglas Haig might now have turned his attention to his intended attack in Flanders. By this, his main project, he hoped to secure the Belgian coastline and deprive the Germans of the submarine bases they were using so effectively. For this the Navy, at the worst crisis of its struggle against the submarine, was extremely anxious, and he would have been glad to start operations in Flanders in May. Actually troops and guns and shells had to be expended on the Arras front, where British troops were sacrificed to shoulder their Allies' burden. If the French could point to their inadequately supported efforts of 1915, the boot was on the other foot now.

The 2nd Hampshire were immediately affected by this prolongation of the Arras battle, as in the big attack ordered for April 23rd their Division was tackling Infantry Hill and other ground East of Monchy where the German position was by now fairly strong and held in some force. The 88th Brigade

[1] There was hardly any relieving them by Divisions from other Armies, as on the Somme.

was attacking between Monchy and the Cambrai road, with the Worcestershire leading, the Hampshire in support and a weak composite battalion formed from the Essex and Newfoundlands in reserve. On the 88th's left the 87th Brigade was attacking Infantry Hill itself, and the 88th aimed at securing its Southern slope, including the Bois du Vert, and keeping touch to their right with the Fifteenth Division, who were attacking Guemappe beyond the Cambrai road.

The 2nd Hampshire had been relieved in front line by the Worcestershire early on April 22nd and had spent the day at Feuchy Chapel. The enemy's shelling was heavy and the Brigadier, General Cayley, was incapacitated by gas, so Lt. Colonel Beckwith took his place, Lt. Colonel McCammon [1] commanding the battalion.

' Zero ' was at 4.45 a.m., (April 23rd) and the Worcestershire, attacking with great dash, quickly forced their way up the slope ahead, advancing nearly a mile and reaching a copse on the crest about 600 yards West of the Bois du Vert. They had done splendidly but had lost heavily, and to hold their gains they needed all the support the Hampshire could give, so there could be no question of the Hampshire pushing on to the Red Line, beyond the Bois du Vert, especially as the Division on their right was not up level. Before advancing, the battalion had nearly 20 casualties from the German barrage, chiefly in Y Company on the right of the leading wave, C.S.M. Toogood being killed. In crossing a sunken road more casualties were caused by flanking machine-guns, but the men pressed on vigorously, many following the Worcestershire to the copse, while one platoon of X, the left support company, actually joined the 87th Brigade on Infantry Hill. The right support company, W, under Captain Cuddon, having captured Pick Trench, started bombing to the right flank and after two hours hard fighting cleared most of String Trench, capturing 50 prisoners. Sergeant Rowe and Private Bicknell [2] were much to the fore in this, supporting Captain Cuddon splendidly. Unluckily the Division on the right had still failed to get forward, so the Twenty-Ninth's success had accentuated the already pronounced salient. German shelling was now heavy and the Hampshire had hard work to retain their gains, let alone consolidate them effectively. Several counter-attacks were checked nevertheless, but in the afternoon the enemy came forward in great force, following a heavy bombardment by big howitzers, and despite the stubborn resistance of the Worcestershire and Hampshire they recovered the copse, most of Y and Z Companies being overwhelmed and both company commanders taken.[3] North of the copse the defence held, and in Shrapnel, Pick and String Trenches the Hampshire, mainly W Company, and some Worcestershire, reinforced by a company of the 16th Middlesex (86th Brigade), succeeded in checking the counter-attack, Captain Cuddon doing much to achieve this and maintain our hold on the

---

[1] 5th R. Irish Rifles, (attached).

[2] They received the M.M., also awarded to Private Primmer, for keeping up communications with Brigade H.Q. by repairing wires under heavy shell fire, and to Private Ferry.

[3] Captains Cornish and Robertson, the latter being badly wounded.

captured ground.[1] With the enemy checked, the Worcestershire's C.O. organized a night attack to recover the copse, in which some 40 Hampshire joined. It went forward well, but the enemy were too firmly established to be ousted and the 88th Brigade had to be content with maintaining a flank running back from Infantry Hill, where the 87th had secured and held a good position, to the Cambrai road, including String Trench and Pick Trench, over 400 yards forward from the starting line. This line they secured, their remnants, except W Company who remained behind for 24 hours, being relieved that evening by the 86th Brigade, when the battalion was taken back by bus to Simoncourt, to rest and reorganize. Losses had been severe, over half those in action ;[2] Lt. Colonel McCammon died of wounds, Lt. Halcrow, 2/Lt. Todd and 13 men were killed, Captains Cornish and Robertson,[3] 2/Lts. Simmonds and Snyder and 67 men were missing, Lts. Fawcitt and Saunders, 2/Lts. Darracott, Hughes, G. H. James,[4] McAvoy, Swann, Watts and Yates and 200 men wounded.

If the attack of April 23rd had nowhere reached its final objective, ground had been gained all along the front ; the Twenty-Ninth Division had advanced 800 yards on Infantry Hill, while Guemappe had eventually been secured by the Fifteenth Division's persistence, and North of the Scarpe the Fifty-First had gained ground beyond Fampoux, it it had not reached Roeux. Casualties had been heavy, but 2500 prisoners had been taken, our guns had had some fine targets in infantry advancing to counter-attack and if the enemy had dislodged it from its advanced position the 88th Brigade had taken its toll of them. Tactically the local position was therefore more than ever secure and we could have well discontinued our attacks, whose difficulties increased in proportion to their progress, especially as no fresh Divisions were available to relieve those already so severely tried and thereby give them the respite they so badly needed. The French situation, however, required the improvisation of another big attack, and for this on May 3rd the Fourth Division was brought forward again with Roeux and Plouvain as objectives, while the much depleted Twenty-Ninth, after the briefest of rests, also came up to Arras in readiness to exploit success

The Fourth Division had had ten days ' out ', the 1st Hampshire being at Izel les Hameau 12 miles West of Arras, but it had received few reinforcements and hardly a battalion was within 50% of establishment. The Hampshire, apart from nearly 200 casualties, had sent another 150 to hospital, drafts and returns from hospital had not totalled 60 and, with C Company detached to help the R.A.M.C. and A detailed as carriers, only 200 men were available for the attack.

On May 3rd the 10th Brigade was making for Roeux, with the 12th on its left, the Hampshire being in support, in trenches just North of the Fampoux-

---

[1] For this and for his good work in the defence of Monchy on April 14th he received the M.C.
[2] The strength on paper on April 30th was 23 officers and 565 other ranks. Colonel Beckwith being still acting as Brigadier, Captain Lord was in command.
[3] Died of wounds as a prisoner of war.
[4] Died of wounds.

Athies road. Colonel Armitage [1] being with the 'battle nucleus', Major Earle was commanding.

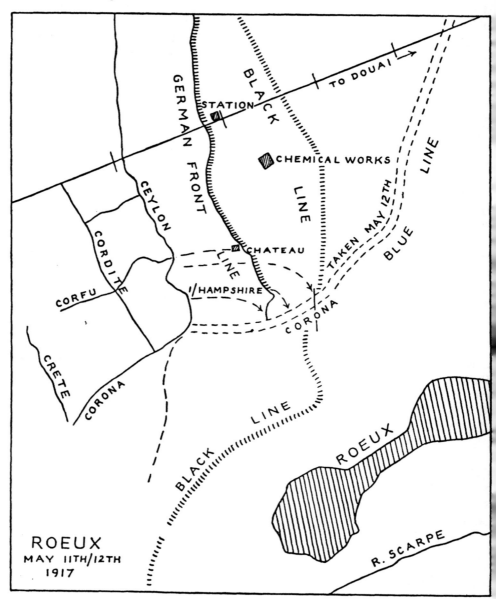

ROEUX
MAY 11TH/12TH
1917

Too early an hour, 3.45 a.m., had been fixed for 'Zero', the darkness causing much confusion and loss of direction. A heavy barrage showed that the attack was expected and it was held up just beyond the first objective, while

[1] He was awarded the D.S.O. for his skilful leading and good work on April 9th.

even this was not finally maintained in face of vigorous counter-attacks. The Hampshire were not engaged but moved up after dark to support the Rifle Brigade, who were to make another attack on Roeux Chateau. This could not be started till 3.30 a.m. (May 4th) and made little headway, and that evening the 11th Brigade took over the front facing the Chateau and Chemical Works North of Roeux, the Hampshire having their left on the Arras-Douai railway and extending South to the junction of Corona and Ceylon Trenches. The enemy's snipers were active and both sides did some intermittent shelling, the Hampshire having a dozen casualties, including 2/Lt. Mooney died of wounds, in four days in line. The Chemical Works were steadily shelled, but patrols which reconnoitred them found them still held in force and could achieve nothing.

After two days in reserve the battalion went up into line late on May 10th for a fresh attack next day, having C (right) and D (left) Companies in front in Ceylon Trench and B in support in Cordite, A being still detached. Its task was to swing round to the right and form a defensive flank along Corona Trench, facing Roeux.

' Zero ' this time was 7.30 p.m. (May 11th), which surprised the enemy completely ; they had not detected the assembly of the attackers and these, despite their long sixteen hours' wait, went forward with much dash behind an excellent barrage, while, the counter-barrage being slow to open, our men suffered little from it. It was a lovely evening, with the ground dry enough to allow of rapid movement. The Hampshire, on the 11th Brigade's right, ably directed by Major Earle, soon mastered their objective which included Roeux Chateau, till now a real stone of stumbling, capturing 150 prisoners and seven machine-guns with trifling casualties, though 2/Lt. Hawke was killed and 2/Lts. Fall and Stringer [1] wounded. The consolidation of the line taken, ' the Black Line ', was covered by Lewis gunners in shell-holes out in front, who kept off all attempts to regain lost ground. Trouble was threatened by a big concrete emplacement near the Chateau with walls six feet in thickness and seven feet of roof cover, the first of the ' pill-boxes ' afterwards so prominent in ' Third Ypres ' which the battalion had met. However, moppers-up who were detailed to tackle it caught its occupants trying to bring a machine gun into action and disposed of them, capturing the ' pill-box ' and with it four machine-guns. Its capture aroused considerable interest as it was clear that this new form of defence was likely to give trouble. Many officers of other units came up to have a look at it.

The rest of the Division had been equally successful and next morning the 11th Brigade, attacking at 6.30 a.m. along with the Seventeenth Division on its left, advanced another 500 yards and captured Cupid Trench, North of the railway and 700 yards East of the station. [2] The enemy offered but little resist-

[1] 2/Lt. Stringer's batman, in his anxiety to get his wounded officer to safety, overlooked the fact that he was taking all the company officers' rations with him.
[2] Approximately the ' Blue Line ' on Sketch (42): This success led to the Germans retiring between the railway and the Scarpe, the ruins of Roeux being occupied during the night of May 12th/13th.

ance and were quickly driven out, though further North the left of the Seventeenth was less successful. Captured machine-guns were used most effectively and the position was consolidated and maintained. Major Earle had again handled the attack admirably and was largely responsible for its success, and the D.S.O. awarded to him was greatly welcomed by the battalion. Once again casualties were low, 2/Lt. Bishop and three men being killed and 2/Lt. Bray and 25 men wounded.

This success was the more creditable because the Fourth Division's battalions were all far below establishment, in neither attack had the Hampshire exceeded 250 of all ranks, and to have secured all objectives and inflicted very heavy casualties on its opponents, the 4th Ersatz Division, over 500 prisoners being taken, was a satisfactory finish to the battalion's highly successful share in the Arras offensive. That night the Division's much reduced battalions were relieved by the Fifty-First Division. When it returned to the Roeux-Fampoux area in June the Arras front had become ' quiet '.

The 2nd Hampshire had also seen something of these closing stages of ' Arras '. No openings being made on May 3rd for their Division to exploit, they had remained at Arras till May 7th and then moved back to Berneville, where a welcome draft of 102 men replenished the depleted ranks, only 270 men would have been available on May 3rd. They were back at Arras by May 11th, occupying the old German front line taken on April 9th. This needed much repairing to make it habitable, while large carrying parties were called for, and then on May 17th the battalion took over reserve trenches between the Scarpe and Monchy, where its Division was now relieving the Twelfth, besides taking over Infantry Hill from the Third. Nearly 240 men from the Base had arrived at the Corps Depot and a trickle of returns from hospital had about balanced admissions.

Its first four days here the 2nd spent in digging communication trenches and shelters and in salvage work. The area had seen heavy fighting and much salvage was collected. Four days in front line (May 22nd to 25th) from Bit Lane to the Scarpe brought much hard work and heavy shelling, which caused few casualties, though 120 yards of Halberd Trench were blown in, while our guns replied vigorously. Our patrols were active and an advanced post was established in No Man's Land. The battalion was back in reserve for five days, during which it was sorry to lose its M.O., Captain Sturdy, whose gallantry and devoted work, particularly at Monchy, where he had searched houses and cellars under very heavy fire and rescued over 100 wounded, had just won him the M.C. Being in reserve meant much hard work on the trenches with large carrying-parties and much digging and was little of a relief. A dozen officers had reported, among them Major Spring, who became second in command, Lt. Colonel Beckwith having rejoined, and other ranks were up over 800 again. Lt. Askew had now taken over duty as Quartermaster, while Captain Knight, R.A.M.C., succeeded Captain Sturdy.

From May 30th to June 2nd the 2nd was in support on this front ; with plenty to do as before, repairing and improving the line, the whole battalion was thus employed on the night of May 31st/June 1st, and little rest, as the enemy's guns were active, partly in retaliation, though casualties were trifling. On the other hand the enemy had given the battalion but few chances of hitting him, rarely exposing himself. The Division made some local attacks during this spell at Monchy, but the 88th Brigade was not employed and its hard-hit units were getting a chance to assimilate their large drafts.

June 3rd saw the 2nd Hampshire at rest but under orders for the North. Like the 1st Battalion, the 2nd had had its chance at Arras and had taken it, more than once; if both had had severe losses, neither had been as hard hit as on the Somme, while both had left their mark on the enemy to some purpose.

CHAPTER XVIII

THE FLANDERS OFFENSIVE

MESSINES AND THIRD YPRES

THE prolongation of 'Arras', if unavoidable, had entailed serious disadvantages. Our heavy casualties in the later attacks had naturally diminished considerably the substantial balance in our favour of the opening stages, though the Germans had had to pay high for stopping us and their counter-attacks had often been heavily punished. The postponing of the Messines attack was another grave misfortune ; the Second Army had long been ready and could have attacked much earlier could Sir Douglas Haig have closed down 'Arras' after the first fortnight and transferred to Flanders the guns which the Third Army could not yet spare, while to crown all unusually bad weather set in just as 'Third Ypres' actually started, making conditions in the Ypres Salient a worse handicap than usual to attackers.

The Flanders offensive was eventually to give opportunities to all five Hampshire battalions in France and to win the regiment two more V.C's, but in its opening phase at Messines only the 11th and 15th Battalions were engaged, the Thirty-Ninth Division's frontage being beyond that of the attack, so that the 14th did not take part in it, while the 2nd Battalion had only just reached Flanders and the 1st was still with the Third Army.

A Pioneer battalion in Flanders had naturally seen much of the preparations, and during April and May the 11th Hampshire had been busy, the snow and sleet of April making things hard for them. Besides Major Hazard the Quartermaster, Lt. Davies, had also rejoined and the normal routine had gone on almost unchanged and with trifling casualties. On June 7th the Sixteenth Division was in the middle of the attacking line, facing Wytschaete Wood with the ruins of Wytschaete behind it. Directly the success of the attack was known,[1] C and D Companies went forward to make tracks across No Man's Land, by which guns, ammunition, rations and R.E. stores might be sent up, and so energetically did they work that by 3 p.m. one track was being used by artillery most of the way across. Work was pushed on at night, A and B taking their turn, and after a day's rest the whole battalion started on June 9th laying tramways under the supervision of the Chief Engineer of the Ninth Corps. Several bridges were constructed and, though at times impeded by shell-fire,[2] the work was so vigorously carried on that by June 18th it could be suspended and the battalion could rejoin its Division, which was enjoying a rest at Strazeele. This rest was not long extended to the Pioneers, who were dispatched on June 21st to Poperinghe to work under the Nineteenth Corps, now preparing for the next stage in the offensive. Its work now was largely

---

[1] The Division's objective was just across the Messines—St. Eloi road.
[2] The battalion diary only records half a dozen casualties from gas shelling.

road making, but wells had to be sunk, several having to be abandoned on reaching blue clay.

The 15th Battalion had had one quite sharp fight during the period of preparation and waiting. It was in front line at St. Eloi on April 20th when an attack developed in some force, aimed, it appeared, at capturing a mine-shaft in the line held by the 11th Royal West Kent on the battalion's right. After a quiet day a violent bombardment had suddenly started, knocking the trenches about badly and cutting all telephone wires. Luckily Captain Barber, who was commanding the 15th's right company, C, sent up the SOS. signals so promptly that our barrage caught the Germans just as they were leaving their trenches, while our rifles and Lewis guns also took toll of them. Sergeant Collis was quick to enfilade the attack with a Lewis gun, while Lance Corporal Windebank showed great gallantry and leadership.[1] A few Germans entered the R.W.K's front line, which the bombardment had almost obliterated, but they were either killed or driven back, the 15th's Lewis guns doing some effective shooting at the retiring raiders, catching them in flank. A second attempt was also checked, the enemy facing the 15th Hampshire hardly getting beyond his own wire, and C Company were warmly commended for their gallantry and steadiness.

If this affair cost the 15th about 30 casualties, five men being killed and Lt. Seers wounded, the enemy had been sharply punished and the damaged trenches were soon repaired. After a small patrol had had a sharp bombing encounter with a rather larger German party on April 22nd, the battalion was ' out ' from April 23rd to May 20th, two marches of over 13 miles, no small trial after a long spell in trenches, taking the 122nd Brigade back to Tournehem. Here it did some vigorous training, including open warfare and musketry, both much needed at this period in the war, but recreation was not neglected.

Returning to the St. Eloi sector the 15th were in reserve, either at Voormezesle or at Chippewa Camp, till May 31st, when they took over the front line. May had passed almost without casualties, but the 15th's total losses during its first 12 months in France came to 760, fifteen officers and 190 other ranks killed and missing, 19 officers and 536 men wounded, mainly in their two spells on the Somme.

The week before our attack was lively enough : our guns were pounding away steadily and the bombardment was clearly being effective, for our patrols, though hampered by bright moonlight, found the wire extensively cut and in places almost demolished. Gas shelling prevented attempts to penetrate the enemy's lines but useful information was obtained. The enemy retaliated vigorously, shelling our support and reserve lines almost as heavily as the front and using much gas shell, and the 15th Hampshire had had nearly 30 casualties, including 2/Lt. Collier gassed before, early on June 5th, they went back to Middle Camp for a brief rest and clean up before moving up next evening to their assembly position.

[1] Both got the M.M.

On June 7th the Forty-First Division was on the left of the attack, with only one other Division beyond it ; its objectives lay South and West of the Ypres-Comines Canal and included the Dammstrasse, SE. of St. Eloi, which was to be taken by the 123rd and 124th Brigades, after which the 122nd would go through them, making for a line of trenches NE. of Oosttaverne and along the back crest of the Messines ridge. This taken, the Twenty-Fourth Division would go through and make for a final objective beyond Oosttaverne.

' Zero ' was at 3.10 a. m. (June 7th), but before that the 15th Hampshire, lying out in the open to avoid the zone where the enemy's barrage usually fell, had had several casualties, including two subalterns wounded. At ' Zero ' the mines so long in readiness were exploded all along our front with devastating

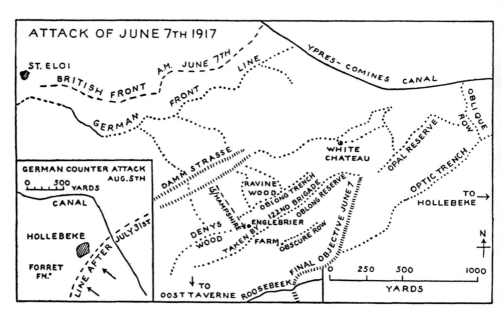

results and the Forty-First's leading brigades dashed forward, meeting only slight resistance until they reached the Dammstrasse. This, after a fierce struggle, they succeeded in mastering and, as they started consolidating, the 122nd Brigade came up in artillery formation in readiness to go through. That brigade had advanced at 5 a.m. and had only trifling casualties before deploying to attack. The 15th were in the centre, between the 11th R.W.K. and 12th East Surrey, and had Englebrier Farm as objective with Oblong Trench to be crossed on the way. They had about 500 yards of fairly flat ground to cross and their objective overlooked the valley of the little Roosebeek.

Our barrage was now rather ragged and delayed the left and centre battalions on whom it inflicted several casualties. Oblong Trench was carried nevertheless by 7 a.m. after some sharp fighting, and the attackers, pushing on, secured Englebrier Farm with Oblong Reserve behind it, overcoming some quite stuborn resistance and capturing many prisoners from dug-outs in Ravine and Denys Woods. By 9 a.m. the Division's last objective was being consolidated, and patrols were collecting prisoners from shell-holes and trenches in front ; R.S.M. Greenwood supported only by one man captured 20, while another large party who were trying to get away were intercepted and taken by 2/Lt. Whaley,[1] who pushed forward although our barrage was still falling just beyond the objective and cut off their retreat. Enemy were now seen gathering for a big counter-attack and about 10.15 a.m. a large body advanced over a ridge to reinforce those already in Obscure Row just ahead. Rifles and guns were quickly on to them and halted them, inflicting heavy casualties. Other attempts were equally successfully repulsed, though in the intervals the battalion was heavily bombarded, most of the day's casualties being due to this shelling. Then in the afternoon, just as another German advance was starting, the Twenty-Fourth Division came through the Forty-First to attack the final objective, beyond Oosttaverne, which it duly secured.

The Forty-First Division's substantial success had been fairly cheaply achieved, the 15th Hampshire, who had 2/Lts. Keep and Wright (died of wounds) and 41 men killed and missing, Captain Gorman, Lt. Newman, 2/Lts. Coope, Daniels and M. S. Moore, the M.O., Captain Hudson, and 135 men wounded, were about the battalion hardest hit, consolidating having, as so often, cost more than capturing. The battalion was back in reserve for four days, June 8th–11th, spent another four consolidating our new support line at the White Chateau, nearer the Canal,[2] and then on June 16th it took over Optic Trench, taken by the 11th R.W.K. two days earlier in an exploiting attack. This line was consistently shelled, and the 15th were lucky to escape with only 35 casualties in four days here, including five killed and 2/Lt. Powell Jones wounded. They were attacked late on June 17th, but our rifles and Lewis guns, aided by our barrage, caught the enemy as he left his trenches at dusk and drove him back. Hostile aircraft were troublesome until ours asserted themselves very effectively, while our guns replied most satisfactorily to the enemy's shell-fire.

From June 21st until July 23rd the 15th were out of trenches, though the large working parties they had to supply were usually in the shelled areas and had several casualties, 2/Lt. Warren being killed the very day after joining. Part of this time they were right back at Schakken, training hard but getting some rest and recreation. Two big drafts joined, with one of 20, and the battalion had reached a reasonable strength when, on July 23rd, its Division took over the St. Eloi–Hollebeke sector from the Forty-Seventh. The final preparations for the big attack were being completed and though the enemy plastered our lines with mustard gas, by July 31st all was ready.

The Forty-First Division, this time on the extreme right of the attack, had only to advance its line astride the Ypres-Comines canal far enough to cover the flank of the main attack. Two battalions of the 122nd Brigade sufficed to

[1] Both 2/Lt. Whaley and the R.S.M. received the M.C.
[2] To our left of the frontage attacked by the Forty-First Division on June 7th.

take Hollebeke,[1] though to accomplish this they had to fight quite hard, and the
15th Hampshire remained in support,though late that evening A and D Companies moved up to occupy Optic Trench and Oblique Row, from which the
attack had started.

Thus the 14th was the only Hampshire battalion actively engaged in the
day's attack ; their Division, now in the left centre Corps, the Eighteenth, was
advancing from just NW. of Wieltje towards St. Julien, over 3000 yards away.
This was the ground over which ' Second Ypres ' had been fought, and its
villages and farms had long ago been knocked to pieces and their ruins converted
into ' strong points ', while of the woods only shattered stumps remained. It
was largely open, barren or at best covered with weeds and rough grass, but
bad going in rainy weather. Unfortunately the start of the Flanders offensive
of 1917 coincided with some unusually bad weather, including quite torrential

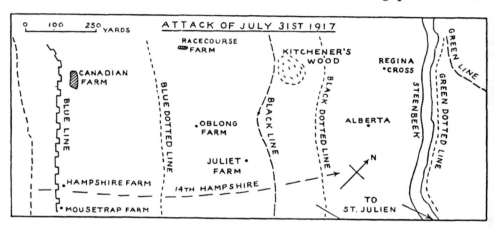

falls of rain, and throughout its course the weather was a recurrent handicap,
if at times the ground dried sufficiently to be no real hindrance, while in September dust was once actually reported. But in the Salient, with the streams
often so dammed up by debris as to have been converted into swamps or lakes,
with the surface pitted with shell-holes which rain speedily converted into
pools above a bottom of foul mire, with the natural drainage ruined by the
shelling and the digging of trenches, even a little rain went a long way. The
soil, if less glutinous than that of the chalk uplands of the Somme, had its own
abominations ; less adhesive, it was looser and softer, and if men slipped and
slithered less, those who fell into shell-holes were hard to extricate. Those few
battalions who went ' over the top ' in ' Third Ypres ' without finding the going
a serious impediment were fortunate.

The 14th Hampshire had had two turns in the line on Observatory Ridge
in the first half of April before their Division shifted North to the Canal Bank-

---

[1] The 123rd Brigade was attacking between the Canal and Klein Zillebeke and secured its
second but not its final objective.

Wieltje front, the 116th Brigade being on the Canal Bank when in support or in the Hill Top sector when in line. The enemy's guns were fairly active but ours replied effectively, an SOS. from the 14th on April 24th being so promptly answered by our barrage that a threatened attack never really got going, while we cut much wire and generally damaged his trenches as much or more than he damaged ours. From April 25th to May 16th the Division was ' out ' near Arques,[1] the 14th Hampshire getting a welcome respite from the trenches with a good spell of recreation as well as work and doing very well in Brigade Sports and competitions. They then had ten days at Wormhoudt, continuing training, and finished May with four fairly quiet days in the Wieltje sector, having only three men hit and these in retaliation for an intense bombardment. June passed uneventfully, though in the digging of a new support trench at a very exposed spot on the nights of June 2nd/3rd and 3rd/4th Captain May and Lt. Lovelace and six men were wounded and several killed, though the line was dug all the same. About the same time 2/Lt. Wallis-Wilson distinguished himself again when in charge of a party covering the digging of an advanced line close up to the enemy's wire. He cleared the enemy out of a sap, which he prevented them from retaking and thus enabled the digging party to carry out its task.[2] The Messines attack provoked some vigorous retaliation without many casualties. Indeed, one turn in support on the Canal Bank brought double the casualties, mainly in working parties, as did the next four days in front line at Hill Top, when the 14th gained great credit by establishing safe communication by day with the Division on the left near Turco Farm. From June 21st to July 15th the 14th was at Houlle near Watten, training, mainly rehearsing its projected attack over practice trenches.

The battalion was then back close behind the front, ' training under company arrangements ', and on July 29th it moved up to the Canal Bank to take up next evening its position for the attack. It was in second line, behind the 11th R. Sussex, with the 13th R. Sussex on its right and the 17th Sherwood Foresters on its left. The 116th and 117th Brigades were to capture four of the Division's five objectives, up to a ' Green Dotted Line ' 200 yards beyond the Steenbeek, the final objective, the ' Green Line ', well NE. of and including St. Julien, being left to the 118th Brigade. From our starting-off line we had a good view to North and East for a full mile, including the ridge running NW from Kitchener's Wood on which was the second objective, the ' Black Line '. This and the ' Black Dotted Line ', 200 yards further on along the slope above the Steenbeek, the 14th had to capture as well as the ' Green Dotted Line '.

' Zero ' was at 3.50 a.m. (July 31st) when the troops, advancing behind ' the biggest barrage of the war ', were also concealed by the darkness. The 11th R. Sussex having taken the ' Blue Line '[3] without much difficulty, the 14th Hampshire, ' leap-frogging ' them, went ahead towards the Black Line. The

---

[1] On detraining at St. Omer the 14th were met by the band of the 1st Garrison Battalion of the Hampshire, later numbered as the 18th Battalion.
[2] He was awarded a bar to the M.C.
[3] This included Mouse Trap Farm.

German trenches had been only lightly held, but the ' pill boxes ', dotted about quite irregularly, which had largely replaced regular trench-lines, presented the attackers with a new problem and gave much trouble. Several farms converted into ' pill-boxes ' lay in the path of the 14th and their capture, mainly effected by getting round behind them and taking them in rear, caused most of the casualties, delaying and disorganizing the later stages of the advance, though the 14th, after taking both the ' Black ' and ' Black Dotted Lines ', pushed on down the slope to the ' Green Dotted Line ' and eventually mastered this also, despite much difficulty at Alberta, a ' defended locality ' NW. of St. Julien, where two tanks were very helpful, crushing uncut wire and subduing the garrison's fire. 2/Lt. Hewitt, after the capture of the ' Black Line ', had reorganized his company and was waiting for the barrage to lift, when a shell burst near him, hitting him and setting fire to the signal lights in his haversack and to his clothing. He not only systematically extinguished the flames but, despite his burns and his wound, led his men resolutely forward in face of heavy machine-gun fire and played a big part in capturing the ' Black Dotted Line '; there, while superintending consolidation, he was sniped and killed. Captain West, finding the attack held up by uncut wire and a ' strong point ', brought up his company from support and carried the position, pushing on over three lines of trenches, and Captain R. H. Freeman, who led his company with much skill, also did much to consolidate the captured objective. Some men went on across the Steenbeek to the ' Green Dotted Line ', while the 118th Brigade took St. Julien and pressed on well across the St. Julien–Poelcapelle road, but the Thirty-Ninth was ahead of the Division on its right and, with its flank exposed, this advanced line could not be held against heavy shelling and vigorous counter-attacks and was eventually evacuated by order, the ' Black Dotted Line ', which the 14th was consolidating, being adopted as the main line of resistance and successfully maintained, our artillery and machine-guns inflicting heavy casualties on the counter-attacking troops.

If the failure to retain St. Julien was disappointing, the Division had gained a substantial success and hit its enemy hard. The 14th alone claimed over 200 prisoners with three guns and 17 machine-guns, their casualties, 2/Lts. Collis, Falconer and Hewitt and 60 men killed and missing, Major Trevor-Roper,[1] Captain Gammon, Lt. Chevalier, 2/Lts. Peet and Tyler and 156 men wounded, though heavy enough, were not the crippling losses of September 3rd 1916 at Hamel, while they had the satisfaction of having carried out all they had been asked to do, and the posthumous V.C. awarded to 2/Lt. Hewitt marked the day in the battalion's record.[2]

For two days the 14th had to hold on here under heavy shelling, another 14 men being killed and 40 wounded, but posts were again established beyond the Steenbeek. Captain Collins, who had been conspicuous in the attack, took a patrol forward to occupy an advanced post where he held on while the ruins of St. Julien were reoccupied. By the morning of August 3rd the battalion was

[1] Died of wounds.
[2] Captains Collins, R. H. Freeman and West were awarded the M.C.

SECOND LIEUTENANT DENIS GEORGE WYLDBORE HEWITT, V.C.

Born on December 18th, 1897 ; elder son of the Hon. George and Mrs. Hewitt, of Field House, Hursley, Winchester. He was educated at Winchester College and gazetted to a commission in the Hampshire Regiment on 1st April, 1916. His decoration was gazetted on September 14th, 1917, when attached to the 14th Battalion, for his actions in an attack, on the Somme, on July 31st, 1917. * IN THE YPRES SALIEN:

' For most conspicuous bravery and devotion to duty when in command of a company in attack.

When his first objective had been captured he reorganized the company and moved forward towards his objective. While waiting for the barrage to lift he was hit by a piece of shell, which exploded the signal lights in his haversack, and set fire to his equipment and clothes. Having extinguished the flames, in spite of his wound and the severe pain he was suffering, he led forward the remains of the company under very heavy machine gun fire, captured and consolidated his objective.

He was subsequently killed by a sniper while inspecting the consolidation and encouraging his men.

This gallant officer set a magnificent example of coolness and contempt of danger to the whole battalion, and it was due to his splendid leading that the final objective of the battalion was gained.'

back on the Canal Bank and next day went further back for a week's rest, partly at Poperinghe, partly at Meteren, after which it came up to the front again, as the Division was relieving the Forty-First at Hollebeke.

The Forty-First's success on July 31st having been cheaply gained, it had been kept in the Hollebeke sector for nearly a fortnight. The 15th Hampshire were at first in support, having two companies in Oblique Row and Optic Trench, trenches taken on June 14th. Here heavy shelling caused 40 casualties, including 2/Lts. S. A. C. Pearce and Adams wounded, while constant rain filled the trenches with mud and water, making some quite untenable. Relieving the 11th R. W. Kent on August 3rd, with two companies in front line and two in close support,[1] the 15th were heavily shelled on the following evening, and early next morning (August 5th) the Germans launched a really vigorous attempt to recover Hollebeke. A mist helping them, an outpost at Forret Farm [2] was over-run and the attackers worked round behind Hollebeke, which Captain Fowler therefore evacuated, though his company checked the interceptors, cutting off and taking some of them, and prevented any further advance. Our left held firm, though one post was overwhelmed, 2/Lt. Martin and a dozen men being killed or taken. Meanwhile Major Amery had arrived from head-quarters to discover what was happening and was arranging counter-measures and the reserve companies had turned out and come forward to counter-attack. Under cover of the mist Captain Oxborrow's company now reinforced Captain Fowler's for an attempt to recover Hollebeke, some East Surrey joining in.[3] This went very well and the village was soon cleared with the bayonet, thanks largely to the good leading of Captains Fowler and Oxborrow and 2/Lt. Shields, several prisoners being taken and the surviving intruders driven out. Major Amery having been badly wounded, Major Pennell came forward to arrange to exploit the recapture of Hollebeke by recovering Forret Farm. This was accomplished by a platoon under 2/Lt. Shields, aided by more East Surreys, a dozen prisoners being added to those taken in clearing Hollebeke. Thus the position was satis-factorily re-established [4] at a cost of no more than 20 killed and missing, in-cluding 2/Lts. Martin, who was later reported to be a prisoner of war, and Sheryer (died of wounds) and Major Amery and 10 men wounded. Some picked *Sturm-Truppen* proved to have reinforced the trench garrison for this attack and its repulse was a creditable effort, seeing that our men were wet and tired and the Germans much fresher. Captains Oxborrow and Fowler and 2/Lt. Shields subsequently received the M.C. and a dozen men the M.M., among them Sergeants Warren, Cross, North and Faulkner, C.S.M. Collis getting a bar.

The Germans despite their repulse, had not relinquished hope of recovering Hollebeke. About 9 p.m. they were observed massing for an attack, but

[1] See Sketch 43 (inset). p. 226.   [2] S.W. of Hollebeke.
[3] The 12th East Surrey were on the 15th's right SW. of Forret Farm and had their outpost line rushed in the fog.
The East Surrey also recovered their outpost line and even advanced it slightly.

directly they started crawling forward our rifles and machine-guns opened up, another company having reinforced our front line, and with our barrage coming down promptly the attack never succeeded in developing. The next four days brought more heavy shelling, the enemy were apparently expecting another attack, so put down some anticipatory barrages, but early on August 10th some posts were slightly advanced beyond Hollebeke, while under cover of a barrage put down to cover an advance on our left, the 123rd Brigade sent out patrols which brought back nearly 30 prisoners. That evening the 15th were relieved, having had 2/Lts. Palmer and Spencer and 26 men wounded since August 5th and nine men killed. By August 14th the battalion was resting at Fletre, where it was inspected by its Corps Commander, Lt General Morland, and by the Divisional Commander and warmly thanked for its recent achievements.

It the 11th Battalion did not ' go over the top ' in this battle it had plenty to do. It had been busy all July, road-making, building bridges and digging wells and working on light railways. Its labours were hindered by counter-bombardments, bad weather and shortage of materials, while lorries might lose their way and fail to deliver their burden even when the required stores were available, but the daily entries in the diary record much steady progress, the result of persistent hard work of a high level of technical efficiency. Battalion head-quarters moved from Poperinghe to Brandhoek Camp on July 23rd, where for several days the 11th rested from their labours and though pestered by bomb-dropping aircraft escaped without casualties.

Shortly after ' Zero ' on July 31st A Company had started work on the roads leading to the positions taken by the Fifteenth Division [1] North of the Ypres–Roulers railway, which included Verlorenhoek and Frezenberg. It was all-important to make them fit for our heavy guns to move up and give better support to our forward troops. While thus engaged the company had the misfortune to be caught in a German barrage in which Major Bell and several men were hit, the Major's wounds unfortunately proving fatal. One of the battalion's mainstays from its earliest days, he was greatly missed. Major Hazard went forward to take his place and direct the work, which was steadily pushed on despite the shelling.

The work also much hampered by the congestion of the roads; even where they were in good repair and had not been damaged by shell-fire, guns and lorries trying to get forward blocked them and prevented materials from reaching the front. Shell craters had to be filled or avoided by making deviations round them and all the time the shelling persisted, causing another 30 casualties, Captain Howson, who did splendid work encouraging his men and refusing to go back, despite his wounds,[2] Lt. Asfield and 2/Lts. Bennett and Pennington being wounded. But much work was done, and on August 4th the battalion handed over to the Fifteenth Division's Pioneers and moved into Ypres to be employed in screening the Menin Road forward to a spot deservedly known as Hell-fire Corner. This meant more casualties, many from gas, and

---

[1] The Sixteenth Division was in reserve. [2] He was awarded the M.C.

the men were sorely tried. Besides more normal pioneer work, parties had at times to help in getting guns into position.

In the next major attack, that of August 16th, which brought the 2nd Hampshire into the battle, the 11th were again detailed to construct tracks across No Man's Land to the captured lines. Where their Division was attacking, in the centre towards Zonnebeke, hardly any ground was gained, but the 11th were kept hard at work nevertheless until August 17th, when all companies were brought back to camp before moving Southward, the Sixteenth Division being now under orders to join the Third Army. Since July 31st 2/Lts. Clarke and Hayman and four men had been killed, Captain Chadwick, Lt. Thorne and over 50 men being wounded or gassed.

Of the two battalions engaged in ' Arras ' the 2nd were thrown into the Flanders fighting many weeks before the 1st, who continued in their old sector North of the Scarpe till the end of June and then, after a brief rest, took over the Monchy sector across the river, which they did not finally leave till the end of August.

The 2nd had spent most of June near Candas, resting and reorganizing. Nearly 200 reinforcements joined them soon after arriving there, but many of them were really only ' C.2.,' mainly under-sized Londoners, and their musketry was little better than their physique ; other drafts and returns from hospital brought the total reinforcements up to 350, against which only 30 were sent to hospital, while the last spell at Monchy had only brought a dozen casualties ; other ranks were up to 960 by July 1st, while with Lt. Colonel Beckwith and Majors Middleton and Spring and Captain Westmorland present the battalion actually had four ' pre-war ' Regulars, of whom the C.O. was ' mentioned ' in the Honours Gazette of June 4th along with the Quartermaster, Lt. A Smith, and Sergeant Merritt,[1] while Major Middleton received the D.S.O.

Reaching Proven on June 27th the battalion went first to Dead Man's Farm near Boesinghe, where it was employed in burying cable and getting a very indifferent reserve line, the X Line, into a defensible condition. This line required almost complete reconstruction and much hard work. The 2nd then took over the Canal Bank from the 87th Brigade and after five days in support were in front line from July 10th to 13th. They found the line fairly quiet and casualties were few, if much hard work was needed. Ten days training West of Proven followed, hampered by lack of ground and of rifle ranges, while at night bomb-dropping aeroplanes were becoming unpleasantly active, on one occasion bombing an ambulance and killing 60 mules which the Hampshire had to bury. By July 24th the battalion was back East of Proven, finding large working parties. Major Middleton now left to command the 10th Northumberland Fusiliers (Twenty-Third Division), and on July 30th Colonel Beckwith received a well-earned promotion, getting the 153rd Brigade (Fifty-First Division), which left Major Spring in command. Drafts amounting to 75 with 11 men back from hospital having joined, against 39 admissions and 28 casual-

[1] Posthumous.

ties,[1] the battalion had on July 31st no fewer than 42 officers and 972 other ranks on its strength, with Captains Cuddon (W), D. Day (Y) and Westmorland (Z), and 2/Lt. Wooldridge (X) commanding companies.

The Twenty-Ninth Division was in reserve on July 31st, being on the extreme British left [2] behind the Guards, who captured Pilckem and pushed forward to the Steenbeek, securing all their objectives without heavy loss, so that the Twenty-Ninth did not have to relieve them for a week. The line it then took over ran along the Pilckem ridge, which was sticky even on top and sloped down to the marsh now formed by the swollen Steenbeek. The so-called ' line ' consisted of isolated trenches and shell-holes, though a few ' pill-boxes '

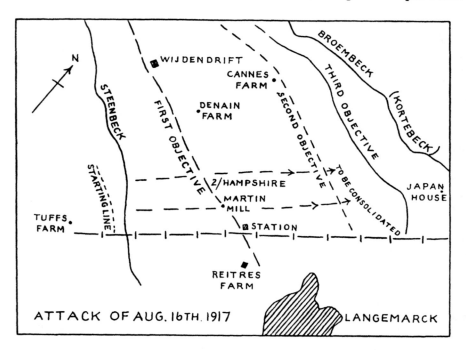

ATTACK OF AUG. 16TH. 1917

had survived the bombardment and could be used as brigade or battalion head-quarters or as 'strong points'. The support line, which the 2nd Hampshire occupied on August 9th, existed mainly on the map and the men had to dig in as best they could. The enemy's fire was heavy and the battalion had 20 casualties, 2/Lts. Wooldridge and Powell being wounded, but the men worked well and improved the position considerably. After four days here, the battalion went forward after dark on August 15th to an assembly position NE. of Pilckem. A tape, previously laid by Captain Day, proved invaluable on a very dark night, the Essex, in support, following the battalion along it. Several men fell into shell-holes or stuck in the bog and had to be hauled out with ropes,

[1] Largely in a working party on the morning of July 10th.
[2] NW. of the frontage attacked by the Thirty-Ninth Division on July 31st.

while shell-fire caused some casualties, but the men were splendidly steady and quiet and the assembly position was reached about 1.30 a.m. (August 16th). Battalion H.Q. were at Tuff's Farm, Y (Captain Day) and W (2/Lt. Whitmarsh) Companies being across the swamps of the Steenbeek, over which the 87th Brigade had previously laid bridges, and X (2/Lt. Reid) and Z (Captain Westmorland) in 'artillery formation' on the near side behind them. On the right, beyond the Ypres–Staden railway, was the Twentieth Division facing Langemarck, the Newfoundlands being on the Hampshire's left. Beyond them was the 87th Brigade, in touch with the French.

Desultory shelling caused several casualties during the wait on the assembly position, but at 4.45 our barrage came down, 'as good as any we ever met during the war', and the men went forward well, taking full advantage of it. The leading companies' objective was a line across the Langemarck–Wijdendrift road, its right being just beyond Martin's Mill ; the supports were to secure a 'Green Line', 500 yards further on and running North to Cannes Farm : on this line the Essex would come through to tackle the third objective, NNW. of Langemarck and short of the Broembeck.[1]

The advance went well, though the right companies suffered some casualties through the Twentieth Division's barrage being ragged and falling outside its proper line, while South of the railway that Division itself had soon fallen behind. In consequence enfilade fire from machine-guns in Reitres Farm and in blockhouses near it caused trouble, but those were dealt with by 2/Lt. Reid, who promptly extended two platoons along the railway and, covered by their fire, 2/Lt. Pine led a party across the railway to attack these obstructing 'strong points'. Well backed up by Corporal Whitaker, he soon captured Reitres Farm, despite stubborn opposition, and after he had been wounded the Corporal carried on, clearing the enemy out of several more posts. Meanwhile Captain Day organized an attack on other blockhouses North of the railway and Sergeant Oram brought Z Company's right platoon across to assist, while Sergeant Finch, leading an attack on another 'strong point', dashed ahead through our barrage, killed four Germans single-handed and took the blockhouses with some 20 prisoners. Thanks to their promptitude and grasp of the situation the opposition was overcome : besides Reitres Farm and the blockhouses near it dug-outs along the railway were taken, Sergeant Holdaway[2] leading a party of bombers splendidly and clearing several dug-outs, with many prisoners and several machine-guns, while with Sergeant Oram's help, Captain Day, who though wounded had continued to lead his company, soon captured his objective. Great work was done by several Lewis gunners, Privates Forrester,[2] Batten[2] and Hoath in[2] particular, who not only assisted in the capture of the battalion's objective but helped the Twentieth Division to advance and, when the enemy retired from near Langemarck Station, fired on them with great effect. Thus the first objective was duly secured and its consolidation could be started, Sergeant Oram's party rejoining their own company for the next advance.

---

[1] This stream is called Kortebeck in some accounts.　　　　[2] Received the M.M.

The first objective had been captured well up to time, so the advance to the Green Line followed at 5.45. The ground was so bad that shallow columns had to be formed to cross one specially marshy bit, wave formation being resumed beyond it. Nevertheless the Green Line was reached on the heels of the barrage, 2/Lt. Reid again leading the advance admirably, while bombers of X Company cleared several more block-houses along the railway. This objective having been secured with more prisoners, bringing the battalion's captures to well over 150, its consolidation was begun, Major Spring coming forward to superintend the construction of 'strong points', while several Lewis gunners took post in front to cover the work. The men worked splendidly and soon had good cover, from which they benefitted when, about 7.30 a.m., the enemy started shelling the captured position with considerable vigour, their fire being largely directed by aeroplanes. This caused many casualties, especially among the stretcher bearers and H.Q. personnel at Tuff's Farm, where Private Gibbs, the Medical Officer's orderly, was conspicuous for good work, and made communication with Brigade H.Q. very hard to maintain. Shortly afterwards the supporting battalions, the Essex (right) and Worcestershire, came forward to attack the Red Line, just short of the Broembeek, which they duly captured, adding substantially to the many prisoners already taken. Rumours of an impending counter-attack now caused the right companies to prepare a defensive line along the railway, where the Twentieth Division, though driven back from the Red Line, was holding on to Langemarck and the Green Line. None developed, however, and the Twenty-Ninth Division was left in possession of its gains [1] and could congratulate itself on a most successful day : its losses had not been very heavy, little over 2000 all told, and the casualties inflicted on the enemy, over and above several hundreds of prisoners, had been substantial. It now retained its position despite considerable shell-fire, easily repulsing some half-hearted counter-attacks, the most threatening being promptly stopped by our artillery, and before daylight on August 17th the 86th Brigade had relieved the attacking brigades, though by some error X Company was not relieved for another 24 hours, when it rejoined head-quarters at Bluet Farm. The Hampshire's casualties, 2/Lt. Feather killed, 2/Lts. Pine and Haddy mortally wounded, 43 men killed and missing, Captain Day, 2/Lt. L. H. Brown and 148 men wounded,[2] though substantial, were not high, considering what had been achieved, and the battalion was most warmly congratulated by the Corps Commander, Lord Cavan, and by General de Lisle, who inspected it on August 19th, bringing a special message of thanks from the G.O.C. Twentieth Division for the great help the Hampshire had given his men. Captain Day and 2/Lt. Reid were given the M.C. and Sergeants Finch and Oram the D.C.M., nine men getting M.M.s.[3] Corporal Whitaker and Privates Gibbs and Wood, a ' runner '

[1] The 87th Brigade on the 88th's left had also captured all its objectives.

[2] The M.O., Captain Knight, 2/Lt. T.C. Pearce and 20 more men, though wounded, remained ' at duty '.

[3] Besides those mentioned, these were Sergeant Paffett, who though wounded had led his men admirably. Private Sheaf, who had taken command of a leaderless section, Privates Everiss and Ratcliffe, ' runners ', and Private Squires, who had done great work as a bomber.

who besides doing admirable work in that line, had rallied a disorganized section, seized a Lewis gun and dispersed a large party of Germans, getting bars.

The battalion was back in front line by August 20th, in the ' Red Line ' taken by the Essex and Worcestershire, where it was severely shelled and sniped and had over 50 casualties, including 2/Lt. Whitmarsh and 17 men killed. It was not inactive, the improvement of the line and of the communications provided plenty of work, while Z Company established a post beyond the Broembeek and did some useful patrolling. August 25th saw the battalion back at Proven, to begin nearly a month's respite from fighting.

The attack of August 16th, highly successful on our left, from St. Julien Northward, had been less fortunate further South, where the enemy's positions astride the narrow ridge running Eastward from Ypres had proved exceptionally strong and his resistance particularly determined. This decided Sir Douglas Haig to extend the Second Army's left Northward, giving General Plumer charge of the attack astride the Menin Road, the Fifth Army continuing the attacks further to the left. Much re-adjustment and re-arrangement was now necessary, while, to meet the pill-box and other new methods of defence, certain modifications in our tactics had to be adopted and practised and this, even more than the rain, postponed the next major attack till mid-September. In the meantime the Divisions in front line, among them the Thirty-Ninth, were kept busy enough ; many local attacks were undertaken, the line being improved at certain points, while the enemy was on the alert to hamper and hinder our preparations, shelling our lines heavily and continually, making local counter-attacks and harassing us with every available weapon, but without gaining much. Meanwhile, by keeping the Germans fully occupied, Sir Douglas Haig was fulfilling one of his major purposes, the Germans were not allowed to recover the initiative and to take advantage of it to attack the still disordered and depressed French Army.

CHAPTER XIX

THE FLANDERS OFFENSIVE, II

THIRD YPRES (continued)

DURING the month's pause which set in after the middle of August only one Hampshire battalion was in the fighting line at Ypres, the 14th, whose Division had taken over the Hollebeke sector from the Forty-First on August 12th, and remained there or at Klein Zillebeke for the next three weeks. Retaliation for the barrage fired to assist our attack of August 16th caused over 30 casualties, and at different times another 20 were suffered,[1] but the enemy was rarely aggressive and the battalion had few chances of hitting back, its main energies being devoted to improving the communications, while when it was in reserve quantities of material had to be carried up to the front line. From September 4th to 8th it was at Chippewa Camp, training, and then had three days in support in Shrewsbury Forest, ground taken on July 31st and North of the sectors it had been holding. After three days in reserve here it held the left sub-sector of this front from September 14th to 16th, when the Forty-First Division, now returning to the line, relieved it. Another attack was now very near, but artillery activity had not been pronounced on either side and the 14th escaped with six killed and a dozen wounded. On relief they went back to Curragh Camp, their brigade being in Divisional reserve during the attack of September 20th, when only the 117th Brigade was actively engaged, securing a rather limited objective SE. of Shrewsbury Forest, on the right of the Forty-First Division.

After being relieved at Hollebeke the Forty-First Division had first been at Fletre and then, on August 21st, marched back to Nieppe, whence buses took the 15th Hampshire to Acquin, where they spent three weeks. Eighty reinforcements had joined before this and another 50 with five officers, among them Major Murdoch of the 11th R.W.K., joined at Acquin, where much useful training was done, especially of signallers and other specialists. Several awards of decorations were announced and on September 9th some were presented after church parade by Brigadier General Towsey.

The return to the front started on September 14th, three marches taking the 15th back to Ridgewood, behind their old sector. Their Division was coming into line between the Twenty-Third, who were astride the Menin road, and the Thirty-Ninth, and was to attack through the Northern part of Shrewsbury Forest, with the Basseville brook to cross. As the 14th Hampshire were in Divisional reserve while the Twenty-Ninth Division was still at rest, the Fourth not yet in Flanders and the Sixteenth already with the Third Army, only the 15th Battalion represented the regiment in the big attack of September 20th.

The Forty-First Division's first and second objectives, the ' Red ' and ' Blue '

---

[1] No officer was hit.

_ines, lay West and East respectively of the Basseville brook : the 122nd
3rigade was attacking on its left, with the 124th on its right, and was using the
_5th Hampshire (left) and 18th K.R.R.C. (right) to capture them, after which
he 11th R.W.K. and 12th E. Surreys would go through and attack a ' Green
_ine ', Tower Trench on the Tower Hamlets ridge beyond. The Tower Hamlets
idge, a flat-topped spur running South from the Menin road, was a position of
:onsiderable natural strength, even without the fortifications. The attackers
iad first to cross the open slope leading down to the Basseville brook and then
o climb the sharp glacis of the spur, equally lacking in cover.

The assembly had been carried out over-night quite quietly and unevent-
ully, except for more rain, and the attack duly started at 5.40 a.m. (September
zoth) in a mist which soon cleared away. Soon after crossing the German front
ine the 15th were held up at Java Avenue by block-houses which the barrage
iad missed. Casualties were heavy, many officers, including all four company
:ommanders, were hit, and the opposition was only overcome and the block-
iouses taken by great gallantry and good leading and with some help from the
R.W.K., whose C.O., Lt. Colonel Corfe, did much to re-organize the attackers,
vhile Captain Wigmore, now Adjutant, went forward to assist and lead the
nen. Before long they had carried the Red Line and, pushing on across the
swampy depression formed by the brook, they mastered the Blue Line also,
z/Lts. Sergeant and Barker distinguishing themselves by good leading and
nitiative.

As consolidation started a counter-attack began to develop from the NE.;
t was checked by our fire, and then the R.W.K. went ahead to take the
Green Line ', where the ' Tower Hamlets ', a mass of concrete dug-outs and
pill-boxes ', promised to give trouble, It was a formidable task, the attackers
iad to mount an open slope quite devoid of cover and many machine-guns
were in action in the ' pill-boxes ', proof against anything short of a ' direct '
from a ' heavy '. The R.W.K. had already lost heavily and, being ahead of
ill other troops on their right, they came under enfilade machine-gun fire, a
strongly fortified ' defended locality ' on that flank having escaped our barrage,
while its fire had also checked the 124th Brigade. However, despite stubborn
opposition they reached Tower Trench and gained a foothold in it, from which
they were soon driven back to the Blue Line, which the 15th were consolidating,
though a few men who had never received the order to retire held on stubbornly
at one point. Late in the afternoon the 15th were ordered to attempt to capture
the Green Line ; only about 130 men could be collected, but these pushed
gallantly forward and established themselves in the Green Line, taking 40
prisoners, among them a battalion commander and his adjutant, a field gun and
two machine-guns ; 2/Lt. M. S. Moore, supported only by half a dozen men,
capturing nearly 30 Germans in one big dug-out. This position they consolidated, repulsing several counter-attacks and getting touch with the Twenty-
Third Division,[1] but without ever getting touch with the handful of R.W.K. who

[1] That Division's *History* (p. 190) is clear on that point : ' the 15th Hampshire ' it writes
' succeeded in capturing their objective '.

had not retired and without our artillery learning that parts of the Green Line were in our hands.

This was only too evident next day, when about 10 a.m. our barrage was put down on the Green Line to assist an advance on the right by the 123rd Brigade, who established themselves across the brook but short of the Green Line, the 'defended locality' South of the Tower Hamlets again proving a stumbling block. 2/Lt. Moore, now the senior officer left in the Green Line, showed great resourcefulness and coolness, withdrawing his men slightly so as to avoid our barrage but reoccupying his position directly it stopped, and despite another bombardment by our guns during the afternoon the position was retained all day. Meanwhile enemy had been seen preparing to counter-attack the Blue Line from the SE. but our rifles and machine-guns had dispersed them even before our barrage answered the SOS.[1]

Early next morning, (September 22nd) another dose of our barrage, which destroyed their rifles and rations, at last forced 2/Lt. Moore and the ten men who alone survived of his party back to the Blue Line, for though they had re-

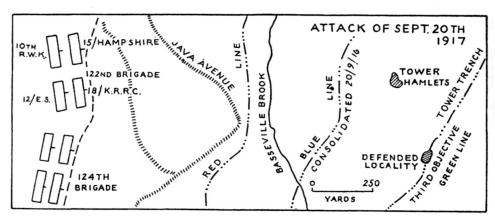

armed themselves with German rifles and bombs, they could not hold on any longer and had very reluctantly to leave behind an anti-tank gun and two machine-guns. They had made a gallant effort and the V.C. shortly afterwards awarded to 2/Lt. Moore was a well-earned recognition of an outstanding exploit.[2] If the Division had only secured part of its objective it had distracted the Germans' attention from the troops on its left and had contributed to their success.

After holding on throughout September 22nd under heavy shelling, though no more counter-attacks developed, the remnants of the 15th Hampshire were relieved by the 14th Battalion and another of the Thirty-Ninth Division, and went back to Ridgewood Camp. Six[3] officers and 83 men had been killed or

---

[1] The regimental histories show that the two German regiments holding the position attacked by the Forty-First Division, the 28th Bavarian Ersatz and the 395th, lost virtually all their front battalions and most of those in support.

[2] Captain Wigmore and 2/Lts. Barker and Sergeant received the M.C.

[3] Major Seers, Captain Daniels, Lts. Bender, Montagu and Stokes and 2/Lt. Savage.

SECOND LIEUTENANT MONTAGUE SHADWORTH SEYMOUR MOORE, V.C.,
Croix de Guerre

He was gazetted to a commission in The Hampshire Regiment from the R.M.C., Sandhurst, on August 16th, 1916. His decoration was gazetted on November 8th, 1917, for his actions on September 20th, 1917, at 'Tower Hamlets', East of Ypres, when attached to the 15th Battalion.
' For most conspicuous bravery in operations necessitating a fresh attack on a final objective which had not been captured. 2nd Lieutenant Moore at once volunteered for this duty, and dashed forward at the head of some seventy men. They were met with heavy machine gun fire from a flank which caused severe casualties, with the result that he arrived at his objective—some five hundred yards on—with only a sergeant and four men. Nothing daunted, he at once bombed a large dug out and took 28 prisoners, 2 machine guns, and a light field gun. Gradually more officers and men arrived, to the number of about sixty. His position was entirely isolated, as the troops on the right had not advanced, but he dug a trench and repelled bombing attacks through-out the night. The next morning he was forced to retire a short distance. When the opportunity offered he at once reoccupied his position, re-armed his men with enemy rifles and bombs, most of theirs being smashed, and beat off more than one counter-attack.
2nd Lieutenant Moore held to this post under continual shell fire for thirty-six hours, until his force was reduced to ten men, out of six officers and one hundred and thirty men who had started the operation. He eventually got away his wounded, and withdrew under cover of a thick mist.

were missing and seven officers and 251 men wounded, leaving the battalion terribly reduced ; indeed, had not 82 men joined on September 24th, the remnant would almost have been outnumbered by the influx on September 25th of twelve officers and 307 other ranks of the 1st Hampshire Carabiniers.

That regiment had continued on home duty all through 1915, though it had volunteered to serve as infantry in any theatre of war. Early in 1916 its squadrons were attached as Divisional cavalry to Second-Line T.F. Divisions, the Fifty-Eighth, Sixtieth, and Sixty-First, all due to go overseas ; B and C Squadrons, however, went out independently in May and June , head-quarters also coming out and becoming head-quarters of the Ninth Corps Cavalry, a composite unit, of which C Squadron also formed part, B being then with the Cavalry Corps and later with the Seventeenth. Eventually in January 1917 A Squadron also came out [1] and the regiment was re-united. It served as Corps Cavalry to the Ninth Corps till late in July, doing useful work during the Messines attack in patrolling, locating the enemy and carrying information. By this time the difficulty of finding drafts was leading to many expedients, and among them the conversion into infantry of several Yeomanry units. The Hampshire Carabiniers were so far allowed to retain their identity that the 15th incorporated their title and became the 15th (Hampshire Carabiniers) Battalion, the Hampshire Regiment.

This was a fine reinforcement ; if many ' originals ' of the Hampshire Carabiniers had obtained commissions or transferred to the cavalry, many remained and the 15th were glad to welcome such splendid material, men of some service and training.

The Thirty-Ninth Division, having had only limited objectives on September 20th, had only employed the 117th Brigade, so that it had two unused brigades available for the next big attack, that of September 26th, when it attacked from the line gained [2] on the 20th by the Twenty-Third and Forty-First Divisions South of the Menin road. The 116th Brigade was on the left, its objectives being the Tower Hamlets and Tower Trench behind them, a formidable task enough. On its right the 118th Brigade had, if possible, an even nastier nut to crack, the ' defended locality ' which had held up the attack of September 20th.

The 14th Hampshire had had two trying days in line here after relieving the remnants of the 15th Hampshire on the evening of September 22nd. The approaches to our advanced positions were exposed to snipers and to machine-gun and artillery fire, and the battalion had been heavily shelled while consolidating a rather imperfect line, having 2/Lts. Chartney and Clarke wounded

---

[1] Its transport was nearly sunk in a collision off Havre and only beached just in time ; the men behaved admirably, several remaining on board with the horses till the vessel could be sufficiently repaired to be berthed. Before this a Divisional squadron had ceased to form part of the Divisional organization, Corps cavalry units being formed instead.

[2] East of the Basseville brook but short of the Tower Hamlets.

with 25 men, six others being killed. After two days in reserve, it took up its position for the attack after dark on September 25th.

Directly the advance started at 5.50 a.m., it met heavy machine-gun fire and casualties soon mounted up : Major Goldsmith, who had given up his leave to be in command in this attack,[1] fell fatally wounded leading the advance, and with him Captain Nichols, Lt. Bainbridge and 2/Lt. Wallis-Wilson, a man of great bravery, who had won the M.C. and a bar, much the oldest subaltern in the battalion. However, despite the fire and the boggy ground, the 14th pressed on and reached and carried the Tower Hamlets, Captain White leading his men splendidly and keeping them close up to the barrage, while 2/Lt. Howard, after reaching his platoon's objective despite mist and smoke by keeping on a compass bearing, organized and led the clearing of several dug-outs, bombing them effectively. Captain Dawson, the next senior officer present, took charge on Major Goldsmith's fall and carried on most efficiently. Parties now pushed ahead to Tower Trench, when 2/Lt. Taberer, finding that one company detailed for this advance had lost heavily and was much disorganized, took his own company forward and by his leadership and initiative did much to ensure the success of this stage of the advance. By 7.30 a.m. about 150 men were consolidating on the left of the final objective, taking up a line just short of Tower Trench itself. Machine-guns on the left front were troublesome but touch had been obtained with the Thirty-Third Division NW. of Gheluvelt Wood, while the supporting battalion eventually reinforced the advanced party of the 14th. The 118th Brigade on the 116th's right had reached but failed to retain possession of the obstructing 'defended locality' on the Southern end of the Tower Hamlets spur, but nevertheless the 116th's gains were retained and consolidation was energetically pushed on, despite the difficulty of getting material forward and the constant shelling and sniping. Counter-attacks developed elsewhere in considerable force and vigour, but the Tower Hamlets lay beyond their frontage, and next evening, (September 27th) on their Division being relieved the 14th Hampshire went back well behind the line. Losses had been fairly heavy, the four officers mentioned and 75 men killed or missing, 2/Lts. Barrass, Butt, Sangster and Thomas and 118 men wounded,[2] but the battalion could feel that it had achieved something substantial despite great difficulties.

The 14th and 15th Hampshire had both finished with 'Third Ypres', for if the 14th were to return to the Salient before the offensive came to its muddy end in the swamps near Poelcapelle and Passchendaele, the Menin road sector had by then become inactive : both Regular battalions, however, were to be present for the next big attack, that of October 4th, when the Twenty-Ninth Division, on our extreme left astride the Ypres–Staden railway, had the Fourth on its right, NE. of Langemarck.

Major operations at Arras had ended before 'Messines' started, but the Arras front did not become really 'quiet' immediately. At several points

---

[1] He had just been through the Senior Officers' School at Aldershot.
[2] 2/Lt. Taberer was awarded the D.S.O., Captains Dawson and White and 2/Lt. Howard getting the M.C.

either Germans or British badly needed to improve their lines or were reluctant to relinquish stubbornly contested positions, and the 1st Hampshire, who remained on this front till the end of August, were active enough. They had returned to their old sector near Roeux in the middle of June. Two companies were in front line, the right, whose flank rested on the Scarpe, holding four disconnected posts, the left's line being more continuous. Patrols were active but did not find the enemy inclined to contest No Man's Land, and though the line was spasmodically shelled by night, the days were quieter and four in line

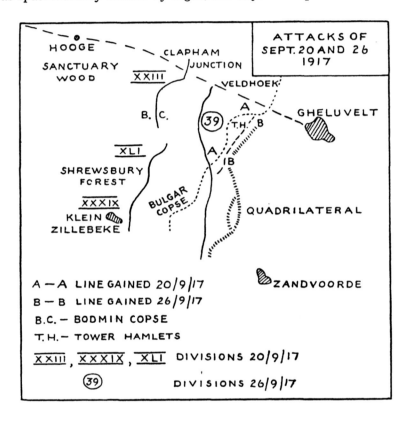

ATTACKS OF
SEPT. 20 AND 26
1917

A — A LINE GAINED 20/9/17
B — B LINE GAINED 26/9/17
B.C. — BODMIN COPSE
T.H. — TOWER HAMLETS
XXIII , XXXIX , XLI DIVISIONS 20/9/17
(39)   DIVISIONS 26/9/17

only brought eleven casualties, but in support the battalion was very hard worked, improving a poor support line. A move back to Balmoral Camp near St. Laurent Blangy, where the battalion remained from June 26th to July 13th, did not bring much rest, an intermediate line needed wiring and cable trenches had to be dug and barges got forward down the Scarpe to Fampoux. Over 120 men, with 20 discharged from hospital, joined during June, when casualties only came to 29.[1] Among the officers who now joined, Captain Smythe and Lt. Collett had been with the battalion before, but the battalion lost Major Earle

[1] 2/Lt. C. A. Huskisson, attached to the Brigade Trench Mortar Battery, was killed.

who was given command of the 1st East Lancashire, so that he remained in the 11th Brigade.

July 13th found the battalion relieving the King's Own in Himalaya Trench South of the Scarpe, and next night it took over the front line NE. of Monchy, having its support company in Bayonet Trench. Despite all the heavy fighting here, the front line was continuous and in good repair, with duck-boards nearly all its length, 1,000 yards. The enemy, who was holding his front line in some strength, as our patrols soon discovered, reserved his activities for the nights, when trench-mortars, rifle grenades and snipers were busy, but again his patrols rarely asserted themselves and ours, who were more enterprising, saw nothing of them. After four days in line and four ' out ' the battalion shifted to the right into Halberd Trench, on July 22nd, with orders to raid Devil's Trench. A barrage on July 23rd on Devil's Trench, South of the point to be raided, provoked heavy retaliation, 2/Lts. Cancellor and Turner being wounded but remaining at duty. Early next morning 2/Lt. Turner was heavily fired on when reconnoitring Arrow Trench with three men. The men must have been hit, but the subaltern escaped and crawled back to report the wire insufficiently cut, so the raid was postponed for 48 hours and the wire again shelled, the gaps being kept under Lewis gun fire at night to prevent repairs. Eventually on July 26th three officers and 78 men, including seven R.E. who were to destroy any dug-outs found, under Captain Icke, carried out the raid. Crawling out 20 minutes before ' Zero ', 10.45 p.m., they lined up 50 yards beyond our wire and at ' Zero ' went forward behind an excellent barrage to find the wire well cut. They were quickly into the front trench, where several prisoners were taken, though most of the garrison had bolted and must have run into our protective barrage, which was being maintained on all known machine-gun emplacements on the flanks. The trench, which was in bad repair and much damaged, was carefully searched, one party advancing nearly 100 yards in a vain search for a suspected machine-gun, while bombers who attacked our left were decisively repulsed, and 25 minutes after ' Zero ' the raiders were back in our lines with their prisoners, having obtained important identifications. Three men were missing and two wounded, but several enemy were left dead and wounded in the trench. Lt. Beatty, whose reconnaissances by day and night had provided most useful information for the raiders, had been conspicuous for his gallantry and leading : he was awarded the M.C., Corporal Holdaway, who had backed up his officers splendidly, getting the M.M.

The battalion spent August 2nd to 14th at Balmoral Camp, training and finding working parties, but was back NE. of Monchy by August 15th, more to the right than on previous occasions, being opposite Arrowhead and Twin Copses, but it shifted to the left again on the 18th. The enemy were quiet, but our Lewis guns and trench mortars were active and, well supported by our artillery, gave them a troubled time.

August 23rd found the battalion in brigade reserve, cleaning up and finding working parties, and then the Division was relieved and had a fortnight's training at Berles au Bois before moving to Flanders. Casualties during July and August had been low, only 12 killed and missing and 2/Lts. Cancellor and Turner and 30 men wounded. However, few drafts had arrived and with 63 admissions to hospital against 30 discharges, companies could not be completed to four platoons till 120 reinforcements joined at Berles au Bois. Lt. Harding now rejoined and half a dozen other subalterns arrived. Before entraining for Flanders on September 19th the opportunity was taken to let all survivors of July 1st 1916 visit Beaumont Hamel and see exactly what they had been facing : enough were present to fill four buses.

On reaching Flanders the battalion had some intensive training with lectures on the new methods of defence to be overcome. Major-General

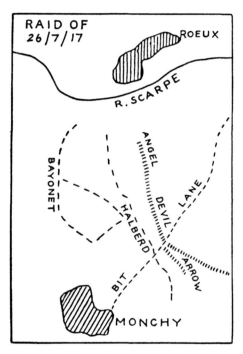

Lambton, who had been commanding the Division for the last two years, had unfortunately been disabled by an accident but his successor, Major-General Matheson, was a tried and capable commander.

A draft of 100 men joined directly the battalion reached Flanders, and with other reinforcements other ranks were up to 960 by October 4th. It illustrates the discrepancy between ' paper strength ' and ' strength in trenches ' that only 520 men ' went over the top ' that day. Sickness and leave accounted for 60, brigade and Divisional employments for 45, 26 were detailed as carriers, 118 were with the battalion transport, ' courses ' and other details accounted for 50, and the remainder formed the ' battle nucleus ' left behind. Of 40 officers 22 were not in action ; Major Hudson, Captains N. Harland and Corner and eight subalterns being ' left out ' and the rest away, on courses or ' employed'.

The 2nd Battalion had spent most of September either near Proven, or at Herzeele or near Elverdinghe. Several officers had joined, among them Lt. Bircham who had been with the battalion in Gallipoli and since then with the 14th at the Schwaben Redoubt, while drafts amounting in all to 175 had brought other ranks up to 900, though as with the 1st Battalion little over half were taken into action.

On returning to the line in the middle of September the Twenty-Ninth Division had relieved the Guards opposite Koekuit, where the 2nd Hampshire had four days in front line before the end of September. The enemy's guns were

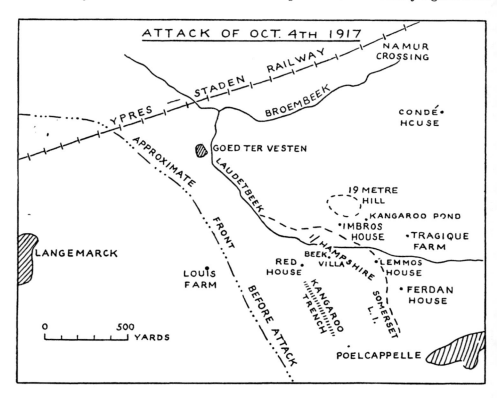

active, especially on the 26th, when a big attack was being made by our right and centre. Our patrols were active, one in particular locating an important German 'strong point'. This turn in front cost the battalion nine killed and 23 wounded, while many men were affected by gas, the area having been drenched before, as well as during, its tenure, indeed the relieved unit's head-quarters had proved almost untenable. The 88th Brigade was relieved on September 29th and was in Divisional reserve on October 4th, the next big 'push', when all that was required of the Division was to make a short advance to cover the flank of the troops on its right, a task successfully discharged by the only two battalions employed.

In that attack[1] the Fourth Division was using the 10th (left) and 11th (right) Brigades. Its starting line was East of Langemarck and its final objective lay NW. of Poelcappelle, which village the Eleventh Division on its right was attacking. The 1st Hampshire were on their brigade's left and their first objective was behind Kangaroo Trench, 350 yards away, the final objective, which included Tragique Farm, being 500 yards further on. Starting at 6.10 a.m., the battalion[2] for once found our barrage ragged and inaccurate and suffered more from it than from the enemy's fire. However, Kangaroo Trench was soon rushed, 30 prisoners and a machine-gun being taken, and by 6.50 the first objective about Beek Villa had been taken, several ' pill-boxes ' being effectively tackled. The Somerset on the right had had much trouble with ' pill-boxes ' but they also had gained their objective. After an hour's pause B Company went forward on the right through C, pushing on past Lemnos House and Imbros House, to be checked by our barrage and forced to come back and dig in short of their objectives, while the Somerset, who also had had to fall back a little way, carried on the line just short of Ferdan House. On the left A Company, after advancing some way, found itself ahead of the 10th Brigade and was checked, but touch was obtained with the troops on both flanks and consolidation was started, the battalion's front line running from Lemnos House (right) to Imbros House, with supporting posts close behind, D Company in battalion reserve being some way in rear near Red House. Some enemy who were sheltering in shell-holes in front were now dislodged by hand-grenades and shot down as they bolted.

About 1 p.m. heavy machine-gun and rifle fire developed against the left, evidently heralding a counter-attack, and the position was endangered by the 10th Brigade being driven off 19-Metre Hill to which it had advanced. The Hampshire and Somerset held on, however, though the Hampshire's left was ' in the air ' Lt. Stannard now showed conspicuous initiative and determination, going out to rally troops who were retiring and leading a counter-attack which helped to check the enemy, and before long the East Lancashire sent up a detachment which covered this exposed flank, while later they assisted the 10th Brigade to bring its line forward again. Pressure on this flank continued, and though the Rifle Brigade's intervention checked a second retirement, the left remained unsettled and the Hampshire had to establish posts behind this flank. This, however, proved sufficient, the enemy did not attempt to press any further, and as the night passed quietly some reorganization was possible and good progress made with the consolidation. Next morning also proved quiet, but the enemy's shelling became heavier in the afternoon and went on till dusk, after which the Rifle Brigade relieved the Hampshire, who spent the next two days at Louis Farm in support under shell-fire, finding parties to carry rations, water and ammunition up to the front,[3] they

---

[1] Officially known as the battle of Broodseinde.
[2] Those actually engaged in the attack came to 18 officers and 522 other ranks : Captains De Gaury (C) and German (D), and Lts. Gullick (A) and Harding (B) commanded the companies.
[3] Pack transport was now being mainly used in the battle area.

then moved back across the canal, on their brigade going into reserve.

The Hampshire's casualties came to 50% of those in action : Lt. Harding, 2/Lts. H. C. Hall, Perrett and Phippard and 64 men killed, 16 men missing, Colonel Armitage, who remained at duty,[1] Lt. Collett, 2/Lts. G. F. Ball, Chester, McCulloch, Middlemass and Scrivens and 187[2] men wounded. But the gain of ground, if less than had been hoped for, was not unsatisfactory, considering all the difficulties to be overcome.[3]

On October 9th when the Fourth Division made its second effort in ' Third Ypres ' and secured nearly all its objectives NW. of Poelcapelle, only the 12th Brigade was engaged, the 11th, who stood to all day in readiness, not being required to assist, and though three days later the Rifle Brigade was attached to the 12th to share in another attack near Poelcapelle, the 1st Hampshire were again not put in but moved back by Proven to Poperinghe to entrain on the 18th for the South, on returning to the Third Army and, as it proved, to familiar ground at Monchy. Nobody was ever very sorry to leave the Ypres Salient, but this time the 1st Hampshire had made some contribution to its expansion.

If the 1st had not shared in the attack of October 9th, that day had given the 2nd some hard fighting. The Twenty-Ninth Division was attacking North of Langemarck, now half a mile behind our front line, with its left brigade, the 88th, astride the Roulers railway. Of its objectives the 4th Worcestershire were to capture two, from Namur Crossing to Koekuit and from Tranquille Farm Westward, after which the Newfoundland Regiment would come through to take a third, from the railway, through Egypt House, to Les Cinq Chemins. It was some indication of the new German methods that both the other battalions were retained to deal with counter-attacks.

The 2nd Hampshire, who left Parroy Camp at 9.15 p.m. on October 8th, found moving up into the assembly positions more than usually difficult : the expanded Steenbeek had to be crossed, the German shelling was fairly heavy and caused both W and X Companies several casualties, while it rained hard all the time ; but if conditions could hardly have been worse,[4] somehow the positions were duly taken up, and at 7 a.m., 100 minutes after ' Zero ', the battalion started forward in ' artillery formation '. The fire was heavy, but it was some compensation for the mud that it partly smothered the shell-bursts, direction was well kept, thanks partly to having the railway line to go by, and before long the Hampshire were digging in on the Namur Crossing Line, which the Worcestershire had taken well up to time, subsequently going forward again.

Advancing again at 8.50 a.m., the Hampshire were heavily shelled but admirably directed by Colonel Spring, established themselves just behind the

[1] The Chaplain, the Reverend A. E. Lawrie, was hit but remained on duty. He was an outstanding figure in the battalion, much loved and respected by all,. He set a wonderful example of courage and devotion to duty and had a remarkable hold on the battalion.

[2] Corrected figures.   [3] Lt. Stannard was awarded the M.C.

[4] Just before the advance hot tea was served out : it had been brought up in tins which were carried in packs stuffed with hay and was thus kept hot.

second objective, which also the Worcestershire had duly secured despite stubborn opposition, taking 200 prisoners. On this line they dug in, 2/Lt. Hicks, though wounded and then buried by a shell-burst near him, set a splendid example, continuing at duty and holding on to his post. Then, about 4 p.m., counter-attacks from the NE. forced the Newfoundlands back from the third objective, which they had reached, their left being pushed back across the Poelcapelle–Cinq Chemins road. They rallied, however, and Colonel Spring was prompt to reinforce them and fill up any gaps in their line, while 2/Lt. Scutt formed a defensive flank on the left with his platoon, rallied officerless men who were retiring and restored the situation. After dark the Hampshire relieved the Newfoundlands in what was now the front line, running about NW.

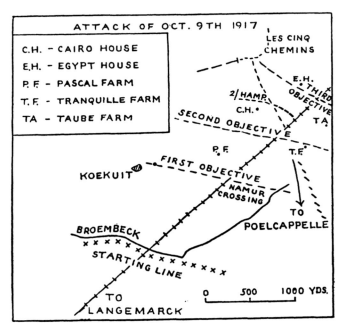

from near Tranquille Farm across the Poelcapelle–Cinq Chemins road,[1] the relief being smoothly effected. During the night, while patrols successfully located the enemy, taking several prisoners, the line was consolidated, with support and reserve lines behind it. Sergeant Sillence, acting as C.S.M., who had been conspicuous during the advance in assisting his officers and setting a fine example, was now much to the fore in directing the consolidation despite heavy shelling.

The enemy's snipers were active, especially from Taube Farm to the right front, causing several casualties, and during the night several times fighting patrols approached our lines, two of about 30 each being dispersed by Private Bray, who was out with a Lewis-gun in front of our line, while Sergeant

[1] i.e. short of the third objective.

Martin beat off another and Lance-Corporal Jerram and Private Smith did useful work in scouting and detecting the enemy's efforts to advance. Except for barraging a line the battalion was not holding, the German artillery was inactive, and though such wet ground made the work difficult, real progress was made next day with the consolidation, very good work being done by the battalion runners in keeping up communications. Early in the afternoon the Brigade Major reached battalion head-quarters, now at Pascal Farm, East of Koekuit, with orders for the capture of a troublesome 'strong point' to the left front near Cairo House. There was barely time to organize an attack before the barrage came down, but Lt. Colonel Spring went forward through a heavy barrage to W Company's head-quarters to arrange the attack, and W was just ready before our barrage began at 5.30 p.m. Advancing with two platoons in a front wave and one supporting, the company, well led and skilfully directed by Captain Cuddon, who was well backed up by Sergeants Trethewy and Parker, mastered its objective, despite stubborn opposition. Many Germans were accounted for, a Lewis gunner, Private Gosling, dispersing one party of 30 single-handed, and a good line was established 50 yards NE. of the buildings and linked up to the rest of the line.

That evening the 7th Lincolnshire (Seventeenth Division) arrived to relieve the Hampshire. A dark night made this difficult, but thanks to good arrangements for guides everything went off smoothly and by 8 a.m. next day (October 11th) the Hampshire were back at Elverdinghe. 2/Lt. Lloyd and 18 men had been killed and Captains C. T. Ball and Mudge, Lt. A. G. Smith, 2/Lts. Cutmore and Hicks and 74 men wounded. One noticeable feature of the action had been the increased expenditure of rifle ammunition ; in bringing up reinforcements the enemy had given better targets than of late and, with more chances of using the rifle, battalions which had been careful to maintain their standards of musketry had reaped the benefit.

Lt. Colonel Spring's skilful handling of the situation was recognised soon afterwards by a D.S.O., while Captain Cuddon was given a bar to his M.C., 2/Lts. Hicks and Scutt receiving the M.C. Sergeant Trethewy, who besides leading his platoon with great determination during the attack had done great work in consolidation, was awarded the D.C.M., while 21 M.M.s were awarded to the battalion, Lance Corporal Fielder, who had worked untiringly to succour the wounded, searching for them under heavy fire, getting a bar, while about the same time Sergeants Oram and Finch and Corporal Whitaker received the French Croix de Guerre.

The Twenty-Ninth Division and the 2nd Hampshire had thus finished their part in ' Third Ypres ' with a satisfactory success ; if the battalion had had less chance at Poelcapelle in October than at Langemarck in August it had done its bit well. Indeed the regiment could congratulate itself on having achieved some substantial success in every episode of ' Third Ypres ' in which it took part, while if its losses had been heavy it had taken a good toll of its enemies and above all won two more V.C's.

CHAPTER XX

CAMBRAI

'THIRD Ypres' continued for some weeks after the Fourth and Twenty-Ninth Divisions had been withdrawn to 'quieter' places. Its closing stages, in which the regiment was fortunate to escape sharing, were like those of the Somme, as much struggles against mud and swamps as against the Germans: the weather, rarely for long favourable to the attack, became worse as the autumn advanced, and what the troops in the front line had to endure rivalled even what the 1st and 2nd Hampshire had gone through in their second experience of the Somme. Attention has, however, been unduly concentrated on these closing stages and the whole offensive judged by its worst moments. That it had to be continued to keep the Germans occupied could not in 1917 be trumpeted abroad on the house tops, and unfortunately, as this essential fact could not then be divulged, it has escaped the notice of many amateur and impatient critics and is perhaps not yet properly appreciated. That the Germans were kept occupied and the French thereby given time to recover was the chief gain from its continuation : its contribution to the wearing down of the hard core of German power, the fighting strength of the German Army, was by their own admissions [1] very considerable : against our own losses and sufferings must be set what the Germans also endured, while their new counter-attacking tactics, especially when unsuccessful, were costly.[2] Very probably, once it became clear that we should not liberate the Belgian Coast, Sir Douglas Haig would have suspended the offensive sooner, if General Petain would have agreed that the state of the French Armies would allow of it, but it is hard to picture General Petain paying much attention to British interests if they clashed in the least with French or sparing the British at any expense to his own men.

Some alternative to 'Third Ypres' might have been tried earlier had General Petain's demands allowed it. For some time the British Commander-in-Chief had been considering attacking in a quarter where the ground would be less unfavourable, where the very strength of the German defences might make surprise easier, where the tank, now greatly improved in design and manufacture and less liable to break down than those used on the Somme, might do more to justify itself than at Ypres, where the bad going was all against it. The Cambrai attack which was to give the 2nd Hampshire yet another battle in 1917, their hardest of the year, was no sudden improvisation.

The Hindenburg Line, skilfully sited and well dug, had been formidable enough in the spring when it had held up the Fourth and Fifth Armies, and such portions as had been captured during the Arras fighting had proved difficult and extremely costly to take. It had been strengthened since then, and besides the Line itself and its Support, the Germans held some strong positions in front and, as the Twenty-Ninth Division was to have reason to appreciate, they had

---

[1] *Official History* 1917. II. chapter 19.   [2] ibid. pp. 362–365.

also constructed a very formidable rearward line, the Masnieres–Beaurevoir This moreover was almost at its strongest immediately SW. of Cambrai, where it ran behind those stretches of the Scheldt and its canal which turn Westward past Crevecoeur and Masnieres to Marcoing and run thence Northward East of Noyelles.

Besides the great concentration of tanks, about whose handling and man-

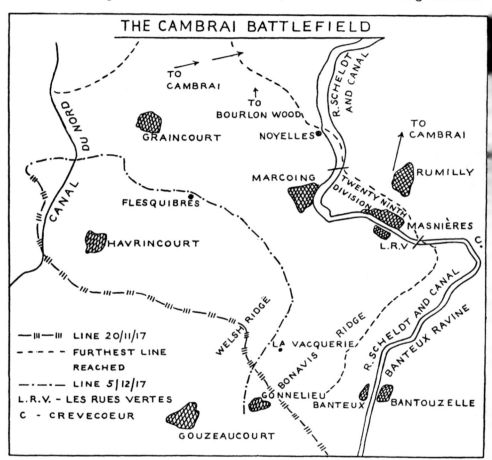

oeuvring in co-operation with guns and infantry much had been learnt by experience and experiment since a solitary tank had led the 15th Hampshire into Flers, other improvements in methods had been devised. The lengthy artillery preparation, which must inevitably give warning of an impending attack, was no longer necessary, previous registration could now be much reduced without diminishing the efficiency of the bombardment, and a complete surprise was achieved when, at 6.25 a.m. on November 20th, our guns opened fire and tanks and infantry went forward : for this the Third Army's Staff deserves enormous credit.

Seven Divisions were being employed in the attack, among them the Twenty-Ninth, which, like the Fourth at Arras, was to go through the leading Divisions of its Corps, the Third, after they had taken the Hindenburg Support Line, its errand being to secure the passages over the Scheldt and its canal and, if possible, exploit that success by breaking through the German third position near Rumilly.

Since leaving Flanders the 2nd Hampshire had been at Bienvilliers for a month ; 164 men and several officers had joined before it left Flanders, and while at Bienvilliers it got reinforcements, including men rejoining from hospital, amounting to 154, together with Captain K. A. Johnston who assumed command on Colonel Spring being suddenly taken ill and having to go to hospital. The training included open-warfare exercises, much needed by nearly everyone in the battalion.

November 17th saw the Hampshire entraining at Boisleux, and after detraining near Peronne they marched to Moislains to encamp, going on next night [1] to Sorel le Grand, where instructions were received and ' battle stores ' issued.

Leaving Sorel le Grand at 2.30 a.m. (November 20th), the Hampshire duly reached the brigade's assembly area at Gouzeaucourt in good time. ' Zero ' was fixed for 6.25, just an hour before sunrise, and a thick autumn mist helped to conceal things even after it began to grow light. The German guns did not open up, even the noise made by nearly 400 tanks had actually escaped notice, and, as on July 14th, 1916, complete surprise had been achieved.

The Third Corps had three Divisions in front, of which the Twelfth and Twentieth, after taking their first two objectives, were to wheel to the right and establish a defensive flank along the slopes above the Banteux Ravine along which the Scheldt and the canal flow North to turn West at Crevecœur. This would clear the front for the Twenty-Ninth Division, whose advance from our old front line was to begin on its receiving news of the capture of the second objective. As usual information was slow to filter back, but General de Lisle was not one to wait, and at 10.30 he started the Division off, Division, brigades and battalions in ' diamond ' formation, the 88th Brigade on the right moving NE. for Masnieres, the 87th (centre) marching North on Marcoing, the 86th (left) having Noyelles and Nine Wood as objectives. In the 88th Brigade the Essex led, with the Worcestershire on their right, the Newfoundland on the left and the Hampshire behind, with Y, X, W and Z Companies in the corresponding positions in the battalion diamond.

In the Brown Line, the second objective, a formidable ' strong point ' at Good Old Man Farm was still resisting, and while the Essex with some support from the flanking battalions dealt with it, taking 150 prisoners, Y Company had a little ' show ' of its own, mopping up some ' strong points ' most successfully and taking 40 prisoners. Re-forming to continue the advance, Lt. Colonel Johnston noticed that it was going too far to the left, so he brought the companies across to the right to recover the true line. Meanwhile the Worcester-

---

[1] To ensure surprise the marches were made at night.

shire had got up level with the Essex and were approaching the canal, making for a lock half a mile SE. of Masnieres. This they secured, and two companies crossed over, while another wheeled towards Les Rues Vertes to try to secure the main bridge by which the Cambrai road crosses the canal from Les Rues Vertes to Masnieres. This the Essex should have taken, but they had diverged to the left and the Germans had had time to demolish it partially, and what they had not finished a tank now completed for them. This prevented the cavalry pushing through to secure a hold in the Masnieres–Beaurevoir Line,

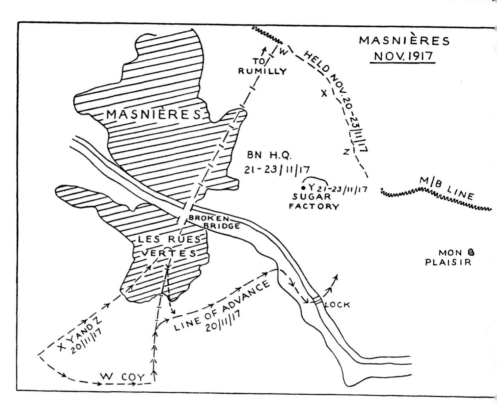

which the supporting infantry might exploit. Indeed, when the Hampshire came up the brigade seemed to be checked, though before long some of the Worcestershire had reinforced the Essex and were forcing their way in to Les Rues Vertes, and the Newfoundland were reaching the canal bank West of Masnieres. Lt. Colonel Johnston's first intention was to press the attack against the main road-bridge, and Y pushed ahead to do this, X and Z following, while W cleared some houses along the main road. However, he now learnt from a Tank officer that the bridge was impassable, so he diverted W, X and Z to the right to cross at the lock and reinforce the Worcestershire, leaving Y under Captain Bircham to help clear Les Rues Vertes and secure our end of the bridge.

Unfortunately, as the lock had to be crossed in single file under machine-gun fire and sniping, it was 3 p.m. before its passage was completed.

Lt. Colonel Linton of the Worcestershire having been killed, Lt. Colonel Johnston took command of the troops across the canal and sent X Company against Masnieres, while W and Z, attacking on the Worcestershire's left, helped them to capture Mon Plaisir Farm and make a lodgement in the Masnieres–Beaurevoir Line, between the lock and the NE. corner of Masnieres. In this stage of the fight Captain Ashling led Z very skilfully and established it in a good position, while Captain Lord took command of officerless men and led them on to the objective, whose consolidation he directed, besides organizing and leading an attack on a ' strong point ' for whose capture he was largely responsible. Thus a good position was established, Lt. Colonel Johnston making very skilful dispositions, going far to secure the right flank of the brigade, line Y, having cleared Les Rues Vertes, rejoined and was placed in reserve at the lock, and X, after clearing the outskirts of Masnieres, formed a defensive flank facing that village.

During the night orders were received that Masnieres must be cleared as a preliminary to further efforts against the Beaurevoir Line, so W and a company of the Worcestershire were detailed for this task. This took some time, the Germans resisting stubbornly, but by 4.30 next morning (November 21st) the village had been practically cleared but for a dug-out below the church which held on for some time longer, so the troops who had done the work could advance against the Masnieres–Beaurevoir trenches across the Cambrai road, which were reported not to be strongly held. Pushing forward to see whether this report was accurate, W, ably led and directed by Captain Singleton-Gates, made some headway but drew heavy fire from near Rumilly and were checked. They held on to their gains, despite having both flanks exposed, and when about 11 a.m. two German battalions came forward against Mon Plaisir our Lewis guns and the artillery helped to check them, no Germans succeeded in getting within 500 yards of the brigade's line. Eventually X came up into the gap on the right of W, where the Worcestershire had diverged to the flank, W and X eventually securing some 200 yards of the Masnieres–Beaurevoir Line, while touch was also gained with the Essex West of Masnieres.

Meanwhile, despite considerable opposition and hard fighting, the 86th and 87th Brigades had on the first day of the battle captured Noyelles and Marcoing and established a bridge-head beyond Marcoing, taking many prisoners, though the 87th's effort on November 21st to break through the Masnieres–Beaurevoir Line had been foiled. The defensive flank had been established above the Banteux Ravine, but on the other flank the Sixth Division,[1] which had taken Ribecourt, had been held up owing to an unfortunate check to the next Division on its left at Flesquieres, which also prevented the exploitation of the substantial successes gained further to the left. A deep re-entrant had thus been left in our front, whereas had it run straight NW. from Masnieres to the Bapaume–Cambrai road, a prompt attack might have been made on Bourlon Wood, the

---

[1] The left Division of the Third Corps.

dominating high ground North of that road : as things were, this Flesquieres
' bulge ' had to be flattened out first, and meanwhile German reinforcements
were arriving. Moreover, the Masnieres–Beaurevoir Line had proved unpleasantly strong : and though the 88th Brigade had established itself securely at
Masnieres and repulsed by fire an attempted counter-attack from the NE., it
could not get on. For two days the situation here remained almost unchanged.
On November 22nd W Company and the Essex tried to push forward along the
Rumilly road and to bomb along a trench, but machine-guns prevented substantial progress. More than once that day a counter-attack seemed to be
starting from the now crowded German trenches, but Lewis guns and machine-
guns quickly quashed every attempt to advance.

Before daybreak on November 24th the brigade had been relieved by the
86th, whom the Sixth Division had replaced at Noyelles ; it now went into
reserve at Marcoing, mainly in cellars, though the houses were as yet little
damaged. The Hampshire's casualties had so far been low : 2/Lt. Howcroft
was missing, 28 men were killed or missing, Captain Bircham and 2/Lts.
McLachlan and Niven and 56 men had been wounded, a light price for what
they had achieved. Altogether the new venture had yielded quite substantial
gains. Even if the Masnieres–Beaurevoir Line had held us up and if Bourlon
Wood had not been cleared, while the rather optimistic projects of passing the
cavalry through to exploit the success had not been fulfilled, the renowned
Hindenburg Line had been well and truly broken, the advance had surpassed
even that of April 9th at Arras, and the experience of liberating from the
Germans hundreds of civilians who had suffered three years under their heel
was both novel and exhilarating. It looked as if, were reserves available, the
opening might yet be exploited to advantage.

After two days in Divisional reserve at Marcoing the Hampshire spent three
uneventful days (November 26th–29th) in front line across the canal. They
were not attacked or even much molested, if the enemy's guns were occasionally
active and caused another 20 casualties, but the really unpleasant feature of the
situation was that the Division had now been in line since November 20th, that
before that it had had three tiring night marches in succession, with little real
rest in between, so that all ranks had earned and greatly needed a relief. No
drafts had appeared to replace the casualties, and the consolidation and improvement of the line had involved much hard and exhausting work. That the two
Divisions holding the long defensive flank on the right needed relief even more
urgently was an additional anxiety to General de Lisle, if it was not realised by
regimental officers and men, who had still less reason to know that tactically
these Divisions' position was weaker than the Twenty-Ninth's ; General de
Lisle's persistent insistence on ' digging in ' properly had driven this idea well
into his Division's heads and its line at any rate was fairly well entrenched.

That no relief was available was partly because all available reliefs and
reinforcements had been sent to the left to continue the effort to exploit our
original success and in particular to secure the key position of Bourlon Wood.
The Third Army may have persevered over long with this effort and failed to

emember that the salient created on November 20th had two flanks, not one
only ; but the ruling factor was that the crisis created by the Austro-German
success at Caporetto had caused French and British Divisions to be hurried to
Italy to prevent collapse developing into disaster. Five British Divisions,
among them the Forty-First, had had to be dispatched to Lombardy ; had they
been at Sir Douglas Haig's disposal to reinforce and relieve the troops who had
gained the success of November 20th, the salient opposite Cambrai might have
been in very different shape on November 30th.

Meanwhile the 11th Hampshire had been employed in an operation which
the Third and Sixteenth Divisions undertook mainly as a diversion to assist the
Cambrai attack. This had also the local purpose of enlarging our lodgement
in the Hindenburg Line near Bullecourt, effected in May after costly efforts.

On joining the Third Army the Sixteenth Division had been posted to the
Sixth Corps. The 11th Hampshire's head-quarters were established at Boyelles
by August 28th and companies were soon busy with different tasks, including
the clearing of debris which blocked the flow of the Sensée river and threatened
to cause flooding higher up. Otherwise its work differed little here from what
was wanted elsewhere, improvement of the trenches, maintenance and development of communications, especially trench tramways and light railways,
erecting huts in camps. Some tasks were never finished ; if any were, another
was immediately forthcoming. Things were ' quiet ' here ; both sides treated
this sector rather as a ' rest area ', and occasional raids and shelling did not
greatly disturb the Pioneers, who only record one casualty in September and
none between October 1st and November 20th. Usually during raids or bombardments working parties were not sent up to the line.

The attack of November 20th was no mere raid : any positions gained were
to be incorporated into our line, which promised the Pioneers plenty to do,
while some of their Lewis guns were employed under the machine-gun companies.

The attack apparently surprised the Germans, whose front line,[1] Tunnel
Trench, was quickly captured on a front of 1800 yards, two important 'pill-boxes'
on the right, Jove and Mars, being rushed from the rear, while many Germans
sheltering in the trench were captured. At 7.30 a.m. a message came back that
the Pioneers could come forward and start work on two communication
trenches, across No Man's Land, Jove Lane on the right to the portion taken
by the Connaught Rangers and Juno Lane to the 2nd R.D.F's lodgement in
the centre. Both were soon started, though counter-attacks were developing
and hampered the work, especially of Captain Howson's party who were
digging Jove Lane, as the Connaught Rangers were being hard pressed by
enemy who emerged from the shelter of the tunnel, and before long ' Jove ' had
been lost. Lt. Hillyer and 2/Lt. Hook, who had previously reconnoitred the
ground to see where the trenches were to be dug, both showed great courage and
initiative, leading their men to the right places and superintending the work

[1] West of Bullecourt.

despite heavy fire.[1] By 2.20 p.m. Juno Lane had reached a depth of over four feet, despite heavy shelling, and the other party was trying to establish connection with the Rangers holding on to Mars,[2] where a stubborn defence was being offered. To reach Mars the 11th had to resort to sapping, as digging from the top was impossible, but by 9.20 p.m. this new trench was well advanced and by 1 a.m. it had been completed, Juno Lane having been reported complete before mid-night. The Rangers had meanwhile formed a defensive flank along a sap leading to Mars and there had held up the counter-attacks, and during November 21st the position was consolidated, the trenches were cleared and Mars Lane improved, while on November 23rd the 7th Leinsters[3] recaptured Jove, so that Jove Lane also would be finished.

If the Pioneers had not had much actual fighting and had only had a dozen casualties, their tasks had made big demands on discipline, endurance and skill

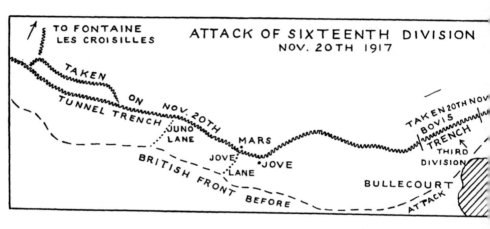

and had contributed appreciably to the retention of the position taken, whereby our line was distinctly improved.

After their spell in front line across the canal the 2nd Hampshire returned on November 28th to Marcoing, where the 88th Brigade was concentrated in reserve. The village was heavily shelled next day, but its cellars provided excellent shelter and the troops escaped loss, while the Germans had left large quantities of stores and food of every kind behind, of which full advantage was taken. It was a lull before the storm.

During the night of November 29th/30th shelling became very much heavier and, warned by its increased violence, the Division was ' standing to ' by 5 a.m. (November 30th). The 86th Brigade were holding Masnieres, the 87th being in the left sector across the canal with their reserve battalion, the K.O.S.B., in

[1] Lt. Hillyer was with the Jove Lane party, Lt. Hook with the Juno. Both received the M.C.
[2] To the left of Jove.
[3] Under Lt. Colonel Buckley, formerly a subaltern in the Hampshire and an original company commander in the 12th Battalion.

Marcoing along with the 88th Brigade. About 7 a.m. German infantry began pressing forward in force, directing their main strength against the long flank thinly held by the two tired and depleted Divisions who had captured it on November 29th and had held on for ten days without reinforcements or relief. Helped by the mist and by the dead ground in the Banteux Ravine in which they could collect unseen, the attackers broke in at several points and were soon thrusting Westwards against the Twenty-Ninth Division's rear, over-running its batteries and head-quarters and threatening to roll up the whole line in the salient. Against the 86th and 87th Brigades their frontal attacks achieved no such success ; even when most of our supporting guns had been taken or forced to move our rifles and Lewis guns could hold the attackers at bay, though the 86th Brigade at Masnieres was desperately hard pressed, Germans, who had over-run the over-matched left brigade of the next Divi-sion, penetrating into Les Rues Vertes behind it. Luckily those in charge of the Twenty-Ninth's reserve were prompt to grasp the emergency and to act, and their battalions responded splendidly to the call, at perhaps the most critical situation they had yet encountered. They turned out promptly, assembling South of the Marcoing–Masnieres road in readiness to attack East-ward and clear the 86th Brigade's rear. This was not easy ; to reach the high ground South of Marcoing, against which the Germans [1] were advancing, companies had to pass through a heavy barrage and some admixture of units resulted ; thus Z Company of the 2nd Hampshire diverged on its own into Marcoing Copse, into which the enemy had penetrated, and cleared it of them after heavy fighting, 2/Lt. Robertson being killed. The other companies fell into place in the general line, being on the right with the K.O.S.B. beyond them on the Northern end of Welsh Ridge, while the Worcestershire continued the line to the left.

Delivered with great vigour, the counter-attack first checked the leading Germans, who were already SW. of Marcoing Copse,[2] and drove them back to higher ground further South.[3] Against this the Hampshire advanced, along with the rest of the brigade, and despite heavy fire they swept the Germans off this rise, the Hampshire capturing 50 prisoners and getting good targets as the baffled attackers retreated Eastward. The fruits of General de Lisle's training were now reaped ; platoons combined ' fire and movement ' as instructed and helped each other, carrying out the attack as if at practice, keeping line and direction admirably and maintaining the advance steadily. Lt. Knott was conspicuous in this counter-attack, leading and encouraging his men, rallying stray men from other units and showing great initiative and resource. C.S.M. Norris also did great work, rallying men and leading them forward to drive the enemy back and then helping to organize a line of defence.[4] The other bat-talions had been equally successful, overcoming stubborn resistance, and the

[1] Mainly of their 30th and 9th Reserve Divisions, the 107th was attacking West of Masnieres.
[2] Approximately A—A on plan 54.   [3] Approximately B—B.
[4] He got a bar to the D.C.M. he had already earned by consistent good work in and out of the line.

promptitude and push of the counter-attack had not only averted the threat to Marcoing and all West of it but had saved from capture many batteries still in action. These had been getting splendid targets in the masses of Germans and doing great execution. Touch was obtained with the 86th Brigade, who were holding on tenaciously at Masnieres, and on the right with the next Division, whose supports and reserves had succeeded in checking the enemy at the Hindenburg Support Line. Further to the right a line had been patched by the remnants of two other Divisions whose line had been pierced. All sorts of troops had thrown themselves into a confused fight, and while much ground and many guns had been lost and several units virtually annihilated, in the end the enemy's advance had been effectively checked. For this relief much credit must go to the splendid defence of the Twenty-Ninth Division and to its vigorous and well-handled counter-attack, for which it may well be claimed that it had averted a major disaster.

Beyond the rising ground which the 88th Brigade's counter-attack had reached, virtually the road from La Vacquerie to Les Rues Vertes, the advance was not pressed and the line was hastily re-organized so that a reserve could be formed, the Hampshire being drawn back to dig in behind the right.[1] Casualties had been fairly heavy, 2/Lt. Robertson had been killed and Captain Scott (at duty) and Lt. Knott and 2/Lt. Yates[2] wounded with 120 other ranks killed, wounded or missing. The Brigade Major having been wounded, Captain Cuddon was acting for him ; he had done good service, rallying the men at a point where the line was breaking and leading them forward again to recover their original line.[3]

This line was consolidated during the night, and though Marcoing and Masnieres were being shelled the work was little impeded, then or on the next day, the Hampshire only having nine casualties, mainly from machine-guns. But the pronounced salient now formed at Masnieres was repeatedly attacked, and the 86th Brigade was hard pressed to hold on, and though it did manage this, repulsing several vigorous efforts and inflicting heavy casualties, so exposed a position was not worth the risk or cost of its retention. Accordingly before morning (December 2nd) Masnieres and Les Rues Vertes were quietly evacuated without the Germans perceiving it. Our line now ran about half way between Marcoing and Masnieres, crossing the canal at the lock West of Masnieres. December 2nd the Hampshire spent in brigade reserve under shell-fire, varied by orders to turn out and counter-attack to re-establish the line of the Essex, falsely reported to have been broken, then to send W Company to reinforce the S.W.B. East of Marcoing and South of the lock and finally to dig in SW. and S. of Marcoing Copse,[4] where Y and Z, the latter having before this rejoined head-quarters, were in line, and X in support. This move was completed by 9.30 p.m. and the entrenching of the new line was begun.

December 3rd brought a renewal of the infantry attacks. About 11 a.m., after a heavy bombardment, infantry swarmed forward in force, pressing

---

[1] Approximately C—C on plan.
[2] Died of wounds.
[3] He received another bar to the M.C.
[4] D—D on plan.

hardest against the S.W.B. and W Company on their left near the lock.[1] These
in hastily dug trenches without wire in front or dug-outs, put up a fine fight,
and after the front line trenches were lost, the survivors rallied on their reserve
at the S.W.B's battalion head-quarters, where a desperate resistance eventually
prevailed ; indeed the Germans fell right back, abandoning the S.W.B's forward
trench and allowing many wounded to be rescued. Elsewhere the German
advance had been held and heavily punished, they could make no progress in
face of our guns and rifles ; X Company had meanwhile been sent forward to
take up a position just NE. of Marcoing Copse to prevent a further advance
along the canal ; this position they reached despite some casualties in going
through a barrage on Marcoing Copse, and held on to it successfully. Even-

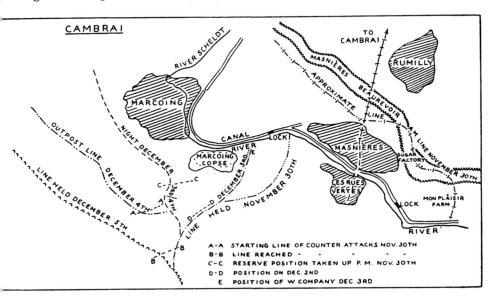

CAMBRAI

A-A STARTING LINE OF COUNTER ATTACKS NOV. 30TH
B-B LINE REACHED -   -   -   - -
C-C RESERVE POSITION TAKEN UP P. M. NOV. 30TH
D-D POSITION ON DEC. 2ND
E   POSITION OF W COMPANY DEC. 3RD

tually at 8 p.m., the rest of the battalion went up to relieve the S.W.B.,[2] now
reduced to about 80.

The Hampshire[3] had hardly taken up this position before orders were received
to fall back to a new line SW. of Marcoing, pivoting on the position retaken
by the battalion and the K.O.S.B. on November 30th. Marcoing with the
other advanced positions had now to be evacuated, as a preliminary to a
further withdrawal roughly to the Hindenburg Support Line. It was clear
that nothing was to be gained by hanging on to the pronounced salient which
our forward line now formed, and that it was imperative to shorten and
straighten out our Cambrai front.

By 1 a.m. on December 4th this first move had been carried out. Lewis
gun posts had been left to cover it but by 5.30 a.m. they too had come back.

[1] E on plan.   [2] Some 20 survivors of W Company were with them.
[3] The day's casualties were well over 80, 2/Lt. Alexander being among those killed.

During the day the Germans frequently tried to push forward but they made little progress, being effectively discouraged by our Lewis guns which, backed by artillery and machine-guns, took advantage of some fine targets, indeed the withdrawal to the Hindenburg Support Line, ordered for that evening, was in no way molested or impeded. Before it started, outposts were posted some way in front of that line, Z Company being detailed for this duty, and soon after midnight, the outposts being in place, the rest fell back through them, to reach the Hindenburg Support Line about 3 a.m. December 5th. Here the Thirty-Sixth Division was in occupation and ready to relieve the outposts also, and when this had been done the Twenty-Ninth was at last fully relieved after a fortnight which had been strenuous even for it.

The 2nd Hampshire now went back to Ribecourt, where Z Company soon rejoined and all had breakfast, after which the battalion marched back to Elicourt and entrained. Their troubles were not over ; about 4 p.m. the train was pulled up suddenly near Farnicourt, shell-fire having torn up the track. The engine left the rails and went down the bank, taking the leading truck off the line : luckily this remained upright as did all behind and no disaster occurred. The enemy went on shelling and their aeroplanes were busy overhead, but the train was unhit and before long the battalion had detrained and shifted to another train beyond the break, so that at 8 a.m. (December 6th) it was safely at Mondicourt and could march to rest billets at Sus St. Leger.

The closing stages of ' Cambrai ' had added 2/Lt. A. H. Alexander and over 50 men to the battalion's killed and missing, mostly in W Company, and with another 50 wounded total casualties came to well over 350. But the 2nd Hampshire could congratulate themselves on their part in the battle, for which the Division was most warmly and deservedly thanked by the authorities from the Commander-in-Chief downward, the value of its tenacious defence and the orderly withdrawal after so long and arduous an effort being emphasized. Lt. Colonel Johnston received the D.S.O., Captains Cuddon and Lord and the M.O., Captain Knight, bars to the M.C., Captains Ashling and Singleton Gates and Lt. Knott the M.C., C.S.M. Milne a bar to his D.C.M., C.S.M. Norris the D.C.M. and a bar, Corporal Ridding and Private Nippard the D.C.M., L/Corporal Hoath a bar to the M.M. and 25 N.C.O's and men the M.M., while Captain Scott got a ' mention ', a list of awards which indicates the enterprise, determination and endurance which the Hampshire had shown and which places ' Cambrai ' among the greatest achievements of the Sixty-Seventh. Whatever the verdict on the battle as a whole it had given the Sixty-Seventh a fine opportunity which they had utilised to the full.

CHAPTER XXI

EGYPT AND PALESTINE, 1916–1917

ALLIPOLI had not given the 8th Hampshire and the rest of the Fifty-Fourth Division much of a chance. Thrown piece-meal into a confused struggle in which the situation was already compromised almost beyond recall, without having been able to reconnoitre the ground or know what was expected of it, the Division had had an unlucky start, and thereafter the difficult conditions with which officers and men had had to contend on the ridges running down from Chunuk Bair in an atmosphere of frustration and disappointment had offered little opportunity to recuperate. Transfer to Egypt had allowed of this, and during 1916 the Division was able to get the training it needed, to benefit by its experiences and to achieve a high standard of efficiency in all its units.

Reaching Alexandria on December 19th the 8th Hampshire were sent to Sidi Bisr Camp, where they remained for six weeks, recuperating, refitting and training. Lt. Colonel Murray of the Black Watch joined on December 22nd and took command, some of the battalion's own base details and convalescents rejoined and eight subalterns with a few men arrived from its 'Third Line' unit. Leaving Alexandria for Cairo on February 2nd, it went to Mena Camp near the Pyramids, where the Division was collecting, its own artillery now coming out from England with other details, including transport men, whom the battalions had left behind. A draft of over 128 men arrived on March 7th, six officers, five attached from the Queen's, joined, and when on March 30th the battalion left Mena Camp for Shallufa and the Canal defences it was rested and up to a fair strength.

By this time a serious Turkish advance against the Suez Canal and Egypt was no longer considered likely. If the Turkish defence at Gallipoli had prevailed, its high cost had gone far to preclude their developing the counter-offensive that had originally been feared, before the incapacity of Turkish administration and communications to organize a large-scale invasion of Egypt had been fully appreciated. If the Canal was not to be attacked, Sir William Robertson, now installed as C.I.G.S., was not leaving troops idle in Egypt, and before long the M.E.F. was mostly on its way to France or Mesopotamia, leaving a much reduced Egyptian Expeditionary Force ('E.E.F.'), including the Fifty-Fourth Division, to secure the Canal and in due time adopt an offensive-defensive by advancing across the Sinai Desert to the gates of Palestine.

The Fifty-Fourth Division were to see 1916 out on the Canal, taking over the Southern section early in April, the 8th Hampshire's H.Q. being at Kubrit. Here 'defence works continued' is the usual entry with which the battalion diary contents itself till it records a move to Serapeum, the central section, late in May. These defence works were being constructed in depth, with one line along the Eastern Canal bank and advanced posts pushed out about five miles into the Desert. Constructing defences in the loose and shifting sand was difficult, much revetting was required, and to keep the line in good order needed constant vigilance and hard work. The forward posts' garrisons ranged from two platoons to two companies, their rations, water and stores being brought up from the Canal by camels, whose acquaintance the 8th now had to acquire. The Yeomanry and the Australian Light Horse, entrusted with the patrolling of the front, may have occasionally sighted an Arab, but the 8th never saw an enemy and worked steadily away, with little to vary the daily routine. The Turkish advance in August, decisively repulsed at Romani by the

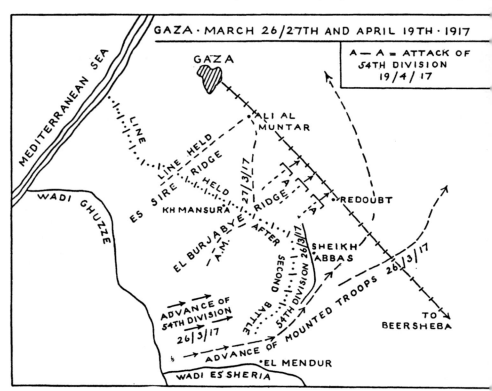

GAZA · MARCH 26/27TH AND APRIL 19TH · 1917

A — A = ATTACK OF
54TH DIVISION
19/4/17

Fifty-Second Division and the mounted troops, did not trouble the Serapeum front, and an extension of the 8th's line to the Southward to relieve the 4th Essex at Toussoum and Deversoir (August 25th) brought little change.

Before this Lt. Colonel Murray had left for France, Lt. Colonel Holland (Devons) replacing him. In September the battalion was withdrawn for a month's training, but it was back in front line by October 12th. Meanwhile the railway and the pipe line which supplied water were being pushed steadily Eastward across the Desert, enabling our front to be advanced, and with another Turkish attack now most improbable the battalion usually has only ' nothing of importance ' to record during these autumn months, except for departures on leave or for courses, with hospital admissions and discharges, or the occasional arrival of drafts.

1916 ended with the British occupation of El Arish, which with further successes at Magdhaba (December 23rd) and Rafa (January 7th) rendered quite unnecessary the retention in the Canal defences of any large force, so that though General Murray had to send a Division to France, he could find troops to replace it in the Eastern Force, now on the Palestine frontier, and could prepare for an attack in force on Gaza, the main bulwark of Southern Palestine. Thus the Fifty-Fourth Division at last left the Canal defences, the 8th Hampshire being relieved by dismounted Yeomanry on January 8th and moving to Moascar, where their brigade spent the rest of January, doing brigade training and route-marching, before starting its advance on February 1st. Five marches took it to Romani, where it spent a week before advancing again. Wire netting, stretched across the sand to form a roadway, made the marching easier, and on February 25th 29 officers and 881 other ranks marched into El Arish, a draft of 62 men having recently joined.

Though the notion of delivering Jerusalem from the Turk had been warmly espoused by Mr. Lloyd George, General Murray had been warned not to expect large reinforcements for an advance into Palestine. However, the force available seemed to warrant the hope of repeating on a larger scale at Gaza the useful successes achieved at Magdhaba and Rafa. The Desert Column [1] was to make the main attack, its mounted troops working round to the East to intercept the garrison's retreat, while the Fifty-Fourth Division covered their right flank and rear against any advance by relieving forces from the South-East.

The 8th Hampshire remained at or in front of El Arish until March 20th and then moved by Rafa and Khan Yunus to Im Seirat, SW. of the place where the Division would follow the Desert Column across the Wadi Ghuzze, the great watercourse covering Gaza from the SW., now dry but a considerable tactical feature.

The 162nd Brigade had reached Im Seirat late on March 26th and moved forward at 5.15 a.m. towards the Wadi. Unluckily a dense mist enveloped everything, preventing reconnaissance, delaying movement, particularly the Fifty-Third Division's, and throwing the whole time-table out of gear. Thus the 162nd Brigade did not leave its assembly position till 7.40 a.m. when it advanced in artillery formation about four miles NE. to the Sheikh Abbas ridge, where the 8th Hampshire took post, with A and C Companies on outpost. Meanwhile the Fifty-Third Division, though much delayed by the fog, was developing its attack. It met stubborn opposition but, reinforced by the 161st Brigade, eventually captured its objectives on the outskirts of Gaza, including the key position of Ali al Muntar, and obtained touch with the mounted troops who had virtually encircled the town on the East and North. Unfortunately the delay in the original advance had sacrificed precious hours of daylight and had given time for strong Turkish reinforcements to advance from NE. and East. On hearing of this the Desert Column's commander, being apparently

[1] The Fifty-Third Division and the mounted troops.

unaware of the Fifty-Third Division's success, warned the Fifty-Fourth to prepare to fall back to the El Burjabye ridge to get closer touch with the Fifty-Third, while he ordered the withdrawal of the mounted troops, partly because their horses were short of water. Actually the Turkish reinforcements did not really exercise any serious pressure till much later, but finding that the mounted troops' retirement was uncovering his flank, the G.O.C. Fifty-Third Division ordered a withdrawal, not knowing that the Fifty-Fourth had occupied the Sheikh Abbas Ridge and could cover his right effectively, so that it was probable that nearly all the ground captured could be retained. Too late next morning it was discovered that this withdrawal had been unnecessary, but efforts to reoccupy the positions evacuated proved unsuccessful and the Fifty-Third Division fell back to a position stretching across from the El Burjabye ridge towards the Rafa-Gaza road, almost at right angles to the Fifty-Fourth's new line, which faced East.

On the Fifty-Fourth evacuating the Sheikh Abbas ridge, the 8th Hampshire were placed in reserve near Mansura, where they remained all day, taking over the outposts after dark. The Turks had established themselves on the Sheikh Abbas ridge but had not advanced further, our guns and machine-guns keeping them at a respectful distance. It had, however, been decided to withdraw both Divisions across the Wadi Ghuzze, as no advantage seemed likely to be gained from retaining so marked a salient whose communications would be under flanking fire.[1] Accordingly during the night both were withdrawn, the 162nd Brigade acting as rear-guard, the 8th Hampshire its rear-party, leaving small covering parties to keep up a desultory fire till the rest had got away. Before midnight they were back at Im Seirat, exhausted and exasperated, if their only casualties were five missing. Next evening (March 28th) they took over an outpost line on our side of the Wadi, near El Breij, with snipers and patrols in advance who took two prisoners in some brushes with the enemy. After 24 hours here, the battalion went back again to Im Seirat ; Lt. Colonel Holland having had to go to hospital, Major Marsh was in command.

General Murray had missed success at Gaza by a narrow margin and could claim that the bad luck of the fog had been a major factor in turning the scales against him. Unfortunately his dispatches rather over-emphasized what had been achieved, greatly exaggerating the Turkish losses and leading the Home authorities to urge him to renew the attempt at once, when another effort should have been postponed until substantial reinforcements and above all much more artillery could be provided. The misfortunes which were to befall the 8th Hampshire in this second attempt must to some extent be attributed to this over-optimistic picture of the first.

Before renewing the attempt General Murray certainly pressed for more guns and more troops ; but, unfortunately, instead of insisting firmly on the urgency of reinforcements he allowed himself to be persuaded to attack without them. The authorities at Home, anxious for a big success and perhaps not

---

[1] Actually on the right the line held after the second attempt on Gaza was almost the same as the position now abandoned.

unwilling to take an optimistic view, would have done well not to urge him to an attack which the strategical situation in Egypt did not require and which had originally only been contemplated should quite substantial reinforcements be available.

Until April 16th the 8th Hampshire remained at Im Seirat, sending out patrols to cover the reconnoitring of a new outpost line beyond the Wadi and finding large parties to work on its crossings and the roads. On April 16th the battalion paraded in readiness to advance to the Sheikh Abbas ridge which its brigade was to secure as a preliminary to the new attack. The three weeks' interval between the attacks had altered the tactical situation for the worse ; whereas in March Gaza only had been prepared with defences, Turkish industry under German direction had created formidable works stretching some way SE. along the Beersheba road, so that instead of open cavalry country a fortified position would confront any turning movement in that direction. Some small additions to the attackers' artillery and even the arrival of eight rather aged tanks did nothing to off-set what the Turks had accomplished.

The attack was to be carried out in two phases, beginning with the securing of the Sheikh Abbas ridge with a line running West across the Mansura and El Sire ridges to the shore. From this in the second stage the Fifty-Fourth Division would advance against the Turkish position SE. of Gaza, the 163rd Brigade on its right making for Kh el Bir,[1] with the two Mounted Divisions covering its flank. On its left the Fifty-Second Division was tackling the defences immediately South of Gaza, with the Fifty-Third between its left and the sea.

The first stage was carried out on April 17th, when, after crossing the Wadi Ghuzze, the 163rd deployed about 4 a.m., with the 8th Hampshire (left) and 5th Suffolks leading and two tanks between them. Advancing steadily, the troops had little difficulty in clearing the Turkish outposts off the Sheikh Abbas ridge, the Hampshire having only two casualties, though one tank was disabled by a direct hit and took fire, stretcher-bearers from C Company helping to rescue wounded members of its crew. The day was spent in consolidating, a good line being established despite intermittent shell-fire. This position was retained next day, shelling causing a few more casualties, and then, early on April 19th, our bombardment opened. Two hours later, at 7.30 a.m., the two Norfolk battalions started to advance towards the Gaza-Beersheba road, with 2500 yards of undulating open ground to cross, A and B Companies of the Hampshire supporting the 5th Norfolks (right) and C and D following the 4th. The Turks, almost silent during the bombardment, started shelling directly the troops went forward, their guns having clearly been unaffected by our fire, while machine-guns soon joined in, developing a very heavy fire. The troops pushed on steadily, nevertheless, crossing a low ridge 500 yards ahead. On the right rather more favourable ground allowed of better progress, while here a tank helped the advance. Casualties, however, were heavy, the open ground providing no cover. The Hampshire were before long absorbed into the attack, which caught heavy fire from a redoubt to our right. This redoubt the tank

[1] Across the road to Beersheba and about North of Sheikh Abbas.

now tackled and with its aid a mixture of Hampshire and Norfolks forced their way in and took it, Sergeant Pearson being greatly to the fore and capturing 20 prisoners single-handed.[1] But the captors of the redoubt were soon hard pressed to maintain their ground, ammunition ran short, our artillery could give little help, and the 163rd Brigade's left and centre, after losing heavily, had been definitely held up 400 yards from their objective. Here the survivors hung on as best they could, pinned to the ground by the Turkish fire without any chance of getting forward. On their left some of the 162nd Brigade had been rather more successful, some men getting well across the Beersheba road, while further West the Fifty-Second Division had made a larger lodgement which it was fighting hard to maintain and extend. On the right the Mounted Divisions had failed to penetrate the defences and the whole attack was brought to a standstill; the 163rd Brigade in particular had lost very heavily, and before long its survivors were forced back, the captured redoubt being retaken and the tank destroyed. Along a slight rise an attempt at a stand was made, about 100 Hampshires with a Lewis gun being rallied by Major Marsh, and here they started to dig in. In the early afternoon the 5th Suffolk, till then in reserve, came up and extended this line to both flanks. The Fifty-Second Division was still beating off counter-attacks, but it was hard pressed and could not maintain all it had gained. The attacking Divisions had still nearly two brigades in hand and the infantry of another Division [2] were in reserve, but to have renewed the attack without far more artillery support could only have swelled the already high casualty list with little chance of achieving any more than the 8th Hampshire had accomplished.

After dark most of those lying out in the open got back to our line, while those wounded who could be reached were brought in. The 5th Suffolk had now taken over the front, and those of the Hampshire who were not collecting the wounded were consolidating part of a support line, taking in the Sheikh Abbas ridge and running thence NW. by Kh Mansura to the shore.

Casualties had been heavy, nearly 6500, well over a quarter in the 163rd Brigade, whose gallantry and determination had been so great but so unavailing. The 8th Hampshire, with 23 officers and 746 other ranks in action, had lost even more heavily than at Suvla: Captains Pittis and C. G. Seeley, Lts. Pakeman and S. G. Ratsey, 2/Lts. Atkin, Attfield, Blofield, Cox, Hills, King, Roberts and Shelton and 248 other ranks were killed and missing, of whom 2/Lts. Atkin, Cox and Roberts and 28 men were later reported as prisoners. Captains Fox, Hylton, Russell (now Adjutant) and Vincent, Lts. Butler and Harker, 2/Lts. Henville, Sutcliffe and Cronin-Wilson and 298 men had been wounded, though after the reserve not engaged in the battle had rejoined the battalion could produce twelve officers and 450 men on May 1st; a fair nucleus on which the work of reconstruction could be once again undertaken.

' First Gaza ' had been a disappointment, ' Second Gaza ' was a disastrous

---

[1] He was awarded the D.C.M.

[2] The incomplete Seventy-Fourth Division, in process of being formed from dismounted Yeomanry.

everse. It finished all prospects of any further advance by the E.E.F., until
much more artillery and substantial reinforcements could arrive. For the 8th
Hampshire it meant settling down to a tedious period of trench warfare opposite
Gaza, waiting for drafts. Still this long wait was far from a time of inactivity,
and the battalion carried out a most successful minor operation and became
most proficient in patrolling and in harassing the enemy.

After three weeks ' out ' training, reorganizing and working on second line
defences, the 8th Hampshire were back in trenches by May 17th, South of
Sheikh Abbas near El Mendur. Here our line faced Eastward over open
country, and with the Turkish defences along the Beersheba road miles away
patrolling was mainly done by mounted troops. After a week here the battalion
was back across the Wadi Ghuzze in reserve till June 13th, when it relieved a
battalion of the Fifty-Second Division in the trenches nearest the coast.
Captains Fox and Vincent and Lt. Butler, wounded on April 19th, had rejoined
before the end of May with about 80 men. Another 100 rejoined during June
and with over 200 transferred from a Garrison Battalion of the Devons,[1] other
ranks available for the trenches were up to 660 by July 1st. Four officers and
270 men of the 2/5th Hampshire, recently arrived from India, were attached
for instruction on June 2nd.

In the coastal sector the battalion was holding a continuous trench with
four posts 800 yards in advance, but communication trenches and a support
line were lacking. The enemy showed little inclination to be active and rarely
interfered with our patrols, which were very enterprising, one under Lt. Brannon
rushing a sentry group near Sugar Loaf Hill on June 17th, taking five prisoners
and returning along the beach. Much information was obtained, which proved
useful in planning a big raid, carried out most successfully on July 14th by B
Company with D Company of the 2/5th, in all 300 officers and men, including
a large covering party and R.E. to blow up the dug-outs. The objectives
included Sugar Loaf Hill and Beach Post. Everything had been carefully
rehearsed, scouts having reconnoitred the ground thoroughly.

Starting off at 11 p.m. (July 14th) behind a most effective barrage which
inflicted heavy casualties and drove the enemy to shelter in their dug-outs, the
raiders first rushed the Sugar Loaf, Sergeant Wheeler leading them splendidly :
five minutes later they were into Beach Post, Rifleman Hawes rushing a machine-
gun before it could open fire, while Sergeants Early and Gray led parties which
blocked the communication trenches. Some enemy showed fight but were
quickly overpowered, Sergeant Palmer accounting for several, while many were
caught in one dug-out and disposed of with the bayonet, on which rather than on
the bomb the raiders had been trained to rely. The R.E. had soon finished their
work and after 19 minutes, the raiders could begin withdrawing, bringing in
19 prisoners and a machine-gun. Casualties, three killed and missing and a
dozen wounded, were very low, while it was estimated that 60 enemy had been
killed, apart from those hit by the barrage during the bombardment or in seeking
to escape.

[1] Several officers also joined.

Lt. Colonel Marsh's arrangements won much praise from the authorities, the raid being regarded as a real model. Lt. Brannon's leadership and his gallantry in bringing in a wounded man won him the M.C. and Sergeants Britten, Early, Gray, Palmer and Wheeler and Rifleman Adams were awarded the M.M.

Apart from this July was uneventful, the battalion twice co-operated by fire in raids on Umbrella Hill in the next sector, its patrols continued to be active but were almost unopposed, casualties were low and discharges from hospital considerably exceeded admissions. Septic sores caused some trouble, but malaria and enteric were infrequent and if conditions were not very comfortable the sea-bathing gave some relief and the sick-rate remained low, despite the heat.

Meanwhile a renewed offensive was in preparation. The War Cabinet hoped for great political results from a major success in Palestine and had at last agreed to provide the reinforcements and additional artillery denied to General Murray. A new, Seventy-Fifth, Division was being formed out of Indian troops already in Egypt and Territorials, including the 2/4th and 2/5 Hampshire, from India, and two Divisions with more Yeomanry were transferred from Salonica. This increase in the E.E.F. naturally involved a tremendous amount of administrative work at the base and on the lines of communication. General Allenby, now in command, was not going to strike prematurely, and as his plans included the outflanking of the Turkish line at and beyond Beersheba, water supply became a more important problem than ever.

The long pause was inevitably giving the Turks time to strengthen considerably their already formidable defences, but their troops were worse off in many ways than their opponents, their sick-rate and losses from disease were much higher, and not even German advice or assistance could introduce efficiency into Turkish administration. Moreover, the strategical deadlock did not preclude a vigorous harassing of the Turks, in which all our Divisions played their part, securing an ascendency in No Man's Land which went far to remove any legacy of discouragement from Second Gaza and its heavy casualties. If the 8th Hampshire did not repeat the Beach Post raid, their continued activity and success in patrolling maintained the feelings that exploit had inspired.

The battalion was 'out' most of August, bathing and training. Drafts brought other ranks up over 900 before the beginning of September, which month was spent in reserve to the left sector, finding large working parties every night to assist the front line battalion. Much of October was devoted to rehearsing the next attack over practice trenches and then, on October 14th, the 8th took over the coastal sector from the sea to Bunker's Hill and promptly started sending out strong patrols to secure the mastery of No Man's Land and cover working parties. After a week of this the battalion was back in the training area, completing arrangements for the attack, now very near at hand, but sending parties up to the front to carry on the patrolling. It only took up its assembly position for the attack on the evening of November 1st.[1]

[1] Its strength on October 31st was 34 officers and 887 other ranks.

Meanwhile both the 2/4th and the 2/5th Hampshire had reached Palestine, being both very different in many respects, above all in personnel, from the raw units which had left England for India in November 1915. Drafts to Mesopotamia,[1] transfers to other units or to special employments, a few deaths and invalidings and many promotions to commissions had changed them almost completely. Even so Lt. Colonel J. B. L. Stillwell, now commanding the 2/4th, had with him twelve of its original officers, including his second in command, Major C. P. Bulley, who had come out as a Captain, as had Captains J. C. Bulley, Ashmore and Goddard, while Captain Bacon, now Adjutant, had come out as a 2nd Lieutenant, but fourteen original subalterns were no longer present and Captain North had been killed with the 1/4th at El Hanna.[2]

The 2/4th had been warned for active service in April 1917, just after having found 150 men for the 2/5th, who preceded them to Palestine. They had earned a good reputation at Quetta for efficiency and for prowess in athletics, for which they owed much to the help of the Quetta Division, especially its G.O.C., General Grover, whose interest in the battalion did not cease when it left his command, but the battalion was glad to be getting a chance to prove itself in the field. It had a great send-off : all Quetta turned out to bid it farewell and wish it luck. Leaving Karachi, where it had had a great variety of guards to find, including one at Hyderabad (Sind), on April 29th, it reached Suez on May 15th [3] and was sent to Zeitoun Camp near Cairo, for a fortnight's equipping and training. New rifles were issued but heavy baggage including most of the band's instruments had to be dumped. From here the 2/4th were sent on to El Arish and thence to Rafa (June 20th), where the Seventy-Fifth Division was being assembled under Major-General Palin. The 2/4th now found themselves in the 233rd Brigade with the 5th Somerset L.I., the 4th Wiltshire and the 3/3rd Gurkhas under Brigadier-General Colston. They had now to find many guards and night outposts as well as to become acquainted with the bomb and the Lewis gun and to do a ' refresher ' musketry course with the short rifle issued to them at Zeitoun, while many officers and men went off to a variety of courses of instruction. It was very hot but the bathing, though at times dangerous, was some relaxation. In the middle of August the battalion moved up to Deir el Belah. The brigade's arrangements involved an unnecessarily exhausting march, started at 10 a.m. and carried out in the worst part of the day, which caused quite considerable suffering to the heavily-equipped men and some cases of heat-stroke. Arrived here officers and men got their initiation into trench warfare under the Fifty-Second Division, whom their Division relieved in the coastal sector on September 11th, holding the left sub-sector, the Apex. The battalion now got its first chance in action, beating off a Turkish patrol on the 20th, while its own patrols were active and several encounters occurred. On October 7th a detachment under 2/Lts. Beauchamp and Fenn

[1] The 2/4th in all sent 17 officers and 700 men.
[2] Three original subalterns, Durnford, Rawlings and Wilkinson, were killed in Mesopotamia or Persia
[3] It mustered 27 officers and 820 other ranks.

acted as a left flank guard in a highly successful raid by the Somerset and 3/3rd Gurkhas, though Turkish retaliation inflicted several casualties, mainly in A Company, which was in support.[1]

The battalion had some days out of the trenches in the middle of October, then taking over trenches at Queen's Hill, subsequently shifting Eastward and taking over the Mansura Redoubt. All was ready now for the big attack. Its Division, now in the Twenty-First Corps, was on its right, on the Sheikh Abbas ridge, with its right flank thrown back facing East, covering the flank of the Fifty-Second and Fifty-Fourth Divisions, who were attacking Gaza from the South-West.

The 2/5th were in Palestine before the 2/4th, having embarked at Bombay on March 19th and reached Suez on April 5th. They went first to Zeitoun, for training and re-equipping, being in the first formed brigade of the Seventy-Fifth Division, the 232nd, under Brigadier-General Huddleston, along with the 5th Devonshire, 2nd Loyal North Lancashire and 2/3rd Gurkhas.

Moving forward in May to El Arish the battalion was employed on the line of communications for a month and then moved up to the front, being attached for instruction from June 3rd to 11th to the 163rd Brigade. Colonel Day and Major Stevenson, the original C.O. and second in command, were still present. Captain Jenner had succeeded Captain Archdale as Adjutant, the latter, now Major, Captains Ellis and Kay, subalterns in 1914, and Lt. Gibbings commanding the companies. Lt. Pigden was still Quartermaster and of the subalterns six were ' originals '.

From June 26th on the battalion took over its own piece of the line, though D Company remained with the 8th Hampshire for the Beach Post raid, in which C.S.M. Graham, who led his section admirably and himself accounted for several enemy, got the D.C.M., while Corporal Wells, who led a bombing section most efficiently, and Ptes. Burgess and Goddard won the M.M.

The 2/5th had seven weeks in line from the end of June onwards, on Samson's Ridge just South of Gaza and at Hart Hill in the centre of the coastal sector. Here it greatly improved the defences, though dead ground just in front of the wire was a trouble. It maintained a steady pressure on the Turks, patrolling and harassing them with fire, to which they replied intermittently, the battalion's total casualties being under 40. Wastage from illness was larger, sand-fly fever being prevalent, and among others the C.O. was invalided. His successor, Lt. Colonel Vernon of the K.R.R.C., soon left to command a brigade, Major Stevenson carrying on until, on October 1st Lt. Colonel G.F. Perkins, who had been for some time on the Staff of the M.E.F., joined. Captain Jenner now going to the Indian Army, Captain Kay replaced him as Adjutant.

During September the battalion was in reserve, working hard on rear lines and getting much useful training, and then in October it took over front

---

[1] Major Parsons, a ' pre-war ' subaltern of the 4th Hampshire, joined in October and became second in command. Captain Bacon had been given a post on the Staff and was replaced as Adjutant by Captain Price.